COURAGEOUS CONVERSATIONS IN THE CLASSROOM

Also Available

Children's Literature in the Reading Program, Fifth Edition:
Engaging Young Readers in the 21st Century

Edited by Deborah A. Wooten, Lauren Aimonette Liang, and Bernice E. Cullinan

The ABCs of CBM, Second Edition:
A Practical Guide to Curriculum-Based Measurement

Michelle K. Hosp, John L. Hosp, and Kenneth W. Howell

Courageous Conversations in the Classroom

USING CHILDREN'S LITERATURE TO SUPPORT SOCIAL AND EMOTIONAL GROWTH, POSITIVE IDENTITY, AND MENTAL HEALTH

Lauren Aimonette Liang
Karen W. Tao
Michelle K. Hosp

THE GUILFORD PRESS
New York London

Printed in the United States of America

This book is printed on acid-free paper.

For product and safety concerns within the EU, please contact *GPSR@taylorandfrancis.com*, Taylor & Francis Verlag GmbH, Kaufingerstraße 24, 80331 München, Germany.

Last digit is print number: 9 8 7 6 5 4 3 2 1

Library of Congress Cataloging-in-Publication Data
Names: Liang, Lauren A. author | Tao, Karen W. author | Hosp, Michelle K. author
Title: Courageous conversations in the classroom : using children's literature to support social and emotional growth, positive identity, and mental health / Lauren Aimonette Liang, Karen W. Tao, Michelle K. Hosp.
Description: New York : The Guilford Press, [2025] | Includes bibliographical references and index. |
Identifiers: LCCN 2024058344 | ISBN 9781462557332 paperback | ISBN 9781462557561 cloth
Subjects: LCSH: Children's literature—Study and teaching | Social skills in children | Affective education | Children—Books and reading—Psychological aspects | Children—Books and reading—Sociological aspects | BISAC: EDUCATION / Teaching / General | EDUCATION / Educational Psychology
Classification: LCC PN1008.8 .L53 2025 | DDC
809/.89282071—dc23/eng/20250312
LC record available at *https://lccn.loc.gov/2024058344*

To Zev, Zoë, and Lexie. May you always be courageous and compassionate!
With love from Mom. —L. A. L.

To Jiajia and Lulu. Lead with love and understanding. To Zac, for seeing me.
To Mom and Dad, for everything. —K. W. T.

For all you courageous educators who see the promise and strength in
every child. You got this! —M. K. H.

About the Authors

Lauren Aimonette Liang, PhD, is Associate Professor in Literacy, Language, and Learning in the Department of Educational Psychology and Director of the Quest Academic Learning Community program for first-year students at the University of Utah. Her research focuses on the selection and educational use of children's literature, particularly as related to student response and comprehension. Dr. Liang is the author or coauthor of many articles, chapters, and books, and has held leadership roles in international literacy and children's literature organizations. She has served as a committee member or chair for several prestigious children's literature awards.

Karen W. Tao, PhD, is Associate Professor in Counseling Psychology in the Department of Educational Psychology at the University of Utah. She is a community-engaged scholar who teaches, conducts research, and facilitates workshops with a commitment to reduce disparities in access, service provision, and quality of mental health and education for historically marginalized groups. Dr. Tao collaborated with PBS Utah to produce an award-winning digital series, "Let's Talk." As the host of this seven-episode series, she met with parents to discuss how to talk with kids about race, racism, and cultural differences.

Michelle K. Hosp, PhD, is Senior Director of Assessment Innovations at Renaissance Learning and Associate Adjunct Professor of Special Education at the University of Massachusetts Amherst. She has over 30 years of experience working directly with students, educators, families, and researchers as a school psychologist, professor, and Director of the Iowa Reading Research Center. Dr. Hosp's research focuses on reading, assessments, and data-based decision making. She has published numerous articles and book chapters on these topics.

Preface

Snapshots from Our Conversations: Why We Care About This Work

KAREN: A Childhood Memory

I was 9 years old when I first learned about the Cold War and nuclear arms race after watching the news about the 1983 nuclear false alarm incident. Frightened by what I had just watched on TV, I ran to my mom and asked her what would happen if a nuclear bomb were dropped on our home. She looked uncomfortable, hesitated, and after several seconds of silence said, "It would be a disaster." I was not satisfied with her response and continued to pepper her with more questions. Later that week, my mom, an elementary school librarian, brought home a book to read with me. It was called *Sadako and the Thousand Paper Cranes* by Eleanor Coerr.

Coerr's book is the retelling of a true story about Sadako Sasaki, a 12-year-old girl from Japan who was 2 when the United States dropped an atom bomb on her home city of Hiroshima in 1945. The bomb immediately killed over 80,000 people and tens of thousands more people in its aftermath. Sadako's exposure to radiation from the explosion resulted in leukemia and her eventual death. The book tells the personal story of Sadako and her family while also confronting the atrocities of war. Through her story, I learned of the horrors of war that impact everyday people, including kids just like me. By reading this book with my mother, I was given a window into another girl's life and her story of trauma and resilience. This book further bridged the ocean's distance between Hilo, Hawaii, where I lived, and Japan. I remember the conversations with my mom about Sadako's story that brought up many emotions. We stopped at certain passages where she asked me how I was feeling or what I would do in Sadako's situation. We spent time talking about how Sadako and I were alike and different. Occasionally, I needed to take a break from reading to cry and express my fear, rage, and sadness. I also remember my building sense of resolve to act upon what I had just read. After finishing the book, I was determined to figure out how I would contribute to a more peaceful world. That summer, I folded a lot of origami cranes! Sadako's story evoked my empathy.

Just like my mother felt when faced with my questions, many adults often feel unsure of how to have meaningful conversations with their children about tough topics. I hope this book will provide some stepping-stones for teachers to leverage the power of books in their classrooms as they delve into dialogue about subjects such as racism, bullying, depression, and war. We encourage educators and families to have these hard and important conversations by reading, crying, and laughing together. Reading quality children's literature in combination with holding meaningful discussions has the power to enhance compassion, foster curiosity, and ultimately strengthen individuals and communities.

MICHELLE: A Parental Experience

As a school psychologist, professor of special education, and parent of a child with a disability, I have a unique perspective on working with adults who have dedicated themselves to helping children. What I know as a professional is that educators want to do the right thing, and they try to do what is best for each one of their students. What I have experienced as a parent is that without the right information or good information, educators are often left fumbling for ways to assist students with issues that are often hard and uncomfortable to discuss.

My son and I experienced this firsthand. My son has muscular dystrophy, and when he was little, his body fought against him, making it difficult and uncomfortable to move and stabilize himself in certain positions like sitting down and getting up from the floor. This is something that is done dozens of times a day in the life of a kindergarten student. However, for my son, this meant falling a lot and often hitting his head and badly scraping his knees and elbows simply because he lacked the muscle strength to brace himself when he fell. He learned early that falling often came with pain so he would try to avoid falling at all costs, which is completely understandable. His kindergarten teacher meant well but did not know how to have the courageous conversation on disabilities and to help my son feel welcome. Nor did his teacher have the knowledge of how to incorporate opportunities for the other students to learn how all people have some things they are good at and some things that are harder for them. Instead, his teacher was at a loss of what to do when my son would grab onto things to help steady himself, including sometimes other kids. Instead, my son was often punished for putting his hands on other students and was labeled as "aggressive." This left my son feeling misunderstood and isolated because his teacher did not have good information on how to support him. I don't blame his teacher since she did not have the tools at her disposal to help her respond differently. I believe she cared, but she needed help in putting that concern into action.

If she had a resource like this book, she would have been able to "go there" in a caring and helpful way that would have benefited my child and, more importantly, all of the children in her classroom. What my son learned was that he is different, and sometimes being different means you get treated differently in ways that are unpleasant and make you feel bad about yourself. It doesn't have to be this way, and for that I am very grateful to be able to contribute to this very important book.

LAUREN: A Professional Perspective

As an ELA teacher and a passionate reader myself, I was on a continual search for titles that hit the trifecta: stories that my students would find highly engaging, accessible, and meaningful. To me, an inherent part of all three of these descriptors were protagonists who reflected the wealth of diversity in the community where I taught.

As a teacher-educator, I quickly found my teachers wanted "trifecta" books, too, but especially ones that addressed specific content: "I need a great book on bullying for my second graders!" "Can you find me an outstanding fifth-grade book that explains self-governance?" As I helped in their searches, I was struck by how passionately educators wanted to find the best book they could. But I noticed that the search for specific content was frequently centered on finding a singular title, and this often eclipsed attention to the diversity of protagonists and their viewpoints.

Reading a particularly good book on a topic *is* an excellent way to begin to introduce a reader to new ideas. Books help confirm for readers that these are universal issues and can present different, new perspectives. That perspective taking, however, happens more easily when readers have *both* the opportunity to see themselves reflected in a story and see the view of others in different stories about the same topic. The focus of many educators on finding the exact content they wanted, combined with issues of limited classroom time, sometimes led to wanting just one book and forgetting the importance of diverse representation.

Until I was in college, I never met a peer living in the experience that I had as a child of a parent with severe disabilities. Families like mine also were rare, and rarely depicted with authenticity, in the books I read or the media I saw. It siloed me. Representation matters; a constant lack can make an individual feel that their story, and ultimately their perspective, are less valued. I am dismayed and frustrated as I see my students of color and my own multiracial children struggle repeatedly to find themselves authentically represented in books—even today, with increased attention to diverse representation in children's publishing. Over time, this can defeat the idea that a variety of perspectives not only matters but even exists.

I wondered what would happen if teachers did not stop at just the one perfect trifecta book that explored the exact topic they wanted, but instead insisted on finding three or four or more? When the focus became finding a *set* of multiple highly engaging, accessible, and meaningful books offering diverse perspectives on a topic? I hope that this book helps educators take that step. The outstanding "trifecta" titles in each unit are carefully sequenced to begin building multifaceted knowledge about the topic: comparing stories, thinking about how perspectives change the nuances, and creating a ladder to greater depth of understanding of the content.

Acknowledgments

This book was born from conversations between us about the power of books to build empathy, awareness, and depth of understanding on topics that are essential to children's development in becoming thoughtful, socially conscious adults. We are grateful for the time and opportunity to talk together and to engage in this work. We are also grateful to our many colleagues, students, and fellow practitioners with whom we have endlessly discussed books and learning and explored new perspectives and ways of understanding. Along those lines, our sincere thanks to the outstanding educators who contributed to this book through trials of various lessons and thoughtful feedback on their experiences. We are grateful for the courageous conversations you held in your classroom that helped inform the work in this volume.

We would especially like to thank Rose Kjesbo, an experienced elementary teacher and doctoral student at the University of Utah, who not only helped author Chapter 10, but also was our resident expert on standards, checking diligently to ensure that the specific CCSS English Language Arts standards and CASEL social and emotional learning standards were correctly aligned for each of our units. University of Utah master's students and middle school teachers Jake Hogan and Elisabeth Wright, and counseling psychology doctoral students Amira Trevino and Camara Chea, were also key in helping craft Chapters 3, 6, 8, and 9, discussing the books and helping create different activities to best offer a variety of perspectives on the topics. Elizabeth Nelson, an assistant professor at Utah Valley University, provided essential assistance in securing permissions for images and helping format figures, as well as always being willing to discuss the importance of selection and sequencing of texts. Grace Cabral's skillful editing helped put the finishing touches on this book.

Finally, we are indebted to Craig Thomas, Senior Editor at The Guilford Press, for supporting this book from the beginning. His patience and encouragement kept our work moving forward, and even resurrected it at one point! Our thanks go to the entire team at Guilford that helped with this book: Laura Specht Patchkofsky, Patti Brecht, Katherine Lieber, Samantha Grossman, and Katie Leonard.

Permission to reproduce covers from the following books has been granted by these publishers:

- *The Rooster Who Would Not Be Quiet!/¡El gallo que no se callaba!* by Carmen Agra Deedy and illustrated by Eugene Yelchin, 2017, Scholastic
- *Maybe Tomorrow?* by Charlotte Agell and illustrated by Ana Ramirez, 2019, Scholastic
- *Maddi's Fridge* by Lois Brandt and illustrated by Vin Vogel, 2018, Flash Light Press
- *When We Were Alone* by David A. Robertson and illustrated by Julie Flett, 2016, High Water Press

Contents

Purchasers of this book can download and print copies of the appendices at *www.guilford.com/liang-materials* for personal use or use with students (see copyright page for details).

COURAGEOUS CONVERSATIONS IN THE CLASSROOM

Welcome to the Conversation

An Introduction to Using Children's Literature for Courageous Conversations

Dear Reader,

We are professors and parents, readers ourselves and those who read aloud. While we come from diverse scholarly and professional backgrounds, all three of us hold in common a strong desire to help young people as they struggle to make sense of the complex situations they face, while also developing a strong sense of identity and the agency to create change in their communities.

As you saw in the Preface, we have thought and talked a lot about this desire from many angles. A common thread in our conversations together has been how to best support the educators, counselors, and other school professionals with whom we work as they encourage their young students' development in both affective and cognitive realms. We find ourselves returning often to two shared beliefs: the power of outstanding books for learning and perspective taking, and the importance of facilitating deep discussion to help build understanding of self, others, and the world around us.

Our world is ever changing, sometimes quickly due to influences like a pandemic, or slowly as with our climate. What is similar is that these changes impact all of us, albeit in different ways based on our own personal views and perspectives. We believe books can be the vehicle that brings us together, helping us consider these shared experiences (and some with which we might be personally less familiar), so we can start the conversations that can feel too big to tackle. As we share research, theories, and instructional strategies, we also share memories, experiences, and perspectives. All of this has led us to the creation of this book, a book that brings together the power of children's literature and that of courageous conversations.

This book was conceived with the idea of encouraging and assisting the adults who courageously enter conversation with children on tough issues. We believe these conversations are vitally important to children's development. We also believe that carefully curated and sequenced sets of outstanding diverse books combined with specific activities, discussion prompts, and guidance can help those conversations to begin.

DISCUSSING CHALLENGING ISSUES WITH CHILDREN: WHY DO IT?

Between the ages of 5 and 12 years old, children undergo major cognitive, social, emotional, and physical changes, which are highly influenced by their environment and relationships with significant adults, such as parents and teachers. Early on, children begin to observe and internalize what they experience within various contexts, including the home, neighborhood, and school. Within these microsystems, they also begin constructing fairly complex narratives about selfhood, understanding where they fit within a social hierarchy, and defining a sense of justice (right/wrong, good/bad). For most children, a major part of growing up involves wrestling with infinite questions related to who they are and will become. Children must negotiate complicated interactions with friends, family, and teachers; within these relationships, they are tasked with defining their personal values and meeting multiple relational expectations. While there are other major sources of influence, much of these identity-formation processes take place by observing how people around them interact and treat each other. One of the consequences of disruptions in schooling (such as during the pandemic and rises in chronic absenteeism) is that students do not have the benefit of being together with other people their age and with caring educators and other school personnel. Students who feel emotionally supported by their teacher report being more motivated and having more positive classroom experiences (Reyes, Brackett, Rivers, White, & Salovey, 2012).

Additionally, Generation Z or iGen, including children born between roughly 1997 and 2012, and the current Generation Alpha or Gen Alpha (around 2010 to the present), are growing up in a fast-paced technologically driven era. Socialization within such a digitally mediated society can be overwhelming for children, as they are forced to sift through unrelenting and sometimes contradicting information. Often, kids' first exposure to social issues (e.g., sexuality and racism) and the initial narratives they create about themselves are facilitated by the internet. Via online platforms, children test the bounds of social rules, try on various personas, and create social networks. While there are some benefits to these online activities, results of longitudinal studies with iGen participants also show a significant link between screen time and mental health disorders; since the invention of the smartphone, rates of adolescent depression and anxiety have increased significantly (Twenge, Martin, & Campbell, 2018). According to the National Survey of Children's Health Data reports collected from parents of children ages 6–17, anxiety diagnoses increased nearly 20% between 2003 and 2012 (Bitsko et al., 2018). Direct explanations for this significant spike in anxiety among youth are unknown; however, experts identify a range of potential correlates including economic volatility (Rajmil et al., 2014), the rise in school shootings wherein lockdown drills are now considered routine (DeVos, Nielsen, & Azar, 2018), academic pressures starting as early as kindergarten (Bassock, Lathan, & Rorem, 2016; Pope, Brown, & Miles, 2015), and cyberbullying (van Geel, Vedder, & Tanilon, 2014). Gen Alpha looks to be even more influenced by the roles of technology in their lives, in addition to being a generation with higher ethnic and racial diversity, more diverse family structures, and higher economic inequality, bringing to the forefront more social issues as well as increased use of technology and its related positive and negative effects. Although daunting to consider these social issues in totality, it is important to contextualize today's social realities as we work to increase awareness of the current adults who assume responsibility for helping today's children cultivate social and emotional well-being.

Why Do We Care About Social and Emotional Competencies?

Social and emotional development, broadly defined, involves children's ability to positively build relationships with peers and adults, understand others' emotions, and regulate their feelings and behavior. Across a lifetime, these social and emotional skills serve as a foundation for success in learning and maintaining healthy relationships. More and more, classroom educators have begun to recognize the importance of teaching the whole child, considering students' emotional, cultural, social, familial, and salient aspects of their identities as integral parts of academic success. Teachers and parents are key individuals in this developmental journey who provide affective roadmaps for children, leading by example and intentional engagement. Over the past two decades, classroom teachers have been at the forefront of addressing the complexities of children's questions about who they are and their readiness to explore identity. For example, students as young as 9 ask themselves questions like "Why do I act differently in different places?" or "Why am I forced to be someone I'm not?" or "Why am I so afraid to share my ideas?" (Kauffman & Short, 2001, p. 1). Resistance to engage in meaningful discussions about identity and controversial social issues often comes from adults who believe children are too young, not ready to talk about things like discrimination or war, do not know how to facilitate tough conversations, feel overwhelmed, or have not confronted their own emotions or opinions about specific topics. Imagine you are a teacher in the following classroom scenario:

> Yesenia, an 8-year-old child in your third-grade classroom is an extremely diligent and friendly student. She has a lot of friends, does well in all academic areas, and is considered a leader among her peers. Over the last 2 weeks, however, Yesenia has been quiet, looks sad, and has participated less in classroom discussions. When you ask her how she's doing, she shrugs and replies, "Fine." After talking to the school counselor, you learn Yesenia's father and uncle were recently deported to Guatemala by ICE. Apparently, there have also been a few playground incidents with sixth-grade boys chanting, "Go back where you came from," which have led to fights between students.

As you read this scenario, what kinds of feelings come up? What are your initial thoughts? What do you believe are your responsibilities? As a teacher, how might you respond—with Yesenia or with your entire class? If you feel like you are a deer in the headlights, you are not alone. Many adults are at a loss for how to discuss such socially charged topics or were taught that any type of conversation about politics, religion, race, and the like is taboo. For many parents and teachers, addressing any of these questions with children is not a simple task, as it requires several important considerations. These include (1) knowing the appropriate terminology to engage in these types of conversations, (2) understanding how to include students from varying backgrounds, (3) appreciating students' emotional thresholds, and (4) identifying "stuck points" that may influence how a topic is discussed (e.g., personal opinions about specific issues). However, the benefits of helping students develop social awareness and emotional competencies outweigh the challenges. By promoting meaningful discussions about hard topics, we better prepare youth for attaining positive educational outcomes and relationships as well as developing ethical responsibility for themselves, peers, family, and community.

The old adage "It's not just what you say, but how you say it" provides a great starting point for engaging in meaningful conversations with children. In each of our chapters, we provide guidelines for the content, including types of questions and focus topics. We also offer some tips on *how* to bring these conversations up as well as keep them going. Research indicates that it is not merely the quantity of time we spend conversing with children, but also the quality of those conversations that lead to positive cognitive, social, and emotional development (Romeo et al., 2018). Children's literature is a particularly useful tool for adults and children to begin having these meaningful conversations. Books provide an ideal context for children and adults to talk about things, which are often difficult to confront head-on.

Where Do Teachers and Other School Professionals Come In?

Thinking back to your own childhood, you may remember specific events that still evoke intense feelings. Perhaps these are painful memories of being bullied or excluded by peers. Maybe it was that horrible time in your life when a beloved family pet died. Ideally, you were able to share what you were going through with a loving adult who sat and listened. We also recognize that for many, these conversations did not happen, as children can find it hard to open up to an adult by saying something like, "It made me so sad when they called me those mean names. I feel so lonely" or "It's so unfair Daisy [the cat] got sick and had to be put down. I'm angry!" Despite how many times we coach children to "use your words," for many under the age of 10, there is a lack of the emotional vocabulary or communication skills to verbally process difficult feelings. Young children's developing brains also can prevent them from completely regulating their emotions on their own (see the Pixar movies *Inside Out* and *Inside Out 2* for great examples). Additionally, a child's home environment and the psychological health of their family are crucial factors in emotional development.

Rather than talk it out, children often show us through action. For example, a child who is experiencing intense bullying at school may lash out toward their siblings at home. The expression of grief for a young child can include a range of behaviors, such as withdrawal from activities they used to enjoy, increased crying or tantrums, intense fear of leaving the house, and catastrophizing about all the worst (and unlikely) possible life events. For other children, difficult feelings may emerge as physiological complaints, including stomachaches, headaches, trouble sleeping, bed wetting, and restlessness. Broadly, these emotional, cognitive, and physical manifestations are a child's way of saying, "I'm having a really hard time and need help." For many of us working in classrooms, we know how challenging it can be to know how and when to intervene when we notice students' high emotional needs. There are also times we are overwhelmed by the extent of trauma some of our students have undergone. Sometimes it is too much to hold.

Educators play so many roles in students' lives, which extend beyond the traditional definitions of your professional title. We know many of you have worn various hats, resembling something more like a close aunt or uncle, mentor, coach, and even a mental health counselor. A common thread through all of these roles, however, is one of a caring adult. Each new school year, you are lucky to get to spend an intense amount of time with a specific group of kids who are going through a lot—emotionally, physically, cognitively, and socially. And you also get to help them figure out a lot of this by being a consistent person in their lives who notices when they are not their usual selves, provides them with a rich emotional vocabulary to talk about hard things, and normalizes their full range of emotions ("It's okay—everyone cries because crying is a part of being human").

In the following chapters, we provide you with some starting points to initiate *and* maintain courageous conversations with your students about difficult-to-discuss topics. A major message we want to illuminate here (imagine a large flashing neon sign) is that you do not have to be an expert on all of the tough topics children confront in order to talk about them. What's *most* important is that your students know their opinions, feelings, and endless questions about racism or gun violence or other topics matter. Their feelings are welcome in your classroom and you are going to be one person helping them explore these feelings in ways that instill respect and empathy. Remember, you are not alone when helping your students explore their feelings, grow in their empathetic responses, and develop respect. The children's books that line the shelves of your classroom, office, school, and local library are here to aid you in this process.

WHY CHILDREN'S BOOKS AS STARTING PLACES FOR CHALLENGING CONVERSATIONS?

Discussion around books begins at a very young age. Many caregivers and family members engage babies in lap-sharing of stories as early as infancy, using the soft lull of a story to settle their little one to sleep, or the excitement of a sturdy board book to engage together in shared interaction and the start of early language learning. The first American Academy of Pediatrics' policy statement on literacy promotion, released in 2014 and updated in 2024, led to increasing numbers of pediatricians across the country talking about reading aloud during well-baby checks, and even providing books for their young patients, while early childhood centers and Head Start, local public libraries, and other public and private education or child-serving institutions do the same with story-time programs and literacy-based preschool activities. By the time they enter elementary school, many children are well versed in the idea of discussing the stories that have been read aloud to them and sharing thoughts about the actions of the characters within them.

Books offer a certain advantage over other technological resources in encouraging discussion in part because they foster oral communication between the adult and children and have built-in personal interactions. Children thrive when the person reading aloud to them engages them with the reading at some level, from encouraging the naming of familiar objects, to pointing out a funny or unusual illustration or part of the story, to making connections to the child's world. This sense of reading as a collective and shared experience follows the children into elementary school, where small-group and whole-class discussion of read-aloud continues. Television shows, movies, computers, and tablet games do not necessarily carry this embedded sense of community, in part because they can be experienced by a child without the adult presence to read and communicate the words of the story. Even audio books and ebook apps suffer from this lack of shared experience because the children can experience them without the presence of another human. While outstanding children's programming and technology often encourage participant interaction, it is not inherently responsive at the same level.

Furthermore, books for young children commonly focus on the themes closest to their daily lives: family relationships, feelings and fears, and friendship (Galda, Liang, & Cullinan, 2017). They frequently involve regular routines and childhood milestones, allowing children to explore a particular adventure or milestone first as an observer. Watching Mo Willems's characters Elephant and Piggie, for example, work out how to share their play with another friend in *Can I Play, Too?* (2010) or learn to have patience in *Waiting Is Not Easy!* (2014) can help a child think about their possible reactions in similar situations. Stories about the first day of school, about the arrival of a new sibling, and even about everyday routines such as getting a haircut and going to the park are used by adults to introduce and discuss these events before they happen, and often later enjoyed by children because they mirror experiences with which they are familiar.

The prevalent use of stories for young readers in this way suggests a natural segue into using picturebooks with children to discuss issues that can be more challenging to comprehend. Children's authors and illustrators recognize this. Alongside books about first trips to the dentist sit texts that attempt to illustrate the grief over death and loss, provide context for situations such as family separation and even war, and acknowledge the fact that the world and life within it can be a confusing, and often terrifying, place. The best of these books avoid being too didactic and instead get to the core of the big emotions that swirl around the complex questions that children ask as they seek knowledge, understanding, and a sense of their role in the world. With many children already familiar with sharing their reactions to characters and stories within picturebooks, these beautifully rendered and thoughtfully written books offer caregivers and educators ways to gently enter into natural conversations on topics they might avoid otherwise.

Safe Way to Gently Open the Window

Books can offer a way to start. Books frequently are the mirrors where children find reflections of their life experiences, the windows through which they begin an understanding of others. The "mirrors, windows, and sliding glass doors" metaphor, originally coined and introduced by scholar and educator Dr. Rudine Sims Bishop in 1990, centers on how children see themselves within stories and learn about others, and focuses on the need for a much more diverse portrayal of characters within children's books so that all children have the opportunity to see themselves, their families, and their communities in books as well as step into the worlds of others.

This metaphor is vitally important to remember as we suggest using picturebooks to open challenging conversations with children. First, because it is a reminder about the portrayal and representation of the children within the books themselves. Despite many industry initiatives started around 2015 (see, e.g., the work of We Need Diverse Books over the last several years, or the publishing industry surveys sponsored by publisher Lee & Low), the diversity of characters in children's books in the United States remains woefully unrepresentative. While the number of children's books published yearly with a person of color in a primary character role has increased from the dismal amounts recorded in the past decade (e.g., approximately 15% in 2015), they are still problematic; the most recent statistics report only approximately 40% of children's books published in 2023 have a person of color in a primary character role (Cooperative Children's Book Center [CCBC], 2024; Huyck, Dahlen, & Griffin, 2016). Taking into consideration that teachers and school and public libraries do not always have the newest titles to offer readers, it is easy to see that the books teachers are using do not fully represent the racial and ethnic diversity of the United States youth population. Particularly as we consider using books as entries into conversations about more complicated topics, it is imperative to have a strong collection of books that offer ethnically diverse protagonists in a large range of settings so that children can both more easily identify with situations by seeing themselves represented and see children from different backgrounds than their own. This helps present the universally challenging nature of these topics. In the search of educators for "just the right book" to use for a particular topic, sometimes the importance of attention to diversity gets left out. It is essential that this not happen.

Second, Bishop's metaphor helps us to remember part of the purpose that children's books hold—this idea of opening the door and peering in at someone else's story. Books invite us to imagine ourselves in new worlds and situations and think about our reactions. Readers instinctively evaluate the actions and emotional reactions of protagonists as they read; thus, discussions about characters' actions are an easy start to thinking about how one might react to a challenging situation. These conversations sometimes allow children, and adults, to consider the topic one step removed from experiencing a real-life event, before gently transitioning into discussing the messiness and reality of personal experiences.

The Power of Perspective and the Value of Story

This invitation of books to encourage empathy with characters highlights the power books hold to build perspective and, ultimately, deeper understanding. As children's literature researcher Laura Apol (1998) once explained, "Children's literature is a form of education and socialization, an indication of a society's deepest hopes and fears, expectations and demands" (p. 34). Examining a set of children's picturebooks that represent several different perspectives can help readers identify and better understand many of the cultural, political, and economic aspects to a social issue. This can lead them to think about how to respond and to understand these issues in ways both similar and different from the various viewpoints in the books, as well as to build more empathy for different ways of thinking overall. The offer of varied perspectives combines with books' promotion of the rich imagination of young readers and, ultimately, adds to readers' growth of a broader view of the world (Frye, 1970; Nodelman, 1996, 1997). Perhaps award-winning author Christopher Myers (2013) captures it best: "Books allow us a bird's eye view of our own lives, and especially how our lives relate to those lives around us" (p. 11).

No Book Stands Alone

An outstanding book by itself will not necessarily broaden your students' perspectives and develop their tolerance, respect, and understanding of others. The discussion around the reading is key, as well as the placement of that book within a larger set of texts. Reading a *set* of purposefully sequenced, outstanding, diverse titles that offer various viewpoints helps to encourage automatic comparison, but without conversation that comparison might not include a growth in perspective taking and deep understanding. Conversation with the sequenced reading is necessary.

As we think about your use of this book to help you with the children in your lives, we return to Bishop's famous piece "Mirrors, Windows, and Sliding Glass Doors" (1990), where she ended her essay by writing:

> Those of us who are children's literature enthusiasts tend to be somewhat idealistic, believe that some book, some story, some poem can speak to each individual child, and that if we have the time and resources, we can find that book and help to change that child's life, if only for a brief time, and only for a tiny bit. On the other hand, we are realistic enough to know that that literature, no matter how powerful, has its limits. . . . [Literature] could, however, help us to understand each other better by helping to change our attitudes towards difference. (p. xi)

YOU ARE NOT ALONE: YOU, BOOKS, AND OTHERS

Teachers can't do it all, try as they might. A broader community that fosters working across fields and disciplines within and outside of a school is critical for teachers to get the support they need, even when they are armed with outstanding books.

Help within the School Building

Let's start with the individuals within a school with expertise assisting with students' social and emotional well-being. These include the counselors, social workers, behavior specialists, and school psychologists. While these professionals all have different roles, they all work with individuals and groups and can share helpful tips and techniques on how to approach sensitive topics. This group of professionals can be counted on to provide assistance in how to build a caring environment allowing students to safely express their own views, leading to a caring classroom and school community. They are trained on how to do this, and on how to respond to students who feel threatened or marginalized. Additionally, these individuals often work with other mental health professionals outside of the school and may be able to suggest additional resources on a particular issue or topic. The specialized training of these individuals makes them an invaluable asset and teachers can receive great assistance from such colleagues when addressing sensitive topics with their students.

There is great benefit in including these individuals who have the training to support social and emotional development. However, they are not the only people within the school who can assist teachers. Other professionals within the school include the special education teacher, speech language pathologist, and librarian. The special education teacher and speech language pathologist have experience supporting students who struggle with academics, emotions, and speech and language issues. These professionals have expertise in working directly with students who often encounter negative experiences in school due to their differences. Similar to counselors, social workers, and school psychologists, these professionals frequently have contacts with agencies and professionals outside of the school, making them another valuable resource for teachers seeking help as they address sensitive topics.

Librarians can also be a wonderful asset for teachers. As both unique school professionals and specialty teachers, they have expertise in working with children as well as identifying appropriate books, movies, websites, and local connections on certain topics. They also tend to know all the students in the school at some level since they interact with every classroom in the building. Thus, they are often tuned into what resonates with students in the community and can narrow the search for an appropriate resource much faster than if the teacher were doing it alone.

Resources beyond the School Walls

Outside the school is also a large network of resources for teachers. Local public libraries often have information on authors and guest speakers who are available to come talk to classes. Local advocacy groups that focus on certain topics frequently offer resources specifically for children, such as community counseling centers with a focus on addiction or incarceration. Many of these agencies focus on the family, meaning they are likely to have expertise in assisting children who are innocent bystanders to the stressful situations that teachers may address in their classrooms and can provide additional help.

Connecting with outside resources should start with those individuals we have already identified within the school. Meeting with school professionals one-on-one, or calling for a meeting with everyone, can provide teachers with ideas for how to approach their class on a particularly sensitive topic. Having a meeting with multiple school professionals provides an opportunity for them to share what they know and help the teacher prepare what they need to be successful in supporting their students.

Including Families and Caregivers

Involving families and caregivers requires thoughtful planning by teachers. It is important to inform them about sensitive topics discussed in class, allowing for open communication and support. Teachers can assist caregivers by sharing practical tips and resources to aid children at home, whether through letters announcing upcoming units or hosting informational sessions at school. Collaborating with school professionals and external resources can enhance planning and ensure effective family engagement. Given the sensitive nature of these topics, it is crucial for teachers to rely on experienced professionals who can provide additional support and guidance to families beyond school hours. Furthermore, it is imperative that school leadership, including the principal, is informed and supportive throughout the process, as they may be the first point of contact for concerned caregivers.

STARTING THE CONVERSATION: HOW TO USE THIS BOOK

We hope you are becoming eager to begin courageous conversations with your classes and start using this book. While this type of instruction is based on our professional knowledge and expertise, it also has roots in our personal experiences that have led us to be willing to try out these discussions ourselves. We hear the questions from children and want to help educators to open conversations. We, too, have made many mistakes and often are not sure how to respond to our own children, the children in the schools with whom we work, and our education and psychology undergraduate and graduate students. But we know that the first, and most important, step is the courage to try.

Thus, we designed this book to help support educators in starting this work. It is a self-contained resource to both provide scripted lessons in complete units that you can implement directly in your classroom, and to give you the more general tools to engage with your students around these difficult topics, especially when you are stuck in the moment and do not know what to say. We aim to help you feel more comfortable with a state of being uncomfortable!

Chapters 3–11 offer thematic book sets of carefully curated, purposefully sequenced, high-quality diverse picturebooks with detailed plans for using these titles to introduce the topic, widen third- through sixth-grade students' perspectives surrounding it, and engage them in meaningful discussions and activities that deepen understanding. See Figure 1.1 to learn about the guidelines we followed in selecting outstanding children's picturebooks for each of the thematic book sets found in Chapters 3–11.

The discussions and activities meet national guidelines for the English language arts and social and emotional learning and are suitable for intermediate classrooms and can extend into middle school classrooms as well. (The individual Common Core standards met by each unit are listed for grade 4, as a representative sample, at the end of each chapter. The individual standards for grades 3, 5, and 6 can be found via the QR code that appears with the grade 4 standards.) Each thematic book set unit is designed for approximately 1 hour of instruction per day across 8 to 9 classroom days (approximately 2 weeks of school). Some days might involve more or less instructional time. We encourage you to make adjustments and accommodations if you have students in your classroom who are just beginning to read and write or have difficulty with these tasks (e.g., you might eliminate the requirement of having students read aloud by maintaining a policy that any student may choose to pass when it's their turn if they wish or allow students the option of drawing instead of writing). To lessen any possible stigma for those students who need accommodations, give all students these same options. Finally, we encourage wait time between using the thematic book set units to let children process new information; our recommendation is no more than one unit per month. The nine thematic book set units offered in this book could work well for the duration of 1 school year.

A rich Appendix of Reproducible Materials—with planning checklists, permission slips, reflection pieces for the teachers' and students' well-being, and pre- and post-evaluations—complements the chapters and includes items designed for use in each thematic book set unit. These materials will aid you in making sure that safety nets are in place for your discussions, including setting ground rules, knowing when to stop discussions, and considering when to

<table>
<tr><td colspan="2">What makes a "good" book? This is a question that has been discussed for years. In the field of children's literature, we acknowledge that what one reader considers a favorite ("the best book I've ever read!") might be disliked by another reader. While the field recognizes the power of personal preference, it also reaches beyond and considers quality when selecting and evaluating children's books.

In general, a children's picturebook's "quality" is evaluated in at least three areas: literary merit, artistic merit, and consideration of cultural authenticity and representation. Educators often add an additional consideration around "fit"—considering if the book meets well with the purposes of its use in the classroom and considering the complexity of the book and the intended reader's reading level. For this book, we evaluated "fit" as meeting the particular purposes of use in our units focused on the topic and standards being met.</td></tr>
<tr><td>Fit for These Units</td><td>☐ Does the book address the topic in a genuine way?
☐ Does it respect the multifaceted nuances of the topic?
☐ Does it avoid didacticism, moralistic language, or overly simple "solutions"?
☐ Does it either center on one unique perspective or offer an array of perspectives in an authentic way?
☐ Is the book suitable for a read-aloud in terms of length and pacing?</td></tr>
<tr><td>Literary Merit</td><td>☐ Is the language engaging and full of verve?
☐ Do the pace and pattern of the language used match with the topic and style of the book?
☐ Does the story contain strong characterization, avoiding one-dimensional characters?
☐ Is the plot plausible within the context of the setting?</td></tr>
<tr><td>Artistic Merit</td><td>☐ Are the illustrations artistically excellent with technique and style appropriate to the text?
☐ Do the illustrations relate to the text in a meaningful way?
☐ Do the medium, technique, and style fit with the text?
☐ Do the design elements work to enhance meaning within individual illustrations and across the book as a whole?</td></tr>
<tr><td>Consideration of Issues of Cultural Authenticity and Representation</td><td>☐ Are the author's and illustrator's expertise, qualifications, and attitudes related to the topic addressed in the book appropriate?
☐ Are stereotypes avoided in both the text and in the illustrations?
☐ Are the characters within the story as diverse as one would expect in any culture?
☐ Are the relationships between characters of different cultures portrayed authentically and accurately?
☐ Does the book seem accurate when compared to other similar books, to research, and/or to other knowledge?</td></tr>
<tr><td colspan="2">Note. Criteria adapted from Galda, Liang, & Cullinan (2017); Lehman, Freeman, & Scharer (2010).</td></tr>
</table>

FIGURE 1.1. Guidelines used for selection of picturebooks.

involve other professionals for help with students. They also guide you to meet the goals and purposes of the unit, evaluating the impact these are having on your students' social and emotional development. Additionally, any reproducible materials used in the unit, such as worksheets or writing templates, are available both in the end-of-book Appendix and on the book's companion website (see the box at the end of the Contents for details).

The thematic book set unit chapters are divided into four parts or sections reflecting the current major concerns of today's school professionals around children's social and emotional development, positive identity formation, and children's mental health. The first part, "Supporting Children's Social and Emotional Growth through Literature," features chapters on peer relationships (friendship and bullying) and grief and loss. The next part, "Supporting Children's Understanding of Communities through Literature," focuses on civic engagement and community population changes due to refugee situations. The third part, "Supporting Children's Positive Identity Formation through Literature," includes chapters on identity in the realms of race and ethnicity, gender, and ability. Finally, the fourth part, "Supporting Children's Mental Health through Literature," offers thematic units on beginning to understand anxiety and depression.

In each unit, we provide specific recommendations to help you facilitate the conversations about the specific topic. However, Chapter 2 reviews important overarching concepts to put in place in your classroom discussions *before you start* your first of this book's thematic book set units with students. After reading this chapter and Chapter 2 that follows, we encourage you to consider the priority needs for your students and select the individual unit with which to begin this work in your classroom.

Finally, it is important to note that these units are designed to facilitate discussions among all children about these challenging topics, fostering a broader understanding of commonly encountered issues. They are not meant to substitute therapy. These units aim to cultivate awareness and empathy. Initiating courageous conversations early in childhood can nurture children to become thoughtful and socially conscious adults.

The Time to Start the Work Is Now

Let's Get Started

It's never too early, or too late, to start talking to children about the tough topics we highlight in this book. Many adults are tentative about addressing these topics with children, particularly in the classroom, because it was often taboo to discuss these things when they were growing up. For example, maybe when you were a child and brought up the topic of differences, adults avoided your questions or said, "We are all human" or "We are all the same on the inside." Perhaps these are ideas you continue to carry with you. By starting these conversations early and by leveraging the power of children's literature to assist in the discussion, you are preparing your students to engage in more authentic, compassionate, and empathic relationships. This work to increase emotional awareness and encourage positive mental health also promotes their academic achievement and future success. The research on children's social and emotional development and its relationship to student outcomes is so compelling that social and emotional learning is part of the standards for preschool in most of the 50 states and may be found in the goals of well over half of elementary and secondary schools nationwide. Yet, the implementation of social and emotional learning is often a challenge. We offer this book to help.

As educators, you are in a prime position to help students learn how to ask and think critically about socially charged topics and avoid falling into binary thinking. By using the book sets and guiding students through the outlined discussions and activities, you are helping them foster curiosity, make keen observations, and sit with ambiguity. We all know it is extremely uncomfortable to have unresolved feelings about an issue. Yet, the greatest gift we can give our children is the ability to live in the gray, to wrestle with all sides of an issue, to understand another person's point of view, even when it contradicts our own. In the end, this enables students to make more informed life decisions, have respectful discussions with people who may not necessarily share similar viewpoints, and be advocates for the change they want to see in the world around them. Your decision to embark on this journey demonstrates your commitment to let your students know who they are matters. You will be leading your classroom communities through powerful experiences, and we anticipate your own transformational moments along the way. Together, you and your class will have many courageous conversations and your students will rely on you to provide them with examples of how to engage with respect, inclusion, and compassion. Each of the units in this book will come with its own unique rewards and challenges, depending on who your students are as well as your level of (dis)comfort in talking about each topic. In this chapter, we provide some strategies for how to prepare for these conversations: understanding your experiences and expectations with these topics; thinking about the dynamic and makeup of your classroom; using tips for starting these courageous conversations; and encouraging ways to support similar or follow-up conversations in the home. Let's start with some "warm-up" exercises, which will help you visualize and then implement these units with clear intentions and self-awareness.

SELF-AWARENESS IS KEY: EDUCATOR, KNOW THYSELF

Each of the units you choose to implement will involve both content (the books you read aloud and the activities you implement) and a process. Process involves *how* you talk about the topic, including the language you use, your response to children's questions, and your nonverbal communication. Students' willingness to delve into a topic will likely rely on your own level of comfort, self-awareness, and humility. The following are some common questions to reflect on before beginning. By spending some time reflecting on these questions prior to using any of the units in this book, you will be better prepared to lead your students through the activities and facilitate rich dialogue.

- *What are your social identities?* The more you understand your own social identities, what they mean, and how they operate in our society, the better equipped you will be to talk with students about their identities. In this book, the chapters in Part III offer units that focus on identity as related to race and ethnicity, gender, and ability. Take an inventory of your knowledge and feelings about your cultural heritage, race, ethnicity, ability, gender, politics, religion, and so on. If you have not had time to think about what these identities mean, it is important to begin this work. Such an exploration may involve doing some research: reading books, watching documentaries and movies about the topic, consulting with content experts, or talking with others you identify with, including joining online affinity groups.

- *How do you feel about the topics?* Prior to each unit, identify some of your strengths that will assist you with facilitating open and honest conversations about this topic. Also identify any worries you have about addressing this topic that might limit your effectiveness in having a dialogue with your students. Reflect on the early messages you received as a child about the topic. Then, talk about these strengths and worries with coworkers, family members, and friends. The more conversations you have with others, the more confident you will become in keeping the conversation about each topic going. *Remember, the goal is not to get everyone to share similar views.* What is most important is to help students stay engaged and learn that talking about these topics helps us get to know each other as whole people—it humanizes each of us.

• *How will you stay engaged in conversations?* There will be times when students bring up questions or comments you are not expecting. (Imagine a student shouting out, "I heard being transgender is evil" or "Don't Chinese people eat dogs?") These examples may get your heart racing, and you may not have a response in those moments. This is okay. We have specifically designed activities and discussion prompts for each topic to help you with these conversations as well as offering tips at the end of this chapter. However, it will be important to consider how you will remain open and stay present (vs. changing the subject or avoiding the discussion). You can prepare by first reflecting on what topics may elicit more discomfort. Gather ideas from parents and teachers on how they might have responded to similar questions. Find comfort in the discomfort and know that you don't and won't have all the answers—instead, embrace the opportunity to learn *with* your students.

• *How can I make sure students feel comfortable?* You can start by modeling and inviting them to be brave and take risks. It is also important to recognize the composition of your classroom by tailoring activities and conversations accordingly. The reality is you will not be able to create an absolutely comfortable space, especially for those who are members of societally marginalized groups. Be careful of opening a space where the students with minoritized identities might feel as if they have to defend their point of view or educate others in the classroom, unless they feel good about doing so. (In the Appendices 2 and 9, we offer two Taking the Pulse of the Class checklists to assist you in gauging the comfort level of your students before and after using the units.)

• *What if I make a mistake?* Even with the best intentions, we all stumble over our words and share wrong information. That's okay! Model for your students that you are still figuring out how to talk about these important topics and are so happy you get to have these conversations together. Research shows that cultivating an open, communicative, and trusting relationship (and not being overly vigilant of what we say) is the foundation to having courageous conversations. We also know this from our personal experiences with some of our closest friends—we may have said and done things we did not intend or later realized were offensive. What's vital here is not to tread so carefully around saying everything "right" (that's an impossible task), but rather to demonstrate humility by admitting moments when you don't know or apologizing when you make mistakes. This also provides an excellent role model for your students, so they know it is okay to make mistakes as well as what they can say or do when they make mistakes.

THE CLASSROOM AS COMMUNITY: IDENTITIES AND GROUP DYNAMICS

Who are the current students in your class? Structuring activities will depend on the composition of your group, students' learning and emotional needs, and the classroom relationship dynamics. The following section highlights some student characteristics that should be considered while determining how to organize your class activities—whole class, small groups, partners, or individuals. (Remember, 2 weeks before the unit, complete the Taking the Pulse of the Class: Before Unit form in Appendix 2 to help with these considerations.)

Diversity and Identity Representation

What is the current demographic of your classroom, and how might students respond to the theme of the current unit? It is important to consider students who may be the only individuals holding a specific identity (e.g., there is only one Muslim student in your classroom). For example, if addressing racial-ethnic identity within a predominantly White classroom, it will be important to avoid singling out students of color (despite your best intentions) to speak on behalf of their racial or ethnic group.

Emotional Needs

Which students may be more activated by the topic, especially if they identify with some of the themes in the book? For example, stories related to the experiences of refugees may bring up negative emotions for children who have been displaced from their countries of origin. Recognize how some of the activities will impact your classroom community. Consult with staff in the school who work with your students, including school counselors and learning specialists; they may offer some suggestions for how to attend to students' needs. (Notification forms alerting others to the upcoming unit can be found in Appendices 3–5 for administrators, for school counselors/school psychologists/school social workers, and for other support staff.)

Peer Relationships

How are the students in your class getting along? Which students will work well together on specific topics? Are there any conflicts between specific students? Based on the answers to these questions, you'll be able to optimally group students into pairs or small groups during activities to create productive interactions. For example, it may be ideal to pair students who have had interpersonal differences to work together on an activity that allows them to problem-solve or get to know each other better. (Refer to the Taking the Pulse of the Class and Daily Reflection forms in Appendices 2, 7, and 9 to help you assess group dynamics and peer relationships.)

Social and Political Climate

Are there current news and events that may intensify students' reactions to the selected books? Your students are likely learning about tragic events on apps, the radio, or the TV but are not talking with an adult to help them make sense of what they've heard. For example, school gun shootings are a national crisis with important but overwhelming amounts of news coverage. Many children may not have the language to express what it's like to hear tragedies about kids their age. It will be important to help students make connections between the unit topics and their lived experiences.

KNOW YOUR AUDIENCE: HOW TO FACILITATE COURAGEOUS CONVERSATIONS

In working closely with your class, you have the clearest sense of students' attention span, how much content students can handle, or when they might need a break. There will be moments you will need to pause what you are doing to attend to individual students or move to a different activity altogether. The following section will provide you with some strategies for facilitating activities and discussions, including how long to keep conversations going, how to involve all students, how to attend to students' social and emotional needs during each activity, how you might respond to questions, or what you might say during unexpected moments. Before we get into the finer details of how to facilitate these conversations, take a look at Figure 2.1,

Transparency	Transparency is about being clear and up-front. It means directly preparing your students for the kinds of feelings a topic might bring up and how some of what you talk about may be harder for some than others. Transparency is also about helping students gauge their own level of readiness to talk about specific subjects, so they can tell you where they are at and how they are feeling.
Humility	Humility is about creating a classroom culture of openness, curiosity, and a willingness to learn from each other. Humility means helping students ask questions and admit when they make mistakes or hurt someone's feelings. It is about choosing kindness and love over needing to always be correct. Helping students recognize that saying "sorry" or "I made a mistake" does not diminish their self-worth; it demonstrates courage.
Respect	Respect is about facilitating interactions in which students truly listen to each other and honor each other's differences (e.g., race, gender, (dis)ability, etc.). Nonverbal respect can be demonstrated by paying full attention to the speaker, comforting a classmate who is having a difficult time, or giving someone the time to gather their thoughts without jumping in. Verbal respect involves thanking a person for sharing, encouraging a quiet classmate to say something out loud, and saying, "I'm sorry."
Integrity	Integrity is often defined as a concept comprising several values, including trust, responsibility, and moral uprightness. It also means standing together as a collective. As such, your early discussions can start with helping students talk about what it means to demonstrate trustworthiness as well as see how they each contribute to the classroom dynamic.
Vulnerability	Vulnerability encompasses self-awareness and the sharing of genuine emotions, which can create a deeper connection and authenticity among people. Although this concept is often defined as weakness, we suggest a reinterpretation. For children to build emotional resilience, there will necessarily be times where they will have to learn how to develop healthy relationships that require courage and risk taking. At times, vulnerability means inviting silence and sitting with our emotions, resisting the pull to fill up discomfort with words.
Empathy	Empathy is the ability to understand, identify with, and respect other people's feelings. It is a social and emotional skill slowly nurtured across a lifetime, which may first start by teaching children to recognize their own emotions and tune into how particular interactions make them feel.

FIGURE 2.1. THRIVE in conversation.

which describes a few key ingredients to help cultivate a courageous space. By embodying these values and teaching your students how to embrace these ideas, we know you will THRIVE in these courageous conversations.

How to Start Courageous Conversations

To help students develop a sense of empathy toward one another, it is helpful to establish ground rules that students can remember during each unit (and in general). This will provide a solid foundation to build an inclusive learning community. Make sure these ground rules are easily visible in the classroom, so you can refer to them when needed. Although it is more powerful to ask children to come up with the rules themselves, here are some handy examples:

- *Listen actively.* Pay attention to others with your eyes, ears, and heart when they are speaking.
- *Show respect.* Even if someone's opinion differs from your own, avoid interrupting, talking over others, and use neutral body language.
- *Maintain confidentiality.* What is shared in the room stays in the room. This helps everyone feel more open to talking.
- *Speak from your own experience.* Use "I" statements (e.g., "I feel," "I think").
- *Recognize your impact.* Pay attention to how your words, body language, and actions affect others.
- *Allow for silence.* Provide the space and time for everyone to reflect and respond thoughtfully.

Breathing or mindfulness exercises can be a helpful way to start (and end) classroom conversations about tough topics. These classroom rituals provide cues to your students that you are going to enter into activities that require self-awareness of how they are feeling and attention to what they do with their bodies and minds. Students will also learn to use these mindfulness skills in other situations. Start by having your students place both feet on the ground, sit up tall, and place their hands palms up in their lap. Ask them to close their eyes or relax their gaze while looking at a place in front of them. Then instruct them to (1) breathe in slowly through their nose for 4 seconds, (2) hold their breath for 4 seconds, (3) breathe out slowly through their mouth for 4 seconds, and (4) hold their breath for another 4 seconds. Repeat this several times. This is called *box breathing,* which is a well-established strategy for calming the nervous system.

The composition of your classroom or who your students are will determine the length of classroom discussion. Sometimes discussion on a particular topic only lasts a few minutes. We all know there are days when students have a shorter attention span or are more rambunctious. Rest assured there is no endpoint to these types of discussions, as each unit is intended to plant the seed for ongoing conversations. You'll be nicely surprised by students whom you think were not paying attention come up to you later in the month and show you they were listening. Be open to revisiting a topic if students are showing interest, allowing for additional learning and processing. Perhaps they needed some time to make sense of how these new ideas fit within their own experiences. Distractedness, however, may also be a sign of students feeling overwhelmed by a topic and your cue to take a pause and check in with your class. We discuss how to attend to children's feelings later in the chapter. The goal is not to "get through it," but rather to take cues from your students as you approach each topic and allow yourself the space to stop and start in ways that make sense given the makeup of your classroom.

How to Draw Students In

There are several strategies to help students feel more comfortable and enthusiastic about participating in each unit. Below we share some tips on what you might say to draw them in:

- *Normalize* that there will be moments when students feel uncomfortable or emotional when talking about an issue. Here's an example of what you could say: "Sometimes when we talk about ____________, lots of different feelings come up. You might feel your stomach tighten as you feel sad or confused. This is all okay, and I hope that we can talk about any of those feelings because they are important." Model this for your students with a personal example: "I know when I talk about ____________, I feel my body tense up, I make a sad face, and I avoid looking at others."

- *Show your curiosity* about what students are bringing up by asking open-ended questions or inviting more detail. Students may not have the vocabulary to describe some of what is coming up for them, so you may need to do some exploring. For example, "Tell me more about that." "What did you learn?" "What are you curious to know more about?" "That's so interesting, and I love that you brought that up." "What a fantastic observation!" "Tell me how that makes you feel."

- *Reflect back what is said and invite other students to respond to one another.* There may be moments when you notice students make connections to a story and raise their hands to share similar observations. One way to help students engage with each other is to highlight the commonalities and invite them to talk to one another. For example, "I think I heard a couple of people share something similar about the book. Liv, will you turn to Marco and tell him why you related to this part of the story. (*Pause to allow for interaction.*) Now, Marco, will you share how you related with Willow? (*Pause to allow for interaction.*) Great sharing!"

- *Use self-disclosure* to model vulnerability and share your own experiences, emotions, and in-the-moment reactions. This can often foster more connection with your students and trust within the classroom. It lets students know it's okay to express feelings and to talk about this out loud. Self-disclosure is a powerful and humanizing tool that can also elicit deeper understanding and empathy toward each other. For example, you might share something like "This part of the book made me feel (*sad, angry, happy, scared*) when (*describe the moment*). Anyone else feel something similar?" Or, "What did you feel during the part when (*describe the scene*). I felt so worried about (*the character's name*) and I cried. How about you?"

- *Validate questions and observations* by encouraging more conversation. Here are some examples of how to deepen discussion while also sending the message that you appreciate what they've brought up: "That's such a great observation, Ruth. Why don't you ask some of your classmates what they thought about this part of the story?" or "I hadn't thought of that before! What made you think of it, Ravi?" or "How did you feel when you saw that happen?" or "I'm so glad you brought this question up. I love that you are curious about this. I like that we get to talk about this stuff together."

- *Help your students think critically.* When discussing identity or cultural differences, children often focus on concrete and visible features to describe others, such as skin color or assumed gender. Encourage them to consider other important personal dimensions. For example, if your student refers to a friend as "my friend with brown skin," prompt her to share more about her friend. Ask questions like "What does your friend enjoy doing?" and "What kinds of things do you like doing together?"

- *Identify and take opportunities to keep the conversations going.* After completing a unit, the discussions on themes in this unit do not have to end. Seek opportunities to engage your students in conversations that can deepen their understanding of difficult concepts and draw connections across themes. For example, "Do you remember when we read the story about (*refer to the book from the unit on gender identity*)? Remember when (*give the name of character*) was treated differently because of their gender? Do you think (*give the name of character in current book*) might be feeling similarly? Why or why not?" Let this lead to a richer conversation.

HOW TO PROCESS WHAT'S HAPPENING IN THE ROOM

It is important to observe both the *process* and *content* of the discussion: *how* the conversation is taking place and *what* is being said in the conversation. Some characteristics to look out for include the flow of the conversation, moments of silence, and whose voices are not being heard in the dialogue. The following are some ways to respond to various situations related to classroom dynamics. (At the end of each lesson within a unit, we encourage you to complete the Daily Reflection in Appendix 7; it will help you reflect on what did and did not go well during each activity and inform your approach to subsequent lessons.)

If you notice **tension** in the room, but it is acting as a force for dialogue and learning, choose to monitor the situation while letting the discussion play out naturally. However, if the tension seems to be escalating, react calmly to defuse the situation. You can also refer back to the ground rules for the classroom.

If a student starts **crying or getting really upset**, it will be important to explore these feelings rather than pushing through the lesson. For example, you may respond with a comment like, "This is a tough conversation to have. I wonder if you're feeling sad or scared about what we're talking about. It's okay to have these feelings." Offer the student the opportunity to step out and get a drink of water, take a deep breath, and then join the conversation while also verbally letting them know it is okay to be upset.

If a child says something embarrassing, insensitive, or even racist, it is important to **stay calm, take a breath**, and **remain curious**. The following tips offer examples of how to continue the conversation without shaming a child or suggesting their observations are inherently wrong:

- "Hmm . . . that's an important observation. I wonder where you came up with that idea. Let's explore."
- "I hear what you are saying. I also think this might not be the full story. Let's figure out how we get more information to fill in the gaps."
- "Your ideas are important, and I wonder if that might be hurtful to hear. Is there another way we can ask that question or make that comment?"
- "What makes you feel that way about ____________?"
- "I want to really understand what you're sharing. Can you tell me more about what you mean when you say that?"

Sometimes you might need to **gauge the emotional temperature** of the room. Here are some strategies from Learning for Justice (*www.learningforjustice.org*) to help assess students' feelings and determine the best approach for certain activities.

Fist-to-Five

The *Fist-to-Five* strategy (see Figure 2.2) is a strategy to quickly check in with students' emotional comfort and readiness to continue. Students hold up a **closed fist** to indicate that they are very uncomfortable or overwhelmed emotionally. This could signal they need support. Holding up **one finger** may suggest some mild discomfort or uncertainty with what's being

FIGURE 2.2. Hand gestures used in the Fist-to-Five strategy.

discussed. They are managing their emotions okay. **Two fingers** might indicate students are somewhat comfortable but may have some questions or concerns. Holding up **three fingers** signals that students are feeling comfortable and still engaged in the discussion. **Four fingers** mean students are feeling quite comfortable, relaxed, and confident about what is happening in the room. **Five fingers** indicate emotional comfort and readiness. The students are at ease and ready to learn more.

Traffic Light

Introduce the *traffic light* analogy at the beginning of discussions or activities. Encourage students to silently indicate their emotional state using the colors by asking, "Are you feeling red, yellow, or green about our topic today?" **Red light** (Stop) means they are feeling uncomfortable or experiencing strong emotions that require immediate attention. They may need to take a break or seek support before continuing with the conversation or activity. **Yellow light** (Caution) means students are feeling unsure or uneasy. They may benefit from clarification, reassurance, or a brief pause to address any concerns before proceeding. **Green light** (Go) signals comfort and readiness to continue with the activity or discussion without any immediate emotional needs.

Thumbs Up/Thumbs Down/Thumbs Sideways

The *thumbs up/thumbs down/thumbs sideways* strategy (see Figure 2.3) is used in classrooms to quickly gauge student understanding or feelings about the conversation. You can ask your students to raise their **thumbs up** to show they are following and are okay continuing with the current discussion. **Thumbs down** indicates they are not comfortable with the dialogue, disagree with or do not understand the conversation. **Thumbs sideways** means students are unsure or need more clarification.

How to Gently Confront Inflammatory Remarks

If a student has just made an invalidating, offensive, or minimizing comment, particularly regarding a classmate's identity or a collective group's experience, it is crucial to stop the

FIGURE 2.3. Hand gestures used in the thumbs up/thumbs down/thumbs sideways strategy.

conversation and address the incident immediately. Such comments can negatively impact others in the room and erode trust. Processing the interaction is essential to repairing potential interpersonal ruptures. The following suggestions are adapted from Souza (2018) and can help guide this process:

- First say, "I want to pause for a moment to address something that was just said. It's important for us to slow down and understand how words like that might impact others when they hear them."
- Engage in active and nonjudgmental listening with the commenter. Paraphrase what the student said and check to make sure you have heard them accurately. Example: "I think I heard you say this _____________. Is that correct?"
  - If the child disagrees with your paraphrase and clarifies a different meaning, you could return to the activity by saying, "Okay, thanks for clarifying. I misheard you."
  - If you think they might be trying to "backtrack," you may consider making a statement about the initial comment to encourage learning. "Thank you for thinking this through with me. The statement I thought I heard you say earlier could be hurtful to others, so we must talk about the impact it might have on our friends."
  - If they agree with your paraphrase, explore your student's intent about why they made the comment, followed by what impact it might have on others. Discuss the difference between intent and impact. A helpful approach is to use yourself as an example, saying something like "Imagine I accidentally tripped my best friend because my foot was sticking out. I didn't mean to trip her, but she still fell and hurt herself. Even though it was an accident, my friend is crying and upset. Sometimes the same things happen with our words. We say things we do not mean to be hurtful. But sometimes, those words still do hurt others. What's important is that we take care of our friends' feelings and make sure to be careful with what we say next time, like "I'm sorry I tripped you. Next time, I will be careful of where I put my foot."
    - Exploring **intent:** "Will you tell me what you were hoping to say with that comment?" or "Will you help me understand what you meant by that?"
    - Exploring **impact:** "How might people feel when they hear that type of comment?" or "If you heard something like this said about you, what might you think?"
- Following any exchange involving the process described above, invite the entire class to think about ways they can communicate moving forward. Request a new behavior from all students, such as, "Our class is a learning community. Comments like these make it difficult for us to focus on learning because people feel bad. I am going to ask you to think about how certain words might hurt others and not say them. Will you please agree to this?"

How to Attend to an Emotionally Flooded Student

By monitoring the reactions of your students, you can attune yourself to how emotionally stimulated a child may be in the moment. Students who are emotionally overwhelmed or flooded may exhibit the following behaviors: They will cry, pull their knees into their body and bury their face in their knees, hug their knees and rock back and forth, actively disrupt the conversation, make jokes, fidget more than usual, or say, "I want to stop talking about this." If this happens, stop whatever you are doing and state your intention to put a pause on the conversation. Try to remain calm, take deep breaths, and be as supportive as you can. (You might also utilize the Fist-to-Five, traffic light, or thumbs up/thumbs down/thumbs sideways strategies to gauge the classroom's emotional atmosphere.) You can also use the "box breathing" exercise shared earlier.

- Gently note what you observe in the space, in a nonjudgmental and affirming way, and state your intention to put a pause on the conversation. For example, "I want to take a pause for a moment. I notice that some of us are having a hard time paying attention. Some of us might be feeling a lot of emotions right now." You can also model this by saying, "There are times when I have needed to stop and take a breath. Like when I was talking to a friend about ____________, I began to cry, and I didn't even realize I had those sad feelings until they just came out."

- Validate and normalize how people can become flooded when thinking or talking about challenging topics. For example, "You know, sometimes, when people talk about difficult things like this, they can feel a lot of emotions. These topics can be hard to talk about." Using a personal experience to model this also shows we all get flooded by emotions.

- Depending on the size and dynamic of your group, it may feel better to check in as a group or bring attention to the person in question. "When we are feeling a lot of emotions, it can be helpful to take a moment and check in on how we all are feeling. How are we doing? Do we need to take a break?" If you think students may be reluctant to indicate they need a break, you can say, "I am having a lot of feelings right now, and it would help me if we all take a break. Is everyone okay with a break?"

- Additionally, you may invite the children to take a break and check in with them individually, or to lead the class in a grounding exercise. Some grounding activities include playing calming music, deep breathing (e.g., box breathing), playing with comforting toys, getting a drink of water. "Perhaps we can all take a few deep breaths and bring our attention to our body and feelings."

- If you think that a child would benefit from further debriefing or processing, consult with a school counselor, social worker, school psychologist, or mental health provider in your school.

KEEP THE SUPPORT AND CONVERSATIONS GOING IN THE CLASSROOM AND AT HOME

Now that your students have some practice talking about life's more difficult topics, it is important to continue these conversations and foster students' social and emotional resilience. See Figure 2.4 to learn more about how to continue these types of conversations and attitudes in your classroom regularly. You may notice students referencing stories or perhaps asking questions about other social issues you have yet to explore. This indicates their openness to ongoing

Classroom Culture: Let's Keep Talking
▶ Incorporate mindfulness exercises into students' daily routine with a sustained focus on the present moment (e.g., emotions, physical sensations) without judgment. Research with elementary age youth links consistent mindfulness practice to higher self-esteem, improved mood, decreases in anxiety and stress, as well as improved social and academic skills.
▶ Maintain special classroom rituals that encourage open dialogue. We want children to pay close attention to the world around them and to draw connections with what they see to what they are learning in the class. Start every morning with the question "What did you notice?" and encourage students to ask each other questions about these observations.
▶ Continue to tie relevant conversations back to books you've read and activities you completed. This will remind everyone of their shared experiences and prompt them to reference what they learned during these lessons.
▶ Verbally affirm moments in class when students share relevant personal stories. Schools are interpersonal contexts in which learning is a collaborative process. Children will feel more encouraged to participate in activities when their experiences are validated by others.

FIGURE 2.4. Classroom culture: Let's keep talking.

exploration of things they may be grappling with. The culture created within the classroom, along with developing a common language, has provided an ideal setting for ongoing conversation, normalizing of students' feelings, respecting various opinions, and recognizing cues that signal a student needs to express themself (or needs a break).

After reading books from a unit and completing related activities, it is likely that your students will have more questions. They will be curious to see how their family members think about these issues. Or perhaps a critical event will compel a student's family to address a difficult issue firsthand (e.g., death in the family, deportation). Understandably, some parents may lack the confidence to have these conversations with their kids. Some worry their children are too young to understand. Many parents are emotionally overwhelmed and will avoid these discussions altogether. With the tools you've incorporated into your own classroom discussions and observations about how students have reacted, you can provide the valuable guidance parents need to have these conversations at home.

How to Encourage Ongoing Conversations at Home

You can send resources and tips home, including the topics and list of books you've read, activities that families can do together, and talking points for furthering conversations at home. When sending resources or activities for adults and students to use at home, remember the following tips:

- Include positive affirmations on any resources you send home (e.g., "Parents are the most influential teachers, mentors, and role models," "Five minutes of quality conversation with your child lets them know they are valued"). This helps to instill confidence in families to have these courageous conversations at home. Remind caregivers they are experts and have a wealth of information to share with their children. Reassure them that they do not need to have all the answers but instead must remain available to ask questions and listen to what their child shares.

- Keep information you send home short and sweet. Avoid unnecessary jargon or technical terms.
- Make sure the home activities are cost-free. Say something like the following:
  - "This week we focused on the topic of mental health. During dinner this week, start a 'Mealtime Mood Check-In' by asking each person to share how they are feeling in the moment and why. This may open more conversation about what happened at school."
  - "At bedtime, spend 10–15 minutes with your child talking about something that made them feel good about themself that day, a kind thing they did for someone else, and one thing they were scared, sad, or mad about."
- Request the professional translation of materials into languages commonly spoken in students' homes. Ask individuals who speak these languages to review all materials for clarity.

Many educators know the importance of family engagement as a vital aspect of students' academic and social and emotional development. Research indicates that parental involvement at home (e.g., helping with homework) and in the school (e.g., volunteering) has been associated with more positive classroom behavior and higher attendance. Although not all parents, due to work or other obligations, are able to volunteer at the school, the importance of welcoming parents to contribute to the school community in any way creates a sense of connectedness needed to support optimal learning. A major aspect of creating positive family–school collaborations is to recognize what families contribute to the learning context (cultural capital). Dr. Tara Yosso's model of community cultural wealth (2005) describes the various forms of cultural capital that students and their families possess, such as familial and linguistic capital. Her model serves as a reminder that students and their families bring a wealth of knowledge and experience to school; educators are encouraged to leverage these cultural strengths. By recognizing and valuing these diverse forms of capital, educators can create more supportive learning environments that honor and build on the cultural assets each student brings. Thus, in addition to sending home resources and activities, help to build a bridge between conversations in the classroom and home in other ways, such as:

- Invite a family member (e.g., parent, relative) to read a book aloud to the class or help lead a classroom activity. Involve parents in classroom discussions.
- Invite a parent to share a personal story, reflecting a book you have read to the class. This may require some preparation to ensure the content a guest shares is suitable for the class and the presenter is prepared for students' questions. You might also invite family members to video-record themselves sharing a personal story, which can then be shared with the class and integrated into one of the units.
- Request nonmonetary donations related to a book-related activity (e.g., recyclables for the art project in a unit).
- In your email updates, let parents know what the class has been discussing and encourage parents to continue conversations on these topics at home.

When to Refer Students for Additional Support

As your students become more comfortable sharing personal experiences related to many of the tough topics highlighted in this book, you may identify individuals' needs for professional mental health support, including referrals to mental health providers and community-based organizations. Unfortunately, the stigma about seeking psychological services continues to deter families from asking for professional help. Historical racism and consistent racial disparities in the access to quality health care have also resulted in people of color's distrust in medical providers. It is therefore important to collaborate closely with your in-house mental health professionals (e.g., school counselor, social worker, school psychologist) to develop culturally relevant wrap-around support for students and family members who need it. If your school works with parent liaison groups, you can leverage their social influence by sharing resources with these groups.

A major challenge for some communities is being able to find mental health professionals who are multilingual or utilize culturally responsive practices. Despite these challenges, it is crucial to refer individuals to practitioners who have extensive experience working with specific cultural groups and possess a deep understanding of their unique contexts. This ensures that the care provided is both culturally sensitive and effective.

GET READY, GET SET, GO!

The next four parts of the book offer units for using children's literature to support the development of children's social and emotional growth, to increase their understanding of community relationships, to encourage positive identity formation, and to build empathy for and awareness of mental health issues. While working through these units, please refer to this chapter for extra support. The suggestions outlined here will also be useful for your everyday teaching and learning with your students.

Remember that these units, even after being completed with your students, are just the beginning. Your students will revisit the topics introduced as they gain more knowledge and mature into thoughtful, engaged individuals. The strategies you have learned from this chapter and those included in each unit will serve as exemplars in respecting others, embracing diverse ideas, and seeing differences as beneficial to character development. These classroom experiences will guide your students as they navigate and engage in challenging conversations in the future. Now, choose one unit to start with, fill out the Taking the Pulse of the Class: Before Unit form in Appendix 2, and prepare for rich discussions on a challenging topic with your class. Take a deep breath. You can do this! And, most of all, have fun!

Supporting Children's Social and Emotional Growth through Literature

INTRODUCTION

The next two chapters feature thematic book sets that address important topics within the area of children's social and emotional development. Peer relationships (Chapter 3) and dealing with grief and loss (Chapter 4) are common experiences that children face. Both involve skills and learning related to affective and cognitive growth, and students in the same grade level often can be at quite different points in these domains. Both thematic book sets acknowledge this and are focused primarily on laying a solid foundation of understanding and awareness that will encourage more in-depth conversations on these two topics in the future.

Before beginning these topics, we encourage you to review Chapter 2 for helpful tips on understanding your own feelings on these topics. We also want to stress that the stories within these units are specifically sequenced to build understanding. To have the greatest likelihood of success with these courageous conversations, we ask that you follow the order and complete the entire unit. Good luck: You've got this!

Chapter 3—Bully or Bestie?: Talking About Getting Along

This thematic book set focuses on the tricky area of peer relationships, an important cornerstone of children's social and emotional development and the center of children's school experiences. Peer-directed relational aggression and bullying are particularly problematic at this young age. This book set contains several children's books that could fit into the "dealing with bullying" category, as well as offer perspectives from the bully, the victim, and the bystander.

These books can be used to discuss bullying situations, address relational aggression among peers, and identify ways to speak up and be a supportive friend. This book set is not intended to solve a bullying situation but rather to open classroom conversations about challenges in peer relationships.

Along with focusing on social and emotional development standards (the CASEL 5), this thematic book set embeds English language arts standards that include having collaborative conversations with classmates, using text evidence to make inferences, comparing characters in stories, and discussing how illustrations add depth to the meaning of the text. Activities and discussion questions are suited for a third- through sixth-grade classroom audience and should be adjusted as appropriate for your grade level and students' understanding.

Chapter 4—The Experience of Loss: Talking About Grieving

This thematic book set revolves around feelings of grief and loss. Loss is a common experience for children, ranging from loss due to death (sometimes of grandparents or older relatives and sometimes of friends or relatives close to their own age), loss of friends or family members due to moves and new family situations, loss of pets, or even the annual "loss" of a class and teachers as students move through school. Children often experience big feelings of grief from these kinds of loss and are also strongly affected by the grieving of those around them.

Reading and discussing this carefully selected set of books with children will help them to begin exploring universal reactions of grief and loss, in turn helping them to gain some understanding about these experiences and related emotions. This can support children in learning to be caring and supportive of others facing grief and loss. While the discussions and activities might help children begin to process their own experiences of loss, this thematic book set is meant as an introduction to learning about these complicated emotions and as a building block for more conversations in the future about loss, rather than to engage in individual grieving or healing activities.

Along with focusing on social and emotional development standards (the CASEL 5), this thematic book set embeds English language arts standards that include having collaborative conversations with classmates, using text evidence to make inferences, and comparing themes and plots across several stories. Activities and discussion questions are suited for a third- through sixth-grade classroom audience and should be adjusted as appropriate for your grade level and students' understanding.

AUTHOR AND ILLUSTRATOR PROFILES

Michael Rosen

Students might ask about Michael Rosen, the author of *Michael Rosen's Sad Book*, a picturebook used in Chapter 3. Rosen's son Eddie died of meningitis at age 18. He explains that his resulting grief was the inspiration for this book.

Rosen is a British children's author well known for his collections of children's poetry, as well as his work as a scriptwriter and broadcaster. He was honored as the sixth British Children's Laureate (2007–2009) and has received numerous awards for his books. While serving as Children's Laureate, Rosen's platform focused on "poetry and fun," resulting in the creation of several guides for teachers intended to encourage writing poetry in the classroom, as well as the establishment of the Scholastic Lollies Award (first titled the Roald Dahl Funny Prize) for outstanding humorous children's books.

Consider sharing some of Rosen's poetry with your students. His honest, and frequently funny, tone captures common emotional experiences in childhood. His works are ripe for sharing and discussing with the class and may inspire students to write their own poems.

Jacqueline Woodson

Jacqueline Woodson's powerful picturebook *Each Kindness* is used for a quiet and reflective activity in Chapter 3. Woodson is an author whom your students will encounter throughout their future years of reading if they have not already. She writes not only picturebooks, but also middle-grades and young adult novels, poetry, and adult books.

In 2020, Woodson received the Hans Christian Anderson Award, considered the highest international recognition for lifelong achievement given to an author of children's books. Woodson has been honored with other lifetime achievement awards such as the Margaret A. Edwards Award and the Astrid Lindgren Memorial Award, as well as winning several prestigious awards for her individual books, including multiple Newbery Honors and Coretta Scott King Awards, and the National Book Award. Her books capture the emotions and complications of childhood and adolescence in a voice immediately recognized by young readers as authentic.

Woodson was named National Ambassador for Young People's Literature in 2018 and created the hope-inspired platform "READING = HOPE × CHANGE (What's Your Equation?)" She encourages young people to consider the impact that reading can have in showing them ways to make positive changes in the world around them. Consider sharing Woodson's READING = HOPE × CHANGE idea with your students. Ask them what this "equation" means to them personally and encourage them to share books that have changed them in some way.

IN MY CLASSROOM

A Barrage of Tattling and Reporting

They are lined up right in front of the door, sun-warmed and gently sweating. The line undulates with their moving bodies and there are bits of grass and wood chips clinging to backs and knees and tousled hair. Some smiles, a few grimaces as they squint toward the building, and some half-hearted shoving as they get ready for me to open the door. I brace myself as I swing open the entrance and they rumble past with that distinct sour–sweet smell of warmth and unbrushed teeth, tangy feet, and good dirt. I think I'm in the clear until I see it at the end of the line: the flushed faces, the two in front leaning in and whispering, the faint trace of tears on one and the triumphant look on another behind her. As the line breaks with children slurping from the water fountain, slinging jackets onto hooks, and funneling into the class, I sigh, knowing in just a moment there will be a small gathering of girls at my desk fervently hissing, "Mrs. Lopez, Mrs. Lopez, she said. . . . "

When the barrage of tattling and reporting postrecess occurs, it's often hard to know what to do. What's real? What needs to be followed up? Is someone crying? Why? Is it the same group of children, the same victim? Does it need to be handled now, or more delicately later? These decisions often seem to need to be made on the spot, and often right when instruction needs to begin. The more years that I have taught, the more I have had to create tips for myself.

1. Actual crying or the stain of real tears needs attention. A gentle "Do you want to go wash your face and get a drink" is often enough to allow an emotional child a minute to leave the room and calm down. When done immediately as children arrive after recess, this can often be a good step in defusing the situation.

2. Having a transitional, independent activity that children immediately do upon entering the room is wonderful for multiple reasons but is also a great time to get a handle on the severity of an issue. If students settle into the work quickly, it is often because the grievances were smaller. Fervent upset will show, and the independent seatwork warmup can allow me a chance to follow up with the upset child.

3. Tattlers are often instigators. Make sure that you listen to all children involved in an incident separately, at different times, outside the hearing of the full class, and carefully question the accuser as much as you do the one being accused. It is common to find out there was more to a story and that the accuser may have started the situation.

4. Keep a close and quiet eye on the actions of repeat offenders and repeat victims during class-time interactions and keep notes as well. If relational aggression is occurring, it will likely be showing in the classroom in more subtle ways as well.

5. Be careful how you speak to other adults about the situation. If you reach out to the recess teacher for more information, be careful to frame your query as "Did you notice anything going on with a group of my students this last recess/recently" rather than asking if they saw a specific incident or witnessed a specific student doing something to another. Your goal is to gain unbiased observational data as much as possible. Reaching out to other teachers the students see regularly can be useful to gauge bullying, but again use caution in how you ask for information.

6. If the situation seems manageable but is still upsetting to the class community, consider holding a class meeting or discussion about recess rules, or asking the school counselor to do a few general lessons on friendship and getting along. Sometimes reminders about kindness more generally can be enough to stop smaller disagreements from escalating. Switching up classroom seats and assigning new classroom jobs can interest students in interacting with new children at recess. Introducing fun new cooperative games or activities that might be imitated at recess is also often helpful.

7. If the situation is clearly aggressive, or after conversations with the students and observations in the larger school day it appears to be related to ongoing bullying, then reach out for help from your school counselor and administrative staff. They can support you in helping the students involved, as well as working with families as the situation merits.

—ML, THIRD-GRADE TEACHER

3 Bully or Bestie?

Talking About Getting Along

THE BOOKS

The Rooster Who Would Not Be Quiet!/¡El gallo que no se callaba!

by Carmen Agra Deedy, illustrated by Eugene Yelchin (Scholastic, 2017)

The village of La Paz was once noisy and vibrant, but in Carmen Agra Deedy's work, the newly elected mayor Don Pepe imposes a strict rule that silences everyone. After 7 quiet years, a loud rooster and his family move in, and test the nerves of the mayor, while encouraging the village people to come back to life!

The Invisible Boy

by Trudy Ludwig, illustrated by Patrice Barton (Knopf, 2013)

In Trudy Ludwig's story, Brian is the shyest boy in his class and feels invisible to his classmates and teacher. He wishes he had a friend and is excited when a new student named Justin joins his class. Soon, Justin, Brian, and even the popular kid in the class, Emilio, become great friends.

The Rat and the Tiger

by Keiko Kasza (Puffin, 2007)

The Rat and the Tiger are best friends in Keiko Kasza's tale. They share everything, except the Rat never gets an equal share because he is just a tiny little rat. This inequality starts to bother the Rat, and when the Tiger kicks down his castle made of blocks, the Rat becomes so angry that he no longer wants to be friends with the Tiger. Realizing the impact of his actions, the Tiger decides to prove his friendship by rebuilding the castle and ensuring the Rat gets the biggest share in all their games and activities.

Bully

by Laura Vaccaro Seeger (Roaring Brook Press, 2013)

A little bull is told to "Go away!" by an older and bigger bull. Hurt and saddened by this interaction, the little bull becomes rude to every friend he encounters afterward. Every time he says something mean, he grows larger until finally a goat points out that he is becoming a bully. Shocked and deflated by this realization, the little bull can't believe what he's become. By the end of Laura Vaccaro Seeger's story, he begins treating friends with more kindness and respect.

Each Kindness

by Jacqueline Woodson, illustrated by E. B. Lewis (Nancy Paulsen Books/Penguin, 2012)

In Jacqueline Woodson's book, Maya is the new girl in her class. Her classmates notice her ragged secondhand clothing and refuse to play with her, as poignantly illustrated by E. B. Lewis. After a lesson on kindness and the powerful ripple effect it creates, the main character feels a strong desire to reach out to Maya and show her kindness. Maya, however, does not return to school, and the main character must grapple with her guilt for not being able to make things up to Maya.

Red

by Jan De Kinder, translated by Laura Watkinson (Eerdmans Books for Young Readers, 2015)

A group of elementary school students are playing at recess when they notice how easily Tommy's cheeks turn red. With Paul as their leader, they mercilessly tease Tommy. In Jan De Kinder's story (as translated by Laura Watkinson), the main character, a compassionate little girl, feels troubled by the taunting, just wants it to stop. Gradually, her courage inspires the other students to stand up to Paul. As a result, Tommy feels more included and accepted.

I Walk with Vanessa: A Story About a Simple Act of Kindness

by Kerascoët (Schwartz & Wade, 2018)

This wordless story by Kerascoët portrays an act of kindness through its beautiful illustrations. As one child is being made fun of on her way home from school, another child notices how sad she is. Throughout the day, this character contemplates how to respond to this sad child. Finally, with heartfelt resolve, she decides to extend a hand of friendship.

> ***Note:*** As with all thematic book sets, we recommend that after each book has been shared within the unit, it is placed in an easily accessible display in the classroom for the rest of the unit days. Children should then be allowed access to explore these books on their own during free-choice times.

PLANNING CHECKLIST

Bully or Bestie?: Talking About Getting Along

We suggest the following timeline to prepare and then share and discuss the books and do the related activities with your students. (A reproducible version of this checklist is available in Appendix 1.) Please note that timing for your individual class should be determined by your situation and your schedule, and, most importantly, should be guided by your students' reactions to the books and activities. Plan generally, however, on about 1 hour of daily time with the unit for 7–10 days in a row.

Two Weeks Prior

- ☐ Complete Taking the Pulse of the Class: Before Unit (Appendix 2) for a general sense of your class at this time.
- ☐ Collect and read twice each of the books for the unit.
- ☐ Review the "Unit Plans: Reading, Discussions, and Activities" section of the unit.
- ☐ Send out the Administration Notification Slip (Appendix 3) and School Counselor/Psychologist and Support Staff Notification Slip (Appendix 4).

One Week Prior

- ☐ (Optional) Send out Family Notification Slips (Appendix 5) to the families of your students.
- ☐ Have students complete the Unit Pre-Check with Students (Appendix 6) and review the results carefully. Check in with any students with reactions that cause concern so that you can prepare for extra support.
- ☐ Review Chapter 2 of the book.
- ☐ Collect all materials needed for the unit:
  - ☐ **Daily Reflection forms (Appendix 7):** You will need one for each day.
  - ☐ **Books:** One copy is required, but you may prefer to secure two copies of each book. After each book has been shared during the unit, place it in an easily accessible display in the classroom. Please give students access to explore these books on their own during free-choice times. You will want to keep the display available for some time after the unit is completed.
  - ☐ **Materials already in your classroom:** Please have available and ready to use the following commonplace classroom materials:
    - Chart paper or a section of whiteboard that can remain posted for the duration of the unit
    - Unlined white paper
    - Pencils and pens; colored pencils, crayons, or markers
    - Construction paper or other colored paper
    - Scissors
    - Tape or glue
    - Any additional materials indicated within the unit chapter's detailed description

During: Readings, Discussions, and Activities (approximately 7–10 school days)

- ☐ Follow the detailed plans for each day.
- ☐ One to 2 days after the unit is completed, have students complete the Unit Post-Check with Students (Appendix 8).

One Week Following

- ☐ After reviewing the Unit Post-Check with Students, check in with any students with reactions that cause concern.
- ☐ Refer any students expressing interest or for whom you have concerns at this point for additional, individual discussion with a school support professional. Also consider additional whole-class work if indicated.
- ☐ Complete and review Taking the Pulse of the Class: After Unit (Appendix 9). This will help you reflect on your experience and your students' experiences with the thematic book set.

UNIT OVERVIEW Bully or Bestie?: Talking About Getting Along		
Day	**Books**	**Discussion and Activities**
1	**Introduction and Whole-Class Read-Aloud #1:** *The Rooster Who Would Not Be Quiet!/¡El gallo que no se callaba!*	• Defining *Bullying* and Other Terms
2 and 3	**Small Groups Read-Aloud and Discuss #1:** *The Invisible Boy* *The Rat and the Tiger*	• Getting to Know You Graffiti Wall
4	**Whole-Class Read-Aloud #2:** *Bully*	• If Someone Were Kind . . .
5	**Whole-Class Read-Aloud #3:** *Each Kindness*	• Pebbles of Kindness
6	**Small Groups Read-Aloud and Discuss #2:** *Red*	• Noticing the Bystander
7	**Conclusion and Whole-Class Read-Aloud #4:** *I Walk with Vanessa: A Story About a Simple Act of Kindness*	• Being a Good Ally • Spider Webs

> ***Note:*** Each "day" of this unit is intended to take around 1 hour of class time. Time may vary slightly depending on student discussion, but please keep this time frame in mind as you move through the reading and activities.

BEFORE BEGINNING

1. Make sure you have completed the "Two Weeks Prior" and "One Week Prior" items on the planning checklist, including the Taking the Pulse of the Class: Before Unit and the Unit Pre-Check with Students forms.
2. Remember that the books within these units are specifically sequenced to build understanding. To have the greatest likelihood of success with these courageous conversations, we ask that you follow the order of the books, discussions, and activities and complete the entire unit.
3. Review Chapter 2 to help prepare for navigating the upcoming discussions you will be having with your students. As you complete the Daily Reflection at the end of each school day, consider revisiting Chapter 2 for helpful support in engaging in your own self-reflection and awareness, and ensuring your thoughtful and respectful approach to the topic.

DAY 1

Introduction and Whole-Class Read-Aloud #1: *The Rooster Who Would Not Be Quiet!/¡El gallo que no se callaba!*

Discussion and Activity: Defining *Bullying* and Other Terms

Time: 1 hour total

Introduction and Whole-Class Read-Aloud #1: *The Rooster Who Would Not Be Quiet!/¡El gallo que no se callaba!*

Begin the unit by gathering your students for a whole-class read-aloud. Introduce the book by showing the students its cover and explaining that today you are going to share a story about a rooster who faces a bully.

- Write the word *bullying* on the whiteboard or chart paper and ask students to help you define what this word means and how they feel about the word *bullying.* On the board, write down "Bullying Definition" on one side and "Feelings About the Word Bullying" on the other.
- Encourage all answers from the children and write their answers on the board as each is offered. Students may give examples of when they were bullied; in these cases, ask them to define feelings they have now when they hear the word *bullying.*
- When several answers have been given, read aloud the definitions and feelings on the board. Tell the children that it looks like they have a lot of knowledge and many feelings about bullies and bullying, and that over the next several days, you will be discussing some of the challenges in working and playing with your peers (classmates, community, etc.).

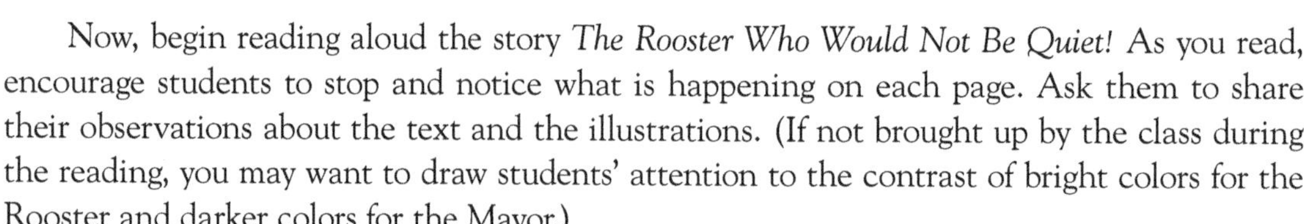

Now, begin reading aloud the story *The Rooster Who Would Not Be Quiet!* As you read, encourage students to stop and notice what is happening on each page. Ask them to share their observations about the text and the illustrations. (If not brought up by the class during the reading, you may want to draw students' attention to the contrast of bright colors for the Rooster and darker colors for the Mayor.)

After you have finished reading the story, engage students in a general share about the story. You might ask, "What page did you especially like? Why?" and "What do you think you will remember about this story?"

After students have shared their open responses, remind them that before you read the story, you asked them to define the term *bully.* Ask them if they think the Mayor is a bully. Why or why not? Encourage students to back up their reasons by pointing to pages in the book or scenes in the story.

Note that answers to this question will vary. Some students may point out that the Rooster was new to the village and broke the law. Others will not view this book as one about bullying and focus more on the aspects of the Rooster's courage or ability to see hope or "good" in all situations. Be open to all responses from students, encouraging them to explain their answers and repeatedly commenting to the whole group on how the way in which we all individually understand and respond to stories is what makes group discussion of them so exciting; it helps us to consider multiple viewpoints.

Discussion and Activity: Defining *Bullying* and Other Terms

After students have discussed their answers for a brief period, have them return to their tables and hand each a piece of blank paper and a pencil. Tell your students they are going to work in pairs with their seatmate.

Have students look at the definitions of bullying they brainstormed at the beginning of class. Tell students that, in general, bullying is defined as having three parts.

- Ask students to write at the top of their paper "Definitions." (Model this on the board.)
- Then tell them to write the word *bullying* and under it list these three parts while you also write them on the board or chart paper:
  1. Unwanted, aggressive behavior
  2. Power imbalance
  3. Repeated over time

  Then ask students what these words mean. Explain each term specifically.
  - *Unwanted*—the victim or target does not want to be treated like this. You can assist students' understanding of the word *unwanted* by pointing out that the prefix *un-* means "not" and therefore *unwanted* is something NOT wanted.
  - *Aggressive*—feels like an attack; feels violent, unpredictable. You can help students understand *aggressive* by describing how the word originates from the Latin *aggress* that means to "attack."
  - *Power imbalance*—one person has more power than their victim or target. You can examine the prefix and root word of *imbalance*. The prefix *im-* means "not" or "no," so *imbalance* is not balanced. Therefore, the bully might have more people standing with them, might be more "popular" in the community, might hold a position of power, might be older or bigger, and so forth than the victim.
  - *Repeated over time*—happens more than once.

Next, ask the students to think again about the Mayor. Was he bullying the Rooster? Ask the pairs of students to go through the three parts of the **Definition of Bullying** and decide. After they have done this, take a class vote. Share for just a minute about the pairs' decisions and examples. The likely conclusion is that the Mayor was demonstrating bullying actions toward the Rooster. Students may disagree on whether the Mayor is a "bully" or talk about the Rooster breaking the rules or "silly laws" (as the Rooster calls them), but help them recognize that the behaviors themselves could be understood as bullying actions.

- Make sure to point out in the discussion that unwanted, aggressive behavior is never a good thing. It is hurtful and wrong. Bullying is those hurtful behaviors aimed at one person and happening repeatedly, much like what happens with the Mayor and the Rooster. Tell students that, as the class talks about friendships and bullying this coming week, there are some other terms they will use.
- Ask students what they might call the Mayor. What is his role in the story? Give the students time to respond, and then write the words *bully* and *aggressor* on the board. Tell students that the Mayor serves as an example of a bully and an aggressor, or "someone who says or does hurtful things." Have students write the word **aggressor** on their sheet of paper and "someone who says or does hurtful things."
- Ask students what they might call the Rooster. What is his role in the story? Give the students time to respond and then write the words **victim** or **target** on the board. Tell students that the Rooster is an example of a victim or target, or the "person who is being bullied or treated in a hurtful way repeatedly and on purpose by someone else." Write this on the board and have the students copy it down.
- Ask students what they might call the Villagers. What was their role in the story? Give the students time to respond and then write the word **bystander** on the board. Tell students that at the beginning of the story, the Villagers were bystanders, or "people who see the bullying happening." Write this on the board and have the students copy it down.
- Ask the students if the role of the Villagers changed during the story. Did they get involved in the bullying? How? Help the students to find where in the story the Villagers stopped being bystanders and stood up for the Rooster. Explain that the Villagers became **allies**, or "people who help or stand up for someone who is being bullied," when they started singing along with the Rooster. Write this on the board and have the students copy it down. Then show the students the book again and have them look for the reactions of the Villagers in the illustrations as the story progresses. When do the Villagers start looking out their windows? Leaving their houses? How do the emotions on their faces change?

Finally, direct students to flip over their paper to its blank back side. Then tell them that the title of *The Rooster Who Would Not Be Quiet!* was almost going to be *The Noisy Little Rooster*. Write both titles on the board (remember that the title *The Rooster Who Would Not Be Quiet!* includes an exclamation point). Ask your students to think about which title they like best and why, and then write down their preferred title with two reasons why they like it best. (Younger students or those who struggle with writing might write down 1 for the actual title or 2 for the "almost" title, and then think about their reasons as they prepare to share.) After they have been writing or thinking for a few minutes, stop them for a moment and circle the exclamation point in the actual title. Tell them to think about what that exclamation point adds to the final title.

- After 1 more minute of writing, ask students to share their papers or verbally share their ideas with their seat partner and discuss them for 2 minutes.
- Then take a class vote on which title they prefer. Have a few students offer the reasons for their choice of favorite title.
- Help students to see how the way the title is worded affects how the Rooster is perceived in the story—someone who stands up versus someone who is simply noisy.

Segue to Next Day and Daily Reflection

Explicitly help your students segue by letting them know you are now moving to the next part of the day, but you will be returning to this topic tomorrow. Collect the student papers and leave up the terms and definitions you wrote on the board or chart paper in one area of the board or hanging on the wall.

When the school day is over, take some time to fill out the Daily Reflection to reflect on this experience. Review it as you prepare for the next 2 days.

DAYS 2 AND 3

Small Groups Read-Aloud and Discuss #1: *The Invisible Boy* and *The Rat and the Tiger*

Discussion and Activity: Getting to Know You Graffiti Wall

Time: 2 hours total

> ***Note:*** Before school begins today, divide your class into small groups. You will read aloud and discuss two books with each of the small groups during center or station time across the 2 days. You will need to arrange for these two read-aloud and discussion time blocks (about 15 minutes each) for each group. Students will also be engaged in creating the Graffiti Wall throughout both days, so take a few minutes to explain this to them today and then give them more time to participate in the activity the next day.

Small Groups Read-Aloud and Discuss #1: *The Invisible Boy* and *The Rat and the Tiger*

Divide your class into small groups of four to five students. Across Days 2 and 3, work with each small group, reading aloud to them and discussing both titles together in two separate small-group meetings: one for *The Invisible Boy* and the other for *The Rat and the Tiger*. All children should have a chance to hear and discuss each book in a small group. (The order of the book read and discussion does not matter.) Both books look at more subtle forms of peer aggression. *The Invisible Boy* concentrates on a student being left out of the classroom community, and *The Rat and the Tiger* highlights issues when a friend does not speak up at first about the unkind treatment of a friend.

- Take plenty of time during each small-group read-aloud and discussion to allow students to explore the pages and talk together with you about the way the author and illustrator use impactful words in the text, or how colors or shapes in the illustrations convey the strong emotions of the main characters. You can do this by asking the students to share what they notice about the words and the pictures and modeling an example to start.
- After you have finished reading the story, engage students in a general share about the story. You might ask, "What page did you especially like? Why?" and "What do you think you will remember about this story?"
- After students have shared their open responses, remind them about the definition of *bullying* they discussed yesterday (or 2 days ago). Ask them to remember the three parts of bullying action: (1) unwanted, aggressive behavior, (2) power imbalance, and (3) repeated over time. Direct them to the board or chart paper where the three parts are listed. Then go through each of these three parts and have students decide if the actions in the story were a form of bullying and, if so, why.
- Remind them that bullying can be subtle, and it can happen even with friends, but also leave open the decision on whether the actions in the stories are truly bullying or not. (The focus is that the actions are unkind and that unkind actions are not okay. While they may not necessarily be fully deliberate actions or add up to bullying, they are actions that end up hurting the victim.)
- After this, encourage students to think about times they might need to speak up, much like the main characters in the two books try to do or have help in doing. Sometimes that can be hard to do and having specific words to use or plans on what to do can help. Hand each student a piece of paper as they work through the book-specific discussion and activities below. (Remind yourself to use the tips from Chapter 2 to help keep your discussions open and honest, while still respecting the feelings of the small group.)

The Invisible Boy:

- Ask the students, "How did Brian feel when he was left out of the kickball teams? How do you know he feels that way?" Open the book to the pages where Brian is waiting to be picked and encourage students to name the physical ways by which they can see Brian is upset.
- Then ask the students, "If you were a teacher on the field at recess, would you tell the kids they have to include Brian in the kickball game? Why or why not?" Ask the students to explain their answers and create possible new rules or suggestions about picking teams and playing at recess. Remind students that these are rules or suggestions for recess time only and not for PE or other class times. (If students mention existing recess rules at your school, allow them the space to discuss the pros and cons of existing rules and explore new suggestions.) Ask students to write down a few new rules or possible changes to existing rules that they think might help in situations like Brian's.
- If time allows, extend this activity to the lunchroom. Ask the students, "If you were a teacher in the lunchroom, would you say something to the kids who made comments about Justin's lunch items? Why or why not? What would you say?" Ask the students to explain their answers and create possible new rules or suggestions for lunch conversations as above.

The Rat and the Tiger:

- Ask the students, "Do you have to do what a friend says? Why or why not?" Discuss their answers to these questions.
- Then ask the students to write down some words and phrases you can use to stop your friend if they keep telling you what to do. Have students share their lists and star the items on the list that they think would work very well.
- Next, ask the students, "Do friends fight? Why or why not?" Discuss this briefly and then ask, "How do friends make up if they fight?" Have each student offer some general examples; be careful to remind them first not to name other classmates. Under their list of words and phrases to stop friends from telling you what to do, create a list of ways to "make up" with friends (acts of forgiveness with friends). Encourage students to be specific.

Whenever you finish a small-group read-aloud and discussion, explicitly help the small group of students segue by letting them know you are now moving to the next part of the day, but you will be returning to this topic of bullying tomorrow.

Discussion and Activity: Getting to Know You Graffiti Wall

During the 2 days that students are engaging in these small-group read-alouds and discussions, have them also contribute to an ongoing activity, the **Getting to Know You Graffiti Wall.**

- Explain that around the room, you have hung chart paper (or made space on the whiteboards) with a question on top. Under the question, they will find yes/no or multiple-choice answers. Read the questions and the possible answer choices to the children, and then give them time to come and write their names next to the answers they have selected.
- Add more topics to the wall several times throughout the 2 days. Give students a short amount of time when they can move about and sign the wall. Also, encourage students to sign their names on the wall whenever they have free time during the day. Be sure to reread the questions aloud and the possible answers (but not the students' names) many times. (For older children and more advanced readers, you may want to pose open-ended questions and allow them to write in their own answers on the wall.) Aim for a total of 10–15 topics/questions. Topics might include:
    - ***Multiple-choice type (provide four choices and an "other" option):*** favorite color, favorite food, favorite cartoon character, favorite emoji, favorite sport, scares me, makes me sad, makes me laugh, number of teeth lost this year, best superhero power, place you want to visit, number of languages you can speak.
    - ***Yes/no or "would you rather" type:*** cat/dog, chips/candy, bike/scooter, singing/acting, righty/lefty, visit Moon/visit Mars, get up early/stay up late, spider/snake, listen/talk.

At the end of Day 3, give students 5–10 minutes to walk around the room and simply look over the wall. Tell students that the Getting to Know You Graffiti Wall has let them see some new similarities and differences they might have with their classmates and helped them learn a little more about each other. Sometimes this is a first step in figuring out how to work with others in the classroom, and an important first step in making new friends.

Segue to Next Day and Daily Reflection

Explicitly help your students segue by letting them know you are now moving to the next part of the day, but you will be returning to this topic of bullying and friendship tomorrow.

When the school day is over, take some time to fill out the Daily Reflection to reflect on this experience. Review it as you prepare for the next day.

DAY 4

Whole-Class Read-Aloud #2: *Bully*

Discussion and Activity: If Someone Were Kind . . .

Time: About 1 hour total

Whole-Class Read-Aloud and Discuss #2: *Bully*

Gather your students for a whole-class read-aloud. Introduce the book by showing the students its cover and explaining that today you are going to share another story about bullying, but this one is short and has very few words. Explain that they will need to pay close attention to the illustrations, so they can capture the nuances of what happens.

Now, begin reading the story aloud. (Note that this book starts before the title page with the image of a large bull telling a smaller one to "Go Away!") As you read, encourage students to stop and notice what is happening on each page. Please encourage them to share their observations. There is little text in this book, so move slowly and allow plenty of time for students to see each illustration.

After you have finished reading the story, engage students in a general share about the story.

- First, ask general questions: "What page did you especially like? Why?" and "What do you think you will remember about this story?"
- Then tell the students that this story was simple but had very strong emotions and was also full of name-calling. Ask them to think about the sound of your voice when you read the story aloud. Speak a bit about the challenge of reading this book aloud and the need to use a harsh, angry voice throughout and how that makes your body feel. Encourage students to discuss a little how anger makes their body feel.
- Then ask students to name the "roles" of the characters. Remind them that earlier this week you discussed bullies, targets or victims, bystanders, and allies when you shared the story *The Rooster Who Would Not Be Quiet!* Ask them to now name what roles the characters in this book played. Return to and show the corresponding page(s) as they label characters and

discuss some of the nuances of the labels they choose. (Students may need help finding the bystander rabbit.)

- "Who was a bully?"
- "Who was a target?"
- "Who was a bystander?"
- "Who was an ally?"

- Ask students if they can, as a whole class, retell the story using this format (below). Call on students to help you fill in the blanks. After they have worked together on this retell, explain that breaking the story down to this simple retell clearly shows the effects that the name-calling action had on the bull and how that spiraled into more unkind actions until finally all the characters called out his behavior.

1. First, . . .
2. Then, . . .
3. Then, . . .
4. Then, . . .
5. Finally, . . .

Discussion and Activity: If Someone Were Kind . . .

Now, tell students they are going to participate in an acting game that highlights kind actions that can be done right in their classroom. Remind them that you have now read a few books illustrating many unkind actions, so it's a good time to think about the kind actions one can take. Kind actions and a community that celebrates kindness can help bullying from happening. Ask students if they can recall the two places in *The Invisible Boy* where small gestures made a big difference for the two students who became the targets of unkind action (Brian's note to Justin about his lunch and Justin speaking up to include Brian, even when Emilio said "no"). Then ask students to return to their seats and pull out a piece of paper.

Ask them to write on the top of their sheet "If Someone Were Kind. . . . " Tell them they are going to work with their seat mate/table partner to create a list or draw a set of pictures of specific acts that would demonstrate kindness.

Help them start by giving a few examples: "If someone were acting kind, they would get scissors for the whole table when picking up a pair from the supplies." "If someone were acting kind, they would smile at their tablemate when they sat down at the table in the morning." "If someone were acting kind, they would hold the door open for people coming into the school building."

After students have worked on their lists for a short period, have them stop. Tell them that each group of partners needs to select one of their specific acts and prepare to dramatize it for the class. One of the partners will do the kind action, and the other partner will receive it. They will have just 1 minute each to act out their **If Someone Were Kind** demonstration for the class. Give them time to select their action and practice it. (If you have a large class, you may want to have the partner groups re-form into groups of four.)

Have students perform their short skits. As each group takes its turn, ask them to clearly say their statement in unison ("If someone were kind, ____________") and write it down on a piece of chart paper. Hang this chart paper on the wall and keep it up for the remainder of the unit.

After all student groups have performed, take the time for a quick class share. Ask students to share how they felt when acting out doing the kind action or receiving it. Point out that these specific acts are ones they can actually incorporate into their everyday school lives.

Segue to Next Day and Daily Reflection

After the discussion, explicitly help your students segue by letting them know you are now moving to the next part of the day, but you will be returning to this topic of kindness tomorrow.

When the school day is over, take some time to fill out the Daily Reflection to reflect on this experience. Review it as you prepare for the next 2 days.

DAY 5

Whole-Class Read-Aloud #3: *Each Kindness*

Discussion and Activity: Pebbles of Kindness

Time: About 1 hour total

Special Materials Needed:

- Large bowl of water
- Small rock or pebble

Whole-Class Read-Aloud #3: *Each Kindness*

Gather your students for a whole-class read-aloud in the first half of the day. Introduce the book by showing the students its cover and explaining that today you are going to share another story about relationships between classmates, friendship, and kind and unkind actions. Tell them that this is a quiet story, and you are going to read it slowly all the way through without discussion this time.

Now, begin reading aloud the story. Make sure to keep the pace slow so that students can hear the rhythm of the sentences in addition to having time to absorb its full meaning. After reading each page spread, take a longer period of time to slowly show the illustrations to the circle or gathered group so that every student has a chance to look closely at the soft illustrations.

After you have finished reading the story, ask the students to return to their seats. Hand each a piece of paper and ask them to fold it into thirds. On the top third, ask them to write or draw their thoughts about the story. Give the students 2–3 minutes to do this.

Discussion and Activity: Pebbles of Kindness

Now, ask students to turn to their desk partner to share briefly their thoughts on the book. Let the pairs share for 2 minutes. Then ask students to write or draw, for 2 minutes, on the second third of the paper their answer to this question: Was Maya a bully?

After students have responded quietly for 2 minutes, have them share and discuss their individual answers with their seat mate/partner.

Next, tell students that what makes this book more unique and a little uncomfortable is that its story is not "resolved." Readers never see Maya have the chance to "make up" or apologize to Chloe. We also never really see Maya being individually mean to Chloe. She mostly explains the actions by saying "we" did it. But we do know at the story's end that Maya feels as if she has been personally unkind to Chloe.

Place the bowl of water you have ready for today in the center of the room and invite students to gather around it for the **Pebbles of Kindness** activity. Drop the small rock in the water so students can see the ripples that form. Explain that, in *Each Kindness*, Ms. Albert, the teacher, taught the children how kindness goes out like a ripple into the world, affecting everything. Maya, though, seemed to understand that acting unkind can also cause a ripple effect. Drop the rock in the water again.

Ask students to return to their seats and think about the small acts of kindness they acted out yesterday and the book they read today. On the last third of their paper, ask them to write down or draw one act of kindness they will do this week. Then they should put their paper response into their folder/desk as a reminder to take the action.

Segue to Next Day and Daily Reflection

Explicitly help your students segue by letting them know you are now moving to the next part of the day, but you will be returning to this topic of kindness and its ripple effect tomorrow.

When the school day is over, take some time to fill out the Daily Reflection to reflect on this experience. Review it as you prepare for the next day.

DAY 6

Small Groups Read-Aloud and Discuss #2: *Red*

Discussion and Activity: Noticing the Bystander

Time: About 1 hour total (this time will be broken down into four 15- to 20-minute blocks when you will be reading and discussing *Red* with small groups of students)

Small Groups Read-Aloud and Discuss #2: *Red*

Divide your class into three to four small groups of students. Across the day, work with each small group to read and discuss *Red*.

- Take plenty of time during the read-aloud to allow students to explore the pages and talk together about the way the author and illustrator use impactful words in the text, or how colors or shapes in the illustrations convey the strong emotions of the main characters. You can do this by asking the students to share what they notice about the words and the pictures as you read and by modeling an example to start.
- While you are reading the story, also stop at the pages listed below to ask and discuss these specific questions:
  - p. 4: "How do you think Tommy felt when his classmates pointed out his face was blushing?"
  - p. 8: "Why do you think Tommy gets quieter every time Paul laughs? What do you notice about how Tommy looks now?"
  - p. 10: "Look at how Tommy is hunched over, putting his hands over his face and covering his eyes. What do you believe he is feeling?"
  - p. 11: "Why do you think the main character is saying that it isn't funny anymore?"
  - p. 15: "Do you find it hard to stand up to people like Paul? What could you do if you noticed your classmate being teased?"
  - p. 21: "Why do you think the main character is worried about saying something to the teacher? How do you think Paul would feel if someone said that they saw what happened? What makes it easier to say something?"
  - p. 26: "How do you think Paul felt when he saw that a lot of people were standing up for Tommy and Lisa? What would you have done if you were Paul?"
  - p. 29: "If you were Tommy, how do you think you would feel?"

Finally, after you have finished reading the story, engage students in one last general share about the story. Ask students about their overall reaction to the story.

Then ask students if the narrator was an aggressor, a bully, a bystander, or an ally. Encourage students to use the definitions chart from Day 1 of the unit as they discuss their answers. Help students to see how the narrator played different roles and discuss how it can be challenging to correct our actions when we are unkind (intentionally or unintentionally) and to move from being a bystander to an ally.

Segue to Next Day and Daily Reflection

Explicitly help your students segue by letting them know you are now moving to the next part of the day, but you will be returning to this topic of unkindness and their response to it tomorrow.

When the school day is over, take some time to fill out the Daily Reflection to reflect on this experience. Review it as you prepare for the next day.

DAY 7

Conclusion and Whole-Class Read-Aloud #4: *I Walk with Vanessa: A Story About a Simple Act of Kindness*

Discussion and Activities: Being a Good Ally; Spider Webs

Time: About 1 hour total

Special Material Needed:

- Skein of yarn

Conclusion and Whole-Class Read-Aloud #4: *I Walk with Vanessa: A Story About a Simple Act of Kindness*

Begin to conclude this unit by gathering your students for a whole-class read-aloud and discussion. Tell the students that, over the last few days, they have talked about some of the challenges of peer relationships, both bullying and kindness, and the roles of bullies and aggressors and of bystanders and allies.

- Ask students to help you list the books they have read. Show them the books on display.
- Ask students to name the three pieces that make something bullying versus an unkind action.
- Ask the students to name specific acts of kindness they could do in their classroom or community.

Tell the students that today you are going to share a story that focuses on being an ally. Tell them the book is a wordless one, so you want them to share what they notice as they examine it together.

As you move through *I Walk with Vanessa: A Story About a Simple Act of Kindness,* stop after each picture or full-page spread and select a student to indicate what is happening in that picture or on that page. After a student answers, pause and ask if any other students notice something else about the illustration they want to share. Allow for just one or two shares to keep the pace moving and then go to the next illustration or page spread. To help students notice certain details in the images, consider also asking these specific questions as you proceed:

- p. 1: "Have you ever been the new kid at school, or have you ever had a new student join your class before? How did you feel?"
- pp. 3–4: "Where is Vanessa? When you look at her face, how do you think she's feeling? Do you see another character in the crowd whose facial expression looks different from Vanessa's and from the other kids in the picture? When you look at his face, how do you think he's feeling?"
- pp. 7–8: "This is an interesting spread, as the three 'scenes' are meant to be read in order from top to bottom as three pieces rather than six. Look across each scene to see

what is happening at the same time. What do you think the child in the yellow dress is thinking? How do you feel when you see a student being mean to another student?"

- pp. 15–16: "How do you think Vanessa and the girl in the yellow dress feel that night? How does the illustrator help you guess their feelings?"
- pp. 23–24: "How do you think Vanessa is feeling now? How does it feel when you hold a friend's hand?"
- pp. 25–26: "Look at all of those children running toward them! How would you feel if you were surrounded by a large group of smiling friends? Find the boy in the red striped shirt. How do you think he's feeling right now? Why do you think he isn't smiling?"
- pp. 27–28: "Can you spot the boy in the red striped shirt? How does he look now?"
- pp. 29–30: "Where is the boy in the striped shirt now? How do you think he's feeling?"

After you have finished reading the story, engage students in a general share about it.

Discussion and Activities: Being a Good Ally; Spider Webs

Point to the list of acts of kindness students have made that hangs on the wall. Tell students that these acts are important to making the classroom a kind place to be. Point to the Graffiti Wall(s) and say that these questions help us to better know each other, to connect with each other, and to create relationships that also help transform the classroom into a kind place. This last book they read today adds one more layer to make the classroom a kind place to be: standing up for each other when unkind things happen. This could be called **Being a Good Ally.**

Ask students to help you create a list of ways to be a "good ally" on chart paper. To start them off, ask what the child in the yellow dress did first (she noticed what was happening). Also, help students to connect to the actions of the narrator in *Red* and the goat in *Bully* and Justin at the end of *The Invisible Boy*. Students might also find inspiration in considering what Maya could have done in *Each Kindness*. Create a class list of five to eight ways in which students can be a good ally in the classroom, school, and their local community.

- During the discussion and list making, take care to mention that these are also ways to be a good friend. Then follow up by stating that good "allies" help support and stand up for others but do not do everything for the "target" or person being bullied, just like good friends do not do everything for each other.
- Hang the list up on the wall.

Ask the students to stand up, stretch, and make a big circle. Pick up the skein of yarn and stand in the circle yourself. Tell the students that each of them will now have a chance to tell another classmate something they appreciate about that person. It can be one of three things. Either they can say: (1) they appreciate an act of kindness they saw that classmate do, or (2) they appreciate something they found out about their classmate from the Graffiti Wall and why they appreciated learning that, or (3) they can say something they appreciated that the classmate did or said during this last week of reading and sharing books about friendship and bullying and getting along.

Give students a minute to think quietly about what has been shared. Then give a few examples but do not throw the yarn yet! For example: "I appreciate how Mackenzie held the door for me when I was walking in with a stack of books." "I appreciate how Layla wrote her name on 'darkness' under 'What Scares Me' because I don't like the dark either." "I appreciate how Carlos noticed, in the first book we read, the way the Rooster always stands tall."

Now, tell the students you are going to start a **Spider Web**. Remind them that each student can only be called on once and they must continue to hold onto the yarn even when they throw it (gently underhand) to someone else in the group. They also need to say their classmate's name and offer their statement of appreciation before they throw the skein. Hold the end of the yarn in one hand and then say, "[*Give student's name.*] I appreciate how ____________ did . . . " and toss the skein gently to the named student. Repeat the instructions as needed to guide the students as they work through the activity until everyone is holding the yarn with one hand, and the final child also has the skein in one hand. Tell that student to hold onto the yarn and then drop the skein to the ground.

Have the students look at the web they have created! Tell them this web shows how connected we, and they, are to each other, and that we appreciate and trust each other. The more we work on these connections, trust, and appreciation for each other, the stronger the web will grow.

Ask the student next to you to hold your end with their other hand. Then tell all the students to continue holding onto the string. Cut the web so that each student will have one piece, and then every student will ask their neighbor to help them tie it on their wrists. These yarn "bracelets" will serve to remind the students that we are a community. Tell students to tie the bracelets loosely so they can take them off at the end of the day and then tape them to the top of their desks or tables. They can be worn on certain days as the teacher or a child requests.

Note: Some teachers also like to tape the spider webs above the whiteboards or on a bulletin board or put them on students' coat hooks. Others like to have their students wear them home to discuss the day's activity with their family.

Segue to Next Day and Daily Reflection, Unit Post-Check with Students, and Taking the Pulse of the Class: After Unit

When the school day is over, take some time to fill out the Daily Reflection to reflect on this experience. The next day or the day after that, ask your students to complete the Unit Post-Check with Students. Finally, about a week to 10 days after the unit is completed, fill out Taking the Pulse of the Class: After Unit to consider more broadly this experience for your current students, yourself, and your future students.

- First, ask the students, "What page did you especially like? Why?" and "What do you think you will remember about this story?"
- Then read to students the last page of the book, "For Children: How You Can Help Someone Who Is Being Bullied."

FINAL SUGGESTIONS

This unit was intended as an introduction to, and the beginning of, courageous conversations around the difficult topic of relational aggression and bullying. Some students may continue to want to discuss this topic. Reach out to your school counselors, psychologists, and support faculty for individual help for students seeking more specific or individualized support in this area. The Unit Post-Check with Students form will help you identify the students needing or wanting this support.

You may decide to expand on this unit with further book sharing, discussions, and activities. The websites that follow may serve as good resources as you do this work.

ADDITIONAL RESOURCES

Anti-Defamation League (ADL). "Bullying and Cyberbullying Prevention." *www.adl.org/education/resources/tools-and-strategies/bullying-and-cyberbullying-prevention-strategies*

Eyes on Bullying (Education Development Center): *http://eyesonbullying.org/index.html*

National Association of Elementary School Principals Bullying Prevention: *www.naesp.org/bullying-prevention-resources*

National Education Association. "Bully Free: It Starts with Me." *www.nea.org/home/neabullyfree.html*

PACER's National Bullying Prevention Center: *www.pacer.org/bullying*

Stop Bullying.Gov: *www.stopbullying.gov*

Teaching Tolerance Bullying and Bias: *www.tolerance.org/topics/bullying-bias*

MEETING COMMON CORE AND CASEL STANDARDS

Common Core English Language Arts Standards for Grade 4

This unit meets specific Common Core State Standards for English Language Arts in grades 3, 4, 5, and 6. We have included the specific ELA standards for grade 4 below to illustrate the strands and items met (similar for all four grades third through sixth). The QR code here will link you to the specific lists for grades 3, 5, and 6.

CCSS.ELA-LITERACY.SL.4.1

Engage effectively in a range of collaborative discussions (one-on-one, in groups, and teacher-led) with diverse partners on grade 4 topics and texts, building on others' ideas and expressing their own clearly.

CCSS.ELA-LITERACY.RL.4.1

Refer to details and examples in a text when explaining what the text says explicitly and when drawing inferences from the text.

CCSS.ELA-LITERACY.RL.4.2

Determine a theme of a story, drama, or poem from details in the text; summarize the text.

CCSS.ELA-LITERACY.RL.4.3

Describe in depth a character, setting, or event in a story or drama, drawing on specific details in the text (e.g., a character's thoughts, words, or actions).

CCSS.ELA-LITERACY.RL.4.4

Determine the meaning of words and phrases as they are used in a text, including those that allude to significant characters found in mythology (e.g., Herculean).

CCSS.ELA-LITERACY.RL.4.9

Compare and contrast the treatment of similar themes and topics (e.g., opposition of good and evil) and patterns of events (e.g., the quest) in stories, myths, and traditional literature from different cultures.

CASEL Social and Emotional Learning Standards for Grades 3–5

This unit meets specific CASEL Core Competence Area goals for Social and Emotional Learning for grades 3–5. We have included the CASEL areas and specific example standards below to show the items met in this unit. (The items are similar for grade 6.)

Self-Awareness: The abilities to understand one's own emotions, thoughts, and values and how they influence behavior across contexts. This includes capacities to recognize one's strengths and limitations with a well-grounded sense of confidence and purpose.

- Identifying one's emotions
- Linking feelings, values, and thoughts
- Having a growth mindset

Self-Management: The abilities to manage one's emotions, thoughts, and behaviors effectively in different situations and to achieve goals and aspirations. This includes the capacities to delay gratification, manage stress, and feel motivation and agency to accomplish personal/collective goals.

- Managing one's emotions
- Exhibiting self-discipline and self-motivation

Social Awareness: The abilities to understand the perspectives of and empathize with others, including those from diverse backgrounds, cultures, and contexts. This includes the capacities to feel compassion for others, understand broader historical and social norms for behavior in different settings, and recognize family, school, and community resources and supports.

- Taking others' perspectives
- Demonstrating empathy and compassion
- Showing concern for the feelings of others
- Recognizing situational demands and opportunities

Relationship Skills: The abilities to establish and maintain healthy and supportive relationships and to effectively navigate settings with diverse individuals and groups. This includes the capacities to communicate clearly, listen actively, cooperate, work collaboratively to problem-solve and negotiate conflict constructively, navigate settings with differing social and cultural demands and opportunities, provide leadership, and seek or offer help when needed.

- Communicating effectively
- Developing positive relationships
- Demonstrating cultural competency
- Practicing teamwork and collaborative problem solving
- Resolving conflicts constructively

Responsible Decision Making: The abilities to make caring and constructive choices about personal behavior and social interactions across diverse situations. This includes the capacities to consider ethical standards and safety concerns, and to evaluate the benefits and consequences of various actions for personal, social, and collective well-being.

- Demonstrating curiosity and open-mindedness
- Identifying solutions for personal and social problems
- Anticipating and evaluating the consequences of one's actions
- Reflecting on one's role to promote personal, family, and community well-being

The Experience of Loss

Talking About Grieving

THE BOOKS

The Rabbit Listened

by Cori Doerrfeld (Dial Books for Young Readers, 2018)

Taylor is very upset when his block tower is suddenly knocked down. He doesn't know how to deal with his grief, and although many of his animal friends try to offer him help, nothing seems to help. Finally, the rabbit's comfort of just listening soothes Taylor's pain. Cori Doerrfeld captures the big emotions Taylor faces, while also displaying many of the stages of grief, and the power of a friend who is simply present.

Michael Rosen's Sad Book

by Michael Rosen, illustrated by Quentin Blake (Candlewick Press, 2005)

Michael Rosen's personal and heartbreaking story captures for readers much of the essence of severe loss. He illustrates through powerful prose how the death of his son and his mom put him in a dark place. With powerful illustrations from Quentin Blake, each page conveys Rosen's attempts to cope with his sadness.

The Rough Patch

by Brian Lies (Greenwillow Books, 2018)

Evan and his dog do everything together, but they especially love working in their garden. One dark day, Evan's dog passes away and, in his grief, Evan destroys his garden. A few months later, a pumpkin vine appears from under the fence. Despite his reluctance to revisit his garden,

Evan can't help but take care of the pumpkins. Later, encouraged by his friends, he brings one to the county fair, where a new friend awaits. In Brian Lies's book, rich oils and acrylic paints help capture the depth of Evan's emotions, while lighter-colored pencil scenes also add detail that shows Evan slowly regaining hope.

The Scar

by Charlotte Moundlic, illustrated by Olivier Tallec (Candlewick Press, 2011)

A sudden torrent of emotions sweeps through a young boy when his mother passes away. Filled with worry about taking care of his dad, and himself, he is equally worried that he will forget his mother. Bright red floods the pages as he struggles with his emotional reactions and simultaneously picks at a scab on his leg as it begins to heal. As the scab turns into a scar, he also begins to move through his grief and find a way to hold onto his memories. Charlotte Moundlic's powerful but often point-blank text captures his immense grief.

The FUNeral

by Matt James (Groundwood Books, 2018)

Norma's Great-Uncle Frank has just passed away and she must go to his funeral with her family. She practices her sad facial expressions for the funeral, but she is mostly excited to miss school for the day and play with her cousin Ray in the beautiful churchyard. The bright colors and mixed-media illustrations of Matt James's book highlight the happiness Norma feels but also begins to capture some of the textured understanding she gains as she learns about the rituals of a funeral service and thinks about death. Pondering these thoughts, Norma decides that Great-Uncle Frank would have liked his funeral.

My Grandma Lives in a Perfume Village

by Fang Suzhen, illustrated by Sonja Daowski, translated by Huang Xiumin (North-South, 2014)

Xiao Le travels with his mother to visit his sick grandmother. After a day of fun enjoying being together, he soon learns that this was his last visit to her and that she has passed away. Xiao Le comforts his mother by telling her that he can imagine his grandmother in heaven washing dishes, doing laundry, and drinking tea. Soft, muted colors give Fang Suzhen's story a dreamy effect.

A Gift for Abuelita: Celebrating the Day of the Dead/Un regalo para Abuelita: En celebración del Día de los Muertos

by Nancy Luenn, illustrated by Robert Chapman (Cooper Square Publishing, 2004) Bilingual version, Spanish/English

Rosita loves her *abuelita* ("grandmother") very much. They make tortillas, braid yarn, and work in the garden together. When her *abuelita* gets sick and passes away, Rosita aches with grief. She yearns to see *abuelita* again, so she makes a braid for her as a part of their family *ofrenda* for the Day of the Dead, just like Rosita's *abuelita* had taught her. The unique collage art by Robert Chapman helps to illuminate how celebrating the holiday begins to heal Rosita's grief.

Maybe Tomorrow?

by Charlotte Agell, illustrated by Ana Ramirez (Scholastic, 2019)

In Charlotte Agell's story, Elba has been grieving for Little Bird for a long time and is tied down by a "block" of grief. Then she meets Norris, who is always happy and offers friendship and support. As their friendship begins to grow, Elba's grief slowly lessens. The brightly colored cartoon illustrations by Ana Ramirez manage to capture the nuances of Elba's emotions and the patience of Norris.

Note: As with all thematic book sets, we recommend that after each book has been shared within the unit, it is placed in an easily accessible display in the classroom for the rest of the unit days. Children should then be allowed access to explore these books on their own during free-choice times.

PLANNING CHECKLIST

The Experience of Loss: Talking About Grieving

We suggest the following timeline to prepare and then share and discuss the books and do the related activities with your students. (A reproducible version of this checklist is available in Appendix 1.) Please note that timing for your individual class should be determined by your situation and your schedule and, most importantly, should be guided by your students' reactions to the books and activities. Plan generally, however, on about 1 hour of daily time with the unit for 7–10 days in a row.

Two Weeks Prior

- ☐ Complete Taking the Pulse of the Class: Before Unit (Appendix 2) for a general sense of your class at this time.
- ☐ Collect and read twice each of the books for the unit.
- ☐ Review the "Unit Plans: Reading, Discussions, and Activities" section of the unit.
- ☐ Send out the Administration Notification Slip (Appendix 3) and School Counselor/Psychologist and Support Staff Notification Slip (Appendix 4).

One Week Prior

- ☐ (Optional) Send out Family Notification Slips (Appendix 5) to the families of your students.
- ☐ Have students complete the Unit Pre-Check with Students (Appendix 6) and review the results carefully. Check in with any students with reactions that cause concern so that you can prepare for extra support.
- ☐ Review Chapter 2 of the book.
- ☐ Collect all materials needed for the unit:
  - ☐ **Daily Reflection forms (Appendix 7):** You will need one for each day.
  - ☐ **Books:** One copy is required, but you may prefer to secure two copies of each book.

After each book has been shared during the unit, place it in an easily accessible display in the classroom. Please give students access to explore these books on their own during free-choice times. You will want to keep the display available for some time after the unit is completed.

☐ **Materials already in your classroom:** Please have available and ready to use the following commonplace classroom materials:

- Chart paper or a section of whiteboard that can remain posted for the duration of the unit
- Unlined white paper
- Pencils and pens; colored pencils, crayons, or markers
- Construction paper or other colored paper
- Scissors
- Tape or glue
- Any additional materials indicated within the unit chapter's detailed description

During: Readings, Discussions, and Activities (approximately 7–10 school days)

☐ Follow the detailed plans for each day.

☐ One to 2 days after the unit is completed, have students complete the Unit Post-Check with Students (Appendix 8).

One Week Following

☐ After reviewing the Unit Post-Check with Students, check in with any students with reactions that cause concern.

☐ Refer any students expressing interest or for whom you have concerns at this point for additional, individual discussion with a school support professional. Also consider additional whole-class work if indicated.

☐ Complete and review Taking the Pulse of the Class: After Unit (Appendix 9). This will help you reflect on your experience and your students' experiences with the thematic book set.

UNIT OVERVIEW
The Experience of Loss: Talking About Grieving

Day	Books	Discussion and Activities
1	**Introduction and Whole-Class Read-Aloud #1:** *The Rabbit Listened*	• Reactions to Loss
2 and 3	**Small Groups Read-Aloud and Discuss #1:** *Michael Rosen's Sad Book* *The Rough Patch* *The Scar*	• Mapping Reactions to Loss • Sympathy Cards for a Character
4	**Whole-Class Read-Aloud #2:** *The FUNeral*	• When Reactions Are Different

5 and 6	**Small Groups Read-Aloud and Discuss #2:** *My Grandma Lives in a Perfume Village* *A Gift for Abuelita: Celebrating the Day of the Dead/Un regalo para Abuelita: En celebración del Día de los Muertos*	• Sharing Grief • I Am Thankful for You Because . . .
7 and 8	**Conclusion and Whole-Class Read-Aloud #3:** *Maybe Tomorrow?*	• Reaching Out to Others

Note: Each "day" of this unit is intended to take around 1 hour of class time. Time may vary slightly depending on student discussion, but please keep this time frame in mind as you move through the reading and activities.

BEFORE BEGINNING

1. Make sure you have completed the "Two Weeks Prior" and "One Week Prior" items on the planning checklist, including the Taking the Pulse of the Class: Before Unit and the Unit Pre-Check with Students forms.
2. Remember that the books within these units are specifically sequenced to build understanding. To have the greatest likelihood of success with these courageous conversations, we ask that you follow the order of the books, discussions, and activities and complete the entire unit.
3. Review Chapter 2 to help prepare for navigating the upcoming discussions you will be having with your students. As you complete the Daily Reflection at the end of each school day, consider revisiting Chapter 2 for helpful support in engaging in your own self-reflection and awareness, and ensuring your thoughtful and respectful approach to the topic.

DAY 1

Introduction and Whole-Class Read-Aloud #1: *The Rabbit Listened*

Discussion and Activity: Reactions to Loss

Time: 1 hour total

Introduction and Whole-Class Read-Aloud #1: *The Rabbit Listened*

Begin the unit by gathering your students for a whole-class read-aloud. Introduce the book by showing the students its cover and explaining that today you are going to share a story about a child who experiences grief after suffering a loss. Write the words *grief* and *loss* on the board and ask students to help you define and understand what these two words mean.

- Encourage all answers from the children. For both terms, try to elicit definitions as well as the types of feelings that accompany these two words. Students may offer examples of when they felt grief or loss, and these can be useful to repeat in a short sentence.
- When several answers have been given, sum up the class meanings. Convey that, overall, grief is very deep sadness, and that loss means not just losing something but can also mean losing someone close to you in some way (e.g., through death, a move, or even a fight between friends). List some of the feelings students mentioned that might be experienced with grief and loss.

Now, begin reading aloud the story *The Rabbit Listened*. As you read, encourage students to stop and notice what is happening on each page. Ask them to share their observations about the text and the illustrations. Below are some questions to stop and discuss as you reach specific parts of the story:

- After p. 8 (the fourth opening of the two-page spreads), stop and ask, "Have you ever worked very hard on something and then something happened that ruined it?" Ask students to raise their hands if this has happened to them. Then ask, "How did you feel when that happened? Tell your neighbor what happened and how it made you feel." After students have shared with a partner, ask the whole group, "Since you know how this feels, how do you think Taylor is feeling right now?" Allow for several students to share the emotions that Taylor might be feeling.
- Around p. 18, stop and ask the students to recall what the chicken, bear, and elephant wanted Taylor to do. Ask the class if talking about the loss of the building, getting mad about the loss of the building, or remembering and then rebuilding it were things that Taylor wanted to do. Then ask the students if there were things that Taylor could have done that might have helped him feel better. (The key here is to help the students understand these are actions that may have helped Taylor, but they were just not what he was ready to do or wanted to do yet.)

After you have finished reading the story, engage students in a general share about the story. You might ask, "What page did you especially like? Why?" and "What do you think you will remember about this story?"

Discussion and Activity: Reactions to Loss

Have students return to their tables and hand each a piece of blank paper and a pencil.

- Using your whiteboard, chalkboard, or large chart paper to model, ask the students to help you create a list of all the animals who came to help Taylor when his building collapsed. (If this is done on chart paper, keep the paper for future use in this unit. If on the whiteboard, please leave the section up for the rest of the unit.) Have the students copy the list on their own paper. (Another option is to copy the list yourself at a later time and then make copies of that for the class or individual students.)
- Then, calling on your students for assistance, write down next to each type of animal the way they wanted to help Taylor (for example, "Chicken—Talk about it," "Bear—Get angry about it," etc.). Again, have the students copy the list on their own sheet of paper. (Or, see the suggested option above: making copies for the class or individual students.)
- Next, ask the students if Taylor ever did any of these things. With student help, reread and show the pages where Taylor, with the rabbit next to him, does all of them.
- Explain to the students that the actions the animals recommended, and that Taylor eventually took with the rabbit next to him, are typical **Reactions to Loss**: the ways many people process or respond to a profound loss and are grieving. Add that it is very common to experience all of these different reactions and emotions, and that this often occurs over a very long time.
- Ask the students to think about a time when they felt very sad and someone comforted them. Have them flip over their paper to its back blank side. Then ask them to draw a picture or write a description of a time they were sad and someone made them feel better.

Segue to Next Day and Daily Reflection

When your students are finished, collect their papers. Explicitly help your students segue by letting them know you are now moving to the next part of the day, but you will be returning to this topic tomorrow.

When the school day is over, take some time to fill out the Daily Reflection to reflect on this experience. Review it as you prepare for the next 2 days.

DAYS 2 AND 3

Small Groups Read-Aloud and Discuss #1: *Michael Rosen's Sad Book, The Rough Patch,* and *The Scar*

Discussion and Activities: Mapping Reactions to Loss; Sympathy Cards for a Character

Time: 2 hours total across 2 days

Special Materials Needed:

- Four to six sympathy greeting cards or computer images of sympathy cards

Small Groups Read-Aloud and Discuss #1: *Michael Rosen's Sad Book, The Rough Patch,* and *The Scar*

> ***Note:*** Before school begins today, divide your class into three small groups. Across 2 days, work with each small group to read aloud and discuss one of the three titles: *Michael Rosen's Sad Book, The Rough Patch,* or *The Scar.* The goal is to have each of the three books listened to and then discussed by one small group. Each read-aloud and discussion will take 15–20 minutes. (Note that these three books are more intense than *The Rabbit Listened,* covering the deaths of a beloved pet, a mother, and a son.) Complete these read-alouds and discussions before moving to the jigsaw activity and sympathy cards for a character.

- Take plenty of time during each small-group read-aloud and discussion to allow students to explore the pages and talk together about the way the author and illustrator use impactful words in the text, or how colors or shapes in the illustrations convey the strong emotions of the main characters. You can do this by asking the students to share what they notice about the words and the pictures and modeling an example to start.
- In the immediate discussion after reading the book, encourage students to think about times they have had strong/big emotional reactions and connect this to the main character in the book. Some questions to discuss, for example, might include:
  - "Have you ever been both mad and sad at the same time, just like the main character? How does that feel? Can you remember what helped you feel better at that time?"
  - "How does your body feel when you're really sad? What can help make those physical feelings go away for you?" (If students struggle to offer examples of things that might help them, you may want to share some ideas. Phrase this as "I know that sometimes people who are sad feel better when they take deep breaths, or go for a walk, or hug a stuffed toy or pillow. Have any of these methods ever helped your body feel better when you were sad?")
  - "What are some important, special times you share with your families or close friends or classmates (such as holidays, or family get-togethers, or special class field trips, etc.)? How might you feel if a particular family member or friend missed that event and was not there with you?"

Following the discussion of the book, have the students work in their small groups on a grief mapping exercise about what they just read.

- Have the students pull out their papers from *The Rabbit Listened* that listed the different ways Taylor's friends suggested he react and/or have them look up at the board or chart from the day before. Give students a new piece of paper and help them fold it vertically in half. On the left side, they should list all those reactions. (It may help to write down the type of animal related to the action; for example, "Chicken—Talk about it," "Bear—Get angry about it," etc. For younger children or children who struggle with writing, you can have them draw the animal.)
- Working together with their small group and the copy of the book, have students now find examples from the book where the main character shows this type of reaction to their loss. When they find one, they should write the page number on the right side of the paper. Model this yourself with the students by finding an example in the book and writing down the page number where the reaction happens. (Students will discover that the main character in each of these books experiences or models most of the emotional reactions found in *The Rabbit Listened*. If students uncover other new reactions, they should list those examples as well.)

Discussion and Activities: Mapping Reactions to Loss; Sympathy Cards for a Character

When all small groups have met for the reading and mapping activity, divide them up into new "jigsaw" groups. That is, each new small group should include one to two students representing each of the three titles. Point on the board or large chart paper to the list of reactions in *The Rabbit Listened*. In the **Mapping Reactions to Loss** activity that will follow, starting with the first reaction, ask students to share together in their small jigsaw group one example where the character in their book wanted to "talk about" the way they felt.

After the groups have shared for a few minutes, ask students to share examples with their group where the character in the three books "got angry" about their loss. Keep going through the sharing process for each of the different reactions. (You may want to remind the students that they are talking about the characters in the stories they read, and not their own experiences.)

Following this small-group share, spend a little time in a whole-class discussion about what the students learned. Did the main characters in the stories experience most of the grief reactions? Did the students identify other types of grief reactions?

Now, pass out construction paper, markers or crayons, and other simple art supplies such as scissors, tape, and glue for the **Sympathy Cards for a Character** activity. Tell students that one way to express caring for someone who is experiencing grief and loss is to be present for that person, just as the rabbit was for Taylor. Being "present" lets the person know that you are thinking about them and care about them deeply and are sorry they are experiencing this strong grief. We cannot always be present physically for someone all the time like the rabbit was for Taylor. Another way to show this is to give the person a *sympathy card*, something that lets the person know you care and are thinking about them. Ask the students to now create a sympathy card for the main character of their book.

- Brainstorm as a class on a few things someone might say in a card like this. Introduce language such as "I am sorry for your loss," "thinking of you," and the like. Show students a few sample sympathy cards you have brought to class. Discuss briefly that, like the rabbit, you are just expressing that you care and will be there for the person. The card can't fix someone's grief, but it could make them feel a little better knowing that someone truly cares.
- Allow students plenty of time to create the cards for their main character. It may help to have them return to their original book groups (*Michael Rosen's Sad Book*, *The Rough Patch*, or *The Scar*) so, together, they can discuss the main character.
- When students are finished with their cards, collect them and place them on display by a copy of each of the books.

Segue to Next Day and Daily Reflection

Explicitly help your students segue by letting them know you are now moving to the next part of the day, but you will be returning to this topic of reaction to loss tomorrow.

When the school day is over, take some time to fill out the Daily Reflection to reflect on this experience. Review it as you prepare for the next day.

DAY 4

Whole-Class Read-Aloud #2: *The FUNeral*

Discussion and Activity: When Reactions Are Different

Time: About 1 hour total

Whole-Class Read-Aloud #2: *The FUNeral*

Gather your students for a whole-class read-aloud. Introduce the book by showing the students its cover and explaining that today you are going to share another story about a child who experiences grief and a sense of loss. Remind students about the definitions of *grief* and *loss* they brainstormed earlier this week. Then explain that this book is about a young girl who attends a funeral for her great-uncle who has recently died. Briefly ask students to share what they know about funerals.

Now, begin reading aloud the story. As you read, encourage students to stop and notice what is happening on each page. Please encourage them to share their observations. There is little text to this book, so give students plenty of time to look at the illustrations. Some questions you might discuss at specific points in the book include the following:

- "What is a great-uncle?" (Help students to understand that a great-uncle would be about the age of a grandparent.)
- "What is a funeral?"
- "Do you think Norma or Ray have been to a funeral before? Why or why not?"

- "What are things kids sometimes do when they have to sit quietly through a long adult meeting or formal situation? What do you notice Norma doing? What about Ray?"
- "How are Norma and Ray related? How does Norma show her care for Ray?"
- "What kind of day is it outside? What colors do you notice the illustrator used in this book as compared to the other books you read in small groups?"
- When you finish reading the story to your students, take off the jacket cover of the book (or lift it up gently so students can see underneath), and ask them what they think about the cloth cover. "How is it different from the jacket cover? Why might the illustrator and author have made this choice? What does it tell us?"

Discussion and Activity: When Reactions Are Different

After you have finished reading the book and examined both of its covers, engage students in a general share about the story.

- First, ask general questions: "What page did you especially like? Why?" and "What do you think you will remember about this story?"
- Then ask the students how they would compare Norma and Ray's grief about their Great-Uncle Frank to the grief displayed by the main characters in *Michael Rosen's Sad Book*, *The Rough Patch*, and *The Scar*. Encourage students to think about whether Norma and Ray are showing reactions to grief like those of the main characters in the prior stories.
- Ask students why their grief reactions might be different. Your goal is to help the students understand that Norma and Ray simply do not appear to know their Great-Uncle Frank quite as closely as the relatives or characters in the other books. (Be careful to help the students not judge Norma and Ray's actions.)
- Ask students to find examples in the book that show Norma is thinking about Great-Uncle Frank. (There are subtle clues in the illustrations, as well as more direct examples toward the end of the story when Norma states that she thinks Uncle Frank "would have liked his funeral.") Take your time finding several of these examples.
- Finally, gently lead students in discussing **When Reactions Are Different**: that people often have different levels of feelings of grief around the death of an individual depending on their relationship with the person, and that this is okay. Have students look for examples where Norma expresses her sympathy and care for her family members who are grieving.

Segue to Next Day and Daily Reflection

After the discussion, explicitly help your students segue by letting them know you are now moving to the next part of the day, but you will be returning to this topic of different responses to loss tomorrow.

When the school day is over, take some time to fill out the Daily Reflection to reflect on this experience. Review it as you prepare for the next 2 days.

DAYS 5 AND 6

Small Groups Read-Aloud and Discuss #2: *My Grandma Lives in a Perfume Village* and *A Gift for Abuelita: Celebrating the Day of the Dead/Un regalo para Abuelita: En celebración del Día de los Muertos*

Discussion and Activities: Sharing Grief; I Am Thankful for You Because . . .

Time: 2 hours total across 2 days

Small Groups Read-Aloud and Discuss #2: *My Grandma Lives in a Perfume Village* and *A Gift for Abuelita: Celebrating the Day of the Dead/Un regalo para Abuelita: En celebración del Día de los Muertos*

Note: Before school begins today, divide your class into two groups. With the first group, you will read aloud and discuss *My Grandma Lives in a Perfume Village* while the second group is engaged in other schoolwork. With the second group, you will read aloud and discuss *A Gift for Abuelita: Celebrating the Day of the Dead/Un Regalo para Abuelita: En celebración del Día de los Muertos* while the first group does other schoolwork. You will need to arrange for these two read-aloud and discuss time blocks to happen first. The reading and discussion blocks will take about 20 minutes each. The goal is to have each of the two books discussed by one-half of the class.

Because both books focus on the loss of a grandmother, many students may bring up their own relationships with their grandparents and possible stories of grandparents passing away. Be careful to give plenty of time to your students for this sharing; also, be sensitive to students who may not know their grandparents at all.

- Take plenty of time during the small-groups read-aloud and discussion to allow students to explore each page and think about the way the author and illustrator show the close relationship of the main characters to their grandmothers through vivid text and soft illustrations.
- While reading and in the discussion that immediately follows, encourage students to consider their relationships with older relatives or with older friends. Also encourage them to think about the ways other adults show their grief in the book as compared to the main character, a child. Some questions to discuss, for example, might include:
    - "How are your relationships with older adults/seniors different from relationships with younger adults? What types of things do you know grandparents and grandchildren might do or experience together?"
    - "How do the adults in this book show their grief about the grandmother dying? What types of reactions do you notice?"

In wrapping up the discussion after reading the book, stress that the story brought up the strong power of memory and highlighted the ways in which the main character, a young boy, remembers his grandmother and how special she was to him and to other characters in the story. Sharing memories can be comforting and remind us in our grief how thankful we are to have had this person in our lives and the special memories of them we hold close.

Discussion and Activities: Sharing Grief; I Am Thankful for You Because . . .

After both books have been shared in small groups, bring all students together for a whole-class activity. Ask students to think of someone for whom they are thankful. This can be someone close to them who has died or someone close to them who is still alive. Then hand out a blank sheet of paper to each of the students, along with pencils and coloring materials such as markers, colored pencils, and crayons, for a **Sharing Grief** activity.

- Ask students to fold the paper in half. Then, on the top half, they should jot down the name of this person and then write or draw a favorite memory they have about this person. This information should all be on the top half of the page. After 10–15 minutes, tell students they may share this written or drawn memory with others in the small group if they would like to.
- After a short period of sharing, have students return to their writing/drawing. Now, on the bottom half of the paper, have students write down a few words or sentences describing how they feel/felt when with this person. For example, they may feel/have felt very loved, or excited, or special, and so forth. (Help students to expand on the word *happy* with other synonyms and emotions.)
- Finally, have students write at the very bottom of the page the words **"I Am Thankful for** (*give name of this special person*) **Because. . . .** " Ask them to complete that sentence. They might be thankful because of how they feel/felt around this person, or because of something they learned from the person, or because of an experience they remember having with this person (retrieving a favorite memory). Allow students to share these sentences if they would like to after everyone in the small group has finished the written activity.
- You may also want to encourage students to take this writing home and share it with the actual person (if still alive) or with other people who loved and cared for this person.

Segue to Next Day and Daily Reflection

After working with the small group, explicitly help your students segue by letting them know you are now moving to the next part of the day, but you will be returning to this topic tomorrow.

When the school day is over, take some time to fill out the Daily Reflection to reflect on this experience. Review it as you prepare for the next day.

DAYS 7 AND 8

Conclusion and Whole-Class Read-Aloud #3: *Maybe Tomorrow?*

Discussion and Activity: Reaching Out to Others

Time: 1.5 to 2 hours total across 2 days

Special Material Needed:

- Large heart stencil

Conclusion and Whole-Class Read-Aloud #3: *Maybe Tomorrow?*

Begin to conclude this unit by gathering your students for a whole-class read-aloud and discussion. Tell the students that, over the last few days, they have learned a lot about grief and loss.

- Ask students to remind you what *grief* and *loss* mean.
- Ask students to help you list the books they have read. Show them the books on display.
- Ask the students to help you recall some of the different reactions and responses to grief that people might have.

Inform the students that today you are going to share a story that includes strategies and ideas on how they could help a friend who is experiencing grief related to a loss. Gather for a whole-class read-aloud and discussion of *Maybe Tomorrow?* Direct students to listen and watch, especially in this book, for clues about the main characters' relationship.

After you have finished reading the story, engage students in a general share about it.

- First, ask the students, "What page did you especially like? Why?" and "What do you think you will remember about this story?"
- Then ask students to comment on what they noticed about Norris and Ella's friendship.
- Ask students to give examples of the ways in which Norris was a good friend to Ella. What did he do to help her? As students offer ideas, write them on the board or large chart paper. Encourage students to be specific and to find the particular page within the book for each idea. When students locate the page, help the whole class notice anything about the art on that same page; it also might illustrate the ways in which Norris is being a good friend.

Point to the original chart the class created about possible reactions to loss after reading *The Rabbit Listened.*

- Read the list aloud (e.g., "get angry," "talk about it," etc.).
- Then ask students to think about all they have observed in the books read this past week

on how a friend could help support someone who is grieving and possibly going through different reactions. Ask students to share a few ideas with the whole class, and push them to think beyond *The Rabbit Listened* and contemplate all the characters they encountered in this week's books.

Now, have the students create a new list with concrete ideas on how they might support a friend or family member who is experiencing one of the specific reactions of grief. As students generate their ideas, write this new list on chart paper or on the whiteboard. (You may also want to try to connect each of the ideas to a specific type of reaction if possible.)

- Encourage the children to think about what Norris and the rabbit did to help Ella and Taylor, and what the grandchildren did to honor their grandmothers and to comfort their parents and families, and themselves.
- Also encourage them to consider the strategies they learned, such as asking them if they would like to share a favorite memory of the person they lost or making them a sympathy card.
- Spend plenty of time in this conversation to develop concrete ways to support the different reactions/responses to loss and processing grief.

Discussion and Activity: Reaching Out to Others

Either on the next day, or once the list is completed, have your students take their seats. Hand out one piece of construction paper to each child. Ask the students to draw a heart (or trace one with the large heart-shaped stencil provided) and then cut it out. Tell them that when someone is grieving, it can feel as if their heart is breaking. Then direct them to carefully cut their constructed heart into five to seven big pieces.

- Ask each child to pick up one of the pieces of their "heart." Tell them to write on one side only with a pencil or marker. Draw students' attention to the reactions to loss listed in the chart on the board. Pick one reaction and read it aloud. Then have students write it down on their piece. (While they do that, check or cross off that reaction on the chart.)
- Tell students to turn that piece over. Then ask them to think of one of the concrete ways you can help or support someone who is grieving. Draw their attention to the list on the board. Pick one of these ways and read it aloud. Then have students write it down on their piece. (While they do that, check or cross off that form of support on the board.)
- Have your students work through this process for all the pieces. You can continue to do this as a whole group or allow students to work independently using the lists on the board for help.

When the students have finished writing on both sides of all the pieces, pass out transparent tape to their tables or desks. Tell them to put their pieces together on the tabletop or desktop like a puzzle until they have re-created the original heart shape. Make sure that the side facing up only has one set of writing—either the reactions to grief or the ways to offer support. Once the students have checked for this, tell them to tape together the pieces of their heart.

Tell students again that when someone is grieving, it can feel as if their heart is breaking. However, the support of friends can help that person heal. The actions written on one side of the heart are the types of things you can do to help. In addition to assisting the grieving person, when you support someone else in this way, a relationship can grow between you.

- Pass out a second piece of construction paper. Tell students to cut out another heart on their own (or using the heart stencil). Then, on one side of this heart, they can draw one person helping or supporting another in one of the ways listed.
- When they finish, on the other side of the heart, they can draw those two people being friends.
- When students have completed their work, collect both hearts from each student. Using a hole punch, create a hole at the bottom of the taped-together heart and one at the top of the heart with a drawing. Connect the two with yarn or string. Then create a hole at the top of the taped-together heart and use yarn or string to make a hanging loop. Hang these connected hearts around the room.

Segue to Next Day and Daily Reflection, Unit Post-Check with Students, and Taking the Pulse of the Class: After Unit

After finishing creating the hearts, explicitly help your students segue by letting them know you are now moving to the next part of the day, and this is the end of the unit on grief and loss. Let them know that the books will remain in the classroom for some time and that they are welcome to revisit them. Also tell them that, although the unit may have been completed, conversations can always continue around its topic, and they should feel free to ask questions or discuss the topic in more detail.

When the school day is over, take some time to fill out the Daily Reflection to reflect on this experience. The next day or the day after that, ask your students to complete the Unit Post-Check with Students form. Finally, about a week to 10 days after the unit is completed, fill out Taking the Pulse of the Class: After Unit to consider more broadly this experience for your current students, yourself, and your future students.

FINAL SUGGESTIONS

During the weeks following this unit, you might want to revisit some of these books or the conversations on them. This unit was intended as an introduction to, and the beginning of, courageous conversations around the difficult topic of loss, especially death, and feelings of grief.

Some students may want to continue to discuss this topic. Reach out to your school counselors, psychologists, and support faculty for individual help for students seeking more specific or individualized support in this area. The Unit Post-Check with Students form will help you identify the students needing or wanting this support.

You may decide to expand on this unit with further book sharing, discussions, and activities. The websites that follow may serve as good resources as you do this work.

ADDITIONAL RESOURCES

Candlewick Press Activity Kit and Teachers' Guide for *Evelyn Del Rey Is Moving Away*: *www.candlewick.com/essentials.asp?browse=title&mode=book&isbn=1536207047&bkview=p&pix=y*

(This outstanding picturebook by Meg Medina *and* Sonia Sanchez *offers a nice extension on the grief and loss unit by exploring the loss of a friend due to a geographic move.)*

Coalition to Support Grieving Students: *https://grievingstudents.org*

The Compassionate Friend. "Supporting Families after a Child Dies": *www.compassionatefriends.org*

HealGrief.org. "Providing Community, Support, and Connections.": *https://healgrief.org*

National Public Radio. "Parenting: Difficult Conversations" episodes: *www.npr.org/podcasts/510334/parenting-difficult-conversations*

Not If But When (Books for Young People about Death and Loss): *www.notifbutwhen.org/#not-if-but-when*

Scholastic and New York Life's Children & Grief Guidance and Support Resources: *www.scholastic.com/childrenandgrief*

Sesame Street Workshop Toolkits. "Grief": *www.sesamestreet.org/toolkits/grief*

MEETING COMMON CORE AND CASEL STANDARDS

Common Core English Language Arts Standards for Grade 4

This unit meets specific Common Core State Standards for English Language Arts in grades 3, 4, 5, and 6. We have included the specific ELA standards for grade 4 below to illustrate the strands and items met (similar for all four grades third through sixth). The QR code here will link you to the specific lists for grades 3, 5, and 6.

CCSS.ELA-LITERACY.SL.4.1

Engage effectively in a range of collaborative discussions (one-on-one, in groups, and teacher-led) with diverse partners on *grade 4 topics and texts*, building on others' ideas and expressing their own clearly.

CCSS.ELA-LITERACY.RL.4.1

Refer to details and examples in a text when explaining what the text says explicitly and when drawing inferences from the text.

CCSS.ELA-LITERACY.RL.4.2

Determine a theme of a story, drama, or poem from details in the text; summarize the text.

CCSS.ELA-LITERACY.RL.4.3

Describe in depth a character, setting, or event in a story or drama, drawing on specific details in the text (e.g., a character's thoughts, words, or actions).

CCSS.ELA-LITERACY.RL.4.4

Determine the meaning of words and phrases as they are used in a text, including those that allude to significant characters found in mythology (e.g., Herculean).

CCSS.ELA-LITERACY.RL.4.9

Compare and contrast the treatment of similar themes and topics (e.g., opposition of good and evil) and patterns of events (e.g., the quest) in stories, myths, and traditional literature from different cultures.

CASEL Social and Emotional Learning Standards for Grades 3–5

This unit meets specific CASEL Core Competence Area goals for Social and Emotional Learning for grades 3–5. We have included the CASEL areas and specific example standards below to show the items met in this unit. (The items are similar for grade 6.)

Self-Awareness: The abilities to understand one's own emotions, thoughts, and values and how they influence behavior across contexts. This includes capacities to recognize one's strengths and limitations with a well-grounded sense of confidence and purpose.

- Identifying one's emotions
- Linking feelings, values, and thoughts

Self-Management: The abilities to manage one's emotions, thoughts, and behaviors effectively in different situations and to achieve goals and aspirations. This includes the capacities to delay gratification, manage stress, and feel motivation and agency to accomplish personal/collective goals.

- Managing one's emotions
- Identifying and using stress-management strategies
- Exhibiting self-discipline and self-motivation

Social Awareness: The abilities to understand the perspectives of and empathize with others, including those from diverse backgrounds, cultures, and contexts. This includes the capacities to feel compassion for others, understand broader historical and social norms for behavior in different settings, and recognize family, school, and community resources and supports.

- Taking others' perspectives
- Demonstrating empathy and compassion

- Showing concern for the feelings of others
- Recognizing situational demands and opportunities

Relationship Skills: The abilities to establish and maintain healthy and supportive relationships and to effectively navigate settings with diverse individuals and groups. This includes the capacities to communicate clearly, listen actively, cooperate, work collaboratively to problem-solve and negotiate conflict constructively, navigate settings with differing social and cultural demands and opportunities, provide leadership, and seek or offer help when needed.

- Communicating effectively
- Developing positive relationships
- Practicing teamwork and collaborative problem solving

Responsible Decision Making: The abilities to make caring and constructive choices about personal behavior and social interactions across diverse situations. This includes the capacities to consider ethical standards and safety concerns, and to evaluate the benefits and consequences of various actions for personal, social, and collective well-being.

- Demonstrating curiosity and open-mindedness
- Identifying solutions for personal and social problems
- Reflecting on one's role to promote personal, family, and community well-being
- Evaluating personal, interpersonal, community, and institutional impacts

Supporting Children's Understanding of Communities through Literature

INTRODUCTION

The next two chapters feature thematic book sets that address important topics around children's development of understanding communities. The notion of community, and how communities change, appears repeatedly in social studies curriculum in the elementary and middle school grades. Community change is the most discussed topic in local news, meaning that students may have particular interest at times in certain local situations, and in generally understanding how communities change over time. The global pandemic has also had a strong impact on children's understanding of concepts of civic engagement and of community membership. Chapters 5 and 6 focus specifically on these two topics.

Before beginning these topics, we encourage you to review Chapter 2 for helpful tips on understanding your own feelings on these topics. We also want to stress that the stories within these units are specifically sequenced to build understanding. To have the greatest likelihood of success with these courageous conversations, we ask that you follow the order and complete the entire unit. Good luck: You've got this!

Chapter 5—*It's Not Fair! What Should I Do?*: Talking About Civic Engagement and Taking Action

This thematic book set focuses on understanding civic engagement and how even young children can take action about the things they believe are just. Children are often passionate about situations they perceive to be inequitable and are eager to make them fair. Likewise, they are frequently invested in global topics that demand quick action such as climate change, the growing extinction of animal species, and other environmental concerns. Our youth yearn to take a stand when they see the social injustices in their world but often are unsure how to do so.

Reading and discussing this carefully curated set of books with your students will help them begin to understand how many children and teens have become effective activists for causes in which they believe. In turn, this can help them think about what concrete actions they might take to start on a path to "be the change you want to see in the world" (as urged by Mahatma Gandhi). The set is not designed to teach students about current issues of social justice, but rather to empower them to understand acts of civic engagement around the inequities and needs they observe. The discussions and activities in the chapter will help inspire children on the path of gaining self-confidence in their personal ability to create meaningful change in their communities and the greater world.

Along with focusing on social and emotional development standards (the CASEL 5), this thematic book set embeds English language arts standards that include comparing various historical events across texts, using text evidence to make inferences, and evaluating the actions of main characters. Activities and discussion questions are suited for a third- through sixth-grade classroom audience and should be adjusted as appropriate for your grade level and students' understanding.

Chapter 6—*And Then We Had to Leave*: Talking About Refugees and Communities

This thematic book set centers on the plight of people facing refugee situations and the resulting changes to their communities. It prompts students to consider what the word home means to themselves and to others and ultimately asks them to consider how they might feel if they had to leave all with which they are familiar in order to be safe. The unit informs students about general occurrences experienced by refugees as they leave their homes, live in temporary places, and find home in new communities. Throughout the reading, discussions, and activities, students are encouraged to develop empathy through listening, learning, and putting themselves in the shoes of others.

Along with focusing on social and emotional development standards (the CASEL 5), this thematic book set embeds English language arts standards related to making connections between text and visual presentation of the text, understanding word choice, and writing with description and sensory details. Activities and discussion questions are suited for a third- through sixth-grade classroom audience and should be adjusted as appropriate for your grade level and students' understanding.

AUTHOR AND ILLUSTRATOR PROFILES

Deborah Hopkinson

Sharing author Deborah Hopkinson's *Butterflies Belong Here: A Story of One Idea, Thirty Kids, and a World of Butterflies*, as featured in Chapter 5, could result in the construction of a monarch way station at your school or local community! Hopkinson weaves together accurate knowledge of the need for these butterfly gardens with details on how to create them, along with a rich set of further resources in the back of her book. At the same time, she adroitly presents the steps for children taking on a community action project.

This careful research and call to social action are notable across the more than 50 titles she wrote for young people. Hopkinson's books are primarily historical fiction and biography; she anchors her stories in facts and then uses those informational details to inspire student engagement and interest. While some of her subjects are well-known figures, more of them are everyday children living in extraordinary times. But with both, she crafts tales bound in accuracy that highlight the courage and creativeness of the main characters in making the world a better place. Hopkinson's dedicated insistence on factual accuracy helps to instill in readers the idea that they, too, can make a difference in their time. Her works subtly teach children that they have the ability and power and strong analytical skills to question, make their own judgments, and take action. In her book *Abe Lincoln Crosses a Creek*, for example, Hopkinson even breaks the fourth wall to demonstrate the importance of carefully questioning the historical "facts" themselves.

Throughout the school year, you may want to consider including some of Hopkinson's stories in your history and social studies readings. Concentrate on how Hopkinson writes of both the successes and failures of her main characters and, together with your students, examine how her portrayals can quietly empower and encourage young people today.

Francesca Sanna

The Journey, featured in Chapter 6, is the first picturebook that award-winning illustrator Francesca Sanna both illustrated and wrote. In describing the process of its creation, Sanna speaks to the importance of the illustration in crafting the story while simultaneously expressing her wish to convey a more universal tale that could emphasize the "idea that everyone has the right to have a safe place to live." The vague setting helps to capture this universality and makes the book a powerful experience.

Sanna offers some of this information in the author's note for the picturebook, but you may want to examine more of her carefully designed artistic decisions in a later reading of the book with your students. This may encourage them to better articulate the decisions they make in creating their own art, as well as build awareness of the way in which all illustrators make aesthetic decisions in their art to bring out the mood of a story, or add a nuanced element to the theme, and more.

Consider exploring more of Sanna's illustrated works, such as *Me and My Fear* (found in this book in Chapter 10) or *My Friend Earth*, and talk about the art and decision making of illustration. Molly Bang's *Picture This: How Pictures Work* could serve as a useful reference.

IN MY CLASSROOM

Meaningful and Messy

In our town, recycling bins are a regular part of the weekly trash pick-up. Buildings and homes each receive one bin for garbage and one bin for recyclables, largely paper and certain plastics.

Glass recycling is only available by personal collection and drop-off to the main recycling center. After a field trip to the recycling center, talk in our fifth-grade classroom developed a definite bent toward environmental issues for several days. Some students checked in classrooms to see if the class recycling bins were being used frequently and correctly. A small contingent examined the signage and use of the recycling sorting area in the lunchroom, something that had been established by another group of fifth graders a few years back. About 2 weeks after the visit, the topic seemed to be dying down. Then Lee raised his hand at the start of the day and asked about glass.

He said he had been thinking about glass recycling and how the lack of glass-collecting bins across our town meant that some people who might want to recycle their glass couldn't because they didn't have the time or a way to get their glass to the recycling center. Lee added that he had looked and there wasn't a bus line that went to the center, and it would be hard to carry bags of glass on a public bus. Lee suggested that the class write to the city to propose large bins at the town's schools for collecting glass that could then be picked up monthly from the recycling trucks. The class rallied around this idea. Within just a few days, a class project began, and I carved out a little time each day for the "Great Glass Recycling Project." Students in teams researched systems for glass collection in other towns, as well as facts about glass recycling and the costs and benefits of pick-up sites. They worked on op-eds to the local paper, spread the word with flyers and posters, did online meetings with the director of the recycling center, and looked into the permitting process. Before I knew it, the students were leading a community campaign and well on their way to making real change in our town. Some afternoons after they left for the day, I would look over at the stacks of flyers ready to be distributed, the posters about the benefits of glass recycling, and the Lego-built model of a recycling bin and be awestruck by their motivation and civic engagement. Then I would take a big sniff and remember that tomorrow I needed to remind them again about fully rinsing out glass before placing it in the boxes lining the wall of our classroom.

Lee and a few friends, eager to get the project moving forward in very concrete ways, had taken to picking up weekly glass bottles, yogurt containers, and jam jars from the residents in the senior apartments near the school grounds. The slightly sour smell permeating the classroom each day was a good reminder of the messy but meaningful work of my fifth-grade activists.

—TD, FIFTH-GRADE TEACHER

It's Not Fair! What Can I Do?

Talking About Civic Engagement and Taking Action

THE BOOKS

Love Is Powerful

by Heather Dean Brewer, illustrated by LeUyen Pham (Candlewick Press, 2020)

In Heather Dean Brewer's story, Mari prepares to attend the Women's March in New York City with her mother. Alongside Mari, the reader learns a little about what it means to participate in a march for a cause, experiencing some wonder at the large size of the crowd. LeUyen Pham's colorful images capture the excitement and even match the photograph and real story of Mari found at the end of the book.

Malala's Magic Pencil

by Malala Yousafzai, illustrated by Kerascoët (Little, Brown, 2017)

Malala Yousafzai tells the story of becoming an activist in her own words, explaining how she became a leader in standing up for women's rights in Pakistan. A story about a magic pencil helps lend a fairytale aura to her story, aided by Kerascoët's captivating and detailed art.

Our House Is on Fire: Greta Thunberg's Call to Save the Planet

by Jeanette Winter (Beach Lane Books, 2019)

Jeanette Winter's picturebook biography captures young activist Greta Thunberg's growing fame. In the beginning, Winter captures Greta as being rather shy, but shows how she soon blossoms into a strong and confident person who inspired many others with her Friday school strikes to advocate for action on climate change.

The Boy Who Grew a Forest: The True Story of Jadav Payeng

by Sophia Gholz, illustrated by Kayla Harren (Sleeping Bear Press, 2019)

This book by Sophia Gholz documents the efforts of Jadav "Molai" Payeng as he works to save the wildlife of the forest surrounding his home that has been ravaged by a flood. As illustrated by Kayla Harren, he cultivates and plants an entire forest, nurturing back to life the ecosystem that had previously thrived. Today, Payeng is famous for the hard work he initiated as a young boy.

Sofia Valdez, Future Prez

by Andrea Beaty, illustrated by David Roberts (Houghton Mifflin Harcourt, 2018)

In this addition to her "The Questioneers" series, author Andrea Beaty portrays Sofia Valdez as a go-getter, someone who loves helping people in her community. After her *abuelo* ("grandfather") gets hurt while running after their dog through the local landfill, Sofia decides to take matters into her own hands and build a park. Sofia learns the steps of engaging in this type of activist work as she convinces her family, neighbors, and local government officials to assist her.

Butterflies Belong Here: A Story of One Idea, Thirty Kids, and a World of Butterflies

by Deborah Hopkinson, illustrated by Meilo So (Chronicle, 2016)

Author Deborah Hopkinson and illustrator Meilo So recount the story of a young girl who has recently moved to the United States and is feeling very much out of place until the school librarian suggests an intriguing book about butterflies. She becomes interested in the migration of monarch butterflies, learns about the danger monarchs now face, and decides to lead her class in building a monarch way station at their school.

Maddi's Fridge

by Lois Brandt, illustrated by Vin Vogel (Flash Light Press, 2018)

Maddi and Sofia are best friends who love to climb and run together. One afternoon, while at Maddi's apartment, Sofia discovers Maddi's family is suffering from food insecurity. Sofia tries to help her friend without letting any adult know but finally asks for help. Lois Brandt's story is well balanced with honesty and humor, as aided by Vin Vogel's illustrations, and offers a sensitive way to open an important conversation.

Let the Children March

by Monica Clark-Robinson, illustrated by Frank Morrison (Houghton Mifflin Harcourt, 2018)

Frank Morrison's gorgeous oil paintings capture the passion and fear of the children who joined the 1963 Birmingham Children's Crusade. Author Monica Clark-Robinson gives readers important details of the courageous event, using the voice of a teenage girl participating in the march alongside her brother. The girl explains why her parents could get in trouble or lose their jobs by marching, so she and her brother feel pride in standing up for the rights of their community.

It Takes a Village

by Hillary Rodham Clinton, illustrated by Marla Frazee (Simon & Schuster, 2017)

In this fictional story by Hillary Rodham Clinton, a community works together to build a playground. Children work alongside adults, families help each other, and eventually, the playground is complete. Everyone supports each other and contributes their unique skills to make the future brighter for the next generation. Marla Frazee's accompanying illustrations draw attention to the collective way the community plans and takes on each step of the process together.

> ***Note:*** As with all thematic book sets, we recommend that after each book has been shared within the unit, it is placed in an easily accessible display in the classroom for the rest of the unit days. Children should then be allowed access to explore these books on their own during free-choice times.

PLANNING CHECKLIST

It's Not Fair! What Can I Do?: Talking About Civic Engagement and Taking Action

We suggest the following timeline to prepare and then share and discuss the books and do the related activities with your students. (A reproducible version of this checklist is available in Appendix 1.) Please note that timing for your individual class should be determined by your situation and your schedule, and, most importantly, should be guided by your students' reactions to the books and activities. Plan generally, however, on about 1 hour of daily time with the unit for 7–10 days in a row.

Two Weeks Prior

- ☐ Complete Taking the Paulse of the Class: Before Unit (Appendix 2) for a general sense of your class at this time.
- ☐ Collect and read twice each of the books for the unit.
- ☐ Review the "Unit Plans: Reading, Discussions, and Activities" section of the unit.
- ☐ Send out the Administration Notification Slip (Appendix 3) and School Counselor/Psychologist and Support Staff Notification Slip (Appendix 4).

One Week Prior

- ☐ (Optional) Send out Family Notification Slips (Appendix 5) to the families of your students.
- ☐ Have students complete the Unit Pre-Check with Students (Appendix 6) and review the results carefully. Check in with any students with reactions that cause concern so that you can prepare for extra support.
- ☐ Review Chapter 2 of the book.

☐ Collect all materials needed for the unit:

☐ **Daily Reflection forms (Appendix 7):** You will need one for each day.

☐ **Books:** One copy is required, but you may prefer to secure two copies of each book. After each book has been shared during the unit, place it in an easily accessible display in the classroom. Please give students access to explore these books on their own during free-choice times. You will want to keep the display available for some time after the unit is completed.

☐ **Materials already in your classroom:** Please have available and ready to use the following commonplace classroom materials:

- Chart paper or a section of whiteboard that can remain posted for the duration of the unit
- Unlined white paper
- Pencils and pens; colored pencils, crayons, or markers
- Construction paper or other colored paper
- Scissors
- Tape or glue
- Any additional materials indicated within the unit chapter's detailed description

During: Readings, Discussions, and Activities (approximately 7–10 school days)

☐ Follow the detailed plans for each day.

☐ One to 2 days after the unit is completed, have students complete the Unit Post-Check with Students (Appendix 8).

One Week Following

☐ After reviewing the Unit Post-Check with Students, check in with any students with reactions that cause concern.

☐ Refer any students expressing interest or for whom you have concerns at this point for additional, individual discussion with a school support professional. Also consider additional whole-class work if indicated.

☐ Complete and review Taking the Pulse of the Class: After Unit (Appendix 9). This will help you reflect on your experience and your students' experiences with the thematic book set.

UNIT OVERVIEW It's Not Fair! What Can I Do? Talking About Civic Engagement and Taking Action		
Day	**Books**	**Discussion and Activities**
1	**Introduction and Whole-Class Read-Aloud #1:** *Love Is Powerful*	• Defining *Social Justice* and *Activist* with "Love Is Powerful" Paper

2, 3, and 4	**Small Groups Read-Aloud and Discuss #1:** *Malala's Magic Pencil* *Our House Is on Fire: Greta Thunberg's Call to Save the Planet* *The Boy Who Grew a Forest: The True Story of Jadav Payeng*	• Changemakers Comparison • Who Can Be a Changemaker?
5 and 6	**Small Groups Read-Aloud and Discuss #2:** *Sofia Valdez, Future Prez* *Butterflies Belong Here: A Story of One Idea, Thirty Kids, and A World of Butterflies*	• Steps to Take Action • Advertisements
7	**Whole-Class Read-Aloud #2:** *Maddi's Fridge*	• Action Steps for Sofia
8	**Whole-Class Read-Aloud #3:** *Let the Children March*	• Why Be a Changemaker?
9	**Conclusion and Whole-Class Read-Aloud and Discuss #4:** *It Takes a Village*	• Project Brainstorms

Note: Each "day" of this unit is intended to take around 1 hour of class time. Time may vary slightly depending on student discussion, but please keep this time frame in mind as you move through the reading and activities.

BEFORE BEGINNING

1. Make sure you have completed the "Two Weeks Prior" and "One Week Prior" items on the planning checklist, including the Taking the Pulse of the Class: Before Unit and the Unit Pre-Check with Students forms.
2. Remember that the books within these units are specifically sequenced to build understanding. To have the greatest likelihood of success with these courageous conversations, we ask that you follow the order of the books, discussions, and activities and complete the entire unit.
3. Review Chapter 2 to help prepare for navigating the upcoming discussions you will be having with your students. As you complete the Daily Reflections at the end of each school day, consider revisiting Chapter 2 for helpful support in engaging in your own self-reflection and awareness, and ensuring your thoughtful and respectful approach to the topic.

DAY 1

Introduction and Whole-Class Read-Aloud #1: *Love Is Powerful*

Discussion and Activities: Defining *Social Justice* and *Activist*; "Love Is Powerful" Paper

Time: 1 hour total

Introduction and Whole-Class Read-Aloud #1: *Love Is Powerful*

Begin the unit by gathering your students for a whole-class read-aloud and discussion. Tell the students that today you are going to share a story about a young girl who takes part in a protest march. But before you do this, the class needs to think about what a few important words mean. These are words that you will be using and learning more about in the next 2 weeks.

Write the words *social justice* and *injustice* close together on your whiteboard. Leave plenty of room underneath them. Then write *taking action*, *activist*, and *civic engagement* on another section of the board also with plenty of room underneath. (You will want to leave this space available across the next 2 weeks. If you have limited board space, use chart paper and hang the charts up on a wall.) Then ask the students to help you define and explain what these two sets of words mean.

- Encourage the students to think about when and where they might have heard these terms before. Write down all ideas, encourage students to look at the affixes and root words, and then ask students if they know any definitions for the terms.
- If students struggle, or you sense only a few are clear on what the words mean, then guide them to find the root word *just* in *social justice* and *injustice*. With student help, explain that *just* can also mean "fair" or "right." An injustice is something that is not fair, or a violation of a person's rights because the prefix *in-* means "not."
- Next, move to the term *social justice*. Tell them that *social* is related to the word *society*, so social justice is basically the rights related to a society or group. Explain that this generally means equal opportunities, equal treatment, and equal rights for everyone in the community, regardless of their race, gender, job, or any other factor. But the concept of social justice goes beyond the concern about fairness and considers how to provide what people need in order to make things more just. Thus, if some people within a community (or in the larger society) are lacking food, health care, housing, or other needs, then someone working to increase social justice would help them find access to fulfilling these needs, and work to inform and educate others about this problem to increase awareness and inspire larger groups of people to organize to help those in need.
- Next, connect these definitions to *activist* and *taking action*. Have students find the common root word: *act*. Explain that *act* means "to do." So, an activist is someone who does something or takes action. Clarify the connection to social justice by explaining that the person working to increase social justice is an *activist*. *Taking action* simply means doing something

to help right the injustice and to inform others about it. Taking action in your community is one way to describe *civic engagement*.

Now, tell students that you are going to share the book *Love Is Powerful*. Indicate that in this first read of the book, you will read slowly and give them plenty of time to carefully notice the details on each page.

- Only read the main text as you read the book aloud. (You will be reading the signs in a later read.) Pause at each page to make sure all the children have time to study the illustrations carefully.
- When you reach the second-to-last page of the book (a two-page spread with the text "Love is powerful" and a large image of Mari's head), stop and engage students in a brief share about the story. Ask students to share aloud some of the careful observations they made about the details in the text and illustrations on each page.

After a few minutes of sharing, tell students that there is more information to this story because it is based on a real event and Mari is a real person.

- Now, turn to the last two pages of the book ("A Note from Mari" on the left page and a photo of the real Mari on the right). Read aloud the note and show students the picture of Mari.
- Tell the class a few facts about this historical event. Explain that the march in the book was part of the Women's March on January 21, 2017, which occurred the day after President Donald J. Trump's first inauguration. This march was a worldwide protest, meaning there were similar protest marches, all for this same reason, held in several places around the world on approximately the same date. The protest was organized in response to several statements President Trump had made about women that some people considered to be offensive and anti-women. The march was organized to call attention to these statements and to support or advocate for government policies that would support the rights of women, as well as the rights of other societal groups that many feared would be treated unjustly by the policies promoted by Trump. It was a historical event because the march was the largest single-day protest in the United States to date.
- Next, slip off the jacket cover of *Love Is Powerful* and show the students the illustrations on the actual book's front and back covers. The overall spread is several boxed illustrations of people protesting. Help students to recognize that the images depict scenes from many different locations. (They might notice the weather in the backgrounds or the different clothing.)
- Then tell students you are going to reread the book so that everyone can look at the signs the marchers carried.

This time as you read the book aloud, stop and pause on each spread after reading its text. Read aloud the messages on the signs seen in the smaller illustrations. (Some of the signs are blurred.)

- When you finish the last spread of the story, turn the page and show the class the picture of Mari again. Read out the words on her two signs: "Be Kind" and "Love Is Powerful."
- Then turn to the inside back flap of the jacket cover. Read aloud the "About the Book" statements, first from the illustrator LeUyen Pham and then from the author Heather Dean Brewer:
    - "I marched in the first Women's March in Atlanta in 2017, but I carried no sign. This book is the sign I wish I'd had with me." —LeUyen Pham
    - "I've often felt quiet and small and that no one could hear me. But when I joined others in the Women's March and saw my friend Mari lifted above the crowd, her voice echoing down the streets of New York City, I learned that even the smallest voice has the power to change the world." —Heather Dean Brewer

Tell your students that Mari, Heather, and LeUyen were all taking action for social justice by participating in the march. They were activists working to inform others about an issue, increase awareness of it, and influence larger groups of people to get involved. (For this protest march, the organizers also had circulated a list of actions people might take after the march to continue to increase awareness and advocate for women's rights.)

Discussion and Activities: Defining Social Justice and Activist with "Love Is Powerful" Paper

Have your students return to their tables or desks and hand out a piece of blank paper to each. As they settle into their seats, ask the children to think quietly about Mari's message: both on her sign and within her note in the book.

- Using your whiteboard, chalkboard, or large chart paper to model, write down the message Mari had written on her sign and shouted out: "Love Is Powerful." Have the students copy the same message at the top of their paper. (Some students might mention that Mari also was holding a sign in the photograph that said, "Be Kind." If they do, tell them that for this activity they will only concentrate on the message that Mari both displayed in public and shouted.)
- Ask your students to share with their seat mate or table group what they think Mari means by "Love Is Powerful." First, ask students to close their eyes and contemplate what Mari means. In a clear loud voice, read aloud the last paragraph from "A Note from Mari." Then tell students to open their eyes and share their thoughts with their seat mate.
- Ask for a few volunteers to share their ideas about Mari's message. Between shares, use a few specific prompts, such as asking, "Why do you think Mari said to remember to speak up not just for yourself, but for other people, too? How does that relate to taking action for social justice?" And, "Why did Mari say to believe in yourself and be confident? Do you think it might be hard to take action for social justice?"
- Continue this whole-class discussion for a few more minutes. Then tell students to think about a time that one of these three things might have happened in their lives:

- They took action to help stand up for another person or for an important cause.
- Someone they knew took action for a social justice cause.
- They read a true or fictional story about a person taking action around a social justice issue. ***Note:*** Give students a few examples, such as helping to collect recyclables and taking them to a collection site, raising money in some way for an important social justice issue, or asking someone to stop using a derogatory term. Include in your examples at least one from a book or story read aloud or shared in your class during the past year. (The examples should make it clear that the action taken was not just "being kind" but taking deliberate action to help raise awareness or in some way address a social injustice.)

- Then ask the students to draw a picture and/or write a description of that incident on their "Love Is Powerful" paper. While the students are working, circle around the room, asking them to tell you about the event they are describing.

Segue to Next Day and Daily Reflection

When students are finished, collect the papers. Explicitly help your students segue by letting them know you are now moving to the next part of the day, but you will be returning to this topic tomorrow.

When the school day is over, find a spot on your classroom wall to hang up each student's "Love Is Powerful" paper. Place them at a level where all students will be able to easily view most of the papers. Then take some time to fill out the Daily Reflection to reflect on today's experience. Review it as you prepare for the next day.

DAYS 2, 3, AND 4

Small Groups Read-Aloud and Discuss #1: *Malala's Magic Pencil, Our House Is on Fire: Greta Thunberg's Call to Save the Planet*, and *The Boy Who Grew a Forest: The True Story of Jadav Payeng*

Discussion and Activities: Changemakers Comparison; Who Can Be a Changemaker?

Time: 3 hours total across 3 days

Special Materials Needed:

- Thinking About the Changemakers (Appendix 10) worksheet

Small Groups Read-Aloud and Discuss #1: *Malala's Magic Pencil, Our House Is on Fire: Greta Thunberg's Call to Save the Planet,* and *The Boy Who Grew a Forest: The True Story of Jadav Payeng*

> ***Note:*** Before starting on Day 2, make enough copies of the Thinking About the Changemakers handout so that each small group has one copy. Before starting on Day 4, make copies of the small group's completed handout so that each member of the small group has a copy of their group work.

On Day 2, begin by giving the students time to quietly view the "Love Is Powerful" papers hung up on the wall. When all students have had time to view the class papers, gather the whole class together for a brief discussion.

First, ask the students if anyone would like to share an observation about the papers. Explain that observations might include statements such as "I noticed that a lot of us have been to the recycling plant," or "I noticed that many people in the class have read books about Martin Luther King, Jr." Call on a few students to share.

After students have shared some observations, ask if anyone has specific questions about the papers. Explain that such questions from classmates might ask for more information, such as "Can you tell us a little more about the fundraiser you helped with?" or "What is the title of the book you read about Harriet Tubman?" (You may also want to add that students can choose to decline to answer any question at this time if they feel uncomfortable.) Allow a few students to ask questions and respond.

End the discussion by reminding the students that the incidents they shared in their "Love Is Powerful" papers are examples of people who are civically engaged as activists working for social justice.

Then tell students that today and the following day, they will be reading and discussing two books in small groups. Explain that these picturebooks are biographies of real people who became activists and civically engaged as teenagers. Malala Yousafzai is an activist for female education, and Jadav Payeng and Greta Thunberg are environmental activists. They will be reading the books and thinking about these individual activists as "changemakers," or people who are taking action to help solve social problems.

Discussion and Activities: Changemakers Comparison; Who Can Be a Changemaker?

Divide your class into three smaller groups of students. The rest of today and on Day 3, work with each small group, reading aloud to them and discussing one of these three titles: *Malala's Magic Pencil*, *Our House Is on Fire: Greta Thunberg's Call to Save the Planet*, and *The Boy Who Grew a Forest: The True Story of Jadav Payeng.* Each group will meet with you to listen and discuss a title, and then, together, complete the first part of the **Changemakers Comparison** activity, using the Thinking About the Changemakers worksheet. Allow 30 minutes for each group.

- Give students plenty of time during each small-group meeting to explore the pages and talk together about the way the author and illustrator use impactful words in the text, or how colors or shapes in the illustrations convey the strong emotions of the main characters. Model an example of this to start.
- After they finish reading the book and have discussed their "noticings," encourage students to think about how the protagonist (the teen activist) learned about the issue involved, how and from whom they first received support in trying to take action, and how taking action affected their lives in positive and negative ways. Discuss these things orally for a few minutes.

- Then hand one student in the group a copy of the Thinking About the Changemakers worksheet. Read aloud the information at the top of the worksheet and ask the student to fill in the blanks. Then read aloud the directions and the first stem/prompt to the group. Ask the group to share answers to the prompt and then have the student write down a few of them. Then pass the paper to the next student. Read aloud the next prompt to the group. Ask the group to share answers to it and have the student write down a couple of those. Continue this pattern until all the prompts have been answered. (Adjust this writing as needed for your class by choosing a "scribe," acting as scribe yourself, etc.)
- After the students finish, collect the completed handouts.

On Day 4, have your students start by sitting in their three small groups. Hand out to each student a copy of their group's Thinking About the Changemakers worksheet. Then divide up the class into new "jigsaw" groups, putting students into small groups that include one student representing each of the three titles.

Tell students that they are now going to compare some of the characteristics of the three teenage changemakers they read about by working together in their new groups on a Venn diagram.

- Pass out to each group a large piece of paper and make sure each group has a red, green, blue, and black marker. Modeling it on the whiteboard or on chart paper, have students create a three-circle Venn diagram.
- First, use the red marker to draw the first circle and explain that it stands for Malala. Use the green maker to draw the second circle and explain that it stands for Greta. Use the blue marker for the third circle and explain that it stands for Jadav.
- Tell students that they should work through each part of their worksheet to help see how the activists are similar and different. Start with the answers to the first prompt ("Some words that could describe _____________ are . . . "). Ask the students to take turns in their group reading aloud their answers. Start with Malala. As the students who read *Malala's Magic Pencil* share with their group the descriptive words they wrote down for Malala, the students in the group for Jadav and Greta should raise their hands whenever they hear a word or phrase that is the same or similar to what they have listed on their worksheet. If the word or a similar word was used for all three changemakers, write it in the middle section where all three circles overlap. If the word or a very similar word or phrase was used for two of the changemakers, write it in the section where those two changemakers overlap. Once finished with Malala, allow the students who read about Jadav to share, and then finally the students who read about Greta.
- Lead the whole class through this process with this first prompt. Then tell students to repeat the process with the next prompts as you circle around the room to help as needed. (***Note:*** If this is your class's first time drawing a Venn diagram, you may need to stop and model a Venn diagram with two items well known to them. You may also want to consider simply doing a two-changemaker comparison with a two-circle Venn diagram with pairs or quads of students.)

When all the students have completed their Venn diagrams, lead a whole-class discussion on their work. Ask the students to share aloud what each group has written in the middle section (where all three circles overlap) and listen for all commonalities between each group's middle section lists. Inform the students that all these traits included in the middle section are characteristics of changemakers! Ask them to think about the changemaker/activist incident they drew and wrote about in the "Love Is Powerful" paper. Does that person share most of these same characteristics? You may even want to think together with the class about other very famous activists they are aware of and decide as a group if those individuals have most of these characteristics. Use these examples to help the class understand that changemakers may be different in their external or "outside" characteristics, but they are all brave and willing to stand up for what they believe in. Ask the students, **"Who can be a changemaker?"** and gently push them to see that anyone can be, including they themselves.

Segue to Next Day and Daily Reflection

At the end of Day 4, explicitly help your students segue by letting them know you are now moving to the next part of the day, but you will be returning to this topic of changemakers tomorrow.

When the school day is over, take some time to fill out the Daily Reflection to reflect on this experience. Review it as you prepare for the next day.

DAYS 5 AND 6

Small Groups Read-Aloud and Discuss #2: *Sofia Valdez, Future Prez* and *Butterflies Belong Here: A Story of One Idea, Thirty Kids, and a World of Butterflies*

Discussion and Activities: Steps to Take Action; Advertisement

Time: 2 hours across 2 days

Small Groups Read-Aloud and Discuss #2: *Sofia Valdez, Future Prez* and *Butterflies Belong Here: A Story of One Idea, Thirty Kids, and a World of Butterflies*

For Days 5 and 6, divide your class again into two half groups. Across the next 2 days, work with each small group independently to read and discuss one of the two titles, *Sofia Valdez, Future Prez* and *Butterflies Belong Here: A Story of One Idea, Thirty Kids, and a World of Butterflies.* (**Note:** *Butterflies Belong Here* is a longer read than *Sofia Valdez* and includes four detailed nonfiction page spreads about monarch butterflies. It also has a subtle secondary theme about the narrator's recent move to the United States and the challenges she faced to learn English.) After their discussion, you will divide these half groups into smaller groups to work together on the advertisement activity.

- Take plenty of time during the small-group read-aloud and discussion to allow students to explore each page and think about the way the author and illustrator show the main character learning about the issue and then deciding to take action. Ask students to point out changes that appear in the illustrations of the character, as well in the colors of the illustrations in general, as they begin to take on leadership roles.
- For both books, stop reading when the story ends. (Do not read the back pages yet.) Then encourage students to talk about the way the main character became a leader. What inspired them to take action? How did they involve others in the community to help?

After this immediate post-reading discussion with the small group, state that the writer added an "Author's Note." Read it aloud to the group. In *Sofia Valdez*, this section appears in the middle of the final illustrated page, right under the dedication. In *Butterflies Belong Here*, it is the next page after the story ends. (This book has quite a bit of extra back-page material. Do stop reading aloud after the "Author's Note." You can tell the small groups reading this book that it includes more resources about monarch butterflies and monarch way stations that they may want to read and explore later. The book will be on display in the classroom for reading and examining along with the other books from this unit, so they can take a look at another time.)

- Then tell the students that the author is actually an activist herself! One part of taking action for social justice is to educate others about the issue and encourage them to take action as well. The authors and illustrators do this here by creating these picturebooks for children and their families.
- For the *Butterflies Belong Here* groups, explain specifically that author Deborah Hopkinson and illustrator Meilo have created another book together with Philippe Cousteau, called *Follow the Moon Home: A Tale of One Idea, Twenty Kids, and a Hundred Sea Turtles*. This book tells the story of a fictional classroom that takes on a community action project.
- For the *Sofia Valdez* groups, explain specifically that author Andrea Beaty and illustrator David Roberts have created a series of other books called the "Questioneer Picture Books," including titles such as *Ada Twist, Scientist* and *Rosie Revere, Engineer*. These books are about fictional children who ask big questions and use their creativity and research to take action and create change.

Discussion and Activities: Steps to Take Action; Advertisement

When all groups have read and discussed the stories, have students sit at their desks and take out a piece of paper and pencil. Working in pairs or individually, ask the students to write down the specific change that Sofia or the girl from *Butterflies* built with their community (a park/a monarch way station and garden) on the top of their sheet of paper. Then, together, have them recall the girls' **Steps to Take Action**, using both the text in the book and the illustrations for reference. Assist the students in creating a list of these action steps. (Some of the steps, particularly in *Sofia Valdez*, are only shown in the illustrations. Make sure that the students notice the girls made advertisements or flyers to help tell others about the cause.)

Now, ask the students to flip their papers over. Remind them that one of the steps each girl took was to tell others in the community about the need for this new action (creating a park or building a monarch way station). You may want to draw students' attention to the illustrations in the book showing this.

- Tell the students that now they are going to imagine that they are one of the children in the classroom featured in *Butterflies Belong Here* or a friend of Sofia's who wants to help with spreading information about the need for the park/monarch way station. This is a very important action step as it gets more people involved, meaning that more of the community becomes personally invested in the project and understands the need for it.
- Explain that to help spread the word, they are going to create either a poster or a flyer. Tell students that posters are usually hung to educate people about the issue in an attention-getting way. Flyers are sometimes handed out to people so they can learn about the project by reading through the brief information in it. Flyers often have a little more writing on them than posters, and posters often include a little more art.
- Using the blank back of their paper and crayons or markers, ask students to spend the next 15 minutes creating a flyer or poster as an **Advertisement** for the park or monarch way station. They should think about the information in the book for why this project is needed and use that to help guide their design. They should also think about what the next action step should be and consider specific ways in which they might encourage others to become a part of the project.
- Students can share their work with their small group when finished.

Segue to Next Day and Daily Reflection

Explicitly help the students in the group segue by letting them know you are now moving to the next part of the day, but you will be returning to this topic tomorrow.

When the school day is over, take some time to fill out the Daily Reflection to reflect on this experience. Review it as you prepare for the next day.

DAY 7

Whole-Class Read-Aloud #2: *Maddi's Fridge*

Discussion and Activity: Action Steps for Sofia

Time: About 1 hour total

Whole-Class Read-Aloud #2: *Maddi's Fridge*

Note: The book *Maddi's Fridge* focuses on the issue of food insecurity. Because the rate of food-insecure households with children is extremely high, this is likely to be an issue for students in your own class. Review the suggestions about observing students to help you best lead this discussion. While reading and discussing, remember to watch students' facial expressions and behaviors carefully, and only call on students who are volunteering. The discussion today is going to focus on moving beyond "helping" to really being an "activist" and not specifically on the issue of food insecurity, but it is possible that your students may be more interested in discussing food insecurity.

Gather your students for a whole-class read-aloud. Introduce the book by showing the students its cover and explaining that today you are going to share another story of a child who learns about an issue of social injustice. Remind students of the definitions they learned at the beginning of this unit for "activists," "social justice," and "civic engagement." Refer to the definitions on the whiteboard/chart paper. Then remind them that if people within a community lack food or health care or housing or other needs, then an activist might be able to assist them in finding access to help meet such needs, and work to inform and educate others about this problem, increasing awareness of it.

Now, begin reading aloud the story. Note that it starts before the title page. Begin by showing the students the first inside cover spread and point out the two little girls chasing each other. Then turn to the title page, and read the title, the names of the author and illustrator aloud. As you read, stop at the following pages to ask questions of the class as indicated:

- On the title page, stop after reading aloud the title and author's and illustrator's names. Ask the students what they notice on the fridge. They will likely comment that the pictures are the same two girls who were chasing each other on the inside cover. Help the students come to the conclusion that these two girls are either sisters, relatives, or close friends. Ask them if they have any predictions to offer about what might happen next in the story. Then continue reading.
- On the second spread, stop after you read "but Sofia was the fastest runner." Ask the students to look closely at Maddi's face. What is her expression? Is she angry at her friend for beating her up the stairs? Or, is she concerned or worried? What do you think she might be worried about? Help students to notice that Maddi seems very concerned that Sofia is going into her apartment. Ask them to consider what might be worrying her, especially since Sofia is her close friend.
- On the fourth spread, stop after you read "all the colors with it." Ask the students to find Maddi in the picture. Have them identify her expression. (She looks sad and worried.)
- On the fifth spread, stop after you read "can of dog food." Tell the students that we cannot see Sofia's face in the illustration. Ask them what they believe she might be thinking. On the seventh spread, stop after you read "but fish is not good for backpacks." Ask the students

what happened. (Sofia brought food for Maddi, but cooked fish does not stay fresh sitting in a backpack all day.) Finish reading the rest of the spread. Ask students what they notice about Maddi's comments to Sofia. Help them to understand that Maddi is encouraging and kind to Sofia.

- After reading the ninth spread, have students explain what happened. (The same thing as the fish, but this time raw eggs were involved.) Help students notice again that Maddi is being very encouraging and supportive of Sofia's attempts to climb the wall.
- On the thirteenth spread, stop after you read "wouldn't be mad." Then put the book down in your lap so students cannot yet see the second half of the spread. Ask the students if Sofia did the right thing in telling her mother about Maddi's secret. Why or why not? After some answers, finish reading the rest of the text on that page and continue on until the end of the story. Skip over the last page after the story ends that is titled "Let's Help Friends Who Have Empty Refrigerators." Turn to the final inside cover spread. Have the students find Maddi and Sofia in the illustration and notice that they are both smiling and talking on the phone to each other.

After you have finished reading the story, ask the students if Sofia is an activist. Take a general vote by having them raise their hands "yes" or "no." Then ask students to explain why they think Sofia is or is not an activist.

- Gently lead students to understand that, while Sofia is very kind and caring, and thoughtfully helped her friend, she is not really an activist. (They may want to debate this a bit because Sofia did tell her mother what was happening.)
- Remind the class that an activist is someone who goes beyond just helping an individual in need and works instead to help advocate for larger change for all people who are suffering a social injustice, like food insecurity, which is a current issue in Maddi's family. (You might clarify that "food insecurity" means that a household doesn't have sufficient food for their family on a regular basis or does not know if they will have sufficient food regularly.)

Discussion and Activity: Action Steps for Sofia

Ask the students what the appropriate **Action Steps for Sofia** might be now that she knows about the issue of food security. Make a list on the whiteboard or on chart paper as the students brainstorm ideas.

- Prompt students to think about the action steps they learned of in the books they have read so far.
- There are also a few suggestions on the last page of the book. After students have offered a few ideas, turn to that last page and read aloud some of those suggestions. Start with the last one on the page and go backward. (The items listed last are true "activist" steps.)

Segue to Next Day and Daily Reflection

After the discussion, explicitly help your students segue by letting them know you are now moving to the next part of the day, but you will be returning to this topic tomorrow.

When the school day is over, take some time to fill out the Daily Reflection to reflect on this experience. Review it as you prepare for the next day.

DAY 8

Whole-Class Read-Aloud #3: *Let the Children March*

Discussion and Activity: Why Be a Changemaker?

Time: About 1 hour total

Whole-Class Read-Aloud #3: *Let the Children March*

Begin the unit by gathering your students for a whole-class read-aloud and discussion. Tell them that today you are going to read aloud a story on an event in U.S. history. Remind your students that last week they learned about individual teen activists who had taken stands for social justice issues despite personal sacrifice. Today, they will hear about a group of children from Birmingham, Alabama, who participated in a march for civil rights in 1963.

These children did this knowing before they took part that they would be yelled at by crowds, might be physically attacked by firehoses or even police dogs, and might be jailed. They had seen on TV what had happened to the adults, some members of their own communities and families, who had participated in the civil rights marches. Yet, they joined the march anyway and took a stand as activists for social justice.

> ***Note:*** If students have learned about the 1960s civil rights movement in the United States or Dr. Martin Luther King, Jr. beforehand, then they will bring that background knowledge to the reading and discussion. The book does provide a little bit of background in its first few pages, but it may be helpful to let students know that the civil rights movement discussed in the book was a social justice movement to give equal rights to Black Americans and occurred primarily in the 1950s and 1960s in the United States. At the time, laws of segregation were preventing Black Americans from having equal justice and equal rights.

- Read the book aloud slowly, giving the students plenty of time to see each spread carefully as you read the text. In this read-aloud, read the book without stopping for student comments or discussion.
- When you finish reading the story, turn to the "Afterword" pages at the end. There are three photographs at the bottom of the spread. If you have access to a document camera or an overhead projector, use that now to show the whole class the photos. If you do not, then you can have smaller groups of students come to you to look closely at each of the photos. (They are too small to be seen well by a whole class during a read-aloud.)

Discussion and Activity: Why Be a Changemaker?

Ask the students to think quietly about how brave the children were to take these risks and participate in the march. Then turn to the inside covers of the book. Show these first inside cover pages to the class and read aloud the timeline entries. Then turn to the back inside cover pages and show them to the class.

- On these back pages, read aloud the first two entries (for June 11 and July 23). Then stop and tell the class that the children of the Children's March in Birmingham had made a difference! The city withdrew its segregation laws.
- Then read aloud the rest of the timeline.

Now, ask the students to share some of their thoughts and reactions to the book. After a short discussion, explain to the class, "The children participating in the Children's March understood well the importance of being changemakers. They recognized the inequalities in their society and fought against them, even risking their own lives in the process. The real teens and people we read about earlier did the same thing in many ways. Malala risked her life and was severely injured as a result. Greta receives threats often. While the fictional characters (Sofia and Maddi and the girl from *Butterflies Belong Here*) might not have been risking their lives, they did risk being made fun of, ignored, or wasting their time and energy trying to get others to help. But they continued to persist even when doing so was a challenge. Do you think that children should be activists for causes they care about? Why or why not? **Why Be a Changemaker**, especially if it is really hard?" Encourage students to respond and discuss with the whole group. To aid their discussion, you might also want to ask what would happen if no one took on the role of an activist.

Segue to Next Day and Daily Reflection

After a brief discussion, tell them to continue thinking about this important question. Explicitly help the students segue by letting them know you are now moving to the next part of the day, but you will be returning to this topic of becoming a changemaker tomorrow. In the meantime, they should not only continue to think about why they might want to be a changemaker and what they would like to change; they might also want to discuss being a changemaker with their family at home, either tonight or in the future.

When the school day is over, take some time to fill out the Daily Reflection to reflect on this experience. Review it as you prepare for the next day.

DAY 9

Conclusion and Whole-Class Read-Aloud #4: *It Takes a Village*

Discussion and Activity: Project Brainstorms

Time: About 1 hour total

Conclusion and Whole-Class Read-Aloud #4: *It Takes a Village*

Conclude this unit by gathering your students for a whole-class read-aloud and discussion. Tell them that over the last several days they have learned a lot about being activists for social justice.

- Ask students to remind you what it means to be an activist or changemaker.
- Ask them to help you list the books they have read. Show them where the books are on display in the room so that they may reread them in the coming weeks if they would like to.

Tell the students that today you are going to share one last story that is about children working as activists. In this book, a small group of children recognize a need in their community and decide on a creative outlet that might fix it. They then speak to their families and their neighbors and friends, and all work together to create something for the entire community to enjoy.

Then begin to read aloud *It Takes a Village*. The text is brief, but the pictures are detailed, so read the story slowly and give students plenty of time to look closely at each spread.

After you have finished reading the story, engage students in a general share about it.

- First, ask the students, "What page did you especially like? Why?" and "What do you think you will remember about this story?"
- Then ask students to comment on what they noticed in the first few pages. What do the illustrations suggest about the children being creative and advocating for others' help to build a community gathering place/playground/park.
- Help the students trace this path of asking: starting with the three children noticing that there is no space for the community to gather, to finding the tree, then by speaking to their families (who then talk to others), and to handing out flyers to neighbors and community members.

Discussion and Activity: Project Brainstorms

Now, tell the students that the authors of all the books they have read in this unit are advocating for children to become changemakers, to notice the issues and problems in the world around them, and to take action to create change.

Send the students back to their tables and desks, and explain to them that, as they return, you would like them to stop and look again at the "Love Is Powerful" posters hanging on the wall.

Once students are at their tables, hand out a piece of blank paper to each. Ask them to fold the paper in half and crease the fold well. Then fold the paper in half again and crease it well. Finally, unfold the paper and note the four sections on each side that have been created.

- In the top left quarter of their paper, ask students to write down some issues that they worry about in their community and the greater society. You may want to encourage your students to share a few examples aloud with the class, or you may remind the class of some of the issues raised in the books read in this unit. Then have students put a star or checkmark next to one or two of the issues on their list that they care the most about right now.

- In the top right quarter of their paper, have students write down the general category of these issues, such as environmental issues, health issues, animal rights, racial inequities, and the like.
- Then in the bottom left quarter of their paper, ask students to write down some facts they know about one or two of the issues they marked.
- Finally, in the bottom right quarter of their paper, have students make a list of the places they could go to learn more about the issue (particular websites, library resources, people to ask, etc.).
- Now, have students turn over their paper. Tell them there are lots of ways to be a change-maker. For example, some people might want to lead a big community protest march, and other individuals might prefer to create flyers to distribute to inform others about the issue. On the whiteboard or chart paper, write down a list of ways to take action as students generate them. To get the class started on **Project Brainstorms**, you might suggest, and write on the board, the idea that someone could raise and donate money to a group already working on the issue, or they might create a petition to address a community need (such as a new crosswalk for the street adjacent to the school, etc.). Help students to come up with several ideas and record them on the whiteboard as they offer their ideas. Then have students write down three or four things on the top half of the back of their paper that they personally would like to do in their civic engagement work as an activist to effect change in their chosen social justice issue.

Now, ask students to stand up with their papers in hand. Help them to move around the room and share quietly with others the areas in which they are interested in making change. As the students share, they should break up into small groups that are concerned with similar issues. When a group of three to five students has formed, they should sit down together.

Once students have all found a small group to join, have them share their individual issue(s) of concern and what types of actions they might want to take.

- When students have completed their share, invite each small group to come forward to the whiteboard/chart paper and write down the issues of concern they shared in their group, and next to each of the name(s) of the students interested in this area of social justice.
- You may also want to have students add the type of action they would like to take to address this issue.

Finally, tell students that you are going to leave this new list up for the next few weeks. Encourage them to consult with you if they, or perhaps a small group of students, would like to propose working together on a project to take action. They should be prepared to share that idea with the class to see if others might be interested as well. Explain that if interest exists, it might be something the entire class or a small group could work on as a future class project, or you might be able to connect them with other children or youth groups already taking action on this issue. Meanwhile, encourage students to keep contemplating their ideas on how to be a changemaker in the school and local community.

Segue to Next Day and Daily Reflection, Unit Post-Check with Students, and Taking the Pulse of the Class: After Unit

Explicitly help your students segue by letting them know you are now moving to the next part of the day, and this is the end of the unit on taking action for civic engagement. Let them know that the books will remain in the classroom for some time and that they are welcome to revisit them. Also tell them that although the unit may have been completed, conversations can always continue around its topic, and they should feel free to ask questions or discuss the topic in more detail.

When the school day is over, take some time to fill out the Daily Reflection to reflect on this experience. The next day or the day after that, ask your students to complete the Unit Post-Check with Students form. Finally, about a week to 10 days after the unit is completed, fill out Taking the Pulse of the Class: After Unit to consider more broadly this experience for your current students, yourself, and your future students.

FINAL SUGGESTIONS

During the weeks following this unit, you might want to revisit some of these books or the conversations on them. This unit was intended as an introduction to, and the beginning of courageous conversations around, the difficult topic of taking action for social justice and understanding civic engagement. It was meant to help encourage students' empowerment to take action around the inequities and needs they observe. The discussions and activities in the chapter will help inspire children on the path of gaining self-confidence in their personal ability to create meaningful change in their communities and the greater world.

Some students may want to continue to discuss this larger topic of taking action or want to talk more about specific inequities and the needs they see surrounding them. Reach out to your school counselors, psychologists, and support faculty for individual help for students seeking more specific or individualized support in this area. The Unit Post-Check with Students form will help you identify the students needing or wanting this support.

You may decide to expand on this unit with further book sharing, discussions, and activities. The books and websites that follow may serve as good resources as you do this work.

ADDITIONAL RESOURCES

Book Suggestions

Dias, Marley. *Marley Dias Gets It Done, and So Can You!* Scholastic, 2018.

Hudson, Wade, and Cheryl Willis. *We Rise, We Resist, We Raise Our Voices*. Random House, 2018.

Moss, Wendy L. *Stand Up! Be an Upstander and Make a Difference*. Magination Press, 2019.

Nagara, Innosanto. *A Is for Activist*. Triangle Square Books for Young People, 2013.

Pimentel, Annette Bay. *All the Way to the Top: How One Girl's Fight for Americans with Disabilities Changed Everything.* Sourcebooks Explore, 2020.

Runstedler, Nancy. *Pay It Forward Kids: Small Acts, Big Change.* Canada Council for the Arts, 2013.

Website Suggestions

Do Something: *https://dosomething.org/us*

Kids for Peace: *www.kidsforpeaceglobal.org*

Marley Dias: *www.marleydias.com*

Taking It Global: *www.tigweb.org*

Youth Activism Project: *https://youthactivismproject.org*

MEETING COMMON CORE AND CASEL STANDARDS

Common Core English Language Arts Standards for Grade 4

This unit meets specific Common Core State Standards for English Language Arts in grades 3, 4, 5, and 6. We have included the specific ELA standards for grade 4 below to illustrate the strands and items met (similar for all four grades third through sixth). The QR code here will link you to the specific lists for grades 3, 5, and 6.

CCSS.ELA-LITERACY.SL.4.1

Engage effectively in a range of collaborative discussions (one-on-one, in groups, and teacher-led) with diverse partners on *grade 4 topics and texts*, building on others' ideas and expressing their own clearly.

CCSS.ELA-LITERACY.RL.4.1

Refer to details and examples in a text when explaining what the text says explicitly and when drawing inferences from the text.

CCSS.ELA-LITERACY.RL.4.3

Describe in depth a character, setting, or event in a story or drama, drawing on specific details in the text (e.g., a character's thoughts, words, or actions).

CCSS.ELA-LITERACY.RI.4.3

Explain events, procedures, ideas, or concepts in a historical, scientific, or technical text, including what happened and why, based on specific information in the text.

CCSS.ELA-LITERACY.RL.4.4

Determine the meaning of words and phrases as they are used in a text, including those that allude to significant characters found in mythology (e.g., Herculean).

CCSS.ELA-LITERACY.RL.4.9

Compare and contrast the treatment of similar themes and topics (e.g., opposition of good and evil) and patterns of events (e.g., the quest) in stories, myths, and traditional literature from different cultures.

CCSS.ELA-LITERACY.RI.4.9

Integrate information from two texts on the same topic in order to write or speak about the subject knowledgeably.

CASEL Social and Emotional Learning Standards for Grades 3–5

This unit meets specific CASEL Core Competence Area goals for Social and Emotional Learning for grades 3–5. We have included the CASEL areas and specific example standards below to show the items met in this unit. (The items are similar for grade 6.)

Self-Awareness: The abilities to understand one's own emotions, thoughts, and values and how they influence behavior across contexts. This includes capacities to recognize one's strengths and limitations with a well-grounded sense of confidence and purpose.

- Identifying personal, cultural, and linguistic assets
- Experiencing self-efficacy
- Developing interests and a sense of purpose

Self-Management: The abilities to manage one's emotions, thoughts, and behaviors effectively in different situations and to achieve goals and aspirations. This includes the capacities to delay gratification, manage stress, and feel motivation and agency to accomplish personal/collective goals.

- Exhibiting self-discipline and self-motivation
- Setting personal and collective goals
- Showing the courage to take initiative
- Demonstrating personal and collective agency

Social Awareness: The abilities to understand the perspectives of and empathize with others, including those from diverse backgrounds, cultures, and contexts. This includes the capacities to feel compassion for others, understand broader historical and social norms for behavior in different settings, and recognize family, school, and community resources and supports.

- Taking others' perspectives
- Demonstrating empathy and compassion
- Showing concern for the feelings of others
- Identifying diverse social norms, including unjust ones

Relationship Skills: The abilities to establish and maintain healthy and supportive relationships and to effectively navigate settings with diverse individuals and groups. This includes the capacities to communicate clearly, listen actively, cooperate, work collaboratively to problem-solve and negotiate conflict constructively, navigate settings with differing social and cultural demands and opportunities, provide leadership, and seek or offer help when needed.

- Communicating effectively
- Developing positive relationships
- Demonstrating cultural competency
- Practicing teamwork and collaborative problem solving
- Standing up for the rights of others

Responsible Decision Making: The abilities to make caring and constructive choices about personal behavior and social interactions across diverse situations. This includes the capacities to consider ethical standards and safety concerns, and to evaluate the benefits and consequences of various actions for personal, social, and collective well-being.

- Identifying solutions for personal and social problems
- Anticipating and evaluating the consequences of one's actions
- Reflecting on one's role to promote personal, family, and community well-being
- Evaluating personal, interpersonal, community, and institutional impacts

And Then We Had to Leave

Talking About Refugees and Communities

THE BOOKS

The Map of Good Memories

by Fran Nuno, illustrated by Zuzanna Celej (Cuento De Luz, 2016)

With the soft wash of watercolor images and lyrical text, Fran Nuno and Zuzanna Celej introduce readers to the importance of memories for holding close positive past experiences in times of trauma. An invasion of armed troops forces Zoe to leave her home and take refuge in another country. Before she leaves, she notes on a city map where she spent her happiest times, sharing these stories with the reader. A decision to draw lines between these spots transforms the map into a special keepsake—and a way she will always remember her childhood community.

Vanishing Colors

by Constance Orbeck-Nilssen, illustrated by Akin Duzakin, translated by Kari Dickson (Eerdmans Books for Young Readers, 2019)

While their city is being bombed throughout the night, a young girl and her mother hide for safety. Trying to ease her daughter's anxiety, the mother tells her a story of a large bird that protects them from danger. The bird encourages the young girl to think of happier times in the past, and with each memory she gains a bit of hope. Akin Duzakin's dramatic dark images gradually lighten as the child remembers and the sun begins to rise. As promised by the bird, a soft rainbow appears, guiding the pair to find their way out of their ruined town.

The Journey

by Francesca Sanna (Flying Eye Books, 2016)

Shattered by the war, a broken family must escape their home. Francesca Sanna's folk art–styled illustrations use sharp line and bold color to capture dramatic images from their perilous journey, as it continues to grow more challenging with each step. Border crossings include hiding from guards; a ferry trip involves a violent, roiling ocean; and the family's belongings disappear with each step. Based on stories that children in a refugee **center** shared with Sanna, *The Journey* captures many of the emotions underlying refugees' experiences.

Marwan's Journey

by Patricia De Arias, illustrated by Laura Borràs (Minedition, 2018)

Marwan walks across the desert surrounded by members of his community, all escaping violent war in their homeland. Marwan does not understand completely where he is going, but he knows he cannot stop walking or look back. Laura Borràs's childlike images, rendered in ink and watercolor, manage to convey both the warmth Marwan finds in his community and the ongoing confusion underlying his plight. Marwan keeps walking to safety and vows that one day he will return to his home.

The Waiting Place: When Home Is Lost and a New One Not Yet Found

by Dina Nayeri, illustrated by Anna Bosch Mirapeix (Candlewick, 2022)

This nonfiction selection brings the experience of a refugee camp to life through the detailed photographs of Anna Bosch Mirapeix. Dina Nayeri's documentary-style text features individual children who live in this "Waiting Place." The book explores their daily lives and activities, as well as conveying how the children combat the painful stress of the "Waiting Place" with friendship and hope.

Lubna and Pebble

by Wendy Meddour, illustrated by Daniel Egneus (Dial, 2019)

Lubna finds a beautiful pebble on the beach as she ends the first leg of her journey across the sea to a refugee camp. She draws a face on her pebble and thinks of it as a friend who can offer comfort and solace through the challenges of refugee camp life. When winter begins, Lubna, with "Pebble," make friends with a young boy who has recently arrived at the camp. When she and her father are given passage to continue their journey to their new homeland, Lubna passes the comforting pebble to her new friend at the camp. Daniel Egneus's full-page spreads of the young children's faces offer an intimate view that engages the reader in empathetic understanding of the emotions at play.

My Beautiful Birds

by Suzanne De Rizzo (Pajama Press, 2017)

Sami loves to take care of his pet pigeons and is devastated when he has to leave them, and his home, due to war. His family takes temporary shelter in a refugee camp, and there Sami grieves the loss of his feathered friends. But slowly, Sami begins to recognize the presence of new birds in the area. He delights in beginning to care for these birds, gradually gaining more interest and increasing his hope. Soon, Sami introduces a new young arrival to the camp to the birds and explains how caring for them can diminish their feelings of loss and sadness. Suzanne De Rizzo's unique use of polymer clay, plasticine, and acrylic paint add a beautiful depth of texture to the illustrations that mirrors the depth of emotion captured within the story.

Four Feet, Two Sandals

by Karen Lynn Williams and Khadra Mohammed, illustrated by Doug Chayka (Eerdmans Books for Young Readers, 2007)

This friendship-centered story, set in a refugee camp, explores the special relationship between best friends. Lina and Feroza are both given an individual sandal by workers and discover each other through making a matched set. As the girls share the pair of sandals, they become close. This friendship buoys both of their spirits, allowing them to navigate the often harsh experience of living in the camp, depicted with realistic images by Doug Chayka, as they await the next step of their journeys.

My Two Blankets

by Irene Kobald, illustrated by Freya Blackwood (Houghton Mifflin, 2014)

Cartwheel is a carefree young girl whose world turns upside down when she and her aunt must move to a new country. For reassurance in this new place, she cuddles with a treasured blanket from home. But soon, a chance encounter with a girl in a nearby park turns into a growing friendship and her new friend helps create a second "blanket" for Cartwheel, one formed from the new words in the local language that Cartwheel is learning. Before long, Cartwheel begins to feel like a member of the new community, buoyed by her friendship and her second blanket.

Mustafa

by Marie-Louise Gay (Groundwood Books, 2018)

Mustafa's new home is very different from his old one—it is not full of fire, smoke, and the loud noises of war. Despite the safety his new home provides, as Marie-Louise Gay's tale opens, Mustafa feels adrift. Venturing into the local park, he hides from a potential new friend at first, but gradually watches and then joins her in play, beginning to feel as if he is now part of this new community.

The Day War Came

by Nicola Davies, illustrated by Rebecca Cobb (Candlewick, 2018)

Studying volcanoes with her class, a young child's happy, typical morning is dramatically shattered when a bomb erupts. Her teacher, classmates, and family disappear into the darkness, and she flees, following the path of other families and individuals heading to a safer place. Images of people running across borders, long rows of cars filled with people, and scenes on an overloaded boat mirror the journeys of many refugees. Rebecca Cobb paints this as a fantastical land, but the scenes of the journey and refugee camp, and the heartbreak the young girl feels, are realistically rendered and heartbreaking. The story closes with the child trying to enter a new classroom in a new country but being initially turned away. The purposeful vagueness of the setting comes into play as the reader is asked to imagine if they would welcome newcomers to their community and "push the war back with every step."

Note: As with all thematic book sets, we recommend that after each book has been shared within the unit, it is placed in an easily accessible display in the classroom for the rest of the unit days. Children should then be allowed access to explore these books on their own during free-choice times.

PLANNING CHECKLIST

And Then We Had to Leave: Talking About Refugees and Communities

We suggest the following timeline to prepare and then share and discuss the books and do the related activities with your students. (A reproducible version of this checklist is available in Appendix 1.) Please note that timing for your individual class should be determined by your situation and your schedule, and, most importantly, should be guided by your students' reactions to the books and activities. Plan generally, however, on about 1 hour of daily time with the unit for 7–10 days in a row.

Two Weeks Prior

- ☐ Complete Taking the Pulse of the Class: Before Unit (Appendix 2) for a general sense of your class at this time.
- ☐ Collect and read twice each of the books for the unit.
- ☐ Review the "Unit Plans: Reading, Discussions, and Activities" section of the unit.
- ☐ Send out the Administration Notification Slip (Appendix 3) and School Counselor/Psychologist and Support Staff Notification Slip (Appendix 4).

One Week Prior

- ☐ (Optional) Send out Family Notification Slips (Appendix 5) to the families of your students.
- ☐ Have students complete the Unit Pre-Check with Students (Appendix 6) and review the results carefully. Check in with any students with reactions that cause concern so that you can prepare for extra support.
- ☐ Review Chapter 2 of the book.
- ☐ Collect all materials needed for the unit:
  - ☐ **Daily Reflection forms (Appendix 7):** You will need one for each day.
  - ☐ **Books:** One copy is required, but you may prefer to secure two copies of each book. After each book has been shared during the unit, place it in an easily accessible display in the classroom. Please give students access to explore these books on their own during free-choice times. You will want to keep the display available for some time after the unit is completed.

- ☐ **Materials already in your classroom:** Please have available and ready to use the following commonplace classroom materials:
  - Chart paper or a section of whiteboard that can remain posted for the duration of the unit
  - Unlined white paper
  - Pencils and pens; colored pencils, crayons, or markers
  - Construction paper or other colored paper
  - Scissors
  - Tape or glue
  - Any additional materials indicated within the unit chapter's detailed description

During: Readings, Discussions, and Activities (approximately 7–10 school days)

- ☐ Follow the detailed plans for each day.
- ☐ One to 2 days after the unit is completed, have students complete the Unit Post-Check with Students (Appendix 8).

One Week Following

- ☐ After reviewing the Unit Post-Check with Students, check in with any students with reactions that cause concern.
- ☐ Refer any students expressing interest or for whom you have concerns at this point for additional, individual discussion with a school support professional. Also consider additional whole-class work if indicated.
- ☐ Complete and review Taking the Pulse of the Class: After Unit (Appendix 9). This will help you reflect on your experience and your students' experiences with the thematic book set.

UNIT OVERVIEW
And Then We Had to Leave: Talking About Refugees and Communities

Day	Books	Discussion and Activities
1	**Introduction and Whole-Class Read-Aloud #1:** *The Map of Good Memories*	• Personal Map Making
2	**Whole-Class Read-Aloud #2:** *Vanishing Colors*	• Defining *Refugee*
3	**Whole-Class Read-Aloud #3:** *The Journey*	• Real-Life Refugees
4	**Whole-Class Read-Aloud #4:** *Marwan's Journey*	• Drawing from Detailed Descriptions
5	**Whole-Class Read-Aloud #5:** *The Waiting Place: When Home Is Lost and a New One Is Not Yet Found*	• Facts about Refugee Camps • Noticing Description as Craft

Day	Books	Discussion and Activities
6 and 7	**Small Groups Read-Aloud and Discuss #1:** *Lubna and Pebble* *My Beautiful Birds* *Four Feet, Two Sandals*	• Describing Refugee Camps with the Five Senses • Five Senses Poem
8	**Small Groups Read-Aloud and Discuss #2:** *My Two Blankets* *Mustafa*	• Diary Writing
9 and 10	**Conclusion and Whole-Class Read-Aloud #6:** *The Day War Came*	• Letters of Welcome

Note: Each "day" of this unit is intended to take around 1 hour of class time. Time may vary slightly depending on student discussion, but please keep this time frame in mind as you move through the reading and activities.

BEFORE BEGINNING

1. Make sure you have completed the "Two Weeks Prior" and "One Week Prior" items on the planning checklist, including the Taking the Pulse of the Class: Before Unit and Unit Pre-Check with Students forms.
2. Remember that the books within these units are specifically sequenced to build understanding. To have the greatest likelihood of success with these courageous conversations, we ask that you follow the order of the books, discussions, and activities and complete the entire unit.
3. Review Chapter 2 to help prepare for navigating the upcoming discussions you will be having with your students. As you complete the Daily Reflections at the end of each school day, consider revisiting Chapter 2 for helpful support in engaging in your own self-reflection and awareness, and ensuring your thoughtful and respectful approach to the topic.

DAY 1

Introduction and Whole-Class Read-Aloud #1: *The Map of Good Memories*

Discussion and Activity: Personal Map Making

Time: 1 hour total

Special Materials Needed:

- Scan of p. 2 from *The Map of Good Memories* to project on the whiteboard for your class (if you do not have an overhead projector in the room, then create paper copies for each table/group to share and view)

Introduction and Whole-Class Read-Aloud #1: *The Map of Good Memories*

Begin the unit by gathering students together for a full-class read-aloud and discussion. Explain to your class that today you will be reading a story about home. Tell students that over the course of the next couple of days, you will be reading different stories and doing different activities related to the idea of home and community. Before starting the full-class read-aloud, ask students what they think the word *home* means. Take responses by a raise of hands. Students will most likely respond by saying something like "my house" or "where my family lives." As students answer this question, write their responses on the whiteboard or on a paper chart hung on a wall where it can remain for the length of the unit.

- Simple responses like these are fine at this point in the unit. Throughout the unit, students will be prompted to question their idea of what *home* means. As the unit goes on, the students' thoughts about home will become more complicated as they read and discuss several related books intended to expand their understanding of refugees and communities.

Tell students that the book you will read as a class today is titled *The Map of Good Memories*. Invite students' attention by saying that it is about the main character and her home. Ask students to pay close attention to the pictures and words of the story, as they will be talking about these in depth later when the class does an activity. Begin reading the book aloud to your class, making sure that each student can easily see the pictures in the story. Take a few minutes to carefully display the pages for a bit of extra wait time after you finish reading each page spread.

- When you get to the second page spread of the book that shows Zoe's map, give students extra time to look at each of the locations. Indicate to them that you will be returning to this page later on.
- As you read through the book, emphasize to students that each of the pages that you are reading include images and descriptions of the locations that they previously saw on Zoe's map. This could be as easy as turning the page and saying, "Here's another place from Zoe's map" or "Remember the park from her map? Here it is!" (Helping students connect these images and descriptions is important, as it will prime them for their own ideas about the maps they will be creating later today.)

- As you read, also take opportunities to help students expand their definition of *home* by commenting that, to Zoe, home means more than just her family's house.
- When you get to the last page of the book, the sharp change in the illustration could catch students by surprise. Emphasize to students that Zoe was making her map so she could remember all that she would be leaving behind, and that she likely knew it would look quite different when she returned. (Some students might point out that the second to last page spread also offers hints about this.)

Discussion and Activity: Personal Map Making

If students are not sitting at their desks, ask them to return to their tables or seats. Pass out the pieces of blank paper and project the scanned version of Zoe's map onto the board so that your whole class can see it. (***Caution:*** Do not pass out your colored pencils yet, or students may start the activity without listening to your instructions.)

Tell students that they are going to be doing **Personal Map Making** of good memories just like Zoe did! While Zoe made a map of many places in her community, your students will create a map of around four to five places. (Depending on the age and work ethic of your students, you may want to adjust the number of places they draw to either more or less than that amount.)

- Tell students they should start this activity by brainstorming places in their community that are important to them and writing one sentence about each place, explaining why it is important.
- Model this to students on the board by writing an example of an important place (e.g., school, park) and adding one sentence underneath that idea explaining its importance (e.g., where I learn important things, where I see my friends and set my energy free).
- Then have students create their own lists and sentences on one side of their blank papers. Tell them to come to you and check off their lists and descriptions, and then they may pick up colored pencils and begin to draw the locations, just as Zoe did.
- As students complete their brainstorming list, check with you, and then begin their drawings, encourage them to look at Zoe's map, projected on the board, as a reference. Make sure that students write their names on the top of their maps in the form of a title: "[*Name*]'s Map of Good Memories."

When all students have finished writing their lists and have started coloring for a little while, begin an informal discussion with them about how and why Zoe had to leave her home. Emphasize to students that she was forced to flee because of the war coming to her town. Stop the class briefly from coloring and write the word *refugee* on the whiteboard (or on your chart paper with the *home* definitions) for all students to see. Explain that being a refugee means that Zoe had to leave suddenly and abruptly, with no desire to do so, because of outside, violent forces (the war) that made her home and community no longer a safe place to live. Ask students to help you create a working definition for *refugee* and write this definition on the whiteboard. (***Note:*** The word *immigrant* may naturally come up here in discussion. If it does, you may want to take a slight detour and explain the difference between the two words. You will return to definitions of both these words during Day 2, so use your judgment of time here to decide the degree of explanation you want to go into today.)

- Your students may ask you questions about where Zoe is from or why she had to leave. This book is a general example of what some refugee children may experience when they are forced to leave their homes, so you will not always have ready answers to the specific questions that your students may ask. If students begin asking you questions like this, guide them to answer their own questions by thinking about what they heard and saw in the book and making inferences. You can also answer their questions by connecting their ideas to real-life examples of refugees leaving their homes. This could be done in a general way: "Many refugees have to leave their homes because of the violence and persecution that are going on around them in their communities," or more specifically: "Zoe had to leave her community like many other people have had to in Syria, Ukraine, Congo, and Palestine."
- When students have finished their maps, begin to hang them up around your classroom for sharing. (If some students want to spend more time on their maps, you may want to give them the option to take them home or turn them in by the end of the day. If that is the case for your class, instead do your "sharing" gallery walk the next day.) Students can hang their maps in a temporary line on the wall in the place that you have designated for maps.
- After all students have hung up their work, ask your class to quietly walk the length of the gallery, looking at their peers' work and selecting three things they notice about the other maps that are either similar to or different from their own map. Give them a couple of minutes to do this walk and then prompt them to return to their seats. Ask students to share their thoughts with the class, calling on them as they raise their hands.

Segue to Next Day and Daily Reflection

Once you have finished discussing the maps with your students, let them know that you are now moving on to the next part of the day, but you will be returning to this topic of home and refugees tomorrow.

When the school day is over, take some time to fill out the Daily Reflection to reflect on this experience. Review it as you prepare for the next day's lesson.

DAY 2

Discussion and Activity: Defining *Refugee*

Whole-Class Read-Aloud #2: *Vanishing Colors*

Time: 1 hour total

Special Materials Needed:

- Projection for watching internet video resources as a class (links listed on the next page)

Discussion and Activity: Defining *Refugee*

Begin today's lesson by asking your students to remember back to yesterday and think silently about one location from their map they would like to share. Tell the class that everyone will get to share the name of just one place on their map in a very fast-paced way. When they are ready, call on students in rapid-fire succession, from one student to the next, with each saying out loud the name of their location the second they hear their own name called. Make sure that all students are given the opportunity to share. This quick callback will help prepare students for today's activity by reminding them of what they did yesterday.

- Remind students that they thought of those locations because of the story that the class read about Zoe yesterday. Mention that Zoe loved all these different places near her home, but she and her family had to leave it suddenly because of a war. Ask your students if they remember what a person who must leave their home without wanting to do so because of, for instance, war or violence, is called. Get their answers by a raise of hands until one student correctly answers (saying, *refugee*) and then refer all students to the vocabulary words on the whiteboard/chart paper.
- Tell students that they will next watch a video that will help them gain more understanding and background information about what it means to be a refugee. Prepare to show students the TED-Ed resource "What Does It Mean to Be a Refugee?": *https://ed.ted.com/lessons/what-does-it-mean-to-be-a-refugee-benedetta-berti-and-evelien-borgman.*
- The following additional video resources may be a better fit for your students or might be used in conjunction with the first one to help deepen their understanding. Please review and use the videos that will work best for your students:
  - *https://sesameworkshop.org/topics/displacement-resettlement*
  - *https://chooselove.org*
  - *www.unhcr.org/what-we-do/build-better-futures/education/teaching-about-refugees/teaching-materials-ages-9-12*
  - *www.ted.com/talks/zarlasht_halaimzai_what_it_s_like_to_be_a_war_refugee?language=en*
- Play the TEDx video (and/or the other video resources at your discretion). The video will offer students a lot of information to think about. Start the class discussion by doing a quick pair-share. Tell students to silently think of one thing that they learned from the video. After 30 seconds, have them turn to their elbow or desk partner. Partner 1 will have 30 seconds to share, followed by Partner 2 for 30 seconds. After this initial share, engage the students in an open discussion for a short period of time to help them process the video.

Be certain to spend some time discussing the difference between refugees and immigrants. This information may be new to students, and they may have questions about the different meanings these words have. Answer your students' questions the best that you can. Let them know that you may not have all of the answers, but you may be able to help them find answers to their questions through the use of the internet, books, and other resources. Also, remind them that the class will be thinking about and discussing topics like this one over the course of the entire unit, so they may be able to answer their own questions in the next week.

Next, draw students' attention to the definitions of the words *home* and *refugee* that you created and wrote on the whiteboard/chart paper yesterday. Have your class read aloud their **Defining of Refugee** with you in unison, and then ask them how they would like to modify it based on what they just learned. Ask students to think quietly about this for 30 seconds and then call on them to share their ideas and modify the definition together as a class. Add these changes to the whiteboard/chart paper. (Do not be concerned with arriving at one solid definition for each of these words; rather, allow each term to have a more fluid definition, with multiple parts.)

Whole-Class Read-Aloud #2: *Vanishing Colors*

Now, have students gather for a full-class read-aloud. Tell them that the book you'll be reading today is *Vanishing Colors*. It is a story about a child who is a refugee, much like Zoe.

- Show students the front cover of the book and ask what they immediately notice about it. Take responses from students by a raise of hands. When they have talked about the things that caught their eye, do the same with the back cover of the book. Ask students what might have happened between the two pictures to make them look so different. Again, take responses by a raise of the hand.
- Tell your students that color is a very important part of this story and that they will need to pay very close attention to the way color is used. Remind students that, in picturebooks, the images or pictures are just as important as the words.
- Begin reading aloud. After you complete the first few pages and reach the page where the girl wakes up and her mother is sleeping, stop and ask students why the illustrator has perhaps included so little color in the pages. Why do they think everything is black and gray? On the next page, the bird prompts the girl to remember the color of her new dress, and over the next several pages, more colors appear. Ask students to notice how the colors highlight the memories she is recalling and provide lots of detail. As you use these pauses to question students about the colors beginning to emerge throughout, ask them what else they are noticing and thinking about the story, using prompts such as "What do you think now about this story?" and "What are you noticing about this page?"
- When you finish reading the book, help the students conclude that whenever the girl remembered the past, the illustrations include color, and when she was in the present, the illustrations were in black and gray. Turn again to the last page of the book where this approach changes (colors are apparent and the setting is the present) and ask students to discuss the change. Prompt them to think about what the rainbow might mean to the girl and the mother, and how the idea of hope is sometimes associated with brighter colors in art and illustrations. Also, draw students' attention to the text a few pages earlier about a bridge and discuss how this could be a literal bridge as well as the idea of a "bridge" to a safer community or new place.

Segue to Next Day and Daily Reflection

Once your discussion begins to come to a natural close, let your students know that you are now moving on to the next part of the day, but you will be returning to this topic tomorrow.

When the school day is over, take some time to fill out the Daily Reflection to reflect on this experience. Review it as you prepare for the next day's lesson.

DAY 3

Whole-Class Read-Aloud #3: *The Journey*

Discussion and Activity: Real-Life Refugees

Time: 1 hour total

Special Materials Needed:

- Scan of p. 16 from Amnesty International's Seeking Safety Unit to project on the whiteboard for your class (if you do not have an overhead projector in the room, then make copies of this page for each table/group to share and view)

Whole-Class Read-Aloud #3: *The Journey*

Gather your class for a whole-class read-aloud. Tell them that today you will be reading and discussing *The Journey* as a group. Ask them to keep their eyes and ears open so they can really understand the story! The illustrations in this picturebook are very detailed and wonderful for class discussions. Make sure to leave plenty of time for students to unpack the illustrations as you move through the book. The specific prompts below will help with this work, but also often ask students, "What are you noticing about this page?" and "Why do you think the illustrator made the decision to draw this particular scene in this way?" and promote student discussion on what they notice and discover about both the story and the craft with which it is told.

As you read, stop at the specific points indicated below and begin student discussion with the prompts listed. These prompts exist to help students notice important aesthetic decisions made by the creators of the book in telling this story, decisions that will increase their understanding of the content and emotional impact of the book.

- Front cover: "What do you notice about the illustrations on the cover? What predictions do they offer you for this book? Why?"
- At the beach: "Look at the color of the ocean. Does this seem typical to you: Is it the way oceans usually appear in books? Why do you think Sanna chose to make it black? Why do you think she made the ocean become hands?"
- Family starting the journey with vehicles: "Why do you think Sanna drew the family traveling in different types of vehicles? What is happening to the vehicles, and to the family, as they travel?"
- Family turned away at the border: "When the family is turned away from the border, why

do you think the illustrator drew the guard so large as compared to the other human characters?"

- Family sleeping at the border: "What are the differences that you notice between the two images on the right and left pages of the spread: of the children sleeping with their mother? Why do you think Sanna decided to show the same image twice? What is she trying to make you as the reader notice here?"
- Family on the boat: "What do you notice about the dark and light colors used on these pages? Why do you think Sanna chose such contrasting colors? How do these colors and the contrast between them make you feel? What is Sanna saying about the family's safety now?"
- When you have completed the pages of the story (do not read the "Author's Note" yet), allow a brief period for a general discussion of the book. Focus this discussion on the way Sanna's illustrations impacted students and how they felt when listening to the story. Then turn to the last page of the book and read the "Author's Note" aloud. Emphasize to students that Sanna based her story on many real experiences.

Discussion and Activity: Real-Life Refugees

After you have finished discussing *The Journey*, let your students know that next the class is going to do an activity where they will learn about a child with a personal experience like those included in Sanna's book, a **real-life refugee**. This child is about the same age as the students are. Have them return to their seats.

- Show students via the projector p. 16 of Amnesty International's Seeking Safety Unit (or have them look at printed copies of it at their tables).
  - Read aloud "Amira's Story" to your class while they follow along.
  - After reading the passage, ask students the following questions listed below. Begin with pair-shares and for the last question start with pair sharing, then leading to a whole-class discussion.
    - "How did Amira feel when she arrived in a new country?"
    - "What do you think Amira misses about her home?"
    - "How does Amira feel people have treated her since she arrived?"
    - "Do you believe Amira has shared with any of her new classmates the details of her journey? Why or why not? If her classmates know, in general, about the experiences and journeys of refugees, how might that change things for Amira?"

(In this part of the class discussion, make sure to emphasize that it is completely up to Amira to decide if she wants to share her journey and experiences. The focus here should be how a classmate would need to be very welcoming for Amira to feel safe to share.)

Segue to Next Day and Daily Reflection

Once your discussion begins to come to a natural close, let your students know that you are now moving on to the next part of the day, but you will be returning to this topic tomorrow.

When the school day is over, take some time to fill out the Daily Reflection to reflect on this experience. Review it as you prepare for the next day's lesson.

DAY 4

Whole-Class Read-Aloud #4: *Marwan's Journey*

Discussion and Activity: Drawing from Detailed Descriptions

Time: 1 hour total

Special Materials Needed:

- Directions to Make a Peanut Butter and Jelly Sandwich document (Appendix 11) to project on overhead (or it can be printed and handed out to students as a hard copy)

Whole-Class Read-Aloud #4: *Marwan's Journey*

Gather your class for another whole-class read-aloud. Tell them that today you will be reading and discussing *Marwan's Journey* as a class. Explain that this is another picturebook where the illustrations and words work together to create a powerful story that features a child who is a refugee. But this book was created by a separate author and illustrator, rather than just one person serving as the author and illustrator. (This is important to convey as you are priming students for today's activity.)

Explain that when authors and illustrators collaborate as a team on a picturebook, they typically do not work together in tandem. Usually, an editor takes the text from the author and delivers it to the illustrator. The illustrator relies on what the author has written to decide how to create the images. The illustrator examines the details in the text and the emotion in the words to help decide what images to create. (If students ask, you can explain that when the illustrator has finished draft artwork, the editor helps the author and illustrator, together, complete the book by guiding both. The focus here is how the illustrator relies on the text to make their aesthetic decisions, so only explain the actual process involving both artists if students directly ask about it.)

- As you read the story aloud, stop every few pages to discuss the book using one or more of these prompts:
  - "What do you notice about this page?"
  - "Why do you think the illustrator made the decision to draw the scene in this way? How does that choice add more meaning to what the words say?"
  - "Why do you think the author used this word (phrase) here? Why does it have an impact? How does the word (phrase) match or work with the illustrations?"
- When you finish reading the story, lead the students in a brief discussion focused on two topics: (1) In what ways did they feel this story was similar to and different from *The Journey*? (2) How do they think the words by the author and the pictures by the illustrator worked together to create the messages and mood of the story?

Discussion and Activity: Drawing from Detailed Descriptions

Have students return to their seats and hand each one three half-pieces of paper. Before starting the **Drawing from Detailed Descriptions** activity, engage students in a warm-up:

- Ask students to write down a list of the steps needed to make a peanut butter sandwich on their first half-sheet. Give them only 2 minutes to do this. Once students have finished, ask the class how many students have arrived at five steps, how many have 10, how many have 15, and so on. Once you have taken stock of how much detail your students have considered in their responses, show on your projector the Directions to Make a Peanut Butter and Jelly Sandwich document (Appendix 11) and read it aloud. Point out to students that these directions include over 50 steps!
- Ask students briefly what differences they notice between their own lists and the list that you displayed for the class. Emphasize to your students that detail is very important in writing directions because, without detail, things can go very wrong.

Explain to the students that now you will be doing an activity working on drawing from detailed descriptions. This activity is sometimes called "Architect–Builder." They should imagine that an author and illustrator work somewhat like this together. In their writing, the author acts a bit like an architect, guiding the illustrator, like a builder, to create images that match their words.

- Give all students 2 minutes to draw something that reminds them of "home" on their second piece of half-paper. They must not let anyone see what they are drawing!
- After the students have finished their drawings, they should flip the page over. Now, give them 3–5 minutes to write down, on the back of their paper, explicit step-by-step instructions for how a person could draw the thing they drew on the front of their page. (Keep the time short and this activity moving quickly, but make sure it is adequate for your students to write down their response.)
- Pair students up with their elbow or desk partners. Have the partnered students face opposite directions, sitting back-to-back. Have each student grab their third blank half-sheet of paper. They will take turns reading their directions to their partner, explaining how to make their drawing. One will be the architect and the other the builder; then the partners will swap roles. The builder cannot ask any clarifying questions; they must only follow the directions being read to them. Student partners cannot look at each other's original or new drawings until the activity is completely finished.
- Ask your students to decide which of them will be the architect first, and which will be the builder first, reminding them that they will get a chance to play both roles. After they have decided on their roles for the first round, give them 3 minutes to issue and follow directions. Once the first round is over, switch to the second round of 3 minutes, where the students should swap roles.
- When both students have given and followed directions, they may reveal their drawings to each other. Prompt students to compare the differences and similarities between their

drawings. Remind them that the builder only followed the directions they were given by the architect!

Then ask your students what was easy about this activity. What was hard about it? Use their answers to segue into asking your students why details are so important to descriptions. After a few answers are shared, ask them to imagine being an illustrator for a picturebook written by another person (the author). How would the specific words and phrases help them decide how to draw the book's images? As students offer answers, you might help them think about particular points in the books they have read so far as examples.

Segue to Next Day and Daily Reflection

Once your discussion begins to come to a natural close, let your students know that you are now moving on to the next part of the day, but you will be returning to this topic tomorrow.

When the school day is over, take some time to fill out the Daily Reflection to reflect on this experience. Review it as you prepare for the next day's lesson.

DAY 5

Whole-Class Read-Aloud #5: *The Waiting Place: When Home Is Lost and a New One Is Not Yet Found*

Discussion and Activities: Facts about Refugee Camps; Noticing Description as Craft

Time: 1 hour total

Special Materials Needed:

- Scan of several photographs from *The Waiting Place: When Home Is Lost and a New One Is Not Yet Found* to project on the whiteboard for your class (if you do not have an overhead projector in the room, then create paper copies for each table/group to share and view). Select photos of several of the 10 different children to highlight as you read.

Whole-Class Read-Aloud and Discuss #5: *The Waiting Place: When Home Is Lost and a New One Is Not Yet Found*

> ***Note:*** Plan to spread this read-aloud across the day in two or three parts to help sustain student engagement. Do the first half of the book in the morning and return to finish the book in the afternoon. Make sure that students have access to the book throughout the day, as they might want to look more closely at the photographs in between. Leave the book accessible as well as in the days that follow as you do with all the books in the unit. Also, be mindful today in particular of students in your class who may have lived in a refugee camp at some point. Because this book is nonfiction, it may bring up vivid memories and past experiences, even more so than the fictional books read earlier in the week.

Gather your class for a whole-class read-aloud. Tell them that today you will be reading and discussing the book *The Waiting Place: When Home Is Lost and a New One Is Not Yet Found.*

Explain that this is a work of nonfiction book, a compilation of the experiences of 10 real children in the Katsikas refugee camp just outside Ioannina, Greece. This is a longer book, so you are going to read and discuss it during a few different blocks of time today. (The total time will still be 1 hour.)

Before starting to read, show the students on your whiteboard a few of the photos from the book. Explain that the children in the photos are refugees who lived temporarily in the camp while waiting to be given permission and passage to a new country.

Discussion and Activities: Facts about Refugee Camps; Noticing Description as Craft

First, go over some basic **Facts about Refugee Camps**. Remind students that this is a different situation than what happens with immigration. As they learned earlier in the week, refugees often remain in a waiting place, or refugee camp, for some time prior to being accepted or assigned to a new country; immigrants, on the other hand, typically go directly to their new country, even if they have to wait at its border for some time in temporary housing prior to officially moving into their new home. Refugee camps are therefore not located in the new country where the people seeking asylum will move. They are intended as temporary shelters, but sometimes refugees end up living in them for a long time while waiting for passage.

- Ask students to think back to the books they have read showing children's journeys as refugees. What were their journeys like? What happened to their belongings along the way? After students have shared, remind them that the book you are about to share is not a story, but rather the actual experiences of 10 children. The text is written by an author who was herself a refugee as a child. She invited a documentary photographer to come with her and capture photos of the children she interviewed while writing the book. In this team of an author and illustrator working together, the same craft happens, with the author writing the words and the illustrator—in this case, the photographer—capturing the photographs that best match the descriptions and details of the text.
- Start reading aloud the text, taking time to show the photographs to the students as you go along. Stop at times to show these photographs on the larger whiteboard projector if you had previously made scans of them. Read slowly and use frequent prompts to start discussion about the topic and **Noticing Description as Craft**:
  - "What are you thinking about now after hearing this part?"
  - "What do you notice about this page/section?"
  - "What is surprising to you?"
  - "Is this how you imagined the camp might look or what it might be like?"
  - "Why do you think the photographer chose this particular photo as the illustration for this part of the text?"
  - "How do the photos and words complement each other and help better describe the camp and experiences?"
- Stop reading the text about halfway or one-third of the way through, depending on whether you have two or only one more available time block(s) left for reading and discussion today.

When you break, be sure to tell students that you will be returning to finish the book later in the day.

Segue to Next Day and Daily Reflection

Once you finish reading the complete book and the discussion comes to a natural close, let your students know that you are now moving on to the next part of the day, but you will be returning to this topic of refugee camps tomorrow.

When the school day is over, take some time to fill out the Daily Reflection to reflect on this experience. Review it as you prepare for the next day's lesson.

DAY 6

Small Groups Read-Aloud and Discuss #1: *Lubna and Pebble*, *My Beautiful Birds*, and *Four Feet, Two Sandals*

Discussion and Activity: Describing Refugee Camps with the Five Senses

Time: 1 hour total

> ***Note:*** Days 6 and 7 focus on the same books and activity. There is a natural break in the activities between days, and thus Day 7 is indicated next, but feel free to combine these days if that works better for your schedule.

Special Materials Needed:

- Three copies of each of the books (today's read-aloud requires more than the usual number of copies; local libraries will likely have these titles available)
- Business-sized envelopes for students to store their group's paper strips

Small Groups Read-Aloud and Discuss #1: *Lubna and Pebble*, *My Beautiful Birds*, and *Four Feet, Two Sandals*

Tell students they will continue to discuss the experience of refugee camps using three different stories. They will be reading and working in small groups today and tomorrow. Next, break up your students into three groups of the same size. Each of the groups will focus on only one of the three titles: *Lubna and Pebble*, *My Beautiful Birds*, and *Four Feet, Two Sandals*.

- Move your students into their specific groups. Hand out three copies of each book to each group: Group 1 receives three copies of *Lubna and Pebble*, Group 2 receives three copies of *My Beautiful Birds*, and Group 3 receives three copies of *Four Feet, Two Sandals*. Each group should then split into three smaller groups, with two to four students. These smaller groups should each take one copy of their group's book.
- Have students read their book together in their small groups. Tell them to take turns reading

aloud and to keep the book spread out on the table, so they can all see the illustrations as they turn the pages. Circle the room while they are reading and provide support as needed.

Discussion and Activity: Describing Refugee Camps with the Five Senses

After most groups have completed reading their assigned books, interrupt and tell students you are going to describe the activity they will work on next. (Explain that, if they have not finished reading the assigned book, they can finish up after you describe the next steps.) Indicate that the activity they will be doing in groups is related to the detailed descriptions that help you imagine scenes when you read a book—and also help picturebook illustrators decide what to create for a book's images!

- Pass out the following to each of the groups: one sheet of lined paper, one pair of scissors, and one business-sized envelope.
- Have each group choose one student to act as the scribe for the group. Then ask all the scribes to list the five senses down the side of the page, writing in the column part of the paper. They should leave about six lines between each of the senses.
  - Review the five senses with the whole class as the scribes write them down: sight, sound, smell, taste, and touch.
- Now, tell students to have their scribe write down the name of the main character in their story at the top of their group's page. Explain that each of the main characters in the three books experienced life in a refugee camp. The job of each group is for its members to imagine themselves as the main character of their book and to consider what the main character noticed about the refugee camp while they were there. They must think about what the main character might have experienced at the camp using their five senses: What did the character see, hear, smell, taste, and touch? Under the headings for each of the five senses, they should identify phrases from the book that capture this and have their group scribe record these on the paper. These can be quotes directly from the book.
  - If students cannot find exact phrases, then they can create their own *textually supported phrases*. Explain to students that this means writing down what they think the character might have seen, heard, smelled, tasted, and touched, based on what is shown in the illustrations or implied in the text. Tell students to try and capture vivid details when they write down these phrases.
  - *Optional:* If you would like to do so, ask students to write down book page numbers for this evidence, or where the exact phrase may be found, next to the phrases they've chosen.
- Give students about 10–15 more minutes to finish reading and to identify the phrases for the five senses and have the scribe for their group record them on the page. Encourage them to include two to three phrases for each of the five senses. Circle the room while they work and provide support.
- Once all groups seem to have completed writing down phrases for **Describing Refugee Camps with the Five Senses**, stop the activity to give the next set of instructions. Tell students they are going to use these phrases tomorrow in creating a "Five Senses Poem" in

the voice of their main character. Now, each group needs to cut their phrases into strips of paper and lay them on their table. Borrow a sample filled-out paper from one of the students and demonstrate how to cut out each phrase into a strip of paper. Then have each group cut their strips and place them in their group's envelope and write the names of the members of their group on it. Collect the envelopes and books from each group.

Segue to Next Day and Daily Reflection

Then let your students know that you are now moving on to the next part of the day, but you will be returning to this topic tomorrow, specifically doing the poem activity.

When the school day is over, take some time to fill out the Daily Reflection to reflect on this experience. Review it as you prepare for the next day's lesson.

DAY 7 (OR AS COMBINED WITH DAY 6)

Small Groups Read-Aloud and Discuss #1: *Lubna and Pebble*, *My Beautiful Birds*, and *Four Feet, Two Sandals*

Discussion and Activity: Five Senses Poem

Time: 1 hour total

Special Materials Needed:

- Five Senses Poem Work Sample: "In My Classroom, by a Teacher" (Appendix 12) document to project on overhead (or can be copied and handed out to students as hard copies)

Discussion and Activity: Five Senses Poem

Begin the day by reminding students that they will now create a **Five Senses Poem** about the experiences in a refugee camp from the perspective of the main character in the book they read yesterday. On the whiteboard, project the Five Senses Poem Work Sample: "In My Classroom, by a Teacher" (Appendix 12). Explain that the teacher had created a list of phrases about their classroom using the five senses, just like the students did for their main character's time in a refugee camp. Then the teacher tried arranging and rearranging the phrases, even editing them a bit, to create a poem. Two examples, or "trials," are shown in the sample document.

- Tell your students that they will now work together with their group to do the same thing. They will move around their strips with phrases to find an organization of lines they like best for their group's poem. They can use as many, or as few, of the strips as they want. They can also cut the strips to create shorter phrases, or cross out (or erase) or add a few words. Show students that the teacher's phrases are very detailed. Encourage them to go back to their book and see if they, too, might want to add more detail to their phrases.
- Each group's members should discuss and work together until they come to a consensus on what they like best in terms of the arrangement and wording of lines, after making changes,

until they all come to agreement on a final poem. As they deliberate, they should keep in mind that this is a poem intended to show the experience of their main character in a refugee camp.

- Hand out the envelopes and books from yesterday, and have students work on their arrangements. Circle the class and support the groups as they mix and arrange lines. Ask them to read their arrangements aloud so they can hear the potential rhythm of the words. Ask them if they think a phrase might need more detail; if so, refer them back to the book to find additional details.
- After students have worked for some time and have decided on a final poem, hand out pieces of blank paper and glue or tape, and tell students to affix their final lines in final order to the blank sheet. They should title the top of their paper "In the Refugee Camp by [*Give name of main character*]."
- When student groups have completed their poems and selected their image, they should begin sharing their work. First, have all the small groups within the larger book group share the poems they created. It can be a lot of fun to see how small groups wrote very different poems about the same experiences! Next, assign numbers to the small groups within each larger book group (1, 2, 3, etc.). Then have all the 1 students from each of the book groups gather together, all the 2s do the same, and so forth, to share their poems as an introduction to the book they read. They should bring a copy of the book with them when they meet and, after the group poems have been shared, tell each other a little more about their assigned book.

Segue to Next Day and Daily Reflection

When group discussions are completed, collect the poems to hang in the room, near wherever you had placed the definitions of home and refugee earlier in the unit. Then let your students know that you are now moving on to the next part of the day, but you will be returning to this topic tomorrow.

When the school day is over, take some time to fill out the Daily Reflection to reflect on this experience. Review it as you prepare for the next day's lesson.

DAY 8

Small Groups Read-Aloud and Discuss #2: *My Two Blankets* and *Mustafa*

Discussion and Activity: Diary Writing

Time: 1 hour and 10 minutes total

Note: Before school begins today, divide your class into two groups. Today, you will read aloud and discuss *My Two Blankets* with the first group while the other group is engaged in schoolwork, and then read aloud and discuss *Mustafa* with the second group while the *My Two Blankets* group engages in other schoolwork. You will need to arrange for these two read-aloud and discuss time blocks, as well as a third time block where all students will be working on a related writing activity. The reading and discussion blocks will take about 20–25 minutes each, the writing block approximately 20 minutes. Today's lesson, including whole-class introduction time and instructions, should altogether take approximately 1 hour and 10 minutes.

Small Groups Read-Aloud and Discuss #2: *My Two Blankets* and *Mustafa*

Begin today by asking your students to look at the definitions of *home* you created at the beginning of this unit. Tell students that they have been learning about refugee situations and ask students to read aloud the definition of *refugee* determined by the definitions of home. Remind students that people in refugee situations leave behind their beloved homes and flee for safety, which often means making a hard journey to a waiting or refugee camp like those they have read about over the last few days. This is not really a new home, as it is intended to be a temporary situation, but sometimes people end up living there for longer than a year. When families are finally able to move from the camp to their new country, they will create a new home that is more permanent. Tell students that today they will hear and discuss one of two stories; both are about a child who is now in their new home in their new country and adjusting to a brand-new life.

- Ask students what they might now want to add to the definition of *home* on the whiteboard/chart paper from earlier in the unit. Write additions to the definition as students share. Encourage them to think about the experiences of children in the refugee camps: both in the nonfiction *Waiting Place* book and in the stories they have read over the last 2 days. How did these children create a temporary sense of home? Reflecting on those experiences, what elements could you add to the growing class definition of *home*? Discuss this briefly and then tell students that, when they listen to the stories today, they should listen closely for how the main characters begin to establish a new sense of home in their new country.
- During your read-aloud with both books and both groups, start by examining the covers. Ask students to consider the colors of both books, as compared to the colors in the books read at the beginning of the unit. (Have students look at those books as they remain on display in your classroom.) After they have noticed the brightness of the new books, ask students to predict what might happen in each book, where the main character is now in a new country. Then begin reading aloud. Stop every few pages to discuss the book using one or more of these prompts to draw attention to both the content of the story and the craft of the book:
  - "What do you notice about this page?"
  - "How do you think the main character is feeling now? What in the illustrations or text helps reveal this to you?
  - "Why do you think the illustrator made the decision to draw this scene in this way? How does it add more meaning to what the words are saying?"
  - "Why do you think the author used this word (or phrase) here? Why does it have an impact? How does the word (or phrase) match or work with the illustrations?"

- At the end of reading and discussing the book, hold a quick general share and then ask students to consider what might have happened if they had started this unit on refugee experiences with this book instead of the ones they read last week. How might reading something like this new book first have changed their understanding of the refugee experience? (Encourage students to talk about the importance of understanding the harsh journeys and experiences of the children and that the children were quite happy in their former homes but were forced to leave. How does that knowledge help them better understand these books about adjusting to a new place?)

Discussion and Activity: Diary Writing

When both groups have participated in the read-aloud and discussions for about 20 minutes total, gather all the students together and distribute paper to them. Tell them they are now going to do some imaginative and detailed writing of their own. They should imagine that they are either Mustafa or Cartwheel and write a diary entry from the character's perspective. In their **Diary Writing,** they will describe what they notice about their new home in their new country. What do they see and hear, but also how do they feel about this new place? Tell students their diary entry can date to the same period of time as the book, thus referring to the events mentioned in the book, *or* the entry could be in the future, with the student imagining what the character might be feeling in a few weeks or months.

- Have students write quietly for about 5 minutes using this prompt. Then tell them they can pair up if they would like to with another student writing from the point of view of the same character. They can share ideas and keep writing, or they can keep writing on their own.
- After 5 additional minutes of writing, have all students stop. Ask them to stand up and find someone in the class who wrote about the other main character. Once they find that person, they should sit down together and exchange papers. After reading each other's diary entry, ask students to discuss these questions:
    - "How are the experiences of the two characters similar? How are they different?"
    - "In each story, how did new friends in the new country help the main character?"
    - "In what specific ways did these new friends make Cartwheel and Mustafa feel as if they were part of a new community?"

  (Write the questions on the board so that students are certain to address all four questions.)
- After about 5 minutes of sharing, ask students to answer the last question as a whole group. On the whiteboard, write down all student answers to the question, creating a list. (This work will help prepare the students for the culminating activity that will take place over the next 2 days.) Leave these answers on the whiteboard.

Segue to Next Day and Daily Reflection

After this discussion, collect the diary entries from your students and let them know that you are now moving on to the next part of the day, but you will be returning to this topic tomorrow.

When the school day is over, take some time to fill out the Daily Reflection to reflect on this experience. Review it as you prepare for the next day's lesson.

DAYS 9 AND 10

Conclusion and Whole-Class Read-Aloud #6: *The Day War Came*

Discussion and Activity: Letters of Welcome

Time: 1.5 hours total

> ***Note:*** The read-aloud, discussion, and activities listed below are intended to take approximately 1.5 hours of class time. You may want to do all of this work in 1 day or spread across 2 days.

Special Materials Needed:

- Two articles from *The Guardian* newspaper's archived website (see links in the descriptions below) to project on overhead (or they can be printed and shared with students as hard copies)

Conclusion and Whole-Class Read-Aloud #6: *The Day War Came*

Begin by reviewing yesterday's final activity, directing students' attention to the list of ways in which the friends of Mustafa and Cartwheel made them feel welcome in their new country. Read aloud the list and discuss with the class that, although these gestures or actions might seem like little things, they were big in the eyes of the main characters. Ask students if they have other ideas that were not included in the books about how someone might make a refugee feel welcome in a new community.

Ask students to think about all the books they have read across the last 2 weeks. Then have them identify the first books that highlighted children having to leave home because of a war or the threat of violence to their family members and homes, and then the next group of books that showed children fleeing to safety with their families, and then those living in a refugee camp, and yesterday's books about adapting to a new home in a new country. Tell students that today they are going to read and discuss a book that includes many of these same experiences in one story. Show students the front cover of *The Day War Came*. Then show them its back cover. Ask students what they notice about the images and what they think might happen in the story. Students will likely see the pictures of volcanoes and may predict a volcano will erupt; if they do, read aloud the title again and ask them what in a war may feel like a volcano. Then open the book to the inside endpapers and ask students to note the differences between the front inside cover and the back. After students have commented, turn to the dedication page and read it aloud to students. Ask them what they are now thinking about the book and what might happen. Now, begin reading the book aloud slowly. Spend extra time showing students each page spread as you read, but do not stop to discuss the book. (For this read-aloud only, you are going to put off the discussion until after the whole story has been read.) When you finish reading the last page of the story, turn to the last page of the book and read aloud Nicola Davies's "Author's Note."

Then on your projector, or in a hard copy, show the students the newspaper article from *The Guardian* titled "The Day War Came: A poem about unaccompanied child refugees" (*www.theguardian.com/childrens-books-site/2016/apr/28/the-day-the-war-came-poem-about-unaccompanied-child-refugees*). Read the beginning of the article to the students and then show them the poem (though you do not need to read it to them). Explain to students that the poem is the same text as in the book you just read. Then show students the painting of a chair by Jackie Morris at the end of the article and read aloud the caption explaining the painting and the brief blurb about the Twitter campaign that then started.

Next, show students this related article from *The Guardian*, "Your #3000chairs for child refugees in pictures" (*www.theguardian.com/world/gallery/2016/may/11/your-3000-chairs-for-child-refugees-in-pictures*). Explain that these are some of the chairs that were drawn. You might want to follow the link to chairs drawn by children's illustrators as well and show a few of these. (***Note:*** If students ask when the book came out, you might want to explain that this poem and the chair campaign happened in 2016, and the book was published in 2018.)

Ask students to consider the chair metaphor: How can offering someone a chair be a sign of welcome? How does this action relate to the things the friends of Mustafa and Cartwheel did to welcome them to their new community? When you are offered a place to sit at the lunch table or asked to join a game, how does that make you feel?

After students have discussed this idea, extend the discussion a little further by telling the students that sometimes people talk about offering someone a "seat at the table." What does this mean? Help students to understand that welcoming someone into a group means more than just including them physically. It also means valuing their contributions, ideas, and selves as equal. When you give someone a "seat," you are also giving them a voice and including them as an equal. Encourage students to discuss a little more about the idea of welcoming a newcomer and really including them as a member of the community. As they discuss, make references back to some of the earlier books read and how understanding the experiences of the main characters can help you imagine the knowledge they could bring to your community with their perspectives from their homes as well as what they have learned on their journeys. (Students may bring up the rejection of refugees as a group in new countries and communities, such as the government actions that spurred Nicola Davies's poem and book. If they do, ask students why they think this might happen. You can help students acknowledge that this can be a complicated situation on a broad level but direct the conversation to concentrate more directly for now on the value that individuals bring to their new communities and ways to welcome and include those that have arrived in the community.)

> ***Note:*** If you are breaking up this day into two, then this is a good place to stop for today. Segue to tomorrow and start the next day's activities here.

Discussion and Activity: Letters of Welcome

Tell students that there are many ways in which people and organizations work to welcome and help establish new refugees in communities. Ask students to share what they might know about this. Then add that these organizations provide support for people as they move into the community by helping them learn about it and then joining as a member. There are organizations like this in their town! Remind students about the maps of good memories, or special places, that they created at the very beginning of this unit (and direct their attention to the wall where these maps are displayed). Explain that sharing about a place can be the first step of welcome—letting someone else know about what is here, but also going further, explaining why you like it, which says a little bit about you! It is also a nice starting place to ask someone else what types of places they like best and begin to learn something about them.

- Have students go to the wall display and find their maps. Ask them to carefully remove the maps from the wall and take them back to their seats. Pass out lined and blank paper to all students, and distribute pencils, pens, and coloring items (markers, crayons, and pencils) as needed. Then tell students that they are going to write **Letters of Welcome** to children who are refugees and moving to their community. If the students give you permission, you will deliver their letters to a local refugee support organization. (There are many in all areas within the United States, and you should be able to find one nearby.) These letters will be shared with local children arriving in the community. If students do not want to give their letters to the refugee organization, that is okay, too. They can write them and then just keep them as examples and reminders for themselves about welcoming newcomers.
- Explain to students that their letters should start by saying "hello" and "welcome." Write on the board the following steps as you also explain them verbally and give examples:
  - **Write a greeting of welcome at the beginning of your letter:** Hi! Welcome to [*Give name of your city*]!
  - **Tell them who you are:** My name is [*Give your first name*], and I am [*Give your grade or age*], and I have lived here for [*Give number*] years.
  - **Explain that you would like to tell them a little about your community:** This is a great place, and I'd like to tell you about some of my favorite things here.
  - **Use your personal map to explain in words a few of your favorite places and why you like them so much:** One of my favorite places is our playground at school. I really like the climbing wall there because it is hard to get to the top and I remember the first time I made it up the wall.
  - **Welcome the child again to the community and tell them you are glad they are here:** There are a lot of good places in [*Give name of your city*], and I hope you find some you like, too! I am glad you are going to be part of our community.
- Tell students to remember as they write their letters that the child reading the letter has had a difficult journey to get here and probably is feeling a little nervous and scared about this new country and new place and might be missing their former homes as well. Ask students

to keep this in mind as they write. Also, encourage them to add pictures to their letters to make it more interesting! They should write first but then draw pictures as well. As students work on their letters, circle the room to encourage them and give support and suggestions.

Note: Students might ask about language issues when writing their Letters of Welcome. Explain that they should write their letters in their own first language and that someone at the organization will read the letter to the child if they do not yet speak that language.

After students have worked for a period, stop everyone and ask them to share their letters with their desk or elbow partners. (Keep all feedback at this time very positive.) Tell students to read their partner's letter and reveal two things they liked about their letters. Then give students 5 minutes to finish their letters.

Segue to Next Day and Daily Reflection, Unit Post-Check with Students, Taking the Pulse of the Class: After Unit

Collect the letters from the students. Then explicitly help your students segue by letting them know you are now moving to the next part of the day, and this is the end of the unit about refugees. Let them know that the books will remain in the classroom for some time and that they are welcome to revisit them. Also tell them that although the unit may have been completed, these conversations can always continue around its topic, and they should feel free to ask questions or discuss the topic in more detail.

When the school day is over, take some time to fill out the Daily Reflection to reflect on this experience. The next day or the day after that, ask your students to complete the Unit Post-Check with Students. Finally, about a week to 10 days after the unit was completed, fill out Taking the Pulse of the Class: After Unit to consider more broadly this experience for your current students, yourself, and your future students.

FINAL SUGGESTIONS

This unit was intended as an introduction to, and the beginning of courageous conversations around, the difficult topic of understanding refugee situations and displacement, and using that knowledge to begin extending a welcome to refugees as they enter our communities.

Some students may want to continue to discuss this topic in class. Reach out to your school counselors, psychologists, and support faculty for individual help for students seeking more specific or individualized support in this area. The Unit Post-Check with Students form will help you identify the students needing or wanting this support.

You may encounter students or families that want more information surrounding the topic that extends past what may have been discussed in the classroom. The websites that follow may serve as good resources for you to share.

ADDITIONAL RESOURCES

Amnesty International: *www.amnesty.org.uk/education*

International Rescue Committee: *www.rescue.org*

Kids in Need of Defense: *https://supportkind.org*

Save the Children: *www.savethechildren.org/us/what-we-do/emergency-response/refugee-children-crisis*

TED Talks: Refugees: *www.ted.com/topics/refugees*

UNICEF: Child Migrants and Refugees: *www.unicefusa.org/what-unicef-does/childrens-protection/child-migrants-refugees*

MEETING COMMON CORE AND CASEL STANDARDS

Common Core English Language Arts Standards for Grade 4

This unit meets specific Common Core State Standards for English Language Arts in grades 3, 4, 5, and 6. We have included the specific ELA standards for grade 4 below to illustrate the strands and items met (similar for all four grades third through sixth). The QR code here will link you to the specific lists for grades 3, 5, and 6.

CCSS.ELA-Literacy.SL.4.1

Engage effectively in a range of collaborative discussions (one-on-one, in groups, and teacher-led) with diverse partners on *grade 4 topics and texts*, building on others' ideas and expressing their own clearly.

CCSS.ELA-Literacy.L.4.4

Determine or clarify the meaning of unknown and multiple-meaning words and phrases based on grade 4 reading and content, choosing flexibly from a range of strategies.

CCSS.ELA-Literacy.RL.4.1

Refer to details and examples in a text when explaining what the text says explicitly and when drawing inferences from the text.

CCSS.ELA-Literacy.RL.4.3

Describe in depth a character, setting, or event in a story or drama, drawing on specific details in the text (e.g., a character's thoughts, words, or actions).

CCSS.ELA-Literacy.RL.4.4

Determine the meaning of words and phrases as they are used in a text.

CCSS.ELA-Literacy.RL.4.7

Make connections between the text of a story or drama and a visual or oral presentation of the text, identifying where each version reflects specific descriptions and directions in the text.

CCSS.ELA-Literacy.W.4.3

Write narratives to develop real or imagined experiences or events using effective technique, descriptive details, and clear event sequences.

CASEL Social and Emotional Learning Standards for Grades 3–5

This unit meets specific CASEL Core Competence Area goals for Social and Emotional Learning for grades 3–5. We have included the CASEL areas and specific example standards below to show the items met in this unit. (The items are similar for grade 6.)

Self-Awareness: The abilities to understand one's own emotions, thoughts, and values and how they influence behavior across contexts. This includes capacities to recognize one's strengths and limitations with a well-grounded sense of confidence and purpose.

- Integrating personal and social identities
- Identifying personal, cultural, and linguistic assets
- Linking feelings, values, and thoughts
- Examining prejudices and biases
- Developing interests and a sense of purpose

Self-Management: The abilities to manage one's emotions, thoughts, and behaviors effectively in different situations and to achieve goals and aspirations. This includes the capacities to delay gratification, manage stress, and feel motivation and agency to accomplish personal/collective goals.

- Managing one's emotions
- Exhibiting self-discipline and self-motivation
- Setting personal and collective goals
- Using planning and organizational skills
- Showing the courage to take initiative
- Demonstrating personal and collective agency

Social Awareness: The abilities to understand the perspectives of and empathize with others, including those from diverse backgrounds, cultures, and contexts. This includes the capacities to feel compassion for others, understand broader historical and social norms for behavior in different settings, and recognize family, school, and community resources and supports.

- Taking others' perspectives
- Recognizing strengths in others

- Demonstrating empathy and compassion
- Showing concern for the feelings of others
- Understanding and expressing gratitude
- Identifying diverse social norms, including unjust ones
- Recognizing situational demands and opportunities
- Understanding the influences of organizations/systems on behavior

Relationship Skills: The abilities to establish and maintain healthy and supportive relationships and to effectively navigate settings with diverse individuals and groups. This includes the capacities to communicate clearly, listen actively, cooperate, work collaboratively to problem-solve and negotiate conflict constructively, navigate settings with differing social and cultural demands and opportunities, provide leadership, and seek or offer help when needed.

- Communicating effectively
- Developing positive relationships
- Demonstrating cultural competency
- Practicing teamwork and collaborative problem solving
- Seeking or offering support and help when needed
- Standing up for the rights of others

Responsible Decision Making: The abilities to make caring and constructive choices about personal behavior and social interactions across diverse situations. This includes the capacities to consider ethical standards and safety concerns, and to evaluate the benefits and consequences of various actions for personal, social, and collective well-being.

- Demonstrating curiosity and open-mindedness
- Identifying solutions for personal and social problems
- Learning to make a reasoned judgment after analyzing information, data, facts
- Recognizing how critical thinking skills are useful both inside and outside of school
- Reflecting on one's role to promote personal, family, and community well-being
- Evaluating personal, interpersonal, community, and institutional impacts

PART III

Supporting Children's Positive Identity Formation through Literature

INTRODUCTION

The next three chapters feature thematic book sets that address important topics in children's positive identity formation.[1] Supporting students' positive identity formation around race and ethnicity (Chapter 7), gender (Chapter 8), and ability (Chapter 9) can be quite daunting, given how politically charged conversations about these topics can be in diverse communities like schools. Research, however, offers a lot of evidence that children develop higher self-esteem, engage with more empathy, and develop healthier relationships when they are clear about who they are and know how to interact with compassion with others who hold different identities and come from communities unlike their own. These thematic book sets will provide students with a richer vocabulary and thoughtful ways to talk about identities, differences, and culture.

As you prepare to facilitate discussions in this section, take time to reflect on your own comfort levels and any discomfort you may feel regarding topics of racism, gender diversity, and disabilities. Although we encourage you to please review Chapter 2 before beginning any unit in this book, please especially do so for the thematic book sets in this section and refer to Chapter 2 as needed throughout. If you encounter challenges or uncertainties, seek consultation from colleagues to ensure a supportive and informed approach. We also want to stress that the stories within these units are specifically sequenced to build understanding. To have the greatest likelihood of success with these courageous conversations, we ask that you follow the order and complete the entire unit. Good luck: You've got this!

[1] When referring to disability, gender, and mental health status, we use person-first language (e.g., "a person with dyslexia"). When referring to a person's race and religion, we use identity-first language (e.g., "Black student" or "Muslim student"), respecting cultural norms that view these identities as integral and inseparable from the person.

Chapter 7—*Where Are You From?*: Talking About Race and Ethnicity and Identity

This thematic book set addresses the topic of race and ethnicity, two concepts individuals often conflate. Each book touches on the ways in which race is simultaneously a social construct and a concept that influence many of our everyday feelings, conversations, relationships, neighborhoods, and laws. The books provide poignant illustrations and language, allowing students an opportunity to explore the explicit and implicit ways in which race and ethnicity affect everyone. The thematic book set invites the class to engage in conversations that help students honor people who have spoken up for racial equity, discover ways they can appreciate their own racial identities, and how to talk about uncomfortable things. In the end, the set encourages the development of advocacy for self, allyship for others, and empathy for all.

Along with focusing on social and emotional development standards (The CASEL 5), this thematic book set embeds English language arts standards where students will engage in collaborative discussions, clarify word meanings, write narratives with descriptive details and clear sequences, produce coherent writing appropriate for task and audience, and analyze text details and perspectives. Activities and discussion questions are suited for a third- through sixth-grade classroom audience and should be adjusted as appropriate for your grade level and students' understanding.

Chapter 8—*I'm Me!*: Talking About Gender and Identity

This thematic book set deals with the topic of gender in a broad sense. It encourages students to think about gender stereotypes and discrimination in the workplace and society. The book set opens the conversation of awareness about gender identification in order to begin to understand and celebrate all identities. As in Chapter 7, the set encourages the development of advocacy for self, allyship for others, and empathy for all.

Along with focusing on social and emotional development standards (The CASEL 5), this thematic book set embeds English language arts standards that have students identifying, organizing, and sharing information, completing graphic organizers, and utilizing images to gain a deeper meaning of the text. Activities and discussion questions are suited for a third- through sixth-grade classroom audience and should be adjusted as appropriate for your grade level and students' understanding.

Chapter 9—*My Name*: Talking About Ability and Identity

This thematic book set covers the topic of ability and identity, with a focus on how we are all different but also alike in many ways. The set opens the conversation of awareness of differences in mental and physical abilities—recognizing that these differences do exist and that they can cause hardships and challenges. At the same time, this book set brings attention to the similarities among people, celebrating identities. Mirroring the other two chapters in this section, this set encourages the development of advocacy for self, allyship for others, and empathy for all.

Along with focusing on social and emotional development standards (The CASEL 5), this thematic book set embeds English language arts standards where students complete timelines, compare and contrast characters, and practice identifying themes. Activities and discussion questions are suited for a third- through sixth-grade classroom audience and should be adjusted as appropriate for your grade level and students' understanding.

AUTHOR AND ILLUSTRATOR PROFILES

Kadir Nelson

Award-winning illustrator Kadir Nelson is the artist behind the powerful *The Undefeated* (authored by Kwame Alexander) included in this unit. Students might recognize his distinctive art not only from his over 30 illustrated titles, but also from his magazine covers, album cover art, animation, postage stamps, and several paintings on display in national museums and notable buildings, such as the Capitol and 3 World Trade Center. Nelson is renowned for the rich palette and beautiful luminosity of his realistically styled oil paintings.

Much of Nelson's illustration work in children's books has been for biographical picturebooks of African American heroes and visionaries, or for stories embedded in African American culture and history. Nelson has explained that he is motivated to illustrate African American narratives of the past and present in part because he recalls as a child not being able to see himself represented in the books available at that time. He also recognizes children's books as the earliest introduction to art for many, and thus how even more important it is that children see a diverse representation of peoples and cultures in their literature.

You might use the sharing of *The Undefeated* in Chapter 7 to later launch a study of Nelson's work as an illustrator. Students can examine several of his illustrated books and develop a better understanding of his unique style and how his illustrations extend understanding of the main figures and work beyond the text to create the emotional setting of the book. At the same time, they can extend the work from this unit to consider the inequitable challenges that Nelson may face in his career as a person of color.

Margarita Engle

Margarita Engle's beautiful poetry sings together with Rafael Lopez's illustrations in *Drum Dream Girl: How One Girl's Courage Changed Music*, a book shared early in the thematic book set found in Chapter 8. Engle's poetic picturebooks and her novels-in-verse capture the experiences of intriguing figures from the past, historical events, and even her own memories from childhood. Frequently tied to the rich history of Latin America, and Cuba in particular, several of her works highlight struggles by individuals to defy prejudiced societal norms and expectations.

Engle served as the United States Poetry Foundation's Young People's Poet Laureate from 2017 to 2019. During an interview at the time, Engle commented that she loves "to write about young people who made hopeful choices in situations that seemed hopeless." The vivid imagery of her poetry often makes her characters and their stories seem timeless in both their challenges and their courage, yet grounded in their historical period at the same time. Students new to Engle's books will find her poems very accessible and relatable.

On her personal webpage, Engle offers videos of teaching tips for writing poetry, bilingual readings of her books, and podcasts and interviews around her work. Many of these include some of her personal experiences and position as a Cuban American woman poet. Consider combining these videos at a later date, along with the Carnegie Medal–winning video of *Drum Dream Girl* by Dreamscape Media, LLC (available in most public and school libraries), to continue the conversation on societal expectations around gender and about the freedom of poetry and verse.

Sydney Smith

Canadian poet and author Jordan Scott's emotional *I Talk Like a River* is based on his own experiences as a child, including a meaningful trip to the Fraser River with his dad. The sparse and lyrical story is brought to fullness with the incredible illustrations by artist Sydney Smith. Smith, a picturebook author himself as well as an illustrator, worked in unusual three-part harmony with Scott and editor Neal Porter to create this outstanding picturebook.

In Chapter 9, *I Talk Like a River* is one of three books told from the perspective of a child with a disability. Students may be particularly drawn to this title because it is a true story. Guided discussion about the book centers on Scott's personal message at the end of the book and encourages students to consider how the illustrations capture the feelings of the narrator. Consider using this focus on illustration as a starting place to later introduce the award-winning work of Smith.

Small in the City, a book both illustrated and authored by Smith, would be a logical choice for the next read of a Sydney Smith selection. The story takes the reader on a mysterious journey that begins with what seems like advice for navigating a large urban area and quickly turns into a heartbreaking journey that highlights Smith's understanding of the complexity of childhood emotions. He neither minimizes nor exaggerates the depth and capacity of children to love, to mourn, and to be courageous. His illustrations in this story, as in his other stories, highlight that understanding. Many of the titles on which he has worked can be additional entryways for discussion of the topics found in the chapters of this book.

IN MY CLASSROOM

Josh the Fifth Grader: Independence and Individuality

I learned that Josh would be joining my classroom 2 weeks before school began. His family had recently moved to our city and he had been enrolled in the past week. While my class list regularly changed in August, I also received an unusual email to give my principal a call immediately as Josh was going to be coming in to visit my classroom the day before school began.

My principal explained the reason for the visit. Josh had a significant visual impairment and would be visiting the school with one of our district's certified teachers for the visually impaired to do a school tour. This would help him orientate more easily when school began and also allow me to make any seating arrangements or classroom set-up modifications that might be needed. A meeting before the visit with all of Josh's teachers would discuss other specific accommodations, and a formal Individualized Education Program (IEP) meeting would follow later. I was apprehensive. I had never taught a student with a significant visual impairment and was concerned that I might not be able to meet Josh's needs in the classroom. How could I adjust some of the larger plans I had already made for the year with community projects and long field trips? Would the rest of the class be not only kind to Josh, but also respectful?

The team meeting took care of some of my immediate concerns, as the district teacher consult led us through the basics of classroom arrangements and explained the braille resources Josh would have easily available. A quick look at Josh's school file was also reassuring, with report cards showing on-level work and comments about his maturity and social nature. Josh had attended a school for the blind for preschool and kindergarten, and then successfully attended his regular neighborhood school in mainstream classrooms since first grade. The district teacher would be available for help when needed, and the school special education team would also assist me with questions and advice. Still, I worried.

Then Josh came to visit with his parents. And immediately, I realized that all of my fears were related to my own preconceived stereotypes. Josh was thoroughly independent and confident. After watching him walk around the room with his parents and the visiting teacher, counting steps and getting oriented to the layout, I asked him what I might do to help support him in the classroom. He quickly asked if he could keep his bell soccer ball in the class recess ball bin. After I said "yes," Josh asked if kids could have water bottles at their desks because in his old school everyone did. He paused and then added that this would be really helpful as that was easier for him than using the water fountain. I realized that Josh was not only quite independent, but that he also was his own advocate.

In the IEP meeting with his parents and the team later that week, I commented on his independence and his clear and polite articulation of his needs. His mom smiled and replied, "Josh was born with both a very strong sense of independence and some visual impairments. Figuring out how to get around in this world is just what he knows. He shouldn't need much more than clear information about the surroundings, and about your expectations like you share with all the students." I nodded and she looked me in the eye. "Just listen to Josh the fifth grader, and he'll let you know."

—NM, FIFTH-GRADE TEACHER

Where Are You From?

Talking About Race and Ethnicity and Identity

THE BOOKS

Where Are You From?

by Yamile Saied Mendéz, illustrated by Jaime Kim (HarperCollins, 2019)

This heartfelt picturebook follows a young girl struggling with questions about her cultural identity. With help from her *abeulo* ("grandfather"), she begins to draw strength from her family's stories and traditions to confidently answer the question and feel positively about her cultural heritage. Yamile Saied Mendéz's poem welcomes the uncomfortable question "Where are you from?" in a circular fashion that is mirrored by Jaime Kim's gently rounding lines, which focus the reader on internal and universal strength.

Leila in Saffron

by Rukhsanna Guidroz, illustrated by Dinara Mirtalipova (Simon & Schuster, 2019)

Leila learns about her cultural identity through stories, food, conversations with her grandmother and relatives in Arabic, and observation of her family's homes. In vibrant illustrations by Dinara Mirtalipova and poignant prose by Rukhsanna Guidroz, this book beautifully explores themes of tradition, family bonds, and the importance of knowing one's cultural heritage.

Alma and How She Got Her Name

by Juana Martinez-Neal (Candlewick Press, 2018)

Alma Sofia Esperanza José Pura Candela is curious about the origins of her long name! As Alma asks her father about the parts of her name, she discovers the unique stories and people that have shaped her identity. Intricate pencil sketches add intriguing details to the family history that Alma's father shares, wrapped in the warm texture of the book's handmade paper.

Each short tale by Juana Martinez-Neal underscores the significance of one's name in shaping their sense of self.

The Proudest Blue: A Story of Hijab and Family

by Ibtihaj Muhammad with S. K. Ali, illustrated by Hatem Aly (Little, Brown, 2019)

On the first day of school, Faizah's big sister Asiya wears a hijab for the first time. Although Faizah admires her sister and her blue hijab, some students at their school respond with bias and misunderstanding. In Ibtihaj Muhammad's story, as illustrated by Hatem Aly, vibrant ink and exquisite use of texture both ground and celebrate the sisters' bond, the power of their mother's words, their courage in the face of prejudice, and a celebration of their Muslim identity.

The Undefeated

by Kwame Alexander, illustrated by Kadir Nelson (Versify-Houghton Mifflin Harcourt, 2019)

Kwame Alexander delivers a poetic tribute celebrating the strength, resilience, and achievements of African Americans throughout history. Powerful verses are rendered in a variety of text types, emphasizing the richness of Kadir Nelson's emotionally moving illustrations. The poem highlights the triumphs and challenges faced by individuals who have shaped history, from athletes and activists to artists and pioneers, inspiring readers with their stories of perseverance and resolve.

When We Were Alone

by David A. Robertson, illustrated by Julie Flett (High Water Press, 2016)

Feeling safe and comfortable helping her grandmother around her garden and home, a young girl begins to ask intimate questions about her grandmother's hair and clothes and language, and soon learns of her past experiences in a Canadian residential school. In David Robertson's short lyrical tales, as illustrated by Julie Flett, the grandmother reveals how she maintained her Cree identity and strength despite the government's efforts to assimilate her. The book poignantly portrays the resilience of Indigenous peoples and the importance of remembering and honoring one's roots.

Something Good

by Marcy Campbell, illustrated by Corinna Luyken (Hachette, 2021)

After something "bad" is graffitied on a bathroom stall, an entire school must figure out how to respond. Marcy Campbell's narrative highlights the many emotions and confusion that students, parents, teachers, and a principal confront as they move toward healing. Corinna Luyken's strong use of color helps to illuminate the importance of courageous conversations when responding to hateful words and actions to build a community of trust and "something good."

Say My Name

by Joanna Ho, illustrated by Khoa Le (Harper, 2023)

Every person's name is unique, often reflecting family history and deep cultural significance. Names can embody hope and the promise of the future. Joanna Ho's precise word choices, and

Khoa Le's illustrations, capture the confidence of six children sharing the rich stories behind their names and cultures, ultimately illuminating the importance of learning to pronounce every person's name correctly to truly understand and honor their identities.

I Am Every Good Thing

by Derrick Barnes, illustrated by Gordon C. James (Nancy Paulsen Books/Penguin, 2020)

With dynamic prose and rich oil illustrations, this book spotlights a confident Black boy who takes pride in his identity. He is funny, smart, creative, and a loyal friend. But at times, he is scared because others don't truly understand him. Despite the obstacles he faces, he remains steadfast in his positive outlook and identity. Derrick Barnes's story, as illustrated by Gordon James, delivers a powerful message about the importance of genuinely listening and learning about others, ensuring that everyone feels as if their whole selves are being seen and respected.

> ***Note:*** As with all thematic book sets, we recommend that after each book has been shared within the unit, it is placed in an easily accessible display in the classroom for the rest of the unit days. Children should then be allowed access to explore these books on their own during free-choice times.

PLANNING CHECKLIST

Where Are You From?: Thinking About Race and Ethnicity and Identity

We suggest the following timeline to prepare and then share and discuss the books and do the related activities with your students. (A reproducible version of this checklist is available in Appendix 1.) Please note that timing for your individual class should be determined by your situation and your schedule, and, most importantly, should be guided by your students' reactions to the books and activities. Plan generally, however, on about 1 hour of daily time with the unit for 7–10 days in a row.

Two Weeks Prior

- ☐ Complete Taking the Pulse of the Class: Before Unit (Appendix 2) for a general sense of your class at this time.
- ☐ Collect and read twice each of the books for the unit.
- ☐ Review the "Unit Plans: Reading, Discussions, and Activities" section of the unit.
- ☐ Send out the Administration Notification Slip (Appendix 3) and School Counselor/ Psychologist and Support Staff Notification Slip (Appendix 4).

One Week Prior

- ☐ (Optional) Send out Family Notification Slips (Appendix 5) to the families of your students.
- ☐ Have students complete the Unit Pre-Check with Students (Appendix 6) and review the results carefully. Check in with any students with reactions that cause concern so that you can prepare for extra support.

- ☐ Review Chapter 2 of the book.
- ☐ Collect all materials needed for the unit:
  - ☐ **Daily Reflection forms (Appendix 7):** You will need one for each day.
  - ☐ **Books:** One copy is required, but you may prefer to secure two copies of each book. After each book has been shared during the unit, place it in an easily accessible display in the classroom. Please give students access to explore these books on their own during free-choice times. You will want to keep the display available for some time after the unit is completed.
  - ☐ **Materials already in your classroom:** Please have available and ready to use the following commonplace classroom materials:
    - Chart paper or a section of whiteboard that can remain posted for the duration of the unit
    - Unlined white paper
    - Pencils and pens; colored pencils, crayons, or markers
    - Construction paper or other colored paper
    - Scissors
    - Tape or glue
    - Any additional materials indicated within the unit chapter's detailed description

During: Readings, Discussions, and Activities (approximately 7–10 school days)

- ☐ Follow the detailed plans for each day.
- ☐ One to 2 days after the unit is completed, have students complete the Unit Post-Check with Students (Appendix 8).

One Week Following

- ☐ After reviewing the Unit Post-Check with Students, check in with any students with reactions that cause concern.
- ☐ Refer any students expressing interest or for whom you have concerns at this point for additional, individual discussion with a school support professional. Also consider additional whole-class work if indicated.
- ☐ Complete and review Taking the Pulse of the Class: After Unit (Appendix 9). This will help you reflect on your experience and your students' experiences with the thematic book set.

UNIT OVERVIEW

Where Are You From?: Thinking About Race and Ethnicity and Identity

Day	Books	Discussion and Activities
1	**Introduction and Whole-Class Read-Aloud #1:** *Where Are You From?*	• Shades of Us
2 and 3	**Small Groups Read-Aloud and Discuss #1:** *Alma and How She Got Her Name* *Leila in Saffron*	• Gallery Walk • A Story for the Next Generation

4	**Whole-Class Read-Aloud #2:** *The Proudest Blue: A Story of Hijab and Family*	• Understanding Microaggressions: Exploring Words and Actions That Hurt
5 and 6	**Small Groups Read-Aloud and Discuss #2:** *The Undefeated* *When We Were Alone*	• Poetic Retelling
7	**Whole-Class Read-Aloud #3:** *Something Good*	• Art for Unity: Messages of Respect and Belonging
8, 9, and 10	**Conclusion and Small Groups Read-Aloud and Discuss #3:** *Say My Name* *I Am Every Good Thing*	• "This Is Us" Poetry Slam

Note: Each "day" of this unit is intended to take around 1 hour of class time. Time may vary slightly depending on student discussion, but please keep this time frame in mind as you move through the reading and activities.

BEFORE BEGINNING

1. Make sure you have completed the "Two Weeks Prior" and "One Week Prior" items on the planning checklist, including the Taking the Pulse of the Class: Before Unit and the Unit Pre-Check with Students forms.
2. Remember that the books within these units are specifically sequenced to build understanding. To have the greatest likelihood of success with these courageous conversations, we ask that you follow the order of the books, discussions, and activities and complete the entire unit.
3. Review Chapter 2 to help prepare for navigating the upcoming discussions you will be having with your students. As you complete the Daily Reflections at the end of each school day, consider revisiting Chapter 2 for helpful support in engaging in your own self-reflection and awareness, and ensuring your thoughtful and respectful approach to the topic.

DAY 1

Introduction and Whole-Class Read-Aloud #1: *Where Are You From?*

Discussion and Activity: Shades of Us

Time: 1 hour total

Special Materials Needed:

- Multiple sets of skin-tone crayons or colored pencils (these are sold in sets such as Creatology Skintone, Lakeshore People Colors, and Crayola "Colors of the World" crayons but could also be a collection you prepared prior to this unit)

Introduction and Whole-Class Read-Aloud #1: *Where Are You From?*

Begin the unit by gathering the whole class for a read-aloud and discussion. Tell the students that today they will be hearing a story whose title is a question: "Where Are You From?" Ask students what they think about when they hear this question. (Note that while a few students may answer your question, others might seem a little uncomfortable.) Allow just a few answers and then explain that this question can mean different things to different people. It can refer to where someone was born, where their family is from, or where they feel they belong.

Next, ask students to consider whether they have ever asked someone else this question, and if so, what were they curious about? (Be careful not to pause in asking students this two-part question; the goal is to allow students to share the reason why they asked the question and what they wanted to learn, rather than to focus on if they have asked it.) After a few students have shared, tell the students:

> *"Some people get asked this question all the time. For some, it makes them feel special because people want to know more about them. For others, it can feel uncomfortable because they get asked it all the time, and after they respond, the person asking the question does not seem satisfied with the answer. It can seem like the person asking the question wants to be able to identify or categorize the person using a specific nationality, which means the country in which they were born or have citizenship, their race, or their ethnicity. That can get pretty frustrating."*

Now, show your students the cover of the book and explain that in this story the main character is asked this very same question quite a bit.

Begin reading the book to the class, making sure that all can see the illustrations well. The text is poetic but sparse, so be careful not to rush your reading and to give the students plenty of time to examine the images on each page and hear the rhythm of the phrases. As you read through the first set of descriptive pages, pause and ask students to notice how the illustrations now depict the places Abuelo is describing. Ask students these questions as you read and pause on each page:

- "What do you notice about the little girl's appearance in each page spread? How do you think she is feeling? Why do you think the illustrator drew her like that?"

- "What do you notice about how Abuelo is looking at the images on each page? What do you think he is feeling?"
- "What do you notice about the shape of the lines of text? How does their shape match the illustrations? Why do you think the text is designed like that?"

When you reach the page that reads, "But, Abuelo, I ask, where am I really from?", question students: "What do you notice about the little girl now? Why do you think she is asking this question?"

Continue reading the last few pages of the book, stopping to ask on the second-to-last spread where Abuelo and the little girl are in this picture. After the students consider this question and answer, read the final page of the story. Then ask students if they notice a change in the narrator. "Who is talking at the end? What do you think she means? How do you think she is now feeling about the question 'Where are you from?' "

Now, tell students that posing this question is one way people can ask questions that center around concepts of race, ethnicity, and identity, which they could see happening in this book. Tell them you are now going to spend a few minutes talking about the first of these words: *race*.

Begin by asking them what the word *race* means other than a "competition" to see who is the fastest. After a few responses, write the word and its definition on the whiteboard: "**Race** is a way of grouping people based on physical features like skin color, hair texture, and facial features."

- Share an example: "For instance, people might be grouped as having light skin, dark skin, or somewhere in between. These groups are often given names like 'Black,' 'White,' 'Asian,' or 'Native American.' "

> ***Note:*** Students might ask questions similar to the following: "Why are people called Black or White when that's not really their skin color?" Consider responding with something like this: "That's a really great question! The terms *Black* and *White* are used to describe different groups of people, but you're right—those words don't exactly match the actual color of our skin."

- Tell students:

  "*A long time ago, people started using these words to make it easier to talk about big groups of people who looked similar in some ways, like having lighter or darker skin. Even though no one's skin is truly Black or White, these words have just stuck around over time. It's important to remember that everyone is unique, and our skin color is just one part of who we are. What's really special is learning more about each other, like our cultures, traditions, and beliefs.*"

- Then advise your students that they are now going to start an art activity to explore who they are.

Discussion and Activity: Shades of Us

- Have students return to their desks or tables. Pass out blank paper and the sets of crayons or colored pencils you prepared before today as well as regular sets of crayons and colored pencils. (It is important that all students have both sets!) Tell students to write their names on one side of the paper.
- Explain to students that everyone's skin color and appearance is unique. There are many different shades of skin, just like there are many different colors in a crayon box. Now, ask students to flip their papers over (so that the names are on the back side) and trace their hand with a pencil. Then use all the colors they want to try to color in their hand picture, matching their own skin tone as closely as possible.
- As students work on their coloring for the next few minutes, walk around the room to help them find shades that fit their skin color. There is a tendency for students to choose a "peach" or "beige" color because they have been socialized to believe these colors are the color of skin (e.g., band-aids advertised as "flesh tone").
  - Engage them in conversation and listen to what students are saying to each other. Encourage them to help their peers find shades that fit them and emphasize that the range in shades will create an even more beautiful picture. Encourage them to use all the colors available and not just the skin tone sets.
- After most students have completed their coloring, ask them to stop for a minute. Tell them they are going to add to their picture now with words. Around the outside of their hand, they will write down words or phrases that help describe the things that make them who they are. It can be anything, including their favorite hobbies, favorite song, or a tradition/holiday they celebrate with their family.
- Tell students: "You are adding these words or phrases to help others get to know who you are." Remind students about the main question in the book they just heard: Where are you from? It seemed at the beginning of the book that the little girl was being asked this question mainly because of how she looked—as if the people around her were only seeing her skin color. Skin color is just one part of a person. And knowing where someone comes from is only one part of knowing about them. There are many ways we can learn about someone in a more meaningful way.
- Write on the whiteboard or on top of a piece of chart paper the phrase, "Getting to Know You." Then with the students, brainstorm and list questions they can ask each other or people they hope to get to know. Start students off with a few examples, and create a list of at least 10 questions, such as:
  - What do you enjoy doing in your free time?
  - What is a tradition or holiday your family celebrates?
  - What's your favorite book?
  - What are some things you like about where you live now?
  - What food do you enjoy the most?
  - What's something interesting about your family?
  - What are some of your favorite hobbies or activities?

  - What's a fun fact about you that not many people know?
  - What's your favorite thing about your culture?
  - What languages do you speak or want to learn?
- Keep the brainstorming session short and turn students back to work on their hand papers. Tell students to now write down words and phrases around their hand picture, using the questions for ideas of what to write. As students begin to write down words and phrases, circle around the room to lend support and encouragement. After about 5 minutes of writing, tell students that it is time to stop.

Segue to Next Day and Daily Reflection

Let students know that you will be moving on to the next part of the day, but you will be returning to this topic tomorrow. Hand out pieces of wall tape and have students tape their hand pictures to the wall.

When the school day is over, take some time to fill out the Daily Reflection to reflect on this experience. Review it as you prepare for the next 2 days.

DAYS 2 AND 3

Discussion and Activity: Gallery Walk

Small Groups Read-Aloud and Discuss #1: *Leila in Saffron and Alma and How She Got Her Name*

Discussion and Activity: Gallery Walk; A Story for the Next Generation

Time: 2 hours total

> ***Note:*** Plan to spend 2 hours total across both days. You can divide this time as works best for your class. On Day 1, allow 10 minutes for the Gallery Walk activity with the whole class. Then plan for a 15- to 20-minute read-aloud and discussions with each of four small groups of students later in the day during center or station time (about 1 hour and 20 minutes total). On Day 2, allow 30 minutes for the whole-class A Story for the Next Generation activity.

Special Materials Needed:

- A Story for the Next Generation (Appendix 13) worksheet to project on overhead (or can be copied and handed out to students as hard copies)

Discussion and Activity: Gallery Walk

Begin today with a short **Gallery Walk** of yesterday's drawings. Give students 3–4 minutes to walk around and look at the different images.

Once students return to their desks, have a brief discussion about the pictures. Tell them:

> *"Our skin color, as shown in the hand pictures, and our physical features are things others can see, and people may think they know who we are just by looking at us. But the words we wrote are even more important! Knowing where someone is from means so many things, not just where they were born or live, but all the amazing parts of their history, family, likes/dislikes, culture, and traditions."*

It is possible that some of your students may have written down their ethnicity. If they did, then ask the first question below. If not, then lead with the second alternate question:

- "I noticed that some students wrote down their ethnicity, such as ____________ (e.g., 'Puerto Rican,' 'Korean'). Do you know what the word *ethnicity* means?"
- "Sometimes people will describe themselves with their ethnicity, using words like ____________ (e.g., 'Puerto Rican,' 'Korean'). Do you know what the word *ethnicity* means?"

After a few responses, go to the whiteboard or chart paper where you wrote down the definition of the word *race* yesterday. Under it, write *ethnicity* and the following: "Ethnicity is about the culture you come from." Then say to your students:

> "***Ethnicity*** *is about the culture you come from. It includes things like the language you speak, the food you eat, the holidays you celebrate, and the traditions you follow. For example, someone might be of Mexican ethnicity, which means they might speak Spanish at home and celebrate holidays like Día de los Muertos. But remember, even if people share the same race or ethnicity, they may look very different from each other, speak different languages, or celebrate different holidays or traditions."*

Then tell the students that today they are going to read and discuss one of two stories, both of which focus on a child who is learning more about her cultural heritage from her family and about being part of a particular ethnic group.

Small Groups Read-Aloud and Discuss #1: *Leila in Saffron* and *Alma and How She Got Her Name*

> ***Note:*** Prior to class today, divide your students into about four small random groups. Across 2 days, work with each small group independently to read and discuss one of the two titles: *Leila in Saffron* or *Alma and How She Got Her Name*. The goal is for each of the two books to be discussed by two smaller groups.

Explain to students that they will move through small-group centers today (and tomorrow if applicable), and at one station they will do a read-aloud and discussion with you about either the book *Leila in Saffron* or *Alma and How She Got Her Name*. Tell them that both books will be available in the room throughout the rest of the unit if they would like to later look at the book that was not read to them today.

During the small-group read-aloud and discussion, prompt students to notice and make comments about what they are hearing and seeing. Use general prompts such as "What do you notice about this page?" and "What do you think the author is trying to tell us about how [Alma or Lelia] is feeling here?" throughout both books, but as well use the specific prompts below for each book as listed:

Alma and How She Got Her Name

- "What do you notice about Alma's facial expressions or body language as she begins to learn more about her name and her ancestors? Does this change over a few pages? Why do you think the illustrator made her respond differently? What do you think these changes tell us about her feelings?"
- "What do you notice about the details in the background of each story that Alma's father reveals about the parts of her name? What do the illustrations add to the words of Alma's story and family history?"
- "When Alma is with her father, what do you notice about their interactions? How are their interactions drawn? What is the illustrator trying to tell us about their relationship? Do you think this helps Alma better understand her ancestor's histories? How about her identity?"
- "In the final illustration on the last page, Alma's whole name is written out in different fonts and takes up a whole page! Why do you think the illustrator did this? What do you think she is trying to tell us about how Alma feels right now?"

Leila in Saffron

- "When Leila looks in the mirror, she thinks, 'Sometimes I'm not sure if I like being me.' On the next page, she observes all her family members and how she resembles them. What do you think the author is trying to tell us about Leila's feelings at this point?"
- "What items in Leila's grandmother's home specifically help connect Leila to her Pakistani culture? How do the author and illustrator show us this?" If students ask where Pakistan is, here is a short description you can offer: Pakistan is a South Asian country bordered by India, Afghanistan, Iran, and China, along the Arabian Sea. Its capital is Islamabad, and its largest city is Karachi. Urdu and English are the main languages."
- "Leila's family members help her learn about her culture and identity. What kinds of things do you notice them saying or doing?"
- "Leila's grandmother selects a special scarf for her. What do you notice about Leila when she sees herself in the mirror wearing the scarf? What do you think the illustrator is trying to tell us about Leila's feelings now?"

When you have finished reading both books, ask students if they noticed that the older relatives in the story help the main character feel pride in their family heritage and culture just like in *Where Are You From*.

Discussion and Activity: A Story for the Next Generation

After all students have read and discussed their book in their group, have them sit in their seats to begin work on this writing activity.

Remind your students that the older relatives in all three books we have read so far use stories and poetic phrases to help their granddaughters better understand having pride in their heritage. Now, tell them to imagine they are an adult or elder, like a parent, grandparent, older aunt or uncle. Then say:

> *"Imagine that you want to tell your grandchildren a little about you and your life so they can feel pride in their family heritage. Think of a story about* **yourself** *that you might share with the next generation. This can be a story of an important event in your life so far, like the first time you rode a bike, or read a book, or when you were extra kind to a friend. It could be a story about your family that your family likes to retell. It could be the story of your name if you know that, or a story about your older relatives or family that has been told to you many times. To pick your story, first think carefully about what message you want to tell your 'grandchildren.' Do you want them to think of their ancestors as being brave? As being kind? As being smart?"*

Now, pass out a copy of the worksheet **A Story for the Next Generation** (Appendix 13) to each student. Ask students to read the first prompt and then write down what they want their grandchildren to know about them and their family. What **message** do they want to send? Offer a few examples: "Lopezes are brave," "We always help others," "Petersons are singers." If students are struggling for ideas, direct them to think about the three books they have read and the messages that Abuelo, Leila's grandmother, and Alma's father shared.

After a few minutes of contemplation and writing, have students stop and put down their pencils. Then ask them to think about the **story** they are going to tell that will send that message. Have them silently consider this for 30 seconds and then record on the worksheet the title of the story or a phrase about that story, for example, "The time I saved the cat," or "when Aunt Tina was on TV" or "when I won the spelling bee."

Then inform your students that they are now going to think about telling this story to their "grandchildren"! Have them fill out the rest of the worksheet, answering the questions listed. Walk around the room as students work, giving individual support and encouragement, and talking about the details of the stories read to them.

After students have had about 10 minutes of writing time, ask them to stop and re-review what they have written. Tell them they are now going to practice telling their story. Each student will get 2 minutes to tell their story to their partner. Have the students pair up with their elbow or desk partners and decide who will be first to go. Remind them that they are supposed to be grandparents telling a story to their imaginary grandchildren, and that the goal is to get across a certain message about their families. They cannot tell this message directly to their partners, and their partners cannot speak while they are telling their story. Ask the first student to begin and set a timer for 2 minutes. At the 2-minute bell, have partners switch. Then ask the students to guess what the message of the story they heard was.

Next, engage the students in a whole-class discussion. Ask students to consider the following questions and take a few student answers for each:

- "How did it feel to tell a story to your imaginary grandchild? Was it easy or difficult to choose a story? Why?"
- "Was it easy or difficult to decide what to say? Why?"
- "When you told your grandchild about how you (or the family member) felt at the beginning and end of the story, what were some of the words or phrases you used?"

Then ask students to consider the following questions and take a few student answers for each:

- "Why do you think it is important for elders to share their stories with younger family members?"
- "How do you think these stories influence or shape the identity of the next generation?"

Segue to Next Day and Daily Reflection

End the discussion as it comes to a natural close and collect the class A Story for the Next Generation papers. Then explicitly help your students segue by letting them know you are now moving to the next part of the day, but you will be returning to this topic of ethnicity tomorrow.

When the school day is over, take some time to fill out the Daily Reflection to reflect on this experience. Review it as you prepare for the next day.

DAY 4

Whole-Class Read Aloud and Discuss #2: *The Proudest Blue: A Story of Hijab and Family*

Discussion and Activity: Understanding Microaggressions: Exploring Words and Actions That Hurt

Time: 1 hour total

Special Materials Needed:

- Understanding Microaggressions: Words and Actions That Hurt (Appendix 14) worksheet to project on overhead (or can be copied and handed out to students as hard copies)

Whole-Class Read-Aloud and Discuss #2: *The Proudest Blue: A Story of Hijab and Family*

Gather your students for a whole-class read-aloud. Introduce the book by showing the students its cover and explaining that today you are going to share a new story, but this one is not about a parent or grandparent and a child! This time the story is told from the perspective of a little sister.

Have students look at the cover of *The Proudest Blue*. Ask them what they notice about the two characters on the cover. How is the little sister looking at her older sister? What do they think of the title? Based on these details, what do they believe the book might be about?

Begin reading by showing the inside cover of the book and asking students to tell you what is happening there. Then show them the title page and have students explain what is occurring on it. Move to the next page and begin to read. Stop after this first two-page spread and help students understand the perspective of the book—this is Asiya's experience of wearing hijab for the first time but as told through Faizah's, her younger sister's, eyes.

At this point, provide a bit of background on what a hijab is and what wearing hijab represents. Offer the explanation below and ask students if they would like to add more information:

> "*A hijab is a special piece of cloth that some Muslim women and girls wear to cover their hair and sometimes their neck and shoulders. It is a way for them to show their faith, be modest, and follow their religious beliefs. Wearing hijab is a personal choice and can be an important part of someone's identity. A Muslim is a person who follows the religion of Islam. Muslims believe in one God, whom they call 'Allah' in Arabic, and they follow the teachings of the Prophet Muhammad. Being a Muslim is an important part of someone's identity and how they live their life. Muslims can be of any race or ethnicity and live in any country in the world.*"

Then continue with your read-aloud, stopping and asking students to share what they notice on the pages as you read. Use the prompts below as well to highlight specific places in the text and illustrations:

- "What are some of the words or phrases the author has Faizah say that show her feelings about this important first day at school?"
- "How do you think Faizah feels about her sister's hijab? What in the text and pictures makes you believe that?"
- "Faizah looks up to her sister Asiya. How do you think Asiya's confidence and pride in her hijab are influencing Faizah's identity?"
- "How do Asiya's classmates react to her wearing hijab?" (Help students notice the different reactions from Asiya's friends and from other classmates.) "What do you think this might tell us as readers about their understanding of different cultures and races?"
- "At the end of the day, Faizah sees Asiya waiting for her. She notes: 'She's smiling. Strong.' Turn back to earlier in the story when Faizah hears mean comments some students make about Asiya's hijab and thinks, 'Asiya's hijab isn't a laugh. Asiya's hijab is like the ocean waving to the sky. It's always there, strong and friendly.' "
    - "How do these two thoughts from Faizah connect? What do you think the author is telling us about how Faizah feels toward her sister, and about her culture and identity?"
- "Faizah and Asiya's mother's lessons also serve as an important part of this story and appear a few times. Remember the story you wrote yesterday and how you created a message? What lesson or message do you think this mother is trying to teach her daughters about their family and who they are?"

After the read-aloud, ask students to return to their seats if they are not currently in them. Hand out pieces of paper and pencils. Tell your students that they should reflect on a few of the questions above. While thinking about them, jot down some words or sentences, or they can sketch pictures.

- First, tell students: "Think of something about your identity that you are proud of and that makes you feel special. Write it down or draw a quick sketch." (Give students 1 minute.)
- "Next, think about times when you felt your friends or classmates supported or celebrated this part of your identity. What did they say or do to show their support? Write this down or draw a quick sketch." (Give students 1–2 minutes.)
- "Now, consider some times when you felt unsupported or teased about this part of your identity. What did people say or do that demonstrated their lack of support or even bias? Write this down or draw a quick sketch." (Give students 1–2 minutes.)

Ask students if they recall the moments in the book when classmates either did or said hurtful things about Asiya's hijab, like pointing and laughing, or calling her hijab a tablecloth. These types of behavior can be called prejudice or microaggressions. Write down the word *microaggression* on the whiteboard or chart paper where you had already written *race* and *ethnicity*. Ask students what they notice about the different parts of the word *microaggression*. Some will say *micro*, and you can ask them what it means.

Guide students to understand that in this context *micro* doesn't mean small or unimportant, but rather refers to something small that can still have a big impact, because after hearing similar negative comments about yourself, it grows into something much more hurtful. One way to think about microaggressions is like germs. We can't see germs, but when we come into contact with enough of them (e.g., lots of mean stares, hearing hurtful comments about who we are every day), the germs can make us sick.

Others will say *aggress* or *aggression*. Ask them what these words mean.

- Discuss with students what *aggression* means—when someone acts in a way that is threatening or says something harmful toward another person. To *aggress* can be physical like hitting or pushing, or it can be verbal.

Now, help your students put together a definition and write it on the board or chart paper. Here is one to use as a starter:

> "A **microaggression** *is when someone says or does something that makes others feel bad or uncomfortable, sometimes without meaning to. It can be a comment or action that shows stereotypes or biases about someone's race, gender, religion, or other parts of who they are. These statements or actions can hurt feelings and make people feel like they don't belong."*

Then tell students the following:

> *"Sometimes we may say things to our classmates without intending to hurt them. However, what matters most is understanding how our words can impact each other deeply. Discussing microaggressions and realizing when we've made them is crucial. It's not about never saying a*

microaggression because we may unintentionally do so at times. Instead, it's about recognizing when we've said something hurtful related to someone's identity or cultural background, apologizing, and trying to learn from the experience. This helps create an environment where everyone feels respected and valued for who they are."

Discussion and Activity: Understanding Microaggressions: Exploring Words and Actions That Hurt

Now move on to the **Understanding Microaggressions** activity by saying:

> *"In our classroom, we believe in treating everyone with kindness and respect. Sometimes, without meaning to, people say or do things that can make others feel uncomfortable or hurt their feelings. Remember, these are sometimes called microaggressions. Microaggressions often happen because of stereotypes—ideas people have about groups of people based on things like their race, gender, religion, or how they look. Remember how Asiya was treated cruelly by some of her classmates because she was wearing a hijab. In this case, the teasing and hurtful words were on purpose, but sometimes microaggressions can be more subtle or unintentional.*
>
> *"Today, we're going to explore microaggressions a bit more and why it's important to think carefully about how our words and actions might impact others. This will help us create a classroom where everyone feels valued and respected for who they are."*

Pass out the Understanding Microaggressions: Words and Actions That Hurt (Appendix 14) worksheet. Students will work with partners, but give each a copy of the worksheet so they can easily read the statements and messages and draw lines.

Explain the instructions to your students while they look over the worksheet:

- In Column 1, they will find statements that people might say. In Column 2, there are explanations that show what these statements could really mean and how they could hurt someone.
- Their job, with their partner, is to match each statement in Column 1 with its corresponding explanation in Column 2 by drawing a line connecting the two.
- As students work on this, they should read each statement carefully and think about why it might be hurtful to someone, consider how such statements could make a person feel excluded.

Walk around the classroom to listen in on how students are working on this activity together. Help students with words or vocabulary they might not know and also assist them in making the connections. Be prepared for the fact that some students may have strong reactions to the statements, especially if they or someone close to them has been the target of one of the forms of microaggression listed. Be ready to support students having big feelings.

Once all the pairs have completed the worksheet, gather as a class for discussion. Ask students to choose a statement to read aloud and the match they made for it. (***Note:*** If you want to cover all the statements in Column 1, this could lead to a richer discussion, but be prepared for the possibility of extending the time you allotted for this activity.)

After sharing a few of the matches, ask students these questions:

- "What did you learn about microaggressions from completing this worksheet?"
- "How might these microaggressions affect someone's self-esteem or sense of belonging?"
- "What can we do as a class to address microaggressions when we hear them or when we make a microaggression toward someone?"
  - *Tip:* Write several of the students' suggestions on the whiteboard or chart paper, so they can see and practice some of these strategies in the future.

Segue to Next Day and Daily Reflection

Draw the conversation to a close and then explicitly help your students segue by letting them know you are now moving to the next part of the day, but you will be returning to this topic of microaggression tomorrow.

When the school day is over, take some time to fill out the Daily Reflection to reflect on this experience. Review it as you prepare for the next day.

DAYS 5 AND 6

Small Groups Read-Aloud and Discuss #2: *The Undefeated* and *When We Were Alone*

Discussion and Activity: Poetic Retelling

Time: 2 hours total

> ***Note:*** Plan to spend 2 hours total across both days. You can divide this time as works best for your class. Plan for a 15- to 20-minute read-aloud and discussions with each of four small groups of students during center or station time (about 1 hour to 1 hour and 20 minutes total). Finally, allow 30–40 minutes for the whole-class Poetic Retelling activity.

Special Materials Needed:

- A Story for the Next Generation (Appendix 13) worksheets that students used earlier in the unit

Small Groups Read-Aloud and Discuss #2: *The Undefeated* and *When We Were Young*

> ***Note:*** Prior to class today, divide your students into about four small random groups. Across 2 days, work with each small group independently to read and discuss one of the two titles: *The Undefeated* or *When We Were Alone*. The goal is to have each of the two books discussed by two smaller groups. Both books present lyrical and beautifully illustrated historical understandings of racism specific to certain cultures.

Explain to students that they will move through small group centers today (and tomorrow if applicable), and at one station they will do a read-aloud and discussion with you about either the book *The Undefeated* or *When We Were Young*. Tell them that both books will be available in the room throughout the rest of the unit if they would like to later look at the book that was not read to them today.

During the small-group read-aloud and discussion, prompt students to notice and comment on what they are hearing and seeing. Use general prompts such as, "What do you notice about this page?" or "What do you think the author and illustrator are trying to tell us here?" throughout both books, but also the specific prompts below for each book as listed:

The Undefeated

- The author wrote this book as a poem. He starts each verse with the statement "This is for" followed by a word that means strong, determined, and/or powerful. "Why do you think the author chose this pattern?"
- Pause on each page with the statement "This is for the unspeakable" and ask students, "What do you notice on this page? What is 'unspeakable'?" After students give an answer for each of the pages, refer to *The Undefeated*'s appendix, which provides short descriptions of what each illustration and page are referring to and read them aloud to the students. These are the unspeakable events Alexander is referring to:
  - The Transatlantic Slave Trade
  - Four little girls killed in the racially motivated 16th Street Baptist Church bombing
  - Deaths of four unarmed Black Americans by police
- Help students notice the alliteration of the words Alexander chooses to describe the resilient Black and African Americans throughout history (e.g., *unforgettable*, *undeniable*, *unflappable*, *unafraid*, *unlimited*) in the title and in his book. Point out to your students that all these words can be connected to the word *resilience*. Help them generate a definition for the word *resilience* if they do not already know what it means.
- You might say:

  > "***Resilience** is the ability to bounce back and keep going, even when things get tough. It's like when you fail trying to accomplish something hard, and you get back up to try again, or use creative ways to accomplish something difficult. Resilience means finding ways to keep moving forward, no matter what obstacles come your way.*"

- Consider writing this word on your whiteboard or chart paper where you had earlier defined race, ethnicity, and microaggression.

When We Were Alone

- "Why do you think Nókom tells Nossim about the clothes she had to wear at her school, 'far away from home'? How do you think it made Nókom feel to not be able to wear her colorful clothes? Why do you believe that?" (Encourage students to point to words in the text that capture her emotions.)
- "Why is Nókom's hair important to her? What do you think it might feel like to have something that makes you proud taken away or destroyed?"
- "Nókom was not allowed to speak her language at school. How do you think this made her feel? How important do you think language is to someone's identity?"
- "The author showed us that Nókom and her classmates found ways to remember their culture. Why is this important?"
- "Do you think that Nossim knew about the experiences her grandmother had had in the past? What do you believe she is thinking about her culture now?"
- When you finish reading the story, introduce the word *resilience* by asking how Nókom demonstrated resilience when attending a school where she was not allowed to speak her language, to keep her hair long in braids, or to wear her traditional clothes. Help students generate a definition for the word *resilience* if they do not already know what it means. You might say:

> "**Resilience** *is the ability to bounce back and keep going, even when things get tough. It's like when you fail trying to accomplish something hard, and you get back up to try again, or use creative ways to accomplish something difficult. Resilience means finding ways to keep moving forward, no matter what obstacles come your way. It also means having the strength and courage to stay strong and true to oneself, even when facing difficult and unfair situations.*
>
> *"For example, Nókom's resilience shows through her ability to maintain her identity, culture, and traditions, despite the rules at the school. She is able to keep her spirit and traditions alive in creative ways, and continues to be proud of who she is, no matter what challenges she faces."*

- Consider writing this word on your whiteboard or chart paper where you had earlier defined race, ethnicity, and microaggression.

Discussion and Activity: Poetic Retelling

After all the students have read and discussed one of the books in small groups, gather the entire class together to briefly review the key definitions discussed over the past several days: race, ethnicity, microaggressions, and resilience.

Read aloud the existing definitions for the first three words. Then tell students that the word *resilience* was very important in the books read today in small groups. Repeat out loud the definitions you wrote down for *resilience*. It was a strong theme in both stories, informing the students of recent historical events that affected many First Nations people (*When We Were Alone*) and African Americans (*The Undefeated*). Both books reveal to their readers some of the things that the two groups have suffered and endured.

Explain that each book used a repeated poetic phrase: either "When we were alone . . . " in the case of the book with a title bearing the same words or "This is for the . . . " in the case of *The Undefeated*. In *When We Were Alone*, the phrase was used by a grandmother talking to her granddaughter; in *The Undefeated*, the voice seemed like that of a grandparent or elder talking to the children of today.

Ask your students what impact each of the phrases might have had on them or others. Say that, from your perspective, the phrase "When we were alone . . . " opens the door to a story about what people did to keep their culture alive and important, despite the oppression of others and their attempts to extinguish that culture. For you, "This is for the . . . " suggests ways to honor African Americans for what they did to preserve and share their culture and to resist those oppressing them. Both books seem to be rallying today's youth to explore and stand up for their culture and heritage, but in different ways.

As a whole class, briefly discuss these questions:

- "How does the repeated phrase change the impact of the story or poem?"
- "What would be different if these phrases were not used?"
- "Why is it important for today's youth to understand and stand up for their culture and heritage?"
- "How do these phrases help convey the themes of resilience and resistance against oppression?"

Now, hand out to your students the Story for the Next Generation papers they had completed a few days ago. Tell them that they are now going to do a **Poetic Retelling** of their stories! Give students a minute to reread their papers and remember the stories they had told as imaginary grandparents.

Indicate that the class, together, is going to brainstorm possible poetic phrases they could use in retelling their stories. Remind them of the repeated phrases in the two books they just read: "When we were alone . . . " and "This is for the. . . . " Ask students what ideas they have. You might help them get started by saying something like this:

> *"A few phrases that you might have heard in other stories are 'once upon a time,' 'a long time ago,' 'when I was young,' 'this is the story of.' "*

Write down student ideas on the whiteboard or on chart paper.

Remind students that the original purpose of their stories was to give a message about their family to their future grandchildren. Discuss how using a poetic phrase as a "lead-in" could change the impact and tone of their stories. Ask them to consider how "This is for the . . . " gave its story a certain tone, just as "When we were alone . . . " did. Direct students to think hard about a phrase they could use that would really capture the message they want to send. You might give them a few examples: for instance, "Because Petersons are very brave . . . " or "But every time I tried again and. . . . "

Have students discuss possible poetic phrases with their partners. Ask them to write down three possible phrases on their worksheets and circle the one they like best. As students come up with their phrases, have them retell a little of their story to their partner, but this time using the poetic phrase.

After students have had time to pick a phrase and try it out in retelling part of their stories to their partners, interrupt them for a whole-class discussion. Invite two to three students to share their poetic phrase and why they selected it. Encourage them to explain how the incorporated phrase now helps to improve the message they want to send with their story. After a few students have shared, reflect as a class on how the use of repeated phrases can result in more meaningful written messages about the importance of resilience and pride in your family. The phrases also help show the power of storytelling. Encourage them to think about sharing their story, using the poetic phrase, with their real families at home.

Segue to Next Day and Daily Reflection

Explicitly help your students segue by letting them know you are now moving to the next part of the day, but you will be returning to this topic of resilience tomorrow.

When the school day is over, take some time to fill out the Daily Reflection to reflect on this experience. Review it as you prepare for the next day.

DAY 7

Whole-Class Read-Aloud #3: *Something Good*

Discussion and Activity: Art for Unity: Messages of Respect and Belonging

Time: About 1 hour

Special Materials Needed:

- Poster boards or large sheets of paper
- Additional art supplies if desired: magazines for making collages, extra glue, paint
- Pictures of community murals to show on projector or printed hard copies to share

Whole-Class Read-Aloud and Discussion #3: *Something Good*

Note: Today's book portrays an incident of hate speech written on a school wall—an event that, unfortunately, is not uncommon. Be prepared to discuss with students that this kind of event really happens. The focus of today's reading and activity is that students begin to understand the importance of discussing these types of incidents openly and honestly, so everyone can figure out how to address them and take the next steps to allow for healing. Thus, be prepared to engage with students in frank discussions about what would happen or has happened around events like this in your school or nearby schools.

Gather your students for a whole-class read-aloud. Explain that the books you talked about the previous day (*The Undefeated* and *When We Were Alone*) focused on historical or important national events. Both of those books depicted how people overcame racism with resilience and courage. In the book you are reading today, a negative experience also happens, but it occurs in a setting everyone is more familiar with: a school just like ours. It also happens in the present time.

Show students the cover of the book. Then show them the front- and back-page illustrations. Encourage them to notice the colors and details of the drawings. Next, share the inside endpages with them (both the inside-front and the inside-back endpages). Then ask students what they think is going to happen based on what they notice. If students struggle, gently lead them to understand that something had been written on a wall and looks as if it was covered up. Tell them that the book is about an upsetting incident that happens at a school and how the students, teachers, and school community figure out how to respond to it.

Now, begin reading aloud the story. As you read, encourage students to stop and notice what is happening on each page and to share their observations. There is little text in this book, so take plenty of time for students to notice the illustrations as they drive the story, particularly through the use of color and line. Some questions you might ask at specific points in the book include the following:

- "What do you notice about the colors on this page? Why do you think the illustrator used these colors? What are the colors making you feel?"
- "What kind of facial expressions do the students have? What do you imagine they are feeling at this point in the story?" (***Tip:*** Encourage students to notice eye contact and the way in which students are sitting and talking to one another.)
- "What kinds of feelings are coming up for you as we read this story and examine the illustrations? Are there parts of this story that you can relate to?"
- "How do you think the parents who come to the school after the "bad thing" happened feel? How does the illustrator draw them that makes you think this?"
- "Does what is happening in the story seem real to you? What do you think would happen if this occurred in your school? What might you say or do if this kind of incident took place in your classroom or at your school?" (***Tip:*** Use these questions throughout the read-aloud and discussion.)

When you have finished the read-aloud, have students aid you in writing out the pattern of events in the book on the chart paper or whiteboard (you do not want to write out the specific events—just the pattern below):

1. The event happened.
2. The school/children/families/community discussed it.
3. The individuals took that discussion to heart and thought deeply about it, using the dialogue to make positive change.

Discussion and Activity: Art for Unity: Messages of Respect and Belonging

Now, have students return to their desks and tables if they are not already seated there. Tell them they are going to engage in an exciting art project inspired by the students in *Something Good*. Explain that, in the book, the children came together to create a mural of belonging and community, which counteracted the hateful words written in the bathroom. They are going to do something similar by creating posters with important messages for their classroom (or school if you have permission to hang up student art outside of your classroom). The focus of their posters will be making **Art for Unity: Messages of Respect and Belonging.** They will need to use their imagination and loving hearts to make posters that will have a positive impact and spread the word.

First, tell students they will brainstorm ideas. Ask them to think about messages important to them as members of the classroom and school, such as being respectful of others, being kind to others, and making everyone feel as if they belong. Invite them to call out any positive ideas they want their posters to highlight. Write these messages on the whiteboard or chart paper where all students can see them. Then ask your students to consider symbols, colors, and pictures that would complement these messages. Add a few of these ideas to the whiteboard or chart paper.

Next, show students just a few examples of community murals that spread positive messages. Project the examples on your whiteboard or share printed copies of them. (Use images of murals that can be found in your community if possible. You can find images easily online by googling "community murals near me" or "community mural examples." Only show a few at this point as you want students to use their own creativity as much as possible.)

Then ask students to select one of the messages on the board that they like best. Form small groups of students by saying each message out loud and asking for four volunteers who want to work on a mural with that message. (If more than four students volunteer, then form two groups to help create such a message.) After groups are formed, tell students to get posterboard from the front of the room and then find a place where their group can work. Pass out typical art materials (crayons, markers, etc.). If desired, also tell students they may want to consider using materials for collage or other decorations, and they should feel free to come to the back of the room to retrieve glue, tape, magazines, or other types of paper to use however they like.

As students work on their posters, circle the room and encourage them to create posters that are eye-catching and convey a clear message of community, acceptance, and respect. Ask them to explain to you what their poster represents and why this message is important. You may also ask where or from whom their inspiration came.

After students have worked for about 20–25 minutes, tell them that it is time to stop working on the posters and put down their materials. Ask, "How can these messages help create a more positive and welcoming environment for everyone?" Ask each group to share where they would like to display their posters within the classroom or school. ***Note:*** You may need to receive permission from the administration to display posters outside of the classroom. After all groups have shared, tell students to put their posters at the front of the room and to store unused materials.

Segue to Next Day and Daily Reflection

Explicitly help your students segue by letting them know you are now moving to the next part of the day, but you will be returning to this topic of responding to a hate incident tomorrow. Also let them know that you will hang up their posters around the room or outside the classroom later today.

When the school day is over, take some time to fill out the Daily Reflection to reflect on this experience. Review it as you prepare for the next day.

DAYS 8, 9, AND 10

Small Groups Read-Aloud and Discuss #3: *Say My Name* and *I Am Every Good Thing*

Discussion and Activity: "This Is Us" Poetry Slam

Time: 3–3.5 hours total

> ***Note:*** Plan to spend 3 hours total. You can divide this time as works best for your class but will want to take at least 2 days. Plan for 15- to 20-minute read-aloud and discussions with each of four small groups of students during center or station time on the first day (about 1 hour to 1 hour and 15 minutes total). Then plan on 1 hour for writing the "This Is Us" Poetry Slam activity, and another hour to 1.5 hour for the Poetry Slam sharing.

Special Materials Needed:

- "This Is Us" Original Poem (Appendix 15) worksheet
- Students' completed copies of A Story for the Next Generation (Appendix 13) worksheet
- Extra copies of all the books used in the unit

Small Groups Read-Aloud and Discuss #3: *Say My Name* and *I Am Every Good Thing*

Prior to class on Day 1, divide your students into about four small random groups. Across 2 days, work with each small group independently to read and discuss one of the two titles: *Say My Name* or *I Am Every Good Thing.* The goal is to have each of the two books discussed by two smaller groups. *I Am Every Good Thing* celebrates personal identity and Black joy, portraying the narrator's pride in both his individuality and his connection to his ancestors. The book's poetic language inspires self-reflection and serves as a catalyst for writing poems that celebrate positive self-identity. Similarly, *Say My Name* also celebrates individuality and ancestral roots through poems beginning with "My name is" and ending with "Say my name." This book highlights the importance of respecting others by learning to pronounce their names correctly, addressing microaggressions, and fostering understanding across cultures. Together, these books encourage empathy, self-affirmation, and cultural appreciation through creative expression.

Explain to students that they will move through small group centers today (and tomorrow if applicable), and at one station they will do a read-aloud and discussion with you about either the book *I Am Every Good Thing* or *Say My Name.* Tell them that both books will be available in the room throughout the rest of the unit if they would like to later look at the book that was not read to them today.

During the small-group read-aloud and discussion, prompt students to notice and comment on what they are hearing and seeing. Use general prompts such as, "What do you notice about this page?" or "What do you think the author and illustrator are trying to tell us here?" throughout both books, but also use the specific prompts below for each book as listed:

Say My Name

Tip: Some of the names in this book might take some practice for you. The book's appendix provides a pronunciation guide. You can also listen to Joanna Ho read her book aloud online, which can help you with pronouncing each name.

- "Each of these pages is a little different! There are different backgrounds, symbols, and colors on each page. What do you notice on this page?"
- "Why do you think each of the children in the book start with 'My name is' and end with 'Say my name'? What is the author trying to tell us by doing this?
- "The children's names have stories connected to them. What are some of these connections?" (Help students to draw connections of the names to nature, ancestors, artwork, religion, music, and immigration.)
- "This image of all six children crossing an ocean is very powerful. What do you think the author means when she writes, 'They are pieces laid by those who looked into the heavens and saw me in the stars, who knew me before they knew me and lived that I might be.'"

When you finish reading this book, ask each student in the small group to say their full name out loud: first name, middle name (if they have one), and last name. Tell them to start as in the book, saying, "My name is ____________," and as at the end, saying, "Say my name." And then have the entire small group repeat that person's name. Remind them to pay close attention to how each person says their name as we want to make sure we pronounce it as accurately as we can. After doing this name sharing, ask students to discuss why it is important that we say a person's name correctly, and how this activity felt.

I Am Every Good Thing

- "What is the narrator wearing on this first page? [A *cape.*] Why do you think the illustrator drew him in a cape? What do you think the illustrator is telling us about how the boy feels about himself?"
- "On the next page, the boy says he is 'good to the core, like the center of a cinnamon roll.' Ask students to describe the middle of a cinnamon roll and then ask a few of them to share what their core is like."
- "The illustrator paints the boy riding a skateboard. Why do you think the illustrator did this? What does riding a skateboard tell us about the boy's character or personality?"
- "What are the boy's relationships with other people like? Consider the pages with his siblings, his grandmother, and his friends. What do we learn from the images on these pages about his relationships?"
- "Spend some time on the page where the boy's positive voice shifts. He tells us that 'every now and then, I am afraid.' Ask students what he might be afraid of and why." (***Tip:*** Be prepared to talk about anti-Black violence and racism toward people who look like the boy in this book. Consider returning to the dedication page and reading aloud the second dedication that is from GCJ, the illustrator. Talk about the Black boys and men and why the illustrator might have written this.)
- "On the last page, the narrator repeats the line 'I am worthy to be loved' two times. Why do you think the author has him say it twice?"

Discussion and Activity: "This Is Us" Poetry Slam

After all students have read and discussed one of the books in small groups, gather the entire class together.

Tell students that to end the unit, they are going to stage a special poetry "slam," called **This Is Us**, celebrating all the hard work you have put into our discussions and activities and reading about some challenging topics: race, racism, ethnicity, microaggressions, and building belongingness. You have shown incredible courage in discussing these challenging issues. Let's wrap up this unit by sharing and perhaps creating spoken word or poetry to remind us of how unique each of you are and to hear the ideas, feelings, and hopes you are going to carry with you as we move forward. Remember, this is not an endpoint for conversations on these topics: We will continue to have rich discussions throughout our time together as a class.

Ask the class if they know what a poetry slam is. Some students may have already participated in one. Explain that a poetry slam is an event where poets perform and share poems and written pieces before an audience, focusing on creativity of expression, emotional impact, and connection with their listeners. Our poetry slam will be a celebration of each person's uniqueness and identities and what we have learned in this unit.

Tell the students to put their heads down or close their eyes as you walk them down memory lane of all the books they read, reminding them briefly of each title and the characters they met in these books. Say a little bit about each of the books (including all titles although students did not read a few of the books on small-group days). Then briefly remind them about the artwork and writing they have produced over the past 2 weeks: their hand drawing, their story for the next generation and the poetic phrase they added to it, the microaggression activity, and art for unity poster.

Then ask your students to raise their heads. Tell them they need to select a short piece to share in the poetry slam. The piece they share should focus on what they wish the world knew about who they are—their unique identities, ethnicity, cultural backgrounds, **or** it can focus on what they hope the world could be for people who are often unseen or discriminated against. Allow less than 1.5 minutes for this read/share aloud.

Students should choose from the following for their piece:

1. Select a few pages, phrases, or passages from one or more of the books read. They can copy down these passages from the books and put them in any order they like. The passages can be from one book or from a few books. When they read their piece aloud, they should say that they themself "mixed" it, but the actual words were "created by" the authors of the books (give their names).
2. They can write out part of their Story for the Next Generation, with or without the poetic phrase addition, and read it aloud.
3. They can also use parts of the books they read as inspiration to write a short mirroring piece, for example, using the stem "This is for . . . " or "My name is. . . . Say my name."
4. They can write an original poem using the "This Is Us" Original Poem (Appendix 15) worksheet to help.

Now give students 30–45 minutes to work on their piece. Pass out the completed A Story for the Next Generation worksheets. Make copies of the "This Is Us" Original Poem worksheet available, as well as plenty of blank paper and copies of the books read in the unit. Circle the room, making sure everyone is getting started and providing support to those who need extra help. Encourage students to consider all the choices they have to create a piece to share. (Depending on what you have done with poetry already this year, guide students to use the skills and strategies they already know to create poetic writing.)

Segue to Next Day and Daily Reflection

When you need to move on to other parts of the day (on Day 1 and/or Day 2), explicitly help your students segue by letting them know you are now moving to the next part of the day, but that you will returning to this topic tomorrow when they hold their poetry slam and share their creative pieces. You may also want to allow students to bring home their poem, to continue working on it there.

When the school day is over, take some time to fill out the Daily Reflection to reflect on this experience. Review it as you prepare for the next day.

Hosting the Poetry Slam

The next day (Day 2 or Day 3) sets the stage for the students' "This Is Us" Poetry Slam! Give them about 5–10 minutes to find their pieces and read through the poems as practice before starting. Also invite them to write their names on the board next to the numbers you have listed, so they will know when it is their turn to perform.

> ***Note:*** You might consider hosting the event in two blocks of about 15–20 minutes each today. This can help maintain student engagement.

When you are ready to begin the slam, remind students about the importance of active listening and respect for each performer. Say that after each student performs, all students will snap their fingers or clap. This is what is done at real poetry slams to show respect for the courage of the performer in sharing their piece. Ask students to start their share by saying their name and then reading aloud their piece.

After all students have shared their pieces, hold a "post-slam" discussion. Ask them to share a few thoughts about their experiences, especially what they learned from their classmates through their pieces and what they learned about themselves in writing and performing their own pieces. Then invite students for any closing thoughts about the unit as a whole—what have they learned over the last 2 weeks about themselves; about others; about race, ethnicity, microaggressions, and resilience? Leave this discussion open-ended.

Segue to Next Day and Daily Reflection, Unit Post-Check with Students, and Taking the Pulse of the Class: After Unit

Collect the poems from the students. Then explicitly help them segue by letting them know you are now moving to the next part of the day, and this is the end of the unit on race, ethnicity, and positive identity. Let them know that the books will remain in the classroom for some time and that they are welcome to revisit them. Also tell them that although the unit may have been completed, these conversations can always continue around its topic, and they should feel free to ask questions or discuss the topic in more detail.

When the school day is over, take some time to complete the Daily Reflection form. The next day or the day after that, ask your students to complete the Unit Post-Check with Students. Finally, about a week to 10 days after the unit was completed, fill out Taking the Pulse of the Class: After Unit to consider more broadly this experience for your current students, yourself, and your future students.

FINAL SUGGESTIONS

During the weeks following this unit, you might want to revisit some of these books or the conversations around them. This unit was intended as an introduction to, and the beginning of courageous conversations around, the difficult topics of race, racism, ethnicity, positive identity, and resilience.

Some students may want to continue to discuss this topic in class. Reach out to your school counselors, psychologists, and support faculty for individual help for students seeking more specific or individualized support in this area. The Unit Post-Check with Students will help you identify students needing or wanting this support.

You may decide to expand on this unit with further book sharing, discussions, and activities. The websites that follow may serve as good resources as you do this work.

ADDITIONAL RESOURCES

Anti-Defamation League: Provides resources for educators and families to address issues of prejudice, bias, and discrimination. *www.adl.org/education*

Embrace Race: Provides resources and supports for parents and educators to raise children who are knowledgeable about race, racism, and identity. *www.embracerace.org*

Facing History & Ourselves: Offers educational resources and professional development to address issues of racism, prejudice, and discrimination through history and literature. *www.facinghistory.org*

Learning for Justice: Provides resources to educators and families to promote diversity and inclusive classrooms. *www.learningforjustice.org*

National Museum of African American History and Culture: Offers educational resources and activities focused on African American history and culture, including topics related to race and racism. *https://nmaahc.si.edu*

PBS Kids—Talking About Race and Racism: Provides articles, videos, and activities to help children understand race, racism, and how to be inclusive. *www.pbs.org/parents/talking-about-racism*

PBS Utah—Let's Talk: A digital series of seven episodes where parents openly discuss their experiences in guiding conversations with their children about race and racism. *www.pbsutah.org/pbs-utah-productions/series/lets-talk*

MEETING COMMON CORE AND CASEL STANDARDS

Common Core English Language Arts Standards for Grade 4

This unit meets specific Common Core State Standards for English Language Arts in grades 3, 4, 5, and 6. We have included the specific ELA standards for grade 4 below to illustrate the strands and items met (similar for all four grades third through sixth). The QR code here will link you to the specific lists for grades 3, 5, and 6.

CCSS.ELA-LITERACY.SL.4.1

Engage effectively in a range of collaborative discussions (one-on-one, in groups, and teacher-led) with diverse partners on *grade 4 topics and texts*, building on others' ideas and expressing their own clearly.

CCSS.ELA-LITERACY.RL.4.1

Refer to details and examples in a text when explaining what the text says explicitly and when drawing inferences from the text.

CCSS.ELA-LITERACY.RL.4.4

Determine or clarify the meaning of unknown and multiple-meaning words and phrases based on grade 4 reading and content, choosing flexibly from a range of strategies.

CCSS.ELA-LITERACY.RL.4.6

Compare and contrast the point of view from which different stories are narrated, including the difference between first- and third-person narrations.

CCSS.ELA-LITERACY.W.4.3

Write narratives to develop real or imagined experiences or events using effective technique, descriptive details, and clear event sequences.

CCSS.ELA-LITERACY.W.4.4

Produce clear and coherent writing in which the development and organization are appropriate to task, purpose, and audience.

CASEL Social and Emotional Learning Standards for Grades 3–5

This unit meets specific CASEL Core Competence Area goals for Social and Emotional Learning for grades 3–5. We have included the CASEL areas and specific example standards below to show the items met in this unit. (The items are similar for grade 6.)

Self-Awareness: The abilities to understand one's own emotions, thoughts, and values and how they influence behavior across contexts. This includes capacities to recognize one's strengths and limitations with a well-grounded sense of confidence and purpose.

- Integrating personal and social identities
- Identifying personal, cultural, and linguistic assets
- Identifying one's emotions

- Linking feelings, values, and thoughts
- Examining prejudices and biases

Self-Management: The abilities to manage one's emotions, thoughts, and behaviors effectively in different situations and to achieve goals and aspirations. This includes the capacities to delay gratification, manage stress, and feel motivation and agency to accomplish personal/collective goals.

- Managing one's emotions
- Exhibiting self-discipline and self-motivation
- Using planning and organizational skills
- Showing the courage to take initiative
- Demonstrating personal and collective agency

Social Awareness: The abilities to understand the perspectives of and empathize with others, including those from diverse backgrounds, cultures, and contexts. This includes the capacities to feel compassion for others, understand broader historical and social norms for behavior in different settings, and recognize family, school, and community resources and supports.

- Taking others' perspectives
- Recognizing strengths in others
- Demonstrating empathy and compassion
- Showing concern for the feelings of others
- Recognizing situational demands and opportunities
- Identifying diverse social norms, including unjust ones

Relationship Skills: The abilities to establish and maintain healthy and supportive relationships and to effectively navigate settings with diverse individuals and groups. This includes the capacities to communicate clearly, listen actively, cooperate, work collaboratively to problem-solve and negotiate conflict constructively, navigate settings with differing social and cultural demands and opportunities, provide leadership, and seek or offer help when needed.

- Communicating effectively
- Developing positive relationships
- Demonstrating cultural competency
- Practicing teamwork and collaborative problem solving
- Seeking or offering support and help when needed
- Standing up for the rights of others

Responsible Decision Making: The abilities to make caring and constructive choices about personal behavior and social interactions across diverse situations. This includes the capacities to consider ethical standards and safety concerns, and to evaluate the benefits and consequences of various actions for personal, social, and collective well-being.

- Demonstrating curiosity and open-mindedness
- Identifying solutions for personal and social problems
- Reflecting on one's role to promote personal, family, and community well-being
- Anticipating and evaluating the consequences of one's actions
- Evaluating personal, interpersonal, community, and institutional impact

I'm Me!

Talking About Gender and Identity

THE BOOKS

Drum Dream Girl: How One Girl's Courage Changed Music

by Margarita Engle, illustrated by Rafael Lopez (Houghton Mifflin Harcourt, 2015)

The gorgeously bright acrylic illustrations from Rafael Lopez, tinged with neon and full of movement, match perfectly with Margarita Engle's poem about drummer Millo Castro Zaldarriaga. Engle uses a rhythmic style that captures the hardships Millo faced in trying to drum in a culture and a time that would not allow women to do so.

I Dissent: Ruth Bader Ginsburg Makes Her Mark

by Debbie Levy, illustrated by Elizabeth Baddely (Simon & Schuster Books for Young Readers, 2016)

This picturebook biography of the famous "RBG" captures Justice Ginsburg's early life, schooling, and legal career before she was appointed to the U.S. Supreme Court. Debbie Levy's text is sprinkled with law-related terms and depicts the sexism RBG faced on a regular basis, and how she persisted in spite of it and excelled. Photos and detailed information can be found in the back of the book and shared for greater depth of understanding.

The International Day of the Girl: Celebrating Girls Around the World

by Jessica Dee Humphreys and the Honorable Rona Ambrose, illustrated by Simone Shin (Kids Can Press, 2020)

This special collective biography celebrates the United Nations' International Day of the Girl with short stories of incredible girls who face issues of gender inequality and economic hardship, violence, and more in their communities, but find solutions to improve the lives of all.

The girls' strength, intelligence, leadership, and courage shine through and will inspire young readers.

Tough Boris

by Mem Fox, illustrated by Kathryn Brown (Voyager Books/Harcourt, 1998)

Tough Boris, one of Mem Fox's iconic characters, is the scruffiest, strongest, and scariest pirate captain around, but he also loves his pet parrot and music. A young stowaway on Boris's ship catches a glimpse of Boris's other side. The sparse text and detailed illustrations of Kathryn Brown offer a poignant lesson about traditional stereotypes.

Big Boys Cry

by Jonty Howley (Random House, 2019)

Levi's father trots out the tired adage "Big boys don't cry" when Levi is scared on the first day of school. While these words do nothing to comfort him, the repeated sight of men expressing sadness and fear while he walks to school begins to help him see that showing your emotions is important and can make you feel better. By the time Levi returns home, his dad has realized his misstep and shares that he made a mistake in responding the way he did—that he actually was the one who was more scared.

Julian Is a Mermaid

by Jessica Love (Candlewick Press, 2018)

Julian loves mermaids! Swimming at the pool is an imaginative delight, and on the train home, he spots three women dressed as gorgeous mermaids. He quickly borrows his *abuela*'s plant and curtains to create a mermaid costume of his own. Upon seeing him, she whisks him out the door—is she angry? No, she takes a gleeful Julian to the Coney Island Mermaid Parade. The use of repeated vignettes and exquisite glimpses of the characters' emotions drive Jessica Love's story.

Sparkle Boy

by Leslea Newman, illustrated by Maria Mola (Lee & Low Books,2017)

Jessie is not sure what to think. When she shows off her new shimmery skirt and polished nails, her little brother Casey is delighted and asks for the same things. Jessie appeals to her parents and grandmother to say "no" but is surprised when they instead support Casey, telling him he can wear the clothes he likes. A trip to the library helps her realize what is most important is loving her brother; when bigger boys tease Casey, Jessie comes to see that her brother should, in fact, wear whatever he wants.

Ho'onani Hula Warrior

by Heather Gale, illustrated by Mika Song (Tundra Books, 2019)

Ho'onani doesn't see herself as *wahine* ("girl") or *kāne* ("boy"); she's comfortable being in-between. While others may not understand, Ho'onani is happy with who she is. When she learns that her school is planning the performance of a traditional *kāne* hula, she wants to perform the chant. But can she, someone perceived as a girl, lead an all-male group? Determined to prove herself, Ho'onani sets out on a journey of self-discovery and leadership. Inspired by a true story, the book celebrates Hawaiian culture and tells the empowering story of a girl embracing her identity and earning respect.

When Aidan Became a Brother

by Kyle Lukoff, illustrated by Kaylani Juanita (Lee & Low Books, 2019)

Aidan is excited to be a big brother! Except that, when Aidan was a baby, everyone mistook him for a girl. Aidan worries that someone might make this same big mistake for this baby and focuses on wanting to get everything right for his new sibling. Eventually, through discussions with his parents and being honest with himself, Aidan learns that the best path forward is for him to be open about trying to do the right thing and remain honest and ready to try again when he makes mistakes.

> ***Note:*** As with all thematic book sets, we recommend that after each book has been shared within the unit, it is placed in an easily accessible display in the classroom for the rest of the unit days. Children should then be allowed access to explore these books on their own during free-choice times.

PLANNING CHECKLIST

I'm Me!: Talking About Gender and Identity

We suggest the following timeline to prepare and then share and discuss the books and do the related activities with your students. (A reproducible version of this checklist is available in Appendix 1.) Please note that timing for your individual class should be determined by your situation and your schedule, and, most importantly, should be guided by your students' reactions to the books and activities. Plan generally, however, on about 1 hour of daily time with the unit for 7–10 days in a row.

Two Weeks Prior

- ☐ Complete Taking the Pulse of the Class: Before Unit (Appendix 2) for a general sense of your class at this time.
- ☐ Collect and read twice each of the books for the unit.
- ☐ Review the "Unit Plans: Reading, Discussions, and Activities" section of the unit.
- ☐ Send out the Administration Notification Slip (Appendix 3) and School Counselor/Psychologist and Support Staff Notification Slip (Appendix 4).

One Week Prior

- ☐ (Optional) Send out Family Notification Slips (Appendix 5) to the families of your students.
- ☐ Have students complete the Unit Pre-Check with Students (Appendix 6) and review the results carefully. Check in with any students with reactions that cause concern so that you can prepare for extra support.

☐ Review Chapter 2 of the book.

☐ Collect all materials needed for the unit:

- ☐ **Daily Reflection forms (Appendix 7):** You will need one for each day.
- ☐ **Books:** One copy is required, but you may prefer to secure two copies of each book. After each book has been shared during the unit, place it in an easily accessible display in the classroom. Please give students access to explore these books on their own during free-choice times. You will want to keep the display available for some time after the unit is completed.
- ☐ **Materials already in your classroom:** Please have available and ready to use the following commonplace classroom materials:
  - Chart paper or a section of whiteboard that can remain posted for the duration of the unit
  - Unlined white paper
  - Pencils and pens; colored pencils, crayons, or markers
  - Construction paper or other colored paper
  - Scissors
  - Tape or glue
  - Any additional materials indicated within the unit chapter's detailed description

During: Readings, Discussions, and Activities (approximately 7–10 school days)

☐ Follow the detailed plans for each day.

☐ One to 2 days after the unit is completed, have students complete the Unit Post-Check with Students (Appendix 8).

One Week Following

☐ After reviewing the Unit Post-Check with Students, check in with any students with reactions that cause concern.

☐ Refer any students expressing interest or for whom you have concerns at this point for additional, individual discussion with a school support professional. Also consider additional whole-class work if indicated.

☐ Complete and review Taking the Pulse of the Class: After Unit (Appendix 9). This will help you reflect on your experience and your students' experiences with the thematic book set.

UNIT OVERVIEW
I'm Me!: Talking About Gender and Identity

Day	Books	Discussion and Activities
1	**Whole-Class Read-Aloud #1:** *Drum Dream Girl: How One Girl's Courage Changed Music*	• Defining and Redefining *Girl*
2	**Whole-Class Read-Aloud #2:** *I Dissent: Ruth Bader Ginsburg Makes Her Mark*	• Introducing Vocabulary • Organizing Information

3	**Small Groups Read-Aloud and Discuss #1:** *The International Day of the Girl: Celebrating Girls Around the World*	• Comparing and Contrasting Girls' Experiences
4	**Whole-Class Read-Aloud #3 and #4:** *Tough Boris* *Big Boys Cry*	• Analyzing Pictorial Storytelling • Expectations for Boys
5	**Whole-Class Read-Aloud #5 and #6:** *Sparkle Boy* *Julian Is a Mermaid*	• Defining *Inclusivity* and *Acceptance*
6 and 7	**Conclusion and Small Groups Read-Aloud and Discuss #2:** *Ho'onani Hula Warrior* *When Aidan Became a Brother*	• Personal Identity • Understanding One Another

Note: Each "day" of this unit is intended to take around 1 hour of class time. Time may vary slightly depending on student discussion, but please keep this time frame in mind as you move through the reading and activities.

BEFORE BEGINNING

1. Make sure you have completed the "Two Weeks Prior" and "One Week Prior" items on the planning checklist, including the Taking the Pulse of the Class: Before Unit and the Unit Pre-Check with Students forms.
2. Remember that the books within these units are specifically sequenced to build understanding. To have the greatest likelihood of success with these courageous conversations, we ask that you follow the order of the books, discussions, and activities and complete the entire unit.
3. Review Chapter 2 to help prepare for navigating the upcoming discussions you will be having with your students. As you complete the Daily Reflections at the end of each school day, consider revisiting Chapter 2 for helpful support in engaging in your own self-reflection and awareness, and ensuring your thoughtful and respectful approach to the topic.

DAY 1

Introduction and Discussion and Activity: Defining and Redefining *Girl*
Whole-Class Read-Aloud #1: *Drum Dream Girl: How One Girl's Courage Changed Music*
Time: About 1 hour

Introduction and Discussion and Activity: Defining and Redefining *Girl*

Begin the unit by having your class gather for a discussion. Explain to your class that today you will be reading a story about a girl. Tell your class that, over the next couple of days, you will be reading books about people of all different kinds of genders.

Write the word *girl* on chart paper, circle it, and post the page at the front of the room so all your students can see it. Ask them to think about what it means to be a girl or come up with examples of things girls like. Encourage all your students to develop a concept **Defining *Girl*** and instruct them to raise their hands once they are ready to share it with the class. Once most (or all) of the hands in your classroom are raised, then you can begin calling on students to share their ideas.

- Grow a word web. All responses that your students give can be branched off the main circle labeled "girl."
- Encourage all responses that you get from students. They may present limited views of what a girl can be, but remember, you are teaching this unit in order to help expand students' ideas of what a girl (or a person) can be, **Redefining *Girl*.**
  - Responses could include "long hair," "likes pink," "strong," "wears makeup," "is a mom," and so forth.

> ***Note:*** Depending on the maturity level/knowledge of your students, some may take the conversation in a direction that is focused on specific body parts. If a student brings up bodies, you can condense any responses they give into a single simple point on the chart, such as "certain kinds of bodies." While you write those words, you can also say them. Or, you might want to add something like this:

"That's one way people might think about it, but it's a bit more complicated. Some girls have a vagina, and some don't. Being a girl is about how you feel inside and how you identify yourself. Just like how some boys might have different bodies, but they still know they are boys. Everyone is unique, and what's most important is how you feel and identify yourself."

- Once you have finished your word web, prompt your students to think of a specific girl they know. Once students have that person in mind, tell them to raise their hands.
  - Have students put down their hands. Ask them this question: "Does the girl you have in mind match up with all of the words/phrases that we wrote on the board?"
  - Prompt your students to show either a thumbs up or a thumbs down or a thumbs sideways

based on their answer to the previous question, with thumbs up meaning "yes," thumbs down meaning "no," and thumbs sideways meaning "not sure" or "sort of."

- Select two students who gave a thumbs down and ask them to identify the differences between the girl they have in mind and the words on the board. Select two students who gave a thumbs up (if any) and ask them to explain how the girl they have in mind is exactly the same as the one described on the board.

Whole-Class Read-Aloud and Discuss #1: *Drum Dream Girl: How One Girl's Courage Changed Music*

Explain to your class that you are now going to listen to and look at pictures regarding a story about a girl who doesn't fit into the usual box of what people think a girl should be.

- Pull up the video for the story *Drum Dream Girl*: *www.youtube.com/watch?v=cfMSbC7T6Jw*.
- Ask your students to pay close attention to the story and to the pictures shown on screen.
- Play the video for your students. Be sure that all students are able to hear the audio and that the room is dim enough for the students to see the details in the illustrations. Be sure to keep the video playing after the story ends while the biographical information about Millo Castro Zaldarriagahe is shared.

Immediately after finishing the video, ask your students to think of things that they noticed about the story and/or illustrations. Direct the students to raise their hands when something comes to mind and then call on them to share with the class.

- Ask your students: "How do you think it made Drum Dream Girl feel to be told that she couldn't do something?" Take responses by a raise of hands.
- Remind your students that this story took place a long time ago. Then ask them: "Are there still things today that girls are told that they can't do because they are girls?" Once again, take responses by a raise of hands. When students name things that girls are told they can't do, ask them: "And can girls do that thing?" In most cases, the answer will be "yes." If the answer is "yes," then add the action or deed they named to the word web that you created earlier.
- Once you have taken a sufficient number of responses from students, tell your class to look at the board and to consider all the different things that a person can be.

Segue to Next Day and Daily Reflection

When the discussion begins winding down, let your students know that you are now moving on to the next part of the day, but you will be returning to this topic of gender and identity tomorrow.

When the school day is over, take some time to fill out the Daily Reflection to reflect on this experience. Review it as you prepare for the next day's lesson.

DAY 2

Discussion and Activity: Introducing Vocabulary

Whole-Class Read-Aloud #2: *I Dissent: Ruth Bader Ginsburg Makes Her Mark*

Discussion and Activity: Organizing Information

Time: About 1 hour

Special Materials Needed:

- *I Dissent: Ruth Bader Ginsburg Makes Her Mark* Vocabulary and Comprehension Chart (Appendix 16)

Discussion and Activity: Introducing Vocabulary

Hand out the *I Dissent: Ruth Bader Ginsburg Makes Her Mark* Vocabulary and Comprehension Chart to each student.

The vocabulary handout includes the following words: *dissent, disapprove, not concur.*

- *Dissent.* To have an opinion that is different from the typical one. (The prefix *dis-* means "to do the opposite of," and the root word sent derives from the Latin word *sentire* that means "to feel." So, dissent is to feel the opposite or differently from others.)
- *Disapprove.* To express an unfavorable opinion about something. (If you approve of something, you agree with it. By adding the prefix *dis-* to the root word, you get the opposite of agreeing or approving.)
- *Not concur.* To disagree with the opinion of a person or group.

The handout also includes *object, protest, resist, persist.*

- *Object.* To say something in order to express disagreement.
- *Protest.* To declare a difference in opinion about something that has been done.
- *Resist.* To fight back against.
- *Persist.* To firmly hold an opinion in spite of opposition.

Before giving students these definitions outright, ask if they have guesses as to what any of the words might mean by using morphological clues or their background knowledge. Write down these words on chart paper or your whiteboard as you discuss them with the class. You will leave up this list throughout the rest of the unit for students to refer back to as needed.

As **Introducing Vocabulary** proceeds with your class, be sure to emphasize that the terms being defined are legal terms. That emphasis will help students connect to the fact that Ruth Bader Ginsburg was a lawyer.

Whole-Class Read-Aloud and Discuss #2: *I Dissent: Ruth Bader Ginsburg Makes Her Mark*

Gather your students for a whole-class read-aloud. Introduce *I Dissent* by showing your students the book's cover.

- As you read the story, stop as each vocabulary word appears and remind the class of its definition in order to help contextualize all the surrounding words.
- As you continue reading the book, stop and ask the students what they are noticing about the story and how it is crafted. "What stands out to you? What do you notice?"
- Ask students to think about how Ruth is treated by the world around her. "How does Ruth react to the discrimination that she sees and the experiences in her life?" Explain to the class that Ruth sees, and also experiences, sexism. Define *sexism* for the students as a "type of discrimination against someone, usually women, based solely on their gender/sex."
- When you have finished reading the book to your class, ask your students for their overall response to it. Students may have more questions about Ruth's life or might want to share stories they know of that connect to the book. Answer their questions to the best of your ability and thank them for making connections.

Discussion and Activity: Organizing Information

Prompt your students to return to their seats and flip over their Vocabulary and Comprehension Charts (Appendix 16) to the other side of the paper, which includes the following questions:

1. "What is this person's name?"
2. "What career did she want? Why?"
3. "How did people react to her wanting this career? Did they disapprove, dissent, or not concur? Why?"
4. "What were her overall goals?"
5. "Ruth faced some problems from others in trying to reach her goals. What were some of these obstacles? Would you say people were objecting to, protesting about, or resisting what she was doing?"
6. "Despite obstacles, Ruth kept trying to reach her goals. Name two ways in which she persisted in trying to reach her goals."

Have students work with a seat or elbow partner to find the answers to these questions by **Organizing Information**. Monitor students' progress to help encourage them to stay focused and to answer any questions that might come up. After about 15 minutes of work, have students share their answers as a whole class.

Segue to Next Day and Daily Reflection

When your students are done sharing, tell them that you are now moving on to the next part of the day, but you will be returning to this topic of gender and, through persistence, overcoming inequality tomorrow.

When the school day is over, take some time to fill out the Daily Reflection to reflect on this experience. Review it as you prepare for the next day.

DAY 3

Small Groups Read-Aloud and Discuss #1: *The International Day of the Girl: Celebrating Girls around the World*

Discussion and Activity: Comparing and Contrasting Girls' Experiences

Time: About 1 hour

Special Materials Needed:

- *The International Day of the Girl: Celebrating Girls around the World* Organizational Chart (Appendix 17)

Small Groups Read-Aloud and Discuss #1: *The International Day of the Girl: Celebrating Girls around the World*

Begin by dividing your students into five groups, all roughly around the same size. Give each student *The International Day of the Girl: Celebrating Girls around the World* Organizational Chart (Appendix 17). One of its five pages will be for the girl on whom their group will focus; the other four pages will be used for the remaining girls in the book and completed in the later comparison activity.

Assign a girl to each group. Here are their names and the pages where you can find information on them:

- Liliya (pp. 14–15)
- Sokanon (pp. 16–17)
- Abuya (pp. 12–13)
- Flora (pp. 8–9)
- Hana (pp. 10–11)

Instruct your groups to read their passages together. Circle the room to help provide support and guidance as needed.

Once groups are finished reading the profile of the girl they were assigned, they will complete the Organizational Chart for that girl. As a group, they will answer the following questions listed on the document:

1. "What career did your girl want? Why?"
2. "How did people react to her wanting this career? Did they disapprove, dissent, or not concur? Why?"
3. "What were her overall goals?"
4. "She faced some problems from others in trying to reach her goals. What were some of these obstacles? Would you say people were objecting to, protesting about, or resisting what she was doing?"
5. "Despite obstacles, she kept trying to reach her goals. Name two ways in which she persisted in trying to reach her goals."

Circle the room to help provide support and guidance and feedback as needed.

Once all the students have completed their work, have them gather together as a whole class for the next activity.

Discussion and Activity: Comparing and Contrasting Girls' Experiences

Explain to your class that they will be taking some time to share on their group's girl and then learn about the other girls highlighted in the book from their classmates, **Comparing and Contrasting Girls' Experiences**.

- (1) Each student will take their Organizational Chart and find someone else in the room whose group was assigned a different girl. (2) Then they will share and write down the information for their partner's girl on the corresponding page in their Organizational Chart. ***Note:*** Students should write down only one of the answers to one of the questions and share the rest of the responses orally with their partner. (3) Then ask students to switch partners, finding another student whose group was assigned yet another different girl. This process will be repeated until all students have, through discussion, learned complete information for each of the five girls included in the appendix form and written down one answer for each of those girls in their Chart.
- When all of your students have shared and copied down their notes on the other groups' girls, ask them to return to their seats. Then ask if they relate to these girls in any way. Take responses by a raise of the hand. Be supportive and positive when your students are sharing their experiences.
- Finally, collect the completed Organizational Charts from all your students.

Segue to Next Day and Daily Reflection

When the discussion has concluded, tell your students that you are now moving on to the next part of the day, but you will be returning to this topic of gender tomorrow.

When the school day is over, take some time to fill out the Daily Reflection to reflect on this experience. Review it as you prepare for the next day.

DAY 4

Whole-Class Read-Aloud #3: *Tough Boris*

Discussion and Activities: Analyzing Pictorial Storytelling; Expectations for Boys

Whole-Class Read-Aloud #4: *Big Boys Cry*

Time: About 1 hour

Special Materials Needed:

- Picture Analysis Chart (Appendix 18)

Whole-Class Read-Aloud #3: *Tough Boris*

Begin by writing the word *pirates* on the board and asking your students what they know about them. "What is the first word that comes to your mind?"

- Take responses from students and write their answers, in list form, on the board below the word *pirates*. Students may say *tough* or *evil*; they could also try to subvert expectations at this point in the unit and offer terms like *friendly* or *kind*. Write **all** student responses on the board and thank them for sharing regardless of the students' perceived intentions.
- Once you have compiled the students' answers in a list on the board, let your class know that today you will be reading a picturebook about pirates.

Remind your students that the books you read over the last 2 days were also picturebooks. Ask them: "What kinds of things are included in a picturebook?" Call on students who are raising their hands to share. You are looking for the answers *words/text* and *pictures/illustrations*. When students have given these answers, let them know that in picturebooks, words and pictures are both extremely important in understanding the full story. The words tell us things that the pictures do not, and the pictures tell us things that the words do not. They are dependent on each other to convey the full meaning. Prompt students to look closely at the pictures and listen closely to the words as you read to them today.

Begin reading *Tough Boris* aloud to the whole class. Let students know that you will discuss the pictures and words as a class when you finish reading the book.

- Be sure to hold the book out for all students to see as always and allow plenty of time, but especially with the next several books in this unit because analysis of the pictures is crucial to their understanding of the stories.

While reading the book, ask student volunteers to share details that they notice as the story is being read. Ask them to comment, in particular, on what they observe about the color of illustrations or the particular word choice used. Encourage comments about craft.

Discussion and Activities: Analyzing Pictorial Storytelling; Expectations for Boys

Once you are finished reading, have students return to their seats. Hand out a Picture Analysis Chart (Appendix 18) to each student. It includes an equation: Text + Picture = Story. Guide them through filling out this graphic organizer. This first one will be done as a class, in order to model how it should be done correctly. Future organizers of this type will be done by the students with less and less guidance each time.

> ***Note:*** This activity does not need to include extensive amounts of writing, maybe only a sentence for each section at most. Decide what is most appropriate and attainable for your students. You might want them to work as partners if the writing becomes a barrier.

- Explain to your class that looking at stories in this way—**Analyzing Pictorial Storytelling**—is a very powerful skill that you will be developing over the next couple of days.
- Model three examples of what they will write in this organizer by giving examples for Tough Boris.
- The text says, "He was tough. All pirates are tough." Write this in the first column. Then in the second column, write down the details you notice in the illustrations on this page. How do the pirates look tough? What details suggest they are tough? Finally in the third column, write down what this means: "The pirates are tough because they are strong and have mean expressions, and are stealing buried treasure."
- On the next page, the text says, "He was massive. All pirates are massive." Write this in the first column. Then in the second column, write down the details you notice in the illustrations on this page. How do the pirates look massive? What details suggest they are massive? Finally in the third column, write down what this means: "The pirates are massive because they are a lot bigger than normal men. Their feet are really big and they have big hands, and you can see this compared to the parrot and the birds."
- Tell students that this pattern will continue for some time. The words are only giving us the briefest of description, and the real description lies in the illustrations.
- Tell students to write down two more examples. Check in on their progress by walking around the room.

Once students have completed their work, prompt them to put down their writing utensils and guide their attention to the board. Hang up a new piece of chart paper and write the word *boy* on it, as the center of a word web. This piece of paper should be the same size as the one on which you wrote *girl* on Day 1 of this unit. (If you are writing on the whiteboard, then use the other side of the board for this activity and leave the *girl* chart on its first side.)

- Ask your students what it means to be a boy—what **Expectations for Boys** are. Or, to name some things that they think about when they hear the word *boy*. All responses that your students give can be branched off of the main *boy* circle of the word web.
- Students might say things like *sports, short hair, stinky*. But because of the work that you

are doing in this unit to help them deconstruct their thinking around gender, they may see behind the curtain, in a sense, and say words like *pink* or *Barbies*. Welcome these kinds of responses! Getting students to think in this expansive sort of way is the goal of this unit.

Whole-Class Read-Aloud #4: *Big Boys Cry*

Tell your class that now you are going to read a story about a boy so that you can see if what they are saying about boys is true. Let them know that they should keep paying attention to the words and pictures and practicing this skill. Pass out a Picture Analysis Chart to each student so they can use it while you are reading *Big Boys Cry*. This chart includes the same equation as the one for *Tough Boris* (Text + Picture = Story).

Tell students that while you read, you would like them to notice and comment on the interactions of the text and pictures. They can write down some of these examples on their charts.

Begin reading *Big Boys Cry* out loud to your class.

- Be sure to let all students get a good look at every page, so they can analyze the pictures. Encourage students to stop and comment on what they are noticing and take the time to have them write down feedback related to using the Picture Analysis Chart. Try to have students write down at least four examples.

When you finish reading the book, ask your students if the words they used to describe boys on the word web apply to the boys that you read about in this book. Take student responses by a raise of hands. Some of the words may fit, some may not. Then ask how the words might apply to the pirates in *Tough Boris*.

Ask students if there are some words they would still like to add to the word web. Take all responses as they come and include new ideas.

Segue to Next Day and Daily Reflection

When you are done with the discussion, tell your students that you are now moving on to the next part of the day, but you will be returning to this topic of gender-related expectations tomorrow.

When the school day is over, take some time to fill out the Daily Reflection to reflect on this experience. Review it as you prepare for the next day.

DAY 5

Discussion and Activity: Defining *Inclusivity* and *Acceptance*

Whole-Class Read-Aloud #5 and #6: *Sparkle Boy* and *Julian Is a Mermaid*

Time: About 1 hour, broken into two 30-minute sections

Special Materials Needed:

- Picture Analysis Chart (Appendix 18)

Discussion and Activity: Defining *Inclusivity* and *Acceptance*

Focus the attention of your class to the front of the room. Write the words *inclusivity* and *acceptance* on the whiteboard or on another piece of chart paper. Ask your students if they know what those words mean.

- Take some responses from the class by a raise of hands.
- Then define both words for your class using the definitions below:
  - *Inclusivity.* Making sure that everyone is included and has an equal say or voice.
  - *Acceptance.* Caring for someone as they are regardless of what other people think.
- Ask your students if they can recall a time when they have been inclusive of another, or have accepted someone else unconditionally or been accepted by someone else as they are. Allow some time for them to share.

Tell your students that you are now going to read two books about acceptance and inclusivity. Ask them to watch for examples of both experiences in both stories that you will talk about after you finish reading.

Whole-Class Read-Aloud #5: *Sparkle Boy*

Gather students for a whole-class read-aloud. As you read the book, encourage your students to raise their hands and point out details or events that they notice, especially with regard to the text and illustrations working together, and about this topic of inclusivity and acceptance. Prompt discussion by asking them a few directly related questions: "Who has experience playing with and/or watching after little children?" "How do these children play?" "How would you react if someone was being rude to a little child in front of you?"

When you have finished reading, have students identify and share a few examples of inclusivity and acceptance they noted.

- If the students say that Jessie accepted Casey wearing a girl's clothes and fingernail polish, challenge that thought. Ask them: "Was that always the case? What made Jessie change her mind about how she felt about her brother? Why do you think that happened?"
- (You might let your students know that, even when someone isn't accepting, as was the case with Jessie at first, there is always room, another chance, to begin accepting someone.)
- "What do you think might happen in the future with Jessie and Casey?"

Thank your class for sharing their thoughts with you. Let them know that you will be reading them a second book today after a short break and they will need to draw on their analysis skills, just as they did with *Tough Boris* and *Big Boys Cry*, while you read it.

Whole-Class Read-Aloud #6: *Julian Is a Mermaid*

Make sure that all students in your class can get a good look at this book from their seats. Pass out a Picture Analysis Chart (Appendix 18) to each student that includes the equation (Text

+ Picture = Story). (You might even have students gather closer and hold their charts in their laps to write.)

- Ask students to fill out this chart while you are reading today. They will do so on their own, but encourage them to comment as soon as they notice the connections between illustration and text, writing down these findings.

Show the class the book's dust jacket. Make sure they see both sides of it and read aloud the text on the back: "Abuela, did you see the mermaids?" asked Julian. "I saw them, *mijo*." Then explain that this book has a different cover on its hardbound cover under the dust jacket. Slide off the jacket and show the hardcover to the students. Then show them the front and back endpages of the book. "What do you notice? How do the pictures appear to be opposites? What do you notice about the mermaid images?" Then point out the image on the inside front flap. "How does Julian look differently in the mirror than he does in person?" Next, show students the inside back flap. "What is happening in this image?"

Now, start reading aloud the book, but move slowly, telling students that there are lots of interesting images like these to put together with the text. Ask them to raise their hands and, as you read, comment when they notice some of these examples.

As you move through the story, ask your students to predict what will happen:

- "Do you think Abuela will be upset at Julian for playing dress-up with her things?"
- "Were you surprised where she took him? Why or why not?"
- "How do you think she feels about his dressing up?"
- "How do you think Julian feels when she takes him to the parade?"

After you finish reading, tell students about the Coney Island Mermaid Parade held each year. Explain that this story is set in Brooklyn in New York City, and Julian lives close enough to get to Coney Island with his grandmother on the subway.

Then return to the ideas presented in the story. Ask students what they think about the story overall. Leave the discussion very open. A student might bring up some ideas around gender expression or identity. If this happens, ask the students if the reader knows how Julian identifies in terms of gender. Help them to understand that it is not explicit in the book, so we don't really know the answer to that question; we only know that Julian specifically likes dressing as a mermaid. Talk for a minute about gender expression (how a person publicly expresses or presents their gender). "How do you think Casey (in *Sparkle Boy*) and Julian are different from or similar to each other in terms of their dressing?" Explain that many young children play dress-up in gender nonconforming ways. "What do you think about that? What do you believe society thinks about that in general?"

Segue to Next Day and Daily Reflection

When the discussion comes to a close, tell students that you are now moving on to the next part of the day, but you will be returning to this topic of inclusivity and acceptance tomorrow.

When the school day is over, take some time to fill out the Daily Reflection to reflect on this experience. Review it as you prepare for the next day.

DAYS 6 AND 7

Small Groups Read-Aloud and Discuss #2: *Ho'onani Hula Warrior* and *When Aidan Became a Brother*

Discussion and Activities: Personal Identity; Understanding One Another

Time: 2 hours across 2 days

Small Groups Read-Aloud and Discuss #2: *Ho'onani Hula Warrior* and *When Aidan Became a Brother*

Note: Before class starts today, divide your class into half. Throughout both Days 6 and 7, read aloud the books *Ho'onani Hula Warrior* and *When Aidan Became a Brother* to each group. All students should have a chance to hear and discuss both stories in their small group over the 2 days. Plan for about 20 minutes of read-aloud and discussion for each book.

- Take plenty of time during each small-group read-aloud and discussion to allow students to explore the pages and talk together with you about the way in which the author and illustrator use impactful words in the text, or how colors or shapes in the illustrations convey the strong emotions of the main characters. To do this, ask students to share what they notice about the words and pictures, drawing on their experience of the previous days when they analyzed the pictures and words of the unit's other books.
- Also use the specific prompts below to help students engage with the story and discuss what is happening.
- After you have finished reading the story, engage students in a general share about it. Ask them to share overall thoughts about the craft of the story (what they notice about the illustrations and words working together) and about the content of the books. These are more unusual stories for picturebooks, so your students might want to discuss that aspect.

Ho'onani Hula Warrior

- "Unlike the characters in the other stories we read over the last few days, Ho'onani is a teenager, not a young child. How does that change the book for you? She is also taking on a leadership role. Does that make the story feel different? In what ways?"
- Tell your students that this book is based on a real person named Ho'onani, and her story was told in a documentary film called *A Place in the Middle*. "How does that change the way you understand the story?"
- "What do you think about Ho'onani's family's reactions to her decision to try out for the lead role in the all-male group and to practice for the audition? How is her family different from the families in the other books we have read recently?"

When Aidan Became a Brother

- Aidan is excited to be a big brother and wants the best for his new sibling. "What are some of the ways you notice this in the words and illustrations?"
- We never know exactly how old Aidan is in the story, but he is portrayed as being likely around 4–6 years old. While he is young, he clearly remembers how hard it was for him when people did not know he was a boy. His worries about this same thing happening to his new sibling are very significant, and hint at how challenging this experience must have been for him. "Have you ever worried about something happening to a younger sibling or cousin because you went through it? How does that feel? Do you think Aidan trusts that things will be okay for his new baby sibling?"
- Kyle Lukoff has said his focus in the book was "on what Aidan and his family do right rather than the mistakes they make." This is important given what happened with Aidan, and part of the reason Aidan wants to make things right for this baby. "Do you see this in the story? Where?" Tell students that Lukoff further said he sees people try so hard to do and say the right thing to be supportive of others' gender identities and expressions, and the best thing you can really do is to try your best, and if you make mistakes, then just keep trying.

Discussion and Activities: Personal Identity; Understanding One Another

When all the students have read both books, write on the whiteboard the main characters' names, Aidan and Ho'onani. Then have students help you come up with three adjectives or descriptive words for each of the characters. Write down these words underneath the names. Record several choices that students volunteer and then, as a class, agree on three for each. Circle these. Then discuss which ones you selected. "Did you choose any words that were related to gender, like *boy* or *girl*? Why or why not?"

Then ask students to think of three words that describe themselves. Give them some examples, for instance, *nice, tall, blonde*; *smart, sports, Mexican*; *hyper, funny, Marvel*. Any three words that describe who they are—their **Personal Identity**—whether it's related to gender or not.

Give them some time to think quietly about their three words while you tape up a new piece of chart paper in the same way that you did for both the *girl* and *boy* word web. Ideally, you should hang this third piece of paper between the two other posters. Put the word *person* in the center of this poster in a circle.

Pass out markers to every student. Have your students go up to the "person" poster and write their three words somewhere on it. Have the students come forward in smaller groups so that the front of the room doesn't get too crowded as they all try to write down their words.

When all of the students have included their words on the poster, have them take their seats. They should look at all of the posters together for an **Understanding of One Another**. Then ask them to turn to their elbow or desk partner and share what words they chose and explain why they chose the words they did.

After students have shared for a few minutes in pairs, ask them if any of the words on the posters apply only to boys or only to girls. See how students respond and try to keep the conversation very open-ended. Encourage students to share any last thoughts they have around this topic of gender. Remind them to think of the books they read as a class, from *Drum Dream*

Girl to *Big Boys Cry*, all the way to Aidan and Ho'onani today. Ask them to comment on some of the things they have learned over the last week.

Segue to Next Day and Daily Reflection, Unit Post-Check with Students, and Taking the Pulse of the Class: After Unit

Explicitly help your students segue by letting them know you are now moving to the next part of the day, and this is the end of the unit on gender and identity. Let them know that the books will remain in the classroom for some time and that they are welcome to revisit them. Also tell them that, although the unit may have been completed, these conversations can always continue around its topic, and they should feel free to ask questions or discuss the topic in more detail.

When the school day is over, take some time to complete the Daily Reflection form. The next day or the day after that, ask your students to complete the Unit Post-Check with Students. Finally, about a week to 10 days after the unit was completed, fill out Taking the Pulse of the Class: After Unit to consider more broadly this experience for your current students, yourself, and your future students.

FINAL SUGGESTIONS

During the weeks following this unit, you might want to revisit some of these books or the conversations around them. This unit was intended as an introduction to, and the beginning of courageous conversations around the topic of gender and identity.

Some students may want to continue to discuss this topic in class. Reach out to your school counselors, psychologists, and support faculty for individual help for students seeking more specific or individualized support in this area. The Unit Post-Check with Students form will help you identify the students needing or wanting this support.

You may encounter students or families that want more information surrounding the topic that extends past what may have been discussed in the classroom. The websites that follow may serve as good resources for you to share.

ADDITIONAL RESOURCES

Ehrensaft, Diane. *The Gender Creative Child.* The Experiment, 2016. *https://dianeehrensaft.com/books*

Human Rights Campaign. "Transgender Children and Youth: Understanding the Basics." *www.hrc.org/resources/transgender-children-and-youth-understanding-the-basics*

Kenney, Lisa, and Stephanie Brill. *The Transgender Teen.* Cleis Press, 2016. *www.simonandschuster.net/books/The-Transgender-Child/Stephanie-Brill/9781573443180*

Movement Advancement Project. "Get the Facts About Transgender Youth" infographic. *www.lgbtmap.org/file/Advancing%20Acceptance%20Infographic%20FINAL.pdf*

Movement Advancement Project and GLSEN. "Separation and Stigma: Transgender Youth and School Facilities." *www.lgbtmap.org/transgender-youth-school*

Trans Youth Family Allies. "Learning the Lingo." *www.imatyfa.org/assets/learning-the-lingo-06-08(1).pdf*

The Trevor Project's Resource Center: *www.thetrevorproject.org/resources/guide/additional-resources/#sm.000ii7pti11knexkwgc2nt870xy2d*

MEETING COMMON CORE AND CASEL STANDARDS

Common Core English Language Arts Standards for Grade 4

This unit meets specific Common Core State Standards for English Language Arts in grades 3, 4, 5, and 6. We have included the specific ELA standards for grade 4 below to illustrate the strands and items met (similar for all four grades third through sixth). The QR code here will link you to the specific lists for grades 3, 5, and 6.

CCSS.ELA-LITERACY.SL.4.1

Engage effectively in a range of collaborative discussions (one-on-one, in groups, and teacher-led) with diverse partners on *grade 4 topics and texts*, building on others' ideas and expressing their own clearly.

CCSS.ELA-LITERACY.RL.4.1

Refer to details and examples in a text when explaining what the text says explicitly and when drawing inferences from the text.

CCSS.ELA-LITERACY.RL.4.3

Describe in depth a character, setting, or event in a story or drama, drawing on specific details in the text (e.g., a character's thoughts, words, or actions).

CCSS.ELA-LITERACY.RL.4.4

Determine the meaning of words and phrases as they are used in a text, including those that allude to significant characters found in mythology (e.g., Herculean).

CCSS.ELA-LITERACY.RL.4.7

Make connections between the text of a story or drama and a visual or oral presentation of the text, identifying where each version reflects specific descriptions and directions in the text.

CASEL Social and Emotional Learning Standards for Grades 3–5

This unit meets specific CASEL Core Competence Area goals for Social and Emotional Learning for grades 3–5. We have included the CASEL areas and specific example standards below to show the items met in this unit. (The items are similar for grade 6.)

Self-Awareness: The abilities to understand one's own emotions, thoughts, and values and how they influence behavior across contexts. This includes capacities to recognize one's strengths and limitations with a well-grounded sense of confidence and purpose. Such as:

- Integrating personal and social identities
- Identifying personal, cultural, and linguistic assets
- Examining prejudices and biases
- Experiencing self-efficacy

Social Awareness: The abilities to understand the perspectives of and empathize with others, including those from diverse backgrounds, cultures, and contexts. This includes the capacities to feel compassion for others, understand broader historical and social norms for behavior in different settings, and recognize family, school, and community resources and supports. Such as:

- Taking others' perspectives
- Recognizing strengths in others
- Demonstrating empathy and compassion
- Showing concern for the feelings of others
- Identifying diverse social norms, including unjust ones
- Recognizing situational demands and opportunities

Relationship Skills: The abilities to establish and maintain healthy and supportive relationships and to effectively navigate settings with diverse individuals and groups. This includes the capacities to communicate clearly, listen actively, cooperate, work collaboratively to problem-solve and negotiate conflict constructively, navigate settings with differing social and cultural demands and opportunities, provide leadership, and seek or offer help when needed. Such as:

- Communicating effectively
- Developing positive relationships
- Practicing teamwork and collaborative problem solving

Responsible Decision Making: The abilities to make caring and constructive choices about personal behavior and social interactions across diverse situations. This includes the capacity to consider ethical standards and safety concerns and to evaluate the benefits and consequences of various actions for personal, social, and collective well-being. Such as:

- Demonstrating curiosity and open-mindedness
- Identifying solutions for personal and social problems

My Name

Talking About Ability and Identity

THE BOOKS

I Talk Like a River

by Jordan Scott, illustrated by Sydney Smith (Holiday House, 2020)

Sydney Smith's watercolor illustrations place us squarely in the perspective of a young boy moving through a difficult "bad speech" day, evoking empathy in the reader for the strong emotional reaction he has to the challenges his stuttering is causing him in the classroom. When his father arrives to pick him up from school, a walk by the river soothes his frazzled and sad feelings. A chance description from his dad ("See how that water moves? That's how you speak") creates a powerful mantra for the boy. Jordan Scott's poetic text rings with both sincerity and verve; a final note in the book explains this is his true story.

I Will Dance

by Nancy Bo Flood, illustrated by Julianna Swaney (Atheneum Books for Young Readers, 2020)

Eva dreams of dancing, especially performing with a group. But her cerebral palsy limits the motions she can make. A local dance class for dancers of all abilities helps make her dreams come true. Nancy Bo Flood's lyrical text, and Julianna Swaney's illustrations, do not shy away from the realities of Eva's situation, including her frustrations with those telling her to pretend or to imagine dancing, making readers fully understand the powerful impact of her ultimate experience with the dance class.

A Friend for Henry

by Jenn Bailey, illustrated by Mika Song (Chronicle Books, 2019)

Henry, like many young students at the beginning of school, searches for a friend in his new class. He quickly discovers that he does not like the way some of his new classmates react or behave, and he feels frustrated in his quest to find someone with whom to connect. Henry's difficulties with social situations make his own more challenging than most, and Jenn Bailey's quiet entry into his thoughts, allows the reader to empathize and better understand his pain. Happily, an encounter at the goldfish bowl leads to the start of a special friendship with Katie.

Emmanuel's Dream: The True Story of Emmanuel Ofosu Yeboah

by Laurie Ann Thompson, illustrated by Sean Qualls (Random House, 2015)

The inspiring 400-mile bicycle journey of Emmanuel Ofosu Yeboah across Ghana is re-told in this picturebook biography that explains Emmanuel's early life and why he undertook this challenge. Born with a limb difference at a time when some in his community viewed this as a curse, Emmanuel faced great obstacles and prejudice. His decision to draw attention to the plight of people with disabilities in his country helped to change legislation and practices. The lyrical text by Laurie Ann Thompson and Sean Qualls's captivating mixed-media illustrations capture readers' interest and draw them to discover more.

Six Dots: A Story of Young Louis Braille

by Jen Bryant, illustrated by Boris Kulikov (Knopf, 2016)

Jen Bryant's picturebook biography of inventor Louis Braille poignantly re-creates the emotional dimension of his childhood and teen years, starting with the accident that left him blind. Braille's determination shines through the story helping the reader to understand both his brilliance and his dedication to creating a system that would improve the opportunities for people with visual impairment to read.

The Girl Who Thought in Pictures: The Story of Dr. Temple Grandin

by Julia Finley Mosca, illustrated by Daniel Rieley (The Innovation Press, 2017)

The rhyming text of Julia Finley Mosca, and engaging cartoon-style illustrations by Daniel Rieley, capture the early life and accomplishments of Dr. Temple Grandin in picturebook format. The focus on Temple's childhood struggles will ring authentically with young readers and highlight the pivotal moments (a move to a ranch, an encounter with an encouraging science teacher) that helped pave her path toward many animal science discoveries. Rich and accessible back matter extends the details conveyed in the book and offers a deeper exploration of Temple's life.

Just Ask! Be Different, Be Brave, Be You

by Sonia Sotomayor, illustrated by Rafael Lopez (Houghton Mifflin Harcourt, 2018)

Supreme Court Justice Sonia Sotomayor offers a collective look at how individual differences can enhance communities. Beautifully illustrated by award-winning artist Rafael Lopez, the book offers a garden metaphor to help consider difference related to ability. A series of questions helps young readers explore individual situations and sends a message about the importance of learning about one another in order to build a stronger and more inclusive community.

What Happened to You

by James Catchpole, illustrated by George Karen (Little, Brown Books for Young Readers, 2021)

How do you address difference? A young boy playing pirates on the playground is confronted by children asking, and guessing, about his missing limb. Finally, a girl thoughtfully asks if he ever gets tired of that question. He admits that constant questions are tiring and that all he really wants right now is a friend with whom to play pirates. Understanding this, the other kids soon join in on the game, focusing on having fun together rather than his limb difference. James Catchpole based his story on his own childhood experiences and tackles the topic with sensitivity and humor.

Awesomely Emma: A Charley and Emma Story

by Amy Webb, illustrated by Merrilee Liddiard (Beaming Books, 2020)

During a class field trip to the museum, Emma is required to enter a different way than her classmates due to her limb differences and the lack of an accessible entrance. She becomes further frustrated when her well-meaning friend then tries to assist her with tasks she can manage on her own. Emma takes this moment to explain how her friend can truly be supportive by becoming an ally and helping her advocate for herself and others with similar challenges. Amy Webb bases her "Emma" stories, illustrated by Merrilee Liddiard, on the real-life experiences of her daughter.

Note: As with all thematic book sets, we recommend that after each book has been shared within the unit, it is placed in an easily accessible display in the classroom for the rest of the unit days. Children should then be allowed access to explore these books on their own during free-choice times.

PLANNING CHECKLIST

My Name: Talking About Ability and Identity

We suggest the following timeline to prepare and then share and discuss the books and do the related activities with your students. (A reproducible version of this checklist is available in Appendix 1.) Please note that timing for your individual class should be determined by your situation and your schedule, and, most importantly, should be guided by your students' reactions to the books and activities. Plan generally, however, on about 1 hour of daily time with the unit for 7–10 days in a row.

Two Weeks Prior

- ☐ Complete Taking the Pulse of the Class: Before Unit (Appendix 2) for a general sense of your class at this time.
- ☐ Collect and read twice each of the books for the unit.
- ☐ Review the "Unit Plans: Reading, Discussions, and Activities" section of the unit.
- ☐ Send out the Administration Notification Slip (Appendix 3) and School Counselor/ Psychologist and Support Staff Notification Slip (Appendix 4).

One Week Prior

- ☐ (Optional) Send out Family Notification Slips (Appendix 5) to the families of your students.
- ☐ Have students complete the Unit Pre-Check with Students (Appendix 6) and review the results carefully. Check in with any students with reactions that cause concern so that you can prepare for extra support.
- ☐ Review Chapter 2 of the book.
- ☐ Collect all materials needed for the unit:
  - ☐ **Daily Reflection forms (Appendix 7):** You will need one for each day.
  - ☐ **Books:** One copy is required, but you may prefer to secure two copies of each book. After each book has been shared during the unit, place it in an easily accessible display in the classroom. Please give students access to explore these books on their own during free-choice times. You will want to keep the display available for some time after the unit is completed.
  - ☐ **Materials already in your classroom:** Please have available and ready to use the following commonplace classroom materials:
    - Chart paper or a section of whiteboard that can remain posted for the duration of the unit
    - Unlined white paper
    - Pencils and pens; colored pencils, crayons, or markers
    - Construction paper or other colored paper
    - Scissors
    - Tape or glue
    - Any additional materials indicated within the unit chapter's detailed description

During: Readings, Discussions, and Activities (approximately 7–10 school days)

- ☐ Follow the detailed plans for each day.
- ☐ One to 2 days after the unit is completed, have students complete the Unit Post-Check with Students (Appendix 8).

One Week Following

- ☐ After reviewing the Unit Post-Check with Students, check in with any students with reactions that cause concern.
- ☐ Refer any students expressing interest or for whom you have concerns at this point for additional, individual discussion with a school support professional. Also consider additional whole-class work if indicated.
- ☐ Complete and review Taking the Pulse of the Class: After Unit (Appendix 9). This will help you reflect on your experience and your students' experiences with the thematic book set.

UNIT OVERVIEW *My Name*: Talking About Ability and Identity		
Day	**Books**	**Discussion and Activities**
1	**Introduction and Whole-Class Read-Aloud #1:** *I Talk Like a River*	• "How I Speak" • Key Terms
2	**Whole-Class Read-Aloud #2 and #3:** *I Will Dance* *A Friend for Henry*	• Common Denominator Game
3	**Small Groups Read-Aloud and Discuss #1 and #2:** *Emmanuel's Dream: The True Story of Emmanuel Ofosu Yeboah* *Six Dots: A Story of Young Louis Braille*	• Timeline
4	**Whole-Class Read-Aloud #4:** *The Girl Who Thought in Pictures: The Story of Dr. Temple Grandin*	• Inner/Outer Self
5	**Whole-Class Read-Aloud #5:** *Just Ask! Be Different, Be Brave, Be You*	• Question and Response
6	**Whole-Class Read-Aloud #6:** *What Happened to You?*	• Post-Reading Discussion
7	**Whole-Class Read-Aloud #7:** *Awesomely Emma: A Charley and Emma Story*	• P.O.V. Diary Entry
8	**Conclusion**	• Accessibility: Noticing and Advocating

> ***Note:*** Each "day" of this unit is intended to take around 1 hour of class time. Time may vary slightly depending on student discussion, but please keep this time frame in mind as you move through the reading and activities.

BEFORE BEGINNING

1. Make sure you have completed the "Two Weeks Prior" and "One Week Prior" items on the planning checklist, including the Taking the Pulse of the Class: Before Unit and the Unit Pre-Check with Students forms.
2. Remember that the books within these units are specifically sequenced to build understanding. To have the greatest likelihood of success with these courageous conversations, we ask that you follow the order of the books, discussions, and activities and complete the entire unit.
3. Review Chapter 2 to help prepare for navigating the upcoming discussions you will be having with your students. As you complete the Daily Reflections at the end of each school day, consider revisiting Chapter 2 for helpful support in engaging in your own self-reflection and awareness, and ensuring your thoughtful and respectful approach to the topic.

DAY 1

Introduction and Whole-Class Read-Aloud #1: *I Talk Like a River*

Discussion and Activities: "How I Speak"; Key Terms

Time: About 1 hour

Special Materials Needed:

- "How I Speak" (Appendix 19) worksheet

Introduction and Whole-Class Read-Aloud #1: *I Talk Like a River*

Begin by gathering your class for a whole-class read-aloud. Show the students the dust jacket cover of the book. Then slip off the jacket and show students the different illustration underneath on the hardcover of the book. Ask students what they notice about the illustrations. What do they think this book might be about?

As you start to read aloud, move through the pages slowly. There are not many words, but there is a lot to take in with the rich illustrations. Stop and pause every few pages to ask students what they notice as they listen and look closely at the illustrations. Keep this sharing very open-ended, but also use some of the prompts below to help evoke your students' meaning-making.

- First spread: "What do you think about how the illustrator arranged this page? Did it surprise you? How did the author capture what it can feel like to first wake up in the morning?" (***Note:*** Some students may comment on the light in the illustrations. Smith's skill with capturing lighting is very strong and something you might want to point out throughout the book.)
- Second spread: "What do you think the boy means when he says, 'And I can't say them at all'? How do you think that relates to the title *I Talk Like a River*?
- Third spread: "How does the close perspective of the boy's face here make you feel? Why do you think the illustrator chose this perspective?"
- Fifth spread: "Look at the difference between the two images. How does the boy feel when everyone turns to look at him? Why do you think the picture is blurry?" (Ask students to think about how they feel when they are put on the spot. Some might comment that the blur could come from tears in his eyes as well.)
- Seventh spread: "The break in the text here slows down your reading. Why do you think the author and illustrator decided to do that?"
- Eighth and ninth spreads: "Look at the difference between the blur in the car illustration and the greater clarity in the walking by the river illustration. What is the illustrator telling you about how the boy feels now?"
- Tenth spread: Stop here for a minute and ask students to discuss the sun image on the left-hand illustration. Ask, "Does looking at this make you squint?"

- Eleventh spread: "What does this statement mean: 'I feel a storm in my belly; my eyes fill with rain'?"
- Take a minute to pause and ponder the middle foldout page. Ask, "What do you notice as you examine this large illustration?" Point out the light and ask students if it reminds them of the sunlight a few pages before that made them squint! Fold the papers back and ask students to look at the light behind the boy as well. Ask, "What do you think the illustrator is telling us with his use of sunlight here?"
- Read slowly through the remaining pages until you reach the end.
- After showing the last illustration, tell students there is an "Author's Note" that you will read aloud to them in just a minute.
- Then ask your students to share their overall thoughts about the book.

Discussion and Activities: "How I Speak"; Key Terms

After students have shared some immediate, overall feedback, have them return to their seats; pass out copies of the **"How I Speak"** (Appendix 19) worksheet. If possible, also project it on your whiteboard. Then turn to the very last page of the picturebook, labeled "How I Speak." Explain to the class that this is a note from the author, Jordan Scott. Read the whole page aloud to the class.

After reading the whole "Author's Note," return to the fifth paragraph that introduces the questions on the worksheet. Ask students to review the questions and then discuss them together with their elbow or desk partners. Give them about 5 minutes to discuss the questions together thoughtfully. Explain that they do not need to write down anything, but that there is space for notes if they would like to make them. Once pairs have concluded their discussions, ask for a few to share their experiences with the entire class.

Now, use this discussion as a starting point for talking about the links between abilities and identities.

- Using the same page in the book ("How I Speak"), reread the first, sixth, and seventh paragraphs to the whole class.
- Tell students that these paragraphs are more focused on how sometimes abilities can make individuals feel isolated and lonely. Ask students to share comments on this idea.

Next, engage students in defining the **Key Words** in the unit: *ability* and *identity*.

- On a piece of chart paper (or on a part of your whiteboard that you can leave up for the next 2 weeks), write the word *ability*. Ask students to help you think through how this word is defined.
- Point out that the root word is *able*, which means "to do or act on something," and the suffix *-ity* expresses the "state of being able"; thus help them understand that ability is

defined as being able to do something. (Write this definition down on the chart paper or whiteboard.)

  - Be sure to guide students to include some phrases around the variability/variance of ability. Emphasize that *ability* changes—with effort, it can improve and change. Be clear with students that the concept of ability is not a "can versus cannot" but rather a "to what extent" one can do something.
  - Help students notice defining words and phrases that seem more negative or positive and discuss that. (**Note:** *Disability* has a **negative** connotation; try to focus on ability.)

- Now, write the word *identity*. Again, ask students to help you think through how this word is defined. (If you have previously defined this word as a class in other units, you can use the definition you arrived at as a class at that time.)
  - Help students come to a definition like this one: *Identity* is all of the parts that make us who we are. Identities can include our family, ancestors, history, and cultural heritage. Identity is also connected to how we want to express ourselves and be viewed by others. This can include our race, gender, and ability.
- Inform students that you will return to your definitions of these words as you continue with the unit.

Segue to Next Day and Daily Reflection

Explicitly help your students segue by letting them know you are now moving to the next part of the day, but you will be returning to this topic of different types of abilities and identities tomorrow.

When the school day is over, take some time to fill out the Daily Reflection to reflect on today's experience. Review it as you prepare for the next day.

DAY 2

Whole-Class Read-Aloud #2 and #3: *I Will Dance* and *A Friend for Henry*

Discussion and Activity: Common Denominator Game

Time: About 1 hour (if possible, break up this time into a 20-minute block for the first read-aloud and then take a break; the second read-aloud and the game will take about 40 minutes)

Whole-Class Read-Aloud and Discuss #2 and #3: *I Will Dance* and *A Friend for Henry*

> ***Note:*** Today, you will read two books aloud to your class as whole-class read-alouds. Both books are on the shorter side, so the read-alouds will move along more quickly than was the case with *I Talk Like a River*. However, still be sure to encourage students to notice things and comment out loud as they are listening to the story.

Begin by gathering your class for a whole-class read-aloud of *I Will Dance*.

- Start by showing the book's cover to the class and ask them what they notice. After a few students have shared, explain that this story is told from the perspective of a young girl who very much wants to be part of a dance class.
- Read the story aloud slowly, pausing from time to time to ask students what they notice about the illustrations. (If a student mentions or asks if these classes are real, explain that many dance companies have all-abilities classes. That information is a surprise to the characters in this book, but such classes are increasingly offered by dance companies and schools.)

Note: Stop reading on the last page of the story. Do not read aloud the "Author's Note" at the back of the book. It is written for adult readers and has a tone that may encourage othering. Stop your read-aloud on the last page of the actual story.

- When you have finished the story, ask students to share their overall reaction with a partner, the student sitting next to them.
- After students have shared in their pair for a few minutes, ask them all to consider something they do now that they thought they would not be able to do before they tried it. First, direct students to think about this in silence for 30 seconds. Then have them share their thoughts with their partner.
- After students have shared with their partner for a couple of minutes, ask if anyone would like to share their personal experience with the class.
- Then ask students to think about the main character's identity. What are some of the identifiers she might use for herself?
    - Students will likely include *dancer* in their responses. Once they do, ask students if they think she would have used that identifier before she started the class. Why or why not?
    - Then ask students to consider how belonging to different groups or communities can be part of determining one's self-identity.

After a short break, gather students to read aloud as a whole class the second book for today: *A Friend for Henry*.

- After reading aloud the title and showing its dust jacket cover, ask students as a class to share the ways they make friends. Students might be hesitant to share at first, but after you have a few comments, then ask students, "Have you ever seen toddlers make friends or engage another toddler to play with them? How do they do it?" After students have responded to this question, ask the class, "How does making friends change when you get older?" Encourage students to think about *where* they make friends (at activities they attend, at school, etc.) and *how* they decide if another person might make a potential friend.
- Tell students that in this story Henry is trying to find a friend. Then begin reading the book.
- Stop a few times during the read-aloud to ask students what they are thinking about Henry and his process of discerning with whom he wants to try and make friends. Help students

notice that this is likely a preschool or kindergarten class (draw attention to details in the setting that convey this) and that Henry is fairly sure of what he likes and does not like.

- After finishing the story, ask students to share their general response to it. Note that some students may notice that Henry might have characteristics that relate to autism. If this is mentioned, encourage students to consider whether this matters to his friend making, gradually helping them to see that Henry simply states more clearly than we might be accustomed to his dislikes and likes, who he thinks might make a good friend. Also, remind students that we are reading the book from Henry's perspective, so we see the things he does not say aloud.

Discussion and Activity: Common Denominator Game

Now, engage students in playing the **Common Denominator Game**.

- Begin by having the class stand up and form a very large circle facing each other.
- Explain to the students that you will call out a variety of identifiers and that students should step into the circle if they feel they "match" the identifier. They do not need to say anything; this is a silent game. They will stand there for a second and then step out when you indicate it is time for the next round.
- Start with one example and then begin the real game. Play 10–15 rounds. Be sure to include plenty of identifiers that you know will apply to several children in the room. Below are a few suggestions:
    - Favorite season is winter
    - Loves to play soccer
    - Likes broccoli
    - Has one or more siblings
    - Prefers indoor recess over outdoor recess
    - Has different vision in both eyes
    - Has been to another state
    - Speaks another language
    - Walks to school
    - Favorite subject is math
- After several rounds, direct students to sit down in their spot. Tell them that this game makes it easy to quickly see that you have things in common with, and different from, others in the circle.
- Ask students if anyone had the exact same identifiers as another person. (There might have been a few that were close!) Then ask students if they were surprised to learn that other people had some of the same identifiers they did.
- Remind students that we are all individuals with many different types of identities and preferences. Together, those characteristics make us who we are and help to create a class community.

Ask students to look at the chart paper with the definitions for *ability* and *identity*. Read both aloud. Then ask students to reflect on the two stories read today and the game they just played. With that in mind, do they want to add any words or phrases to the definitions? What are some other ways to think about identity, for example? Add to the chart as needed.

Segue to Next Day and Daily Reflection

Explicitly help your students segue by letting them know you are now moving to the next part of the day, but you will be returning to this topic of ability and identity tomorrow.

When the school day is over, take some time to fill out the Daily Reflection to reflect on today's experience. Review it as you prepare for the next day.

DAY 3

Small Groups Read-Aloud and Discuss #1 and #2: *Emmanuel's Dream: The True Story of Emmanuel Ofosu Yeboah* and *Six Dots: A Story of Young Louis Braille*

Discussion and Activity: Timeline

Time: 1 hour total (this time will need to be broken into three blocks of about 20 minutes each)

Special Materials Needed:

- Story Timelines (Appendix 20) worksheet

Small Groups Read-Aloud and Discuss #1 and #2: *Emmanuel's Dream: The True Story of Emmanuel Ofosu Yeboah* and *Six Dots: A Story of Young Louis Braille*

Before school begins today, divide your class into two groups. You will read aloud and discuss *Emmanuel's Dream* with the first group while the other group is engaged in different schoolwork, and you will read aloud and discuss *Six Dots* with the second group while the first one is doing other schoolwork. You will need to arrange for these two read-aloud and discussion time blocks as well as a third time block during which all students will work on the related timeline activity. The reading and discussion blocks will take about 20 minutes each, and the timeline activity block about 20 minutes. Today's lesson altogether will take approximately 1 hour.

Start by informing students that the class is going to read three books over the next 2 days (Days 3 and 4), but only one of them will be read aloud to each group today. Explain that all these books are biographies of famous adults who had disabilities from birth or a young age. Two of the figures have physical disabilities, a limb difference and blindness, and one has autism. The class will learn a little bit about all three people.

Conduct today's two read-alouds with each group. During your read-aloud of both books, start by examining their dust jackets. Both books include phrases on the back cover; read these aloud to the class. Ask students to comment on what they notice and to make predictions about the life of the main character.

Then begin reading aloud. Stop every few pages to discuss the book using one or more of these prompts to draw attention to both the content of the story and to the craft of the book:

- "What do you notice about this page?"
- "How do you think the main character feels right now? What in the illustrations or in the text helps tell you this?
- "Why do you think the illustrator made the decision to draw this scene in this way? How does it add more meaning to what the words are saying?"
- "Why do you believe the author used this word (or phrase) here? Why does it have an impact? How does the word (or phrase) match or work with the illustrations?"

In addition, use the specific prompts below for the books read aloud.

Emmanuel's Dream

- First spread: Ask students what they notice about the looks on the mother's and father's faces.
- Fourth spread: "What do you think about Emmanuel getting to school?"
- Eleventh spread: "Why do you think Emmanuel's plan was especially about riding a bike?" (Connect back to the earlier bike scene when he was at school.)
- Twelfth spread: Ask students why Emmanuel might have wanted the king's royal blessing.
- When you have finished reading the story, share the "Author's Note" with your students.

Six Dots

This is a longer picturebook, so you will want to keep the pace moving a bit more quickly.

- Before reading, show students the front and back endpages that give the braille alphabet. Ask them what other places they have seen braille written.
- Then explain that, because the story is about Louis Braille, who was French, it contains many French phrases and names. Show students the pronunciation guide that comes before the title page and explain that, when they look at the book later on their own, they might want to use the guide.
- On the third spread, the pages change to black with faint greenish outlines in contrast to the fully colored pages beforehand. Ask students why they think the illustrator made this design choice. As you read through the book, notice when it happens again and discuss why.
- When you finish the story, read aloud the "Author's Note." Ask students what they believe the author's intent was. Do they think the book captured what Louis Braille might have felt like? (Tell students that more information about Louis Braille appears on the last two pages of the book and they may want to explore those pages later on.)

Discussion and Activity: Timeline

When you have completed the read-aloud and discussion for each of the two books cited above, pass out the Story Timelines (Appendix 20) worksheet. Have students complete the **Timeline** for the life events of whichever character they learned about (Emmanuel or Louis). They might work in pairs or small groups with others who heard the same story. Circle the room while they collaborate, providing support as necessary. Give students about 10 minutes to complete the timelines.

When the students are finished, help them form jigsaw groups of two people who read about Emmanuel and two people who read about Louis. Students will share details about, and compare, the lives of Emmanuel and Louis, using their timelines as a guide for that discussion. Give students about 5 minutes to do this.

Finally, draw students' attention as a whole class to the front of the room. Ask students to look at the definitions of *ability* and *identity* on the chart paper. Ask them to reflect on the two stories read today and the Timeline activity just completed. After having learned about Emmanuel and Louis, are there other ways in which those two men might have thought of the term *ability* or *identity?*

- On the chart paper, include any additions to the definitions of *ability* and *identity* that students suggest.

Segue to Next Day and Daily Reflection

Collect students' timelines and explicitly help your students segue by letting them know you are now moving to the next part of the day, but you will be returning to this topic of ability and identity, as reflected in life events, tomorrow.

When the school day is over, take some time to fill out the Daily Reflection to reflect on today's experience. Review it as you prepare for the next day.

DAY 4

Whole-Class Read-Aloud #4: *The Girl Who Thought in Pictures: The Story of Dr. Temple Grandin*

Discussion and Activity: Inner/Outer Self

Time: About 1 hour

Whole-Class Read-Aloud #4: *The Girl Who Thought in Pictures: The Story of Dr. Temple Grandin*

Today, you will continue learning about famous adults who were born with disabilities or developed them at a young age by reading and discussing our third biography, which is about Dr. Temple Grandin, a person with autism.

On a new piece of chart paper or on the whiteboard, list the three characters' names: Emmanuel, Louis, and Temple. Under each write the words *Physical Traits* and *Personal Attributes*. Explain to the class what these two terms mean:

- *Physical Traits.* "What would you notice and learn about a person after meeting them for the first time and having a short conversation with them?"
- *Personal Attributes.* "What would you learn about a person's personality traits after spending a day with them or reading about their lives?"

Have your students help fill in ideas on the two lists for Emmanuel and for Louis.

Then begin a whole-class read-aloud of *The Girl Who Thought in Pictures: The Story of Dr. Temple Grandin.*

- Before they start to read, ask students to picture a cow in their mind. Show them the cover. Then show them the inside cover and ask if the picture in their mind matches any of the cows depicted there.
- As Temple grows older, we start to see dashed lines in the illustrations connecting her thoughts and ideas. Ask students what Temple is thinking about on each of these pages. The first one shows flies. On the next page, Temple stands next to a cow, and the like.
- When you have finished the story, ask students to share their overall reaction with a partner. Then direct students' attention to the material at the back of the book. Show students the timeline, which is very similar to what they created for Louis and Emmanuel! Next, show them the pages of biographical information and further resources to explore, and suggest that they look at this material when they explore the book on their own at some time over the next few weeks. Then flip back to the page that is titled "Fun Facts and Tidbits From the Author's Chat with Temple!" and say:

  "These are interesting nuggets the author called out and they are all connected to something she portrays in the main pages of the biography. For example, one of the sections addresses the sexism that Temple faced in her work as an animal scientist in the 1970s, a time when there were few women working in that role."

Remind students that people have multiple identities and that Temple's identity as a woman is just one part of who she is in addition to her identity as a person with autism.

Now, have students look at the board where the traits and attributes from Emmanuel and Louis's stories are listed. Ask them to help you add a traits and attributes list for Temple.

Discussion and Activity: Inner/Outer Self

When you have finished listing the physical traits and personal attributes for Temple as a class, have students return to their seats. Tell the class that they will now be participating in an activity called **Inner/Outer Self**.

- Pass out a blank piece of paper to each student. Students should then draw an oval as the outline of a face. Give students a minute to quickly draw in the features of the face.
- Then tell students to draw a line down the middle of the face so it is split in two! One half of the face will represent their inner self; have them label it as such. The other half will represent their outer self; have them label it as such.
- (If possible, model this on the whiteboard or using an overhead projector while students are working.)
- Explain to students that personal attributes are what makes the inner self. Physical traits are the outer self.
- Use the questions from earlier to help each student answer questions about their inner and outer selves: "What would someone notice and learn about **you** after meeting you for the first time? What would someone notice and learn about you after having a short conversation with you? What would one learn about your personality traits after spending a day with you, or reading about your accomplishments and life?"
  - Now, on their faces, students should write or draw the answers to these questions.
  - For their inner self, they could draw ballet slippers if they like to dance, a book if they enjoy reading, a tree if they like going outside, or write the words *brave*, *determined*, and so forth.
  - For their outer self, they could make the features on that half of their face look like them and also write additional descriptive words about themself (*tall*, *9 years old*, etc.).
- Give students about 20 minutes to work on this project. Then have students share their drawings with an elbow or desk partner.

Segue to Next Day and Daily Reflection

Collect the Inner/Outer Self papers and explicitly help your students segue by letting them know you are now moving to the next part of the day, but you will be returning to this topic of revealing your identity tomorrow.

When the school day is over, take some time to fill out the Daily Reflection to reflect on today's experience. Review it as you prepare for the next day.

DAY 5

Whole-Class Read-Aloud #5: *Just Ask! Be Different, Be Brave, Be You*

Discussion and Activity: Question and Response

Time: About 1 hour

Special Materials Needed:

- Question and Response (Appendix 21) worksheet

Whole-Class Read-Aloud #5: *Just Ask! Be Different, Be Brave, Be You*

Gather your students for a whole-class read-aloud. Begin by introducing the book and explaining who Sonia Sotomayor is. Then explain her connection to Emmanuel, Louis, and Temple; explain that she is someone who "lives with a challenging condition but whose courage, determination, and grit sustains them every day." (This is a direct quote from Sonia in the acknowledgments at the end of the book.)

Show your class the book cover and read aloud its title as well as the words on the back cover. Ask students what they notice and briefly discuss that it appears as if this book might be about gardening.

Begin by reading aloud "A Letter to Readers" at the beginning of the book:

- After you finish reading this letter, ask students if they know what the word *inclusive* means. Come to a working definition as a class, something similar to this: *Inclusive means to include all people or to include all groups involved in something.*
- Record the word *inclusive* on the chart where you have defined ability and identity. (You may also want to mention the word *exclusive* and how the prefixes *in-* and *ex-* work in both words.)
- Then ask students how this term inclusive fits with what Sonia Sotomayor is saying in her letter. Discuss that Sotomayor is stressing the inclusive nature of community.

Next, read the introductory spread from Sonia talking about her garden and the subsequent two-page spreads (one about Sonia and one about Rafael). Stop here and tell students that the story will now follow that same pattern: Each spread introduces a new person. Ask them if they noticed that the first two people, Sonia and Rafael, are the creators of the book.

At this point, direct your students to return to their seats as they will now do an activity while you read aloud the rest of the book to them.

Discussion and Activity: Question and Response

First, pass out the Question and Response (Appendix 21) worksheet. This includes the questions asked in the book and space to respond. Tell students to listen as you reread the page about Sonia and to then write down a short response to the first question on the worksheet. Continue by reading the page about Rafael, stopping for students to respond. Continue this pattern for the rest of the book.

When you have finished the book, have students review their completed **Question and Response** worksheet. Ask each to highlight two questions and responses that they would feel comfortable sharing. Then direct them to share these with an elbow or desk partner in a pair-share for a few minutes.

After students have shared, ask them to raise their hands if they learned something new about their classmate. (Do not have them comment about this; only have them raise their hands.)

Next, return to the overall book and discuss why Sotomayor stresses the idea of "Just Ask." Why do students think she wants people to *just ask* about differences they notice? Guide students to consider how knowing more about people's differences helps build a more inclusive community.

Then point out that Sotomayor says not everyone feels ready and comfortable about sharing. Some ways of knowing if it is okay to ask or talk about differences is to notice if the person does not look away or appear upset when the topic is raised. You might also consider if you have ever seen them share with other friends. Or, you might try to recall if you have shared something deeply personal about yourself with them, and if they were open to that conversation. When you don't know if they will feel comfortable about your question, you might ask a parent or teacher or trusted adult first, rather than ask the person directly. And when you ask, you might clarify that it is okay if they do not want to answer you.

Remind students again that knowing more about people and their different identities can help build a more inclusive community. But asking directly can be off-putting or feel uncomfortable, so it is important to think about how you will ask your question(s), and to remember that your intent is to learn and better get to know the person.

Segue to Next Day and Daily Reflection

At the end of today's unit, explicitly help your students segue by letting them know you are now moving to the next part of the day, but you will be returning to this topic of inclusivity and expressing one's identity tomorrow.

When the school day is over, take some time to fill out the Daily Reflection to reflect on today's experience. Review it as you prepare for the next day.

DAY 6

Whole-Class Read-Aloud #6: *What Happened to You?*

Discussion and Activity: Post-Reading Discussion

Time: About 1 hour

Whole-Class Read-Aloud #6: *What Happened to You?*

Begin today by reviewing the message from *Just Ask,* discussed the previous day. Remind students about Sonia Sotomayor's point: that not everybody is comfortable sharing and they should not have to share if they do not want to. Like the Question and Response activity from the previous day, you only had to share two responses you were *comfortable* sharing. You were able to determine what you felt okay revealing.

When we are comfortable and in a safe space, sharing information about ourselves can help us grow closer to one another and improve understanding and empathy in our community, just like the garden in the story from the previous day. (If students ask about empathy, let them know you will return to this term in a little while after you go over some examples.)

Ask students to think about what it means to have good manners. What does that mean to them? Then ask them when is it okay to ask strangers personal questions? Then say:

"Often, we are told not to talk to strangers, so is it always appropriate to 'just ask' someone a personal question especially when we do not know them? Imagine you saw a bald man you didn't know in the street. Would you go up to him and ask, 'What happened to your hair?'"

Write the term *empathy* on the chart paper where you have defined identity, ability, and inclusivity. Ask students to think back to the Common Denominator Game they played on the second day of this unit. What may be uncommon for us is normal or common for others. Similarly, we may view a disability as different or unusual, whereas the person with the disability views it as normal. Ask students what it means to put yourself in someone else's shoes. That idea is very similar to the definition of empathy. Write a definition of empathy on the chart paper similar to these:

- The ability to take on another person's perspective
- The ability to imagine what someone else might be thinking or feeling, to understand and share the feelings of another person

Have students help you put these ideas into words that make sense to them and then write down the final class definition of *empathy* on the chart.

Then gather your students for a whole-class read-aloud of *What Happened to You?*

Start by showing students the cover and asking what they notice. Then tell them that in this book you want them to really focus on how the main character Joe is feeling. Then begin reading, using some of these places below to help students focus on Joe's emotions and reactions:

- When Kid One (Simone) says, "You've only got one leg!", point out Joe's facial cues and discuss what emotions they indicate. Ask students, "How do you think Joe feels here?"
- Help students notice how many questions the other kids are pressing Joe with. Ask, "How does Joe feel after he says, 'It was a thousand lions' and the other kids respond with, 'Really?'"
- Pause on the page with no words and the illustration of Joe's face blown up. Ask students how they believe he feels.
- Ask how they think Joe feels when the other kids start playing the game with him.

Discussion and Activity: Post-Reading Discussion

When you finish the story, ask the following questions to facilitate a whole-group **Post-Reading Discussion:**

- "What did the kids do that Joe felt okay with or appreciated?"
- "What do you think the kids did that Joe was not okay with and did not appreciate?"
- "What could these kids have done differently?"

Then show students the picture of the author on the last page of the book. Tell them that this page, titled "Dear Adult," has some suggestions on what kids might do if they want to ask questions of another child with a visible disability.

- Explain that, for example, James says: "It's good to be curious but be clear that if you do not know this person specifically, then it has to be okay to not know. It is not polite to ask people you don't know personal questions."
- James offers this example: If you saw a bunch of kids asking a child with a disability questions like those asked of Joe, what would you do? James says, "You could tell them to leave the kid alone or mind their own business and ask the kid if they want to play with you or if they're okay."
- James also explains there is a reason in the story why the reader doesn't find out why Joe only has one leg. He says, "Because the reader didn't need to know because it is personal. Joe did not have to share that information if he didn't want to."

Remind students of what they learned about empathy. Knowing more about people and their different identities can help build a more inclusive community. But asking directly can be off-putting or feel uncomfortable, so use empathy to put yourself in the shoes of the individual. It is important to think carefully about how you ask questions and to remember that your intent is to learn and better get to know the person you're questioning.

Show them the definition of *empathy* again on the chart paper:

- Remind students that there is a difference between being kind and being empathetic. When we are talking about empathy, we do not mean just don't be rude. Empathy means considering how another person is feeling or how we might feel if someone made the same statement to or asked the same question of us. Having empathy also means having understanding.
- Refer back to the last couple of pages of the book. There is an exchange between Simone and Joe at the end where she shows an empathetic response. Ask students what they noticed about the way she responded to Joe. When he asked, "Do you need to know?", Simone replied, "No." Bring up the point that perhaps if they were older children, Simone could have said, "No, unless you want to tell me," because she is empathetic enough to realize that Joe should not have to tell anyone about his personal situation if he does not wish to share.

Segue to Next Day and Daily Reflection

Explicitly help your students segue by letting them know you are now moving to the next part of the day, but you will be returning to this topic of empathy tomorrow.

When the school day is over, take some time to fill out the Daily Reflection to reflect on today's experience. Review it as you prepare for the next day.

DAY 7

Whole-Class Read-Aloud #7: *Awesomely Emma: A Charley and Emma Story*

Discussion and Activity: P.O.V. Diary Entry

Time: 1 hour

Whole-Class Read-Aloud and Discuss #7: *Awesomely Emma: A Charley and Emma Story*

Begin by explaining that you are going to read another book about a main character with a limb difference, like Joe from yesterday's story. The central character of today's book, Emma, is based on the author's daughter and some of the experiences her daughter has confronted as a child with limb differences.

Gather students to read *Awesomely Emma: A Charley and Emma Story* as a whole class. This time, show students just the front cover and then jump right into reading.

While you read, invite students to offer comments about what they are noticing in the illustrations and about the story. Specifically, stop and prompt them to consider these particular moments in the story:

- How does Emma's face change from the moment they arrive at the museum to when she and her teacher realize there is no ramp?
- "Think about a time you tried helping a friend. What do you notice about Emma's face when Charley pushes Emma around in her wheelchair?"
- Ask students to think about how it feels when a friend does not want their help. "What do you notice about the differences in Emma's face and Charley's face on the page where Charley says he was just trying to help?"
- Ask students to think about how it feels when they *can* help someone, like the students who helped Emma when she asked them to write and sign a letter to the museum.

When you have finished the story, ask students to share their overall reaction with a partner. Then have students return to their seats.

Discussion and Activity: P.O.V. Diary Entry

Pass out paper to all the students. Then tell them to pretend they are Charley reflecting on the day. Ask the students to write a diary entry or draw a picture from Charley's point of view that describes his day at the museum. As they think about the day from Charley's point of view, encourage them to think especially about how he feels. He was trying to do something nice, but his friend either did not respond or responded negatively.

After about 10 minutes of student writing and drawing this **P.O.V. Diary Entry**, have students stop. Ask them to take a look at the terms and definitions on the chart paper as a whole class. Now write down three new terms on the paper. These terms are *ally*, *advocate*, and *accessibility*.

Tell students that the first two terms (*ally* and *advocate*) are related. Ask students to think about how Emma explained the ways in which Charley could help. She didn't want him to help her, but rather wanted him to be her ally and maybe her advocate.

- Define *ally* for students as "someone who aligns with and supports an individual or group of people." Depending on what students have learned in their history classes, they might recognize the term ally as being related to countries working together as allies united in a cause or action. Explain that, in this case, you are thinking about an ally as an individual. *Ally* as a verb is defined as "forming a connection or uniting two things." As a noun, as you are considering it here, the word is more about being someone who connects to another group or individual by being supportive.
- Define *advocate* for students as "someone who supports or promotes the interests of a group." *Advocating* as a verb can mean defending or standing up for a certain cause.

Tell students that these are two working definitions of *ally* and *advocate* they can use to start thinking about this concept. Ask students to consider ways in which the kids from the previous book (*What Happened to You?*) could have been allies or advocates. Then recall Charley and the rest of Emma's class. How were they allies or advocates?

Now, tell students to think about the word *accessibility*. What does it mean? Help students come to a working definition similar to this: "Accessibility means being able to be reached, entered, used, or understood." Explain to students that accessibility is often used along with the word *inclusive*. When we contemplate places, like the museum in the book, being accessible for use by all community members, we are thinking about how to make the museum inclusive.

- Ask students to explain what Charley, Emma, and Emma's classmates did in the story to advocate for accessibility.

Segue to Next Day and Daily Reflection

Explicitly help your students segue by letting them know you are now moving to the next part of the day, but you will be returning to this topic of accessibility tomorrow.

When the school day is over, take some time to fill out the Daily Reflection to reflect on today's experience. Review it as you prepare for the next day.

DAY 8

Conclusion

Discussion and Activity: Accessibility: Noticing and Advocating

Time: 1 hour

Discussion and Activity: Accessibility: Noticing and Advocating

Start the activity **Accessibility: Noticing and Advocating** by having students reflect on all the books you have read in this unit. With the students' help, list the main characters on the whiteboard. Ask students to think about each character and their unique differences. Then ask students to imagine that these main characters were visiting. What are some challenges they might face in terms of accessibility if they visited our school and local community? Have a few students respond and then tell the class you are going to do a brainstorm and a subsequent walk around the school.

Have students pair up with their desk or elbow partners. Then assign each pair a main character from the list. (Just go down the list in order. More than one pair will share the same character.)

- Now, tell them to imagine that the main character is their friend and coming to visit them at school. They have asked for the student's help: seeing if the school premises will be accessible for them and, if not, then helping to advocate for them.
- Hand out paper to the students. Have them think about their character and what challenges they might face in terms of accessibility around the school. With their partner, each student should make a list of those possible challenges. Give students some examples to help them brainstorm:
  - Entrances, seats, stairs, signs, crosswalks
  - As you give examples, you can ask students other questions, such as "Why is it important for the crosswalk countdown to also have a beeping sound as you walk across the street?" These types of questions can help students identify very specific challenges and accessibility issues.
  - Remember to keep the students focused on the needs of their assigned main character (this can help mitigate the potential feelings of students with particular disabilities who might otherwise feel on the spot with this activity).

Then tell students they are now going on an accessibility walk! Your class will stroll around the school and school grounds very quietly, noticing where areas of challenge might exist for their friend (the main character) when they visit.

Take students out on their walk around the school. Encourage them to carry notebooks where they can write and take notes or draw sketches of areas of potential concern for their friend. Have students work very quietly as they tour the school.

When you return to the classroom, have students and their partners now gather in groups by their main character. They should share together the observations they made about possible areas that may present issues of accessibility for their friend.

After students have shared in their groups for about 5 minutes, interrupt. Ask all of them to think about one area they noticed that might involve accessibility issues for their friend. As an advocate for their friend and for people like their friend who have similar abilities, what steps could they take next? Students will likely suggest writing letters to the school to fix these areas so they will be more accessible.

Tell students that this is their next task. You would like them as a small group to select **one** area of need and write down the following:

1. Describe the area that they noticed would be inaccessible to some people.
2. Describe what needs to happen so it can be made more accessible and inclusive for all.

Give them just 5 minutes to do this as a group.

After groups have completed this task, ask them to select one person to share aloud their group's response. As the groups share, record only the specific area of concern on the board. When all groups have shared, take a look at the board and ask students if there are any spaces in the school or on the school grounds that are listed repeatedly. Then ask the students what action they could next take. Request ideas and then say the following:

> *"You have learned a lot about ability, identity, inclusivity, empathy, accessibility, and being an ally and advocate over the last several days. This new knowledge can help you as a community member.*
>
> *"Some of you may be feeling strongly about what we noticed today on our school grounds and how there might be areas that need improvement so they are inclusive for all. If you would like to do so, you could write a letter or talk to our school board and administration as an advocate to see if these areas can be improved. If you are interested in doing that, we could schedule a meeting during free time or recess to work on this together."*

Segue to Next Day and Daily Reflection, Unit Post-Check with Students, and Taking the Pulse of the Class: After Unit

Explicitly help your students segue by letting them know you are now moving to the next part of the day, and this is the end of the unit on ability and identity. Let them know that the books will remain in the classroom for some time and that they are welcome to revisit them. Also tell them that although the unit may have been completed, these conversations can always continue around its topic, and they should feel free to ask questions or discuss the topic in more detail.

When the school day is over, take some time to complete the Daily Reflection form. The next day or the day after that, ask your students to complete the Unit Post-Check with Students. Finally, about a week to 10 days after the unit was completed, fill out Taking the Pulse of the Class: After Unit to consider more broadly this experience for your current students, yourself, and your future students.

FINAL SUGGESTIONS

During the weeks following this unit, you might want to revisit some of these books or the conversations around them. This unit was intended as an introduction to, and the beginning of courageous conversations around the topics of ability and identity, inclusivity and accessibility, and being an empathetic ally or advocate. It was meant to help students feel more comfortable talking about differences in both physical and personal attributes. It also emphasized that empathy is important. Likewise, it encouraged students to be allies and advocates.

Some students may want to continue to discuss this topic in class in a deeper way. Reach out to your school counselors, psychologists, and support faculty for individual help for students seeking more specific or individualized support in this area. The Unit Post-Check with Students form will help you identify students needing or wanting this support.

You may decide to expand on this unit with further book sharing, discussions, and activities. The websites that follow may serve as good resources as you do this work.

ADDITIONAL RESOURCES

Ability, Disability and Ableism Educational Resources: *www.adl.org/resources/tools-and-strategies/ability-disability-and-ableism-educational-resources*

Article about James Catchpole's *What Happened to You?*: *www.businessinsider.com/i-wrote-a-childrens-book-to-normalize-limb-differences-2023-4*

Autism Speaks: *www.autismspeaks.org*

Interview with Amy Webb, author of *Awesomely Emma: A Charley and Emma Story*: *www.fox19.com/video/2019/04/29/new-book-when-charlie-met-emma-by-local-author-amy-webb*

James Catchpole reading his book *What Happened to You?*: *www.youtube.com/watch?v=H785j9wg-BU*

Just Ask Literature Guide: *www.learningtogive.org/resources/just-ask-be-different-be-brave-be-you-literature-guide*

Neuro and Physical Diversity Toolkit: *www.learningtogive.org/resources/embracing-neuro-and-physical-diversity-toolkit*

MEETING COMMON CORE AND CASEL STANDARDS

Common Core English Language Arts Standards for Grade 4

This unit meets specific Common Core State Standards for English Language Arts in grades 3, 4, 5, and 6. We have included the specific ELA standards for grade 4 below to illustrate the strands and items met (similar for all four grades third through sixth). The QR code here will link you to the specific lists for grades 3, 5, and 6.

CCSS.ELA-LITERACY.SL.4.1

Engage effectively in a range of collaborative discussions (one-on-one, in groups, and teacher-led) with diverse partners on *grade 4 topics and texts*, building on others' ideas and expressing their own clearly.

CCSS.ELA-LITERACY.RL.4.1

Refer to details and examples in a text when explaining what the text says explicitly and when drawing inferences from the text.

CCSS.ELA-LITERACY.RL.4.3

Describe in depth a character, setting, or event in a story or drama, drawing on specific details in the text (e.g., a character's thoughts, words, or actions).

CCSS.ELA-LITERACY.RI.4.3

Explain events, procedures, ideas, or concepts in a historical, scientific, or technical text, including what happened and why, based on specific information in the text.

CCSS.ELA-LITERACY.RL.4.4

Determine the meaning of words and phrases as they are used in a text, including those that allude to significant characters found in mythology (e.g., Herculean).

CCSS.ELA-LITERACY.RL.4.9

Compare and contrast the treatment of similar themes and topics (e.g., opposition of good and evil) and patterns of events (e.g., the quest) in stories, myths, and traditional literature from different cultures.

CCSS.ELA-LITERACY.RI.4.9

Integrate information from two texts on the same topic in order to write or speak about the subject knowledgeably.

CASEL Social and Emotional Learning Standards for Grades 3–5

This unit meets specific CASEL Core Competence Area goals for Social and Emotional Learning for grades 3–5. We have included the CASEL areas and specific example standards below to show the items met in this unit. (The items are similar for grade 6.)

Self-Awareness: The abilities to understand one's own emotions, thoughts, and values and how they influence behavior across contexts. This includes capacities to recognize one's strengths and limitations with a well-grounded sense of confidence and purpose. Such as:

- Integrating personal and social identities
- Identifying personal, cultural, and linguistic assets
- Identifying one's emotions
- Experiencing self-efficacy

Social Awareness: The abilities to understand the perspectives of and empathize with others, including those from diverse backgrounds, cultures, and contexts. This includes the capacities to feel compassion for others, understand broader historical and social norms for behavior in different settings, and recognize family, school, and community resources and supports. Such as:

- Taking others' perspectives
- Recognizing strengths in others
- Demonstrating empathy and compassion
- Showing concern for the feelings of others
- Identifying diverse social norms, including unjust ones

Relationship Skills: The abilities to establish and maintain healthy and supportive relationships and to effectively navigate settings with diverse individuals and groups. This includes the capacities to communicate clearly, listen actively, cooperate, work collaboratively to problem-solve and negotiate conflict constructively, navigate settings with differing social and cultural demands and opportunities, provide leadership, and seek or offer help when needed. Such as:

- Communicating effectively
- Developing positive relationships
- Practicing teamwork and collaborative problem solving
- Standing up for the rights of others

Responsible Decision Making: The abilities to make caring and constructive choices about personal behavior and social interactions across diverse situations. This includes the capacities to consider ethical standards and safety concerns, and to evaluate the benefits and consequences of various actions for personal, social, and collective well-being.

Such as:

- Demonstrating curiosity and open-mindedness
- Identifying solutions for personal and social problems
- Reflecting on one's role to promote personal, family, and community well-being

Supporting Children's Mental Health through Literature

INTRODUCTION

The next two chapters feature thematic book sets that address important topics within the area of children's mental health. Both anxiety (Chapter 10) and depression (Chapter 11) are increasingly prevalent mental health concerns, affecting a significant percentage of young people today. Children struggling with anxiety and depression, or living with someone with these diagnoses, often have feelings of being unseen and/or misunderstood. Both thematic book sets acknowledge this and demystify these issues while acknowledging we all experience frightening and troubling thoughts and feelings. Students have the capacity to empathize and understand serious mental health issues. This is especially important as the data indicate that these issues are on the rise.

Before beginning to address these topics, we encourage you to review Chapter 2 for helpful tips on understanding your own feelings on them. We also want to stress that the stories within these units are specifically sequenced to build understanding. To have the greatest likelihood of success with these courageous conversations, we ask that you follow the order and complete the entire unit. Good luck: You've got this!

Chapter 10—Feeling Fragile: Talking About Anxiety

This thematic book set covers the topic of living with anxiety. Anxiety is an increasingly common mental health issue for both teens and children. The goal of the set is to illuminate this issue through collaborative conversations and engaging activities centered around the characters' experiences in the sequenced, outstanding picturebooks. This set is not designed to solve individual students' anxiety but does introduce ways to reduce feelings related to worry in situations as well as to promote preventive actions. The unit ultimately helps students learn more about anxiety and provides a stepping stone for future conversations about mental health and its challenges.

Along with focusing on social and emotional development standards (The CASEL 5), this thematic book set embeds English language arts standards whereby students will complete plot diagrams and story maps, compare and contrast characters, and practice identifying themes. Activities and discussion questions are suited for a third- through sixth-grade classroom audience and should be adjusted as appropriate for your grade level and students' understanding.

Chapter 11—Losing Hope: Talking About Depression

This thematic book set covers the topic of depression. Like anxiety, depression is a rising mental health concern among children and teens. The goal of this set is to better understand depression as a behavioral and mental health issue and how it might affect students' families or peers or even themselves. This text set is not designed to address individual students with depression, but to increase all students' understanding and awareness. This unit introduces preventive actions and general practices for increasing self-knowledge related to emotional well-being, and can serve as an introduction to further conversations around mental health.

Along with focusing on social and emotional development standards (The CASEL 5), this thematic book set embeds English language arts standards whereby students will work on writing procedural texts, understanding cause-and-effect structures, and considering word choice. Activities and discussion questions are suited for a third- through sixth-grade classroom audience and should be adjusted as appropriate for your grade level and students' understanding.

AUTHOR AND ILLUSTRATOR PROFILES

Dan Santat

After the Fall, a fractured fairy tale version of the Humpty Dumpty rhyme, is shared at the beginning of Chapter 11. Close attention to each page reveals hidden depths to the story, and students will further enjoy exploring additional details on the jacket cover, endpages, and hardcovers. Some may notice and ask about the small dedication on the wall marked "For Leah."

As Santat did with his Caldecott Medal–winning picturebook *The Adventures of Beekle: The Unimaginary Friend*, he has woven stories from his own life into *After the Fall*. With *Beekle*, Santat discussed how the story had parallels to his experiences and feelings around the birth of his first son, as well as relating to that same son's experience years later, worrying on the first day of school about fitting in and finding a friend. With *After the Fall*, Santat has connected the story to the postpartum depression and anxiety faced by his wife Leah. In fact, Santat has called the book a "love letter to my wife." This personal experience helped him to better understand and write a story that quietly and powerfully discusses living with depression, the challenges in tackling anxiety and fear, and the huge amounts of courage it takes to try to live fully despite these mental health illnesses.

Santat's emotional honesty is clearly evident in the art and the text of all of his books and add a level of underlying connection in even his most humorous titles that his readers inherently feel. You may want to consider sharing with your students his many award-winning picturebooks, chapter books, and graphic novels.

Christian Robinson

Christian Robinson and Adam Rex's *School's First Day of School* takes a special twist on the typical first-day-of-school picturebook and presents a fresh perspective on this often anxiety-ridden event. "School," built over the summer, is a quite happy building until he learns about this upcoming "first day" and the arrival of students and teachers. His worried and pessimistic reaction to this, and the roller coaster of emotions as he experiences his first day, cleverly mirror the worry of many students attending school for the first time.

Your students might immediately recognize this book as one of Robinson's by his colorful collages and cut-outs, and then mention some of his most well-known titles, such as *Last Stop on Market Street*, *The Smallest Girl in the Smallest Grade*, or *You Matter*. This can present an opportunity to discuss how Robinson portrays his main characters. They are often sensitive and caring and kind, but more than anything they are observant. They notice and wonder about the world around them. Robinson's stories celebrate this trait, showing his young readers that this is the way to learn about others, broaden your perspective, and take action to be kind.

Robinson's firm handle on the emotional scope and needs of young children shines in his books, and he directly addresses challenging topics they might face, but always with an underlining tone of love and gentle joyfulness. It is not surprising then that his personal website is called "The Art of Fun," or that he does animation for *Sesame Street*. He is well established as a modern picturebook creator to whom we might turn for wonderful books, especially when seeking books to use with regard to social and emotional development in your classroom.

IN MY CLASSROOM

My COVID Classroom

Along with other teachers across the world, I was never taught in my teacher preparation program about how to pivot my classroom from in-person to online during the midst of a global pandemic. But in the spring of 2020, that is exactly what I did.

For me, the hardest piece was continuing to support my students as a class community. Technological issues abounded in my district, and throughout the spring, we struggled to connect all the students with devices and reliable internet access, making it nearly impossible to hold regular meetings online with all students present. It took nearly a month before most of the class was able to join in the occasional Zoom-supported meeting. Once we began, the newness of the space and unusual situations at home made teaching tough, but we were able to slowly regain some sense of community, in large part due to our relationships that had been well formed from August through February.

The fall of 2020, however, was harder. High COVID-19 infection rates in my area meant my school began the year online. Buoyed by a summer of training, and the reassurance my students would be fully technologically supported, I felt more prepared to engage my new class in solid academic pursuits in a mainly synchronous online setting. But I knew that the ability to form relationships as a new class would be difficult. I turned to techniques I had used in the past, sending out letters about myself to the students before class began and encouraging them to write back, but this time using school email. I created a welcoming Google Classroom site, including my Bitmoji avatar, and set up a classroom-like space in a corner of my family room for Zoom. I relied on the heavy use of interactive discussion apps to get students talking to each other. I also made use of flexible scheduling to plan a weekly individual Zoom meeting with each student and family to simply check in and chat for a few minutes. These pieces helped to form relationships, and the resilience and adaption of my young learners showed. This is simply how they learned to do school that year.

But there was often a persistent weariness and sadness present behind our lessons that quietly permeated the day. Many students' family members were ill. Jobs were lost or salaries cut, and students felt the stress in their households. While I know the students enjoyed the escape of my read-alouds of humorous books and sharing of fun videos, discussing together some of the titles that appear in Chapters 10 and 11 here allowed for conversations to open up, and the sharing of difficult, complicated feelings emerged. For many students, this seemed like a needed release and resulted in a deeper connection to each other and to me. Now back in the classroom in person, I have continued to address mental and behavioral health issues on a conversational basis with students, something I used to avoid. I have learned that honestly discussing this with my young scholars can be as much a relationship-builder as sharing the funniest cat video.

—EV, SECOND-GRADE TEACHER

Feeling Fragile

Talking About Worry and Anxiety

THE BOOKS

School's First Day of School

by Adam Rex, illustrated by Christian Robinson (Roaring Book Press, 2016)

Children experience the anxiety of going back to school through another perspective: a school! With Christian Robinson's reassuring, warm, and comforting palette of colors, Adam Rex's book flips the typical first-day-of-school narration to the voice of the actual "School," providing novelty and keeping the reader one step removed from the situation in an observant stance.

Wemberly Worried

by Kevin Henkes (Greenwillow Books, 2000)

Wemberly, a young mouse, worries about everything, but recently, especially about starting school. As Wemberly prepares for the big day, her anxieties reach a climax, as illustrated in a two-page, black-and-white spread that capture her worries the night before, and reflect many feelings common to children in new situations: what if no one looks like me ("has spots"), what if "no one else wears stripes," what if "they make fun of my name"! While Kevin Henkes brings the story to happy resolve with a new friend and lessening of Wemberly's fears, he is careful to note that Wemberly still worried "but no more than usual," allowing the young readers to begin to understand the concept that anxiety may not simply disappear.

The Day You Begin

by Jacqueline Woodson, illustrated by Rafael Lopez (Penguin, 2018)

Jacqueline Woodson's always perfect word choice sets the tone for this exploration of a young girl's worries as she prepares to return to school after the summer. Through the colorful illustrations of Rafael Lopez and vivid storytelling, the book draws attention to layers of identity and belonging, and the anxieties that can arise from feeling different due to social class and race. Use of the second-person "you" brings the concept closer to home and prompts identification with understanding these worries.

Oops I Dropped the Lemon Tart

by An Swerts, illustrated by Eline van Lindenhuizen (Clavis, 2020)

Based loosely on a true experience in an Italian restaurant, this captivating story explores anxieties around performance and perfection. A young girl working in her father's restaurant, and already struggling with issues of anxiety, drops a lemon tart in front of a visiting food critic. To her surprise, the critic thinks her mistake makes the dessert even more wonderful and writes an amazing review for the restaurant. An Swerts's story gently emphasizes the importance of accepting and learning from mistakes.

Jabari Jumps

by Gaia Cornwall (Candlewick Press, 2017)

Jabari's fear of jumping off the diving board at the public pool has become a situation of high distress and rising anxiety. He feels he must jump! Beautifully rendered perspectives by Gaia Cornwell (even inducing a bit of vertigo) help the reader empathize with Jabari's struggles. With his father's love and encouragement, Jabari gains self-confidence and eventually takes the "leap" into the pool.

Saturday Is Swimming Day

by Hyewon Yum (Candlewick Press, 2018)

Hyewon Yum's skill with capturing her character's emotions through just the simple placement of a line comes to the fore here as she masterfully portrays the anxieties and fears of a young girl facing swimming lessons. Every Saturday, she feels ill, until her savvy instructor reassures her it's okay to sit out the lesson if she's not ready and, with gentle encouragement, the girl slowly gains confidence. Readers can see her body grow increasingly relaxed until, by the story's end, she floats happily in the pool. Yum softly suggests that support and patience can help someone bravely overcome their fear.

Me and My Fear

by Francesca Sanna (Flying Eye Books, 2018)

Fear is a heavy load that a young child has carried on her back for some time. When she moves to a new country, "fear" grows bigger and bigger and simply will not leave. But when she meets a friend in her new city, she discovers that he, too, has a companion named "fear." Their shared commonality brings her comfort and a sense of hope, as poignantly conveyed by Francesca Sanna, and even reduces the size of her fear.

Ruby Finds a Worry

by Tom Percival (Bloomsbury, 2019)

When Ruby first noticed Worry, it was rather small. But over time, it began to grow and take over her thoughts. While Worry is not malevolent, it is a problem. Then Ruby learns that talking about Worry will help it shrink just a bit, and she begins to express her concerns. Her self-confidence increases as her empowerment grows, and soon Worry is back to a size Ruby can handle. Tom Percival's clever casting of "Worry" as a bloblike, bright character helps to neutralize the emotional impact just a bit, allowing readers to think about their own worries and anxieties in a more objective way.

The Girl and The Wolf

by Katherena Vermette, illustrated by Julie Flett (Theytus Books, 2019)

Enjoying a walk in the woods, a young girl treks farther away from her mother than she intends and panics when she suddenly cannot find her way home. As she tries to find her way back, she encounters a surprising ally in the form of a friendly wolf. Author Katherena Vermette and illustrator Julie Flett turn traditional castings of fairytale wolves on their side, and this wolf helps the young girl tap into her inner wisdom as she navigates her way, learning to trust her instincts and overcome her anxieties and initial self-doubt.

> ***Note:*** As with all thematic book sets, we recommend that after each book has been shared within the unit, it is placed in an easily accessible display in the classroom for the rest of the unit days. Children should then be allowed access to explore these books on their own during free-choice times.

PLANNING CHECKLIST

Feeling Fragile: Talking About Worry and Anxiety

We suggest the following timeline to prepare and then share and discuss the books and do the related activities with your students. (A reproducible version of this checklist is available in Appendix 1.) Please note that timing for your individual class should be determined by your situation and your schedule, and, most importantly, should be guided by your students' reactions to the books and activities. Plan generally, however, on about 1 hour of daily time with the unit for 7–10 days in a row.

Two Weeks Prior

- ☐ Complete Taking the Pulse of the Class: Before Unit (Appendix 2) for a general sense of your class at this time.
- ☐ Collect and read twice each of the books for the unit.

☐ Review the "Unit Plans: Reading, Discussions, and Activities" section of the unit.

☐ Send out the Administration Notification Slip (Appendix 3) and School Counselor/Psychologist and Support Staff Notification Slip (Appendix 4).

One Week Prior

☐ (Optional) Send out Family Notification Slips (Appendix 5) to the families of your students.

☐ Have students complete the Unit Pre-Check with Students (Appendix 6) and review the results carefully. Check in with any students with reactions that cause concern so that you can prepare for extra support.

☐ Review Chapter 2 of the book.

☐ Collect all materials needed for the unit:

  ☐ **Daily Reflection forms (Appendix 7):** You will need one for each day.

  ☐ **Books:** One copy is required, but you may prefer to secure two copies of each book. After each book has been shared during the unit, place it in an easily accessible display in the classroom. Please give students access to explore these books on their own during free-choice times. You will want to keep the display available for some time after the unit is completed.

  ☐ **Materials already in your classroom:** Please have available and ready to use the following commonplace classroom materials:

  - Chart paper or a section of whiteboard that can remain posted for the duration of the unit
  - Unlined white paper
  - Pencils and pens; colored pencils, crayons, or markers
  - Construction paper or other colored paper
  - Scissors
  - Tape or glue
  - Any additional materials indicated within the unit chapter's detailed description

During: Readings, Discussions, and Activities (approximately 7–10 school days)

☐ Follow the detailed plans for each day.

☐ One to 2 days after the unit is completed, have students complete the Unit Post-Check with Students (Appendix 8).

One Week Following

☐ After reviewing the Unit Post-Check with Students, check in with any students with reactions that cause concern.

☐ Refer any students expressing interest or for whom you have concerns at this point for additional, individual discussion with a school support professional. Also consider additional whole-class work if indicated.

☐ Complete and review Taking the Pulse of the Class: After Unit (Appendix 9). This will help you reflect on your experience and your students' experiences with the thematic book set.

UNIT OVERVIEW *Feeling Fragile*: Talking About Worry and Anxiety		
Day	**Books**	**Discussion and Activities**
1	**Introduction and Whole-Class Read-Aloud #1:** *School's First Day of School*	• Building a Story Map • "Facing the Unknown"
2 and 3	**Small Groups Read-Aloud and Discuss #1:** *Wemberly Worried* *The Day You Begin*	• Comic Strip • Character Web • Letter to a Character
4	**Whole-Class Read-Aloud #2:** *Oops I Dropped the Lemon Tart*	• Mindfulness Practice • Researching a Mistake
5 and 6	**Small Groups Read-Aloud and Discuss #2:** *Jabari Jumps* *Saturday Is Swimming Day*	• "Around the World" Collaborative Discussion • Compare/Contrast • Quick-Write • Breathing Exercise
7	**Whole-Class Read-Aloud #3:** *The Girl and the Wolf*	• Class Brainstorm • "Face Your Fears"
8	**Small Groups Read-Aloud and Discuss #3:** *Me and My Fear* *Ruby Finds a Worry*	• Themes and Big Ideas Discussion
9	**Conclusion**	• Reader's Theater

Note: Each "day" of this unit is intended to take around 1 hour of class time. Time may vary slightly depending on student discussion, but please keep this time frame in mind as you move through the reading and activities.

BEFORE BEGINNING

1. Make sure you have completed the "Two Weeks Prior" and "One Week Prior" items on the planning checklist, including the Taking the Pulse of the Class: Before Unit and the Unit Pre-Check with Students forms.
2. Remember that the books within these units are specifically sequenced to build understanding. To have the greatest likelihood of success with these courageous conversations, we ask that you follow the order of the books, discussions, and activities and complete the entire unit.
3. Review Chapter 2 to help prepare for navigating the upcoming discussions you will be having with your students. As you complete the Daily Reflections at the end of each school day, consider revisiting Chapter 2 for helpful support in engaging in your own self-reflection and awareness, and ensuring your thoughtful and respectful approach to the topic.

DAY 1

Introduction and Whole-Class Read-Aloud #1: *School's First Day of School*

Discussion and Activities: Building a Story Map; "Facing the Unknown"

Time: About 1 hour

Special Materials Needed:

- Story Map (the blank story map in Appendix 22)
- *School's First Day of School* Quick-Write/Reflection (Appendix 23) handout

Introduction and Whole-Class Read-Aloud #1: *School's First Day of School*

To begin this unit, gather your whole class for a read-aloud and discussion. Explain that, over the next several days, the class will be exploring the topic of *anxiety*. Explain that the first few books they will be reading are about the anxiety or worry caused by the first day of school. Today, the class will together read a story that portrays this anxiety from the point of view of a most unlikely character. Before you begin, define the word *anxiety* with the class.

- Students may share synonyms for the word *anxiety* or past experiences where they have personally felt anxiety. Encourage students to offer such stories so that others who are unfamiliar with the term can connect and begin to form their own definition of it.
- After the class brainstorms, display this definition of anxiety from the Merriam-Webster dictionary: "a feeling of worry or unease about an uncertain outcome." Compare students' ideas to the official definition. Help them understand the definition by looking at the words *unease* and *uncertain* more closely. Remind students that we can look at different parts of words (morphology) to give us clues about what they mean. For example, we know the root word *certain* in uncertain means "to be sure of." If you put the prefix *un-* in front of *certain*, it changes the word to mean "something we cannot be sure of," or in the context of the definition, "an outcome that is not for sure." (Feel free to add more or less about the morphology of these words depending on your class needs.) Discuss how uncertain outcomes can make someone feel worried.
- Gently encourage students to differentiate between *worry* and *anxiety*. Ask students how a worry and anxiety might be the same or different. Some classrooms might not be quite ready for this distinction yet, so you will need to judge your students' ability and provide guidance, or save the discussion of this distinction for when you are reading the stories over the next few days or discussing them afterward. If you do discuss this issue now, add a few notes about the differences between anxiety and worry under the anxiety definition.
- Leave the definition of *anxiety* posted in the classroom so students can refer back to it throughout the unit.

Now, begin reading the story. Explain that this book is *fiction*, which means it is a made-up story and has a plot. A fictional story also includes characters, a setting, a problem, a turning point/climax, a solution, and a theme or themes. Reference the class definition of anxiety and describe how anxiety stems from a "problem" or a "worry." Tell students that the purpose of reading this book is to define the problem or worry in the story and analyze its evolution or development throughout the story.

- On p. 4, take a brief moment to discuss character and setting with the class. "Who is the character in this story? How do you know? Where does this story take place?" Make students aware that they will be experiencing the first day of school through another's perspective: the School itself! Encourage students to use both the images and the words to help them answer your questions.
- After reading p. 8, ask students, "Why does School think the janitor is wrong about him liking the children when they arrive on the first day? How can you see this in the illustrations?" Students will need to make an inference, using what they know from the text and their own personal experiences.
- On p. 15, ask, "Why did School squirt water at the boy?" Have students share their ideas. Then inquire, "Have you ever felt like School and tried to 'get back' at someone or retaliate? Why did you do something like this? Did you regret your action in the end?" Students should recognize that School's worries caused it to become angry and retaliate. After discussing, continue reading.

Once the complete story has been read, ask your students, "What emotions has School gone through on its first day?" Students will likely mention emotions such as worry, anger, sadness, happiness, interest, excitement. Press them, asking "Did School's problem or worries in the beginning get resolved? How do you know?"

Discussion and Activities: Building a Story Map; "Facing the Unknown"

Now, pass out a copy of the blank Story Map (Appendix 22) document to each student. Project your copy on the board, so you can complete **Building a Story Map** with your students. Guide students through the plot, prompting them to write about each element of the map: from the problem to the solution (leave the theme for last). Then add the emotions felt by School at the appropriate places on the map. Students can apply smiley faces (as seen in the sample in Figure 10.1) or use words. Have students use another color to add the face emotions or write the emotion words.

After students have completed each element on their map and included the corresponding emotions, direct them to think about the story's theme. Define *theme* as the lesson of the story. Ask, "What did the author want us to learn from this story?" Remind students that the topic the class will be discussing over the next several days is anxiety and again repeat the class definition. Then have students think–pair–share to answer your question.

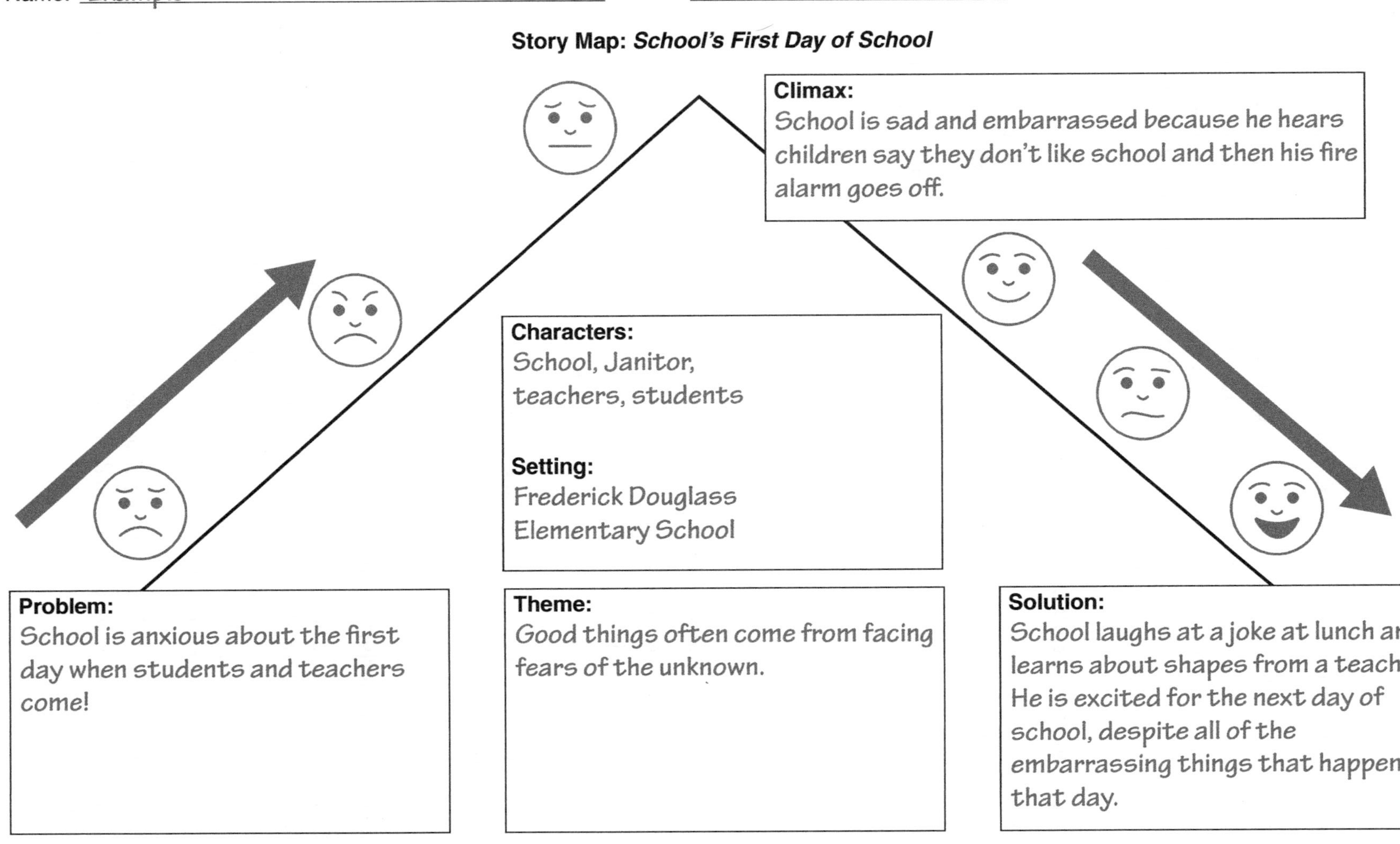

FIGURE 10.1. Completed Story Map for *School's First Day of School*.

In the end, students will come up with many ideas for the story's theme, but the most common will be **"Facing the Unknown,"** facing your worry, or being exposed to your fears can often turn out to be rewarding.

Next, pass out *School's First Day of School* Quick-Write/Reflection (Appendix 23). Ask students to answer this question: "What did you learn about anxiety today?" Allow them to write for 5 minutes. Then have them share their writing and summarize the lesson with a partner. When prompting them to pair-share, refer to the definition of *anxiety* and the theme of the story. Share as a whole class to end the lesson for Day 1.

Segue to Next Day and Daily Reflection

At the conclusion of today's unit, explicitly help your students segue by letting them know you are now moving to the next part of the day, but you will be returning to this topic of anxiety tomorrow.

When the school day is over, take some time to fill out the Daily Reflection to reflect on today's experience. Review it as you prepare for the next day.

DAY 2

Discussion and Activity: Comic Strip

Small Groups Read-Aloud and Discuss #1: *Wemberly Worried* and *The Day You Begin*

Time: About 1 hour total (or 2 hours total if all activities are done on Day 2)

Special Materials Needed:

- Writing Prompt/Comic Strip (Appendix 24) handout

> ***Note:*** Days 2 and 3 focus on the same books. There is a natural break in the activities between days, and thus Day 3 is indicated next, but feel free to combine these days if that works better for your schedule.

Discussion and Activity: Comic Strip

Remind students that we have been talking about worry and anxiety, especially anxiety caused by the first day of school. Pass out the Writing Prompt/Comic Strip (Appendix 24) handout. Explain that before reading today, you would like them to respond to the prompt on this page and create a **Comic Strip** to display their feelings on the first school day of the new year. Read aloud the handout's prompt to the students:

> *"Think of the first day of school. What feelings did you have? Was one of your feelings anxiety or worry? If you felt anxious, what did you do to conquer your anxiety? If you did not feel anxious, describe why."*

Small Groups Read-Aloud and Discuss #1: *Wemberly Worried* and *The Day You Begin*

Tell the class that they will now split into two groups to read two more books about the first day of school. Half of the class will read *Wemberly Worried*, and the other half will read *The Day You Begin*.

During the read-aloud of either of the books, start by examining its cover with the students. Ask students to predict what might happen in their story. Pause in the read-aloud every few pages to discuss the book with the students, using one or more of the following prompts to draw attention to both the content of the story and to the craft of the book:

- "What do you notice about this page?"
- "How do you think the main character (Wemberly or Angelina) feels right now? What in the illustrations or in the text helps tell you this?"
- "Why do you think the illustrator made the decision to draw this scene in this way? How does it add more meaning to what the words are saying?"
- "Why do you think the author used this word (or phrase) here? Why does it have an impact? How does the word (or phrase) match or work with the illustrations?"

Once the reading of and discussion about the book are complete, hold a quick general share. Ask your students how this book was similar to or different from *School's First Day of School.*

Segue to Next Day and Daily Reflection

After all students have drawn their comic strip and read one of the books with their group, the class can continue to the next step or stop here for the day. If you choose to end the activities for now, collect the comics and explicitly help your students segue by letting them know you are now moving to the next part of the day, but you will be returning to this topic of anxiety and worry tomorrow.

When Day 2 is over, take some time to fill out the Daily Reflection to reflect on today's experience. Review it as you prepare for the next day.

DAY 3 (OR AS COMBINED WITH DAY 2)

Small Groups Read-Aloud and Discuss #1: *Wemberly Worried* and *The Day You Begin*

Discussion and Activities: Character Web; Letter to a Character

Time: About 1 hour total

Special Materials Needed:

- Character Webs: *Wemberly Worried* and *The Day You Begin* (Appendix 25)
- Letter to a Character (Appendix 26) handout

Now that both groups have completed their comic strips and read their assigned book (*Wemberly Worried* or *The Day You Begin*), pass out the Character Webs (Appendix 25) document to all students in the class. Ask each to now fill out their individual **Character Web**, recording the worries that the main character in their assigned book had about going to school.

- Tell students to write down a worry that Wemberly or Angelina had and draw a circle around it, then draw a line to connect this worry to the big circle in the middle of the page.
- Have students jot down three worries they remember their character experienced. Then they need to quickly find someone else who read the same book and sit down next to them. Together, the pair should try to arrive at a total of six worries.

Once each pair has settled on six worries for the same central character, they should seek out a different pair of students that read the other book. They will then share their character webs with this new pair of students.

Tell students that the class is now going to discuss the similarities and differences between the worries of Wemberly and Angelina. Ask students to look at their character webs together to find the answers to the questions you ask below. Then ask a few groups to share aloud their answers with the whole class.

- "What **similar** worries did both characters have on the first day of school?"

> ***Note:*** One important example that students may want to discuss further: Wemberly worried about her spotted fur, and Angelina worried about the color of her skin.

- "What were some **different** worries the characters had?"
- "Were any of these worries similar to those you have experienced about the first day of school?" (Students have been sharing their answers as a group, but here you might ask if any individual students want to share with the whole class if their group did not have similar worries.)
- "In the end, what did each character discover about their anxiety on the first day of school?" (Students should discuss this as a group first before you call on any of them to answer.)

Guide students in this discussion to notice that despite the fact that these two characters were different and dealing with a range of issues, each one had to face the unknown and was exposed to their fears on that first day of school. Tell students that something we know from research is that exposing yourself to a situation that makes you uncomfortable can actually help you decrease your worry. Explain that such an experience can be valuable because it can help you change your avoidance behaviors and deal more directly with your discomfort.

By the end of this discussion, you want your students to understand that, although new situations can create all different types of worries, exposure to them can often be rewarding in the end. Wemberly and Angelina may still have worries at the conclusion of their stories, but they also come away from the first day of school with a new friend or positive experience.

Now, ask students to return to their seats. Explain that they will write a letter to Wemberly or Angelina with advice for facing their fears or anxiety on the first day of school. Students can use ideas from today's discussions and/or their own experiences. Pass out the Letter to a Character (Appendix 26) worksheet.

- Have students fill in the name of the character on their worksheet.
- Brainstorm a list of ideas as a class that students could share with the characters before students begin the assignment. Remind students that they are not trying to fix the character's anxiety; rather, they are just suggesting ideas that might help them work through their worry. Not every strategy or coping mechanism will work to completely extinguish anxiety, and that is okay. Like Kevin Henkes writes at the end of *Wemberly Worried*, "Wemberly still worried. But no more than usual. And sometimes even less" (p. 27). In their **Letter to a Character**, they want to simply capture a few of the ideas that worked for Wemberly or Angelina, and remind them of what they are, or share some ideas they have used with success or that School applied when worried.
- Give students about 10 minutes to write. If time allows, have students share their letters in pairs.

Segue to Next Day and Daily Reflection

At the conclusion of today's unit, explicitly help your students segue by letting them know you are now moving to the next part of the day, but tomorrow you will be returning to this topic of worry and anxiety.

When the school day is over, take some time to fill out the Daily Reflection to reflect on today's experience. Review it as you prepare for the next day.

DAY 4

Whole-Class Read-Aloud #2: *Oops I Dropped the Lemon Tart*

Discussion and Activities: Mindfulness Practice; Researching a Mistake

Time: About 1 hour and 30 minutes

Special Materials Needed:

- Mistakes! Research (Appendix 27) handout
- Chromebooks, iPads, computers, or computer lab

Whole-Class Read-Aloud #2: *Oops I Dropped the Lemon Tart*

Gather students together and direct their attention to the definition of *anxiety*. Discuss the theme of the last 3 days: that facing the unknown can often lead to positive results. This happened for School, Wemberly, and Angelina. Have students offer examples of how exactly this worked for all three characters.

Explain that the next three books they will be reading together on Days 4–6 are also about worry and anxiety but a little bit different:

> *"Each of these books also addresses anxiety, but I want you to think about how these books are different from the first three we read as we dive into them over the next few days. We will discover what the characters in these books do to alleviate or ease their anxiety."*

Then introduce the book *Oops I Dropped the Lemon Tart.* Before you start to read and discuss it, tell students that this is a picturebook set in Italy and written by a woman from Belgium. Before they start reading it, have students examine the dust jacket on the cover and notice its illustrations. Can they predict what it is about? What clues in the title and on the cover make them think about anxiety? Conduct a think–pair–share so that all students can share their ideas. Then call on two to three children to share with the class what they just told their partner.

Begin reading the story. Encourage students to comment on what they notice in the illustrations and text, but also stop with specific prompts at these places:

- First spread: "What about the special extra page flap? Why do you think the illustrator added this? What does it help us understand about Lucy?"
- Fourth spread: "What do you think happened to Lucy? How would you describe Evan and Lucy's friendship?"
- Seventh spread: "It doesn't seem like Lucy's teacher thinks Lucy has anything to worry about. And Nonna doesn't either. What do you think is happening with Lucy? What message do you think both Nonna and the teacher are trying to tell Lucy?"

Stop reading for a minute on this page for a longer discussion. As a class, discuss why it is important to keep trying even after you make a mistake. Have students recall a time they made a mistake but didn't give up and then share about that experience in pairs. As students share their stories, tie them back to the topic of anxiety by asking how each student felt as they made their mistake and how they felt after they kept trying.

Then pick up the book again and continue reading aloud:

- Ninth spread: Stop after you read, "Lucy gained confidence. She felt useful." Do we know what happened to Lucy? We actually don't know if something happened. What we do know is that Lucy was suffering from anxiety, and it was affecting her day-to-day life in a big way. And, we also know that working at the restaurant was helping her feel better.
    - Ask your students if they think her worries were small or big. Help them to realize that the worries might have been small, but they began to have a "compounding" effect as more and more worries consumed her. Mention that there are ways to combat such small worries with activities that can help lessen them, so they don't turn into something unbearable. (At the end of the read-aloud and discussion, you will come back to this topic; here, you are simply planting a seed.)
    - Also direct students' attention to Lucy's dad. Ask, "Why do you think Lucy's dad offered Lucy's help in the kitchen?" Students will observe that Lucy likes working in the kitchen,

that it seems to make her less worried. Guide students to appreciate how supportive Lucy's dad is, and how he helps alleviate her anxiety just as much as Evan and Nonna.

- Tenth spread: "What did you think Lucy's dad (Robert) was going to say? Were you surprised?"
- After you read the second-to-last spread with Nonna's letter, turn the page and show students the box that says, "Inspired by a True Story." Then read this aloud and on the next page the quote from Taka Kondo.

At the story's conclusion, have students discuss mistakes they've made that have actually turned out to be good! Ask two to three students to share their examples with the class.

Then request that the class come up with a theme or "big topic takeaway" for this story. Have students discuss their ideas briefly in pairs to get started, and then offer a few ideas to the whole group. Students will likely identify this theme: that making mistakes can, in fact, turn out for the best. You might also try to help them consider the idea of how friends and family can be of assistance when you are anxious, can make things feel a little better.

Take out a new poster paper and write down "Themes" and "Big Ideas" on the top. Then underneath, jot down the theme from *School's First Day of School* and the theme from *Oops I Dropped the Lemon Tart* on the list:

- Facing the unknown or your worry can often turn out to be rewarding!
- Making mistakes can sometimes turn out for the best!

Post this list near the definition of anxiety your class had earlier come up with. You will continue to add themes and big ideas to this poster throughout the remaining lessons, so be sure to leave plenty of room.

Discussion and Activities: Mindfulness Practice; Researching a Mistake

Now, have students return to their seats. Remind them that you had mentioned there are some small activities one can use to help alleviate stress when little worries bother you, some of which are called *mindfulness techniques*. Emphasize that mindfulness techniques can be used during those times when worries stack up and begin to overwhelm you.

Tell students you are all going to practice the "Away in a Bubble" technique. This is something they could try if they start to feel worried about a particular thing and it is bothering them a lot.

> Instructions: *Sit comfortably in your chair with your back straight and arms relaxed. Breathe in slowly three times and close your eyes. Think of a worry or something that is bothering you. Imagine a bubble forming around your worry, fully enclosing it. Then picture the bubble with your worry completely enclosed inside of it, floating away into the sky and getting smaller and smaller. Keep your eyes closed as you imagine the bubble floating away in the breeze and then whisper goodbye to your worry. Take two more deep breaths and open your eyes when you are*

ready. (This idea appears in Huebner's Outsmarting Worry: An Older Kid's Guide to Managing Anxiety *on p. 59.)*

Once the class has tried the "Away in a Bubble" **Mindfulness Practice**, ask how it made them feel. Keep this discussion relatively short, with just a few students sharing with the whole class. You might also want to share how it helps you/makes you feel like a good model for the students to demonstrate that everyone has worries from time to time.

> ***Note:*** Today's lesson is a little longer at an hour and a half. If needed, you can move this activity to the next day as a 30-minute research and writing activity.

Tell students that you are now going to return to the topic of mistakes after the mindfulness practice. Say:

> *"One thing we learned about today was that often mistakes lead to amazing discoveries, just like how the lemon tart became famous in the story. The lemon tart story is based on a true story about a food mistake! Now you will research some other food mistakes in the past and share your discoveries with your classmates."*

Pass out the Mistakes! Research (Appendix 27) worksheet. Then ask students to pull out their Chromebooks, iPads, or computers, or have them share devices from the computer lab. Have students work together in pairs with one device.

> ***Note:*** If your students do not have 1-1 devices or devices available in the room for small-group use, they can complete their research during other computer-access time.

On your whiteboard, model going to the website *Kiddle.co* to find something that was invented as the result of a mistake. Help them search using the term "mistake inventions." You might also specifically ask them to look into inventions such as chocolate chip cookies or ice cream cones. After seeing a few examples together, tell students to continue **Researching a Mistake** in pairs and write down one of their discoveries on their worksheet. Circle the room to give support and encouragement.

Segue to Next Day and Daily Reflection

At the conclusion of today's unit, collect these worksheets and explicitly help your students segue by letting them know you are now moving to the next part of the day, but tomorrow you will be returning to this topic of actions taken to minimize anxiety over a mistake.

When the school day is over, take some time to fill out the Daily Reflection to reflect on today's experience. Review it as you prepare for the next day.

DAYS 5 AND 6

Small Groups Read-Aloud and Discuss #2: *Jabari Jumps* and *Saturday Is Swimming Day*

Discussion and Activities: "Around the World" Collaborative Discussion; Compare/Contrast; Quick-Write; Breathing Exercise

Time: 2 hours across 2 days

Special Materials Needed:

- Story Map (Appendix 22); Compare and Contrast: *Jabari Jumps* and *Saturday Is Swimming Day* (Appendix 28) worksheet
- Six blank posters
- Three copies of each of the books

Small Groups Read-Aloud and Discuss #2: *Jabari Jumps* and *Saturday Is Swimming Day*

To begin, display both books for students to see. Ask them what the two books seem to have in common. (Swimming!)

Remind students that part of the purpose for their reading of *Lemon Tart* yesterday, and these two books today, is to recognize how anxiety might look and feel, and discover more strategies that people use to help decrease its impact. Have a student volunteer to share again what the theme of *Oops I Dropped the Lemon Tart* was, as discussed yesterday in class. (Point to the theme poster you have hung up in the room, so students see the themes they have already discussed in class.)

Explain to your students that today they will read one of two books in a small reading group. Some groups will read *Jabari Jumps*; some groups will read *Saturday Is Swimming Day*. As students read, they will fill out the blank Story Map (Appendix 22) handout, much like they did for *School's First Day of School*.

Divide up the students into six groups. (***Note:*** It is best to determine these groups the night before, so you can carefully consider how the group dynamics will work.) Then pass out one Story Map handout to each group. Ask for a student volunteer or two from each group to be the "scribes"; they will write down what the group decides for each part of their story map. Next, give a copy of one of the two books to each group.

Tell students they are going to read the book together. They can take turns reading aloud or let a few students who would like to read do the job. However, they must make sure that everyone can see the pages.

Explain to your students that, together, they will read the story first and then complete the blank Story Map. Let them get started and circle the room to encourage and support their work.

Segue to Next Day and Daily Reflection

This is likely the best place to end today. When you finish, collect the story maps and explicitly help your students segue by letting them know you are now moving to the next part of the day, but tomorrow you will be returning to this topic of lessening anxiety.

When the school day is over, take some time to fill out the Daily Reflection to reflect on today's experience. Review it as you prepare for the next day.

Discussion and Activities: "Around the World" Collaborative Discussion; Compare/Contrast; Quick-Write; Breathing Exercise

The following day, once every student has had a chance to read one of the books and complete their story map, students will participate in an **"Around the World" Collaborative Discussion.**

- Before starting this activity in your class, be sure you label each element of a narrative on a poster board. You will have one poster for each of these elements: (1) Characters, (2) Setting, (3) Problem, (4) Turning Point/Climax, (5) Solution, (6) Theme.
- After labeling the elements, split each poster down the middle. Label one half *Jabari Jumps* and the other half *Saturday Is Swimming Day*.
- Have students sit in their groups from yesterday. Pass out markers to each group. Then assign each group a poster to start with. Each group will move "around the world" (classroom) and write their answers on the half of the poster that corresponds to the book they read. Give students 20 minutes to complete this activity (about 3 minutes for each poster, with a minute for transition in-between).
- As students rotate from poster to poster, circle the room, conversing with groups and asking the students questions about the story and the element of the text they are describing. Make sure that each person in the group has a chance to write something on the poster or to participate in the discussion with you.
- When the 20 minutes are up, have students come back to their seats, leaving the posters hanging up around the classroom.

Then direct students' attention to the posters, starting with characters and setting. Pass out the Compare and Contrast (Appendix 28) worksheet. Explain that now students will begin to fill out the Venn diagram within it while everyone else looks at the posters. If possible, project a copy of the worksheet on the whiteboard.

Call on students to point out similarities and differences—do a **Compare/Contrast**—between the two stories for each of the elements. (If possible, write down their ideas and display your teacher's annotated copy of the Venn diagram via a projector.) As they find the similarities and differences, students can record them in a **Quick-Write** on their own copies of the Venn diagram worksheet.

Once the Venn diagram is complete, have students first reflect on what they noticed as similar themes in the two stories. Students will have many responses, but the idea of taking small steps to decrease anxiety will be predominant. Students may also notice that each main character had a strong support system, whether that was a family member or friend or teacher. These people were influential in helping each character work through their worries/complete their goals; however, emphasize that these individuals did not solve the characters' problems for them directly.

Then ask, "What are some things we learned from these characters, and the ones we met in earlier books this week, to help combat worries and anxiety?" Guide students as they consider what they have learned from the books read so far. Help them out as well by looking at the poster where you wrote the themes/big ideas from *School's First Day of School* and *Lemon Tart*. As the students suggest ideas, add them to this poster. Ideas might include:

- Take small steps to achieve a scary goal or work through anxiety.
- Don't be afraid to ask for help from a friend or a loved one.
- Adjust your steps if they still feel too big.

Collect the worksheets from your students.

Now, tell students that you are going to do one more **Breathing Exercise**, similar to the bubble you created yesterday. This breathing exercise is one that the main characters in *Jabari Jumps* or *Saturday Is Swimming Day* could have tried in their most anxious moments to calm down.

Explain to students that this is a quick way to reduce tension in your body. It is an idea called "Draining." Put your arms out straight, holding your hands in fists. Pretend your hands are faucets, and when you straighten your fingers, water begins to run out of them. Squeeze your hands, arms, face tightly, and then open your fists. If you want, you can even blow through your mouth and make a "shhhhhh" sound, as if water is running out of your hands or your "faucets." Let out all the tension and worry you have!

Segue to Next Day and Daily Reflection

At the conclusion of today's unit, explicitly help your students segue by letting them know you are now moving to the next part of the day, but tomorrow you will be returning to this topic of how they can alleviate stress on their own.

When the school day is over, take some time to fill out the Daily Reflection to reflect on today's experience. Review it as you prepare for the next day.

DAY 7

Whole-Class Read-Aloud #3: *The Girl and the Wolf*

Discussion and Activities: Class Brainstorm; "Face Your Fears"

Time: About 1 hour

Special Materials Needed:

- Class Brainstorm: Animals We Fear (Appendix 29) handout
- Facing My Fears: *The Girl and the Wolf* (Appendix 30) handout

Whole-Class Read-Aloud #3: *The Girl and the Wolf*

Gather your students for a whole-group read-aloud. Remind them that you have been talking about anxiety the last few days and direct their attention to the definition of anxiety from the first day of the unit. After that, review the poster with the themes/big ideas the class has collected throughout the unit from the books they have read so far. Let students know that over the next few days they will be adding more to the "theme" poster as they read a few more books together.

Introduce the story *The Girl and the Wolf.* Allow students to study the illustrations on its cover. Then discuss the background of the author and illustrator.

- This book is written by a Canadian author and the story highlights Indigenous people and their traditions.
- Read aloud the "Author's Note" (found in the back or the beginning of the book depending on your copy) to the students before you begin to help them better understand its context. Make sure to define *Indigenous* if your students are unfamiliar with this word.
- Also, briefly discuss the typical role of a wolf in folklore (often known as an evil or witchlike character). Ask your students what they think of when they recall wolves in fairy tales. Then ask students to keep this in mind as the book is read aloud.

Begin reading the story. Have students comment on what they notice about the illustrations and stories, and also stop at the places below to ask specific questions:

- After completing the fourth spread (when the wolf asks if the little girl knows her way home), have your students make a prediction about the wolf, especially considering your earlier discussion about a wolf's typical characterization in fairy tales. Ask, "Do you predict that the wolf will help or harm the girl? Why?"
- After completing the fifth spread, take some time to think aloud in front of your class on how this wolf seems compared to the evil character usually portrayed in folklore. Point out that the author writes his breath "stank of meat" and it was starting to get dark. The author's elaboration here still makes the reader think the wolf is going to harm the girl. You might also discuss with the class that it seems as if the main character feels helpless due to her responses to the wolf and her body language.
- After completing the seventh spread, ask, "What has changed in the story?" You will want to direct students to the fact that the wolf is being helpful, guiding the girl to breathe and take small steps to find her family.
- After completing the ninth spread, as a class, summarize how the wolf was encouraging and helpful. Ask students, "In what ways was the wolf being encouraging? Show me specific places in the text where this happened. How did he help the girl alleviate some of her anxiety? Again, tell me about specific places in the text where this happened."

When you have finished the story, discuss the wolf and the girl's relationship further.[1] Ask questions such as, "How does the girl show she likes the wolf?" and "Was your prediction from the beginning of the story correct?" and "Was the wolf helpful or harmful toward the girl?" You will want your students to come to the conclusion that sometimes the very things you fear might end up being okay. The girl faced her fear of both being lost and of the wolf, and the wolf ended up coming to her rescue. Some students will also recognize her ability to slow down, breathe, and tackle her fear step-by-step. The wolf helped the girl do this by reminding her of these steps. As students share these ideas, have them write them on the themes/big ideas class poster for the unit.

Discussion and Activities: Class Brainstorm; "Face Your Fears"

Have students return to their seats and pass out the Class Brainstorm: Animals We Fear (Appendix 29) handout (the topic "Animals We Fear" appears within a circle in the center of the page). Explain that for this **Class Brainstorm**, students will practice turning an animal they fear into a helpful supporter, mirroring what happened in the book. Brainstorm together animals that students fear as a class. As students think about such animals, ask them to add the animals to the web by writing down the word for them and drawing a line to the circle in the middle. If students have a hard time coming up with an animal they fear, they can just pick a widely feared animal or one that a family member is scared of.

After brainstorming, when students have decided on an animal, they can circle the word for it on their handout. Then pass out the next worksheet: Facing My Fears: *The Girl and the Wolf* (Appendix 30). In this activity, "**Face Your Fears**," students will fictionalize the animal to match the story just read, but they must make sure that their animal behaves in the way it really acts in nature. It can talk, but otherwise needs to be similar in appearance and actions to real life, much like the wolf in the story was. (A great white shark, e.g., would need to be in a body of water during any story about it.)

Direct students to the opening line of the worksheet: "If I were the author of this story, I would get lost in the woods with a _____________." They will need to cross out the word *woods* and write in the correct habitat for their animal!

Instruct students to think about their story and then fill in the worksheet with what will happen first, next, and at the end. Remind them that their story should be a retelling of *The Girl and the Wolf*, but with a different animal and in their own words. How will they alleviate some of their fears of this animal by turning its actions that are "scary" into being supportive, following the example of *The Girl and the Wolf*?

Give students 15–20 minutes to complete their work and circle the room to support and encourage them.

When most of the class has finished their story, have students do the "Stand Up–Hand Up–Pair Up" activity to share their ideas with more classmates. Students will stand up when you say "Stand Up"; then they will put up their hands and find a partner. They will share their

[1] Students might have questions about the tobacco gift on the last page. There is an "Author's Note" addressing this that you can read aloud as needed.

ideas for 2 minutes and then raise their hand when they finish to find another partner. After students have shared for two rounds, collect their worksheets.

Segue to Next Day and Daily Reflection

At the conclusion of today's unit, explicitly help your students segue by letting them know you are now moving to the next part of the day, but you will be returning to this topic of facing one's fears tomorrow.

When the school day is over, take some time to fill out the Daily Reflection to reflect on today's experience. Review it as you prepare for the next day.

DAY 8

Small Groups Read-Aloud and Discuss #3: *Me and My Fear* and *Ruby Finds a Worry*

Discussion and Activity: Themes and Big Ideas Discussion

Time: About 1 hour

Special Materials Needed:

- Story Map (Appendix 22)
- Three copies of each of the books

Small Groups Read-Aloud and Discuss #3: *Me and My Fear* and *Ruby Finds a Worry*

To begin, display both books for students to see. Ask students what the two books seem to have in common. This might be difficult to tell at first. Read the titles aloud and help students find in the cover illustrations the blob-type "fear" and the squiggle-type "worry." Assist students in realizing that in both books the ideas of fear/worry are actual characters.

Explain to your students that today they will read one of two books in a small reading group much like they did with *Jabari Jumps* and *Saturday Is Swimming Day*. As students read, they will fill out the blank Story Map (Appendix 22) handout as a group for their book.

Divide up the students into six groups. (***Note:*** It is best to determine these groups the night before, so you can carefully consider how the group dynamics will work.) Then pass out one Story Map handout to each group. Ask for a student volunteer or two from each group to be the "scribes"; they will write down what the group decides for each part of their story map. Next, give a copy of one of the two books to each group.

Tell students they are going to read the book together. They can take turns reading aloud or let a few students who would like to read do the job. However, they must make sure that everyone can see the pages.

Explain to your students that, together, they will read the story first and then complete the blank Story Map. Let them get started and circle the room to encourage and support their work.

Discussion and Activity: Themes and Big Ideas Discussion

Once the story map is completed, ask students to engage in a **Themes and Big Ideas Discussion** in their groups with regard to their story. After a few minutes of small-group discussion, ask them to share their thoughts with the whole class.

Students might suggest that talking or sharing your fear/worry can help reduce it, or that everyone has fears/worries. As they share, they will quickly come to realize that the books are very similar in their message! Write down the two themes/big ideas on the class list.

Then have some students switch their groups. Ask two people from each of the *Ruby* book groups to stand up and join each of the *Me and My Fear* groups. Next, send two people from the *Me and My Fear* groups to the *Ruby* groups. Once everyone is situated in their new groups, tell students to share about their books with each other. They should talk about two things: (1) explain what happened in the book and then (2) explain how the book made them feel. Give students about 10 minutes for this discussion, allowing the *Ruby* people to talk for 5 minutes and then the *Me and My Fear* students to speak for 5 minutes.

Segue to Next Day and Daily Reflection

At the conclusion of today's unit, explicitly help your students segue by letting them know you are now moving to the next part of the day, but tomorrow you will be returning to this topic of coping with fear/worry.

When the school day is over, take some time to fill out the Daily Reflection to reflect on today's experience. Review it as you prepare for the next day.

DAY 9

Conclusion

Discussion and Activity: Readers' Theater

Time: About 1.5 hour

Special Materials Needed:

- Completed story maps from previous days

Discussion and Activity: Readers' Theater

> ***Note:*** For today's activity, students will work in small groups. Plan for small groups of around four people and decide on the group members the night before.

To begin, review the themes/big ideas on the poster one more time. Emphasize with the students how much they have learned about worry and anxiety after the last several days! Then tell students that today this unit will conclude, but that worry and anxiety is a topic they can circle back to discuss many times in the school year.

Next, tell students that today in ending the unit, they will stage a **Readers' Theater.** Students will work in small groups to act out one of the stories read over the last 2 weeks. Their performances must be 5 minutes or less.

Using the story maps they completed for the books as a guide, students will take the following steps:

- First, select a story.
- Second, analyze their story maps from that book to consider what part of the story is most important for them to tell. As a group, they must decide what they are going to highlight in their retelling of the story. What message/theme/big idea about anxiety and worry are they going to convey?
- Third, assign each member of the group a character plot.
- Fourth, together decide orally on the brief scenes they are going to enact for their retelling, focusing on the part of their story that they chose as most important.
- Fifth, write out a script together. (Tell students that one way to do this is to fold a piece of paper in half vertically. List the student/character on one side and the lines each will say on the other side.)
- They will have 30 minutes to complete these components.

Write these steps on the whiteboard as students listen to the directions. Then pass out the story maps from the previous days to each student and direct students to work in their groups.

When the 30 minutes are up, announce to the class that they will have 10 minutes to practice their story before they perform for the class. Students can use their scripts during their performance if they would like to. Each group's performance should be about 5 minutes long. Have each group perform for the class.

- After each performance, ask the performers to identify the major lesson or theme or important point about anxiety that their group focused on in their performance.

When the performances are completed, have students return to their seats and tell them to reflect on what they've learned about anxiety.

Ask, "What are some of the most valuable things you've learned about living with anxiety in this unit?" Have a few volunteers share with the class. As the teacher, feel free to model for your students by sharing what you felt was the most valuable information about anxiety in the unit and why it spoke to you.

To conclude the discussion, remind students that feeling worried is normal for everyone, and while anxieties may not go away completely, there are many strategies to help alleviate them. In this unit, they have learned some of those strategies from the characters and the themes in the stories they've read.

Segue to Next Day and Daily Reflection, Unit Post-Check with Students, and Taking the Pulse of the Class: After Unit

Explicitly help your students segue by letting them know you are now moving to the next part of the day, and this is the end of the unit on anxiety and worry. Let them know that the books will remain in the classroom for some time and that they are welcome to revisit them. Also tell them that although the unit may have been completed, these conversations can always continue around its topic, and they should feel free to ask questions or discuss the topic in more detail.

When the school day is over, take some time to complete the Daily Reflection form. The next day or the day after that, ask your students to complete the Unit Post-Check with Students. Finally, about a week to 10 days after the unit was completed, fill out Taking the Pulse of the Class: After Unit to consider more broadly this experience for your current students, yourself, and your future students.

FINAL SUGGESTIONS

During the weeks following this unit, you might want to revisit some of these themes, books, or the conversations around them. This unit was intended as an introduction to, and the beginning of courageous conversations around, the difficult topic of the mental health issue of anxiety. It was meant to bring light to the issue and to help students feel more comfortable talking about it. It also emphasized that struggling with anxiety is very challenging and that your teachers, school staff and administration, friends and families are here to support you if you are experiencing anxiety. Likewise, students themselves are encouraged to become the support for others in need.

Some students may want to continue to discuss this topic in class in a deeper way. Reach out to your school counselors, psychologists, and support faculty for individual help for students seeking more specific or individualized support in this area. The Unit Post-Check with Students will help you identify students needing or wanting this support.

You may decide to expand on this unit with further book sharing, discussions, and activities. The websites that follow may serve as good resources as you do this work.

ADDITIONAL RESOURCES

American Academy of Child and Adolescent Psychiatry—Anxiety Resource Center: *www.aacap.org/AACAP/Families_and_Youth/Resource_Centers/Anxiety_Disorder_Resource_Center/Home.aspx*

American Psychological Association: Psychology Topics—Anxiety: *www.apa.org/topics/anxiety*

Centers for Disease Control and Prevention: Children's Mental Health—Anxiety and Depression in Children: *www.cdc.gov/childrensmentalhealth/depression.html*

Child Mind Institute: Family Resource Center—Anxiety: *https://childmind.org/topics/anxiety*

Mental Health Foundation (United Kingdom)—The Anxious Child: *www.mentalhealth.org.uk/explore-mental-health/publications/anxious-child*

National Association of School Psychologists—Anxiety: *https://apps.nasponline.org/search-results.aspx?q=anxiety*

MEETING COMMON CORE AND CASEL STANDARDS

Common Core English Language Arts Standards for Grade 4

This unit meets specific Common Core State Standards for English Language Arts in grades 3, 4, 5, and 6. We have included the specific ELA standards for grade 4 below to illustrate the strands and items met (similar for all four grades third through sixth). The QR code here will link you to the specific lists for grades 3, 5, and 6.

CCSS.ELA-LITERACY.SL.4.1

Engage effectively in a range of collaborative discussions (one-on-one, in groups, and teacher-led) with diverse partners on grade 4 topics and texts, building on others' ideas and expressing their own clearly.

CCSS.ELA-LITERACY.RL.4.1

Refer to details and examples in a text when explaining what the text says explicitly and when drawing inferences from the text.

CCSS.ELA-LITERACY.RL.4.2

Determine a theme of a story, drama, or poem from details in the text; summarize the text.

CCSS.ELA-LITERACY.RL.4.3

Describe in depth a character, setting, or event in a story or drama, drawing on specific details in the text (e.g., a character's thoughts, words, or actions).

CCSS.ELA-LITERACY.RL.4.4

Determine the meaning of words and phrases as they are used in a text, including those that allude to significant characters found in mythology (e.g., Herculean).

CCSS.ELA-LITERACY.RL.4.9

Compare and contrast the treatment of similar themes and topics (e.g., opposition of good and evil) and patterns of events (e.g., the quest) in stories, myths, and traditional literature from different cultures.

CASEL Social and Emotional Learning Standards for Grades 3–5

This unit meets specific CASEL Core Competence Area goals for Social and Emotional Learning for grades 3–5. We have included the CASEL areas and specific example standards below to show the items met in this unit. (The items are similar for grade 6.)

Self-Awareness: The abilities to understand one's own emotions, thoughts, and values and how they influence behavior across contexts. This includes capacities to recognize one's strengths and limitations with a well-grounded sense of confidence and purpose.

- Identifying one's emotions
- Linking feelings, values, and thoughts
- Having a growth mindset

Self-Management: The abilities to manage one's emotions, thoughts, and behaviors effectively in different situations and to achieve goals and aspirations. This includes the capacities to delay gratification, manage stress, and feel motivation and agency to accomplish personal/collective goals.

- Managing one's emotions
- Identifying and using stress-management strategies
- Exhibiting self-discipline and self-motivation

Social Awareness: The abilities to understand the perspectives of and empathize with others, including those from diverse backgrounds, cultures, and contexts. This includes the capacities to feel compassion for others, understand broader historical and social norms for behavior in different settings, and recognize family, school, and community resources and supports.

- Taking others' perspectives
- Recognizing strengths in others
- Demonstrating empathy and compassion
- Showing concern for the feelings of others

Relationship Skills: The abilities to establish and maintain healthy and supportive relationships and to effectively navigate settings with diverse individuals and groups. This includes the capacities to communicate clearly, listen actively, cooperate, work collaboratively to problem-solve and negotiate conflict constructively, navigate settings with differing social and cultural demands and opportunities, provide leadership, and seek or offer help when needed.

- Communicating effectively
- Developing positive relationships

- Practicing teamwork and collaborative problem solving
- Resolving conflicts constructively

Responsible Decision Making: The abilities to make caring and constructive choices about personal behavior and social interactions across diverse situations. This includes the capacities to consider ethical standards and safety concerns, and to evaluate the benefits and consequences of various actions for personal, social, and collective well-being.

- Demonstrating curiosity and open-mindedness
- Identifying solutions for personal and social problems
- Reflecting on one's role to promote personal, family, and community well-being

Losing Hope

Talking About Depression

THE BOOKS

Outside, Inside

by LeUyen Pham (Roaring Brook Press, 2021)

Filled with small hints and nuanced details, LeUyen Pham's brightly colored scenes of the days right before the pandemic and the first days of it complement her consideration of this unique time when everyone went inside. Pham does not shy away from the scariness of the period, yet, despite everything, a sense of hope prevails. An important "Author's Note" at the back of the book explains that the people and their stories portrayed within her illustrations are real, underscoring the title's emotional heft.

After the Fall: How Humpty Dumpty Got Back Up Again

by Dan Santat (Roaring Brook Press, 2017)

What happened next? Dan Santat fractures the well-known nursery rhyme of Humpty Dumpty to create a masterfully crafted story of facing fears and overcoming a traumatic experience. Humpty's miserable state after his fall, and the way the trauma affects his daily life and takes away his favorite hobby, is painfully, but humorously, captured in detail, only serving to create greater delight for readers when Humpty is finally "put back together" again in a joyful new way.

Big Bear Was Not the Same

by Joanne Rowland, illustrated by John Ledda (Beaming Books, 2021)

Big Bear is trapped in a forest fire, and although he escapes, he is not the same. Joanne Rowland's tale gently follows the confusion of Little Bear as he learns to adapt to the new changes in his friend that are a result of posttraumatic stress disorder (commonly called PTSD). Rowland does not promise a perfectly happy ending for either bear, but her messaging about having time and patience offers hope. The bears and beautiful wilderness backdrops created by John Ledda also hold a hint of realism that helps to ground the story.

Maybe Tomorrow?

by Charlotte Agell, illustrated by Ana Ramirez Gonzalez (Scholastic, 2019)

Elba has been grieving for Little Bird for a long time and is weighed down by a "block" of grief. Then she meets Norris, who is always happy and offers friendship and support. As their friendship begins to grow, Elba's grief slowly lessens. The brightly colored cartoon illustrations of Ana Ramirez Gonzalez manage to capture the nuances of Elba's emotions and the patience of Norris.

A Blue Kind of Day

by Rachel Tomilson, illustrated by Tori-Jay Mordey (Kokila, 2022)

Coen feels more than just blue today. Rachel Tomilson's details sketch a young main character who is experiencing severe symptoms of depression, and his caring family tries but is unable to help at first. Eventually, Coen feels their warm presence and begins to reach out, asking for some time to quietly coexist together with them and in time gaining some sense of peace and a bit of hope. Tori-Jay Mordey's images movingly capture Coen's pain, as well as his family's, and pack an emotional punch.

The Cat Who Couldn't Be Bothered

by Jack Kurland (Frances Lincoln, 2024)

Gareth the cat can't be bothered, but really that is because he *is* bothered. In fact, he is quite sad. Jack Kurland's sparse text and dramatic cats create a deceivingly simple story that demonstrates the importance of trying to verbalize your emotions when you are not feeling well. Young readers will enjoy the imaginative ideas the cats present to Gareth, as well as the relief Gareth feels when he finally explains why he is staying home.

When Sadness Is at Your Door

by Eva Eland (Random House, 2019)

When the green bloblike monster appears to have come for a visit, a young boy is not so sure he would like his guest to stay. But Sadness appears to be sticking around for a while, and eventually the child finds that acknowledging his presence makes things just a bit easier. Eva Eland's handwritten-style font and softness of the images help keep the book from becoming too didactic and instead evoke the sense of a warm reminder that all emotions are okay, and noticing and naming them might help.

Rain Before Rainbows

by Smriti Prasadam-Halls, illustrated by David Litchfield (Candlewick Press, 2020)

The lyrical text of Smriti Prasadam-Halls offers a more generalized tale of struggle and hope, but David Litchfield's detailed painted illustrations show the reader a young girl and a fox displaced by warfare and violence and now seeking refuge. Each page highlights a new obstacle on their journey until they finally reach a new land where they are welcomed. Once there, they do not simply rest but rather begin to work and care for the land to create an even better place for all. Litchfield's masterful control of light gives a reality to the images that shimmer and dance in true sunlight.

> ***Note:*** As with all thematic book sets, we recommend that after each book has been shared within the unit, it is placed in an easily accessible display in the classroom for the rest of the unit days. Children should then be allowed access to explore these books on their own during free-choice times.

PLANNING CHECKLIST

Losing Hope: Talking About Depression

We suggest the following timeline to prepare and then share and discuss the books and do the related activities with your students. (A reproducible version of this checklist is available in Appendix 1.) Please note that timing for your individual class should be determined by your situation and your schedule and, most importantly, should be guided by your students' reactions to the books and activities. Plan generally, however, on about 1 hour of daily time with the unit for 7–10 days in a row.

Two Weeks Prior

- ☐ Complete Taking the Pulse of the Class: Before Unit (Appendix 2) for a general sense of your class at this time.
- ☐ Collect and read twice each of the books for the unit.
- ☐ Review the "Unit Plans: Reading, Discussions, and Activities" section of the unit.
- ☐ Send out the Administration Notification Slip (Appendix 3) and School Counselor/Psychologist and Support Staff Notification Slip (Appendix 4).

One Week Prior

- ☐ (Optional) Send out Family Notification Slips (Appendix 5) to the families of your students.
- ☐ Have students complete the Unit Pre-Check with Students (Appendix 6) and review the results carefully. Check in with any students with reactions that cause concern so that you can prepare for extra support.
- ☐ Review Chapter 2 of the book.
- ☐ Collect all materials needed for the unit:

- ☐ **Daily Reflection forms (Appendix 7):** You will need one for each day.
- ☐ **Books:** One copy is required, but you may prefer to secure two copies of each book. After each book has been shared during the unit, place it in an easily accessible display in the classroom. Please give students access to explore these books on their own during free-choice times. You will want to keep the display available for some time after the unit is completed.
- ☐ **Materials already in your classroom:** Please have available and ready to use the following commonplace classroom materials:
  - Chart paper or a section of whiteboard that can remain posted for the duration of the unit
  - Unlined white paper
  - Pencils and pens; colored pencils, crayons, or markers
  - Construction paper or other colored paper
  - Scissors
  - Tape or glue
  - Any additional materials indicated within the unit chapter's detailed description

During: Readings, Discussions, and Activities (approximately 7–10 school days)

- ☐ Follow the detailed plans for each day.
- ☐ One to 2 days after the unit is completed, have students complete the Unit Post-Check with Students (Appendix 8).

One Week Following

- ☐ After reviewing the Unit Post-Check with Students, check in with any students with reactions that cause concern.
- ☐ Refer any students expressing interest or for whom you have concerns at this point for additional, individual discussion with a school support professional. Also consider additional whole-class work if indicated.
- ☐ Complete and review Taking the Pulse of the Class: After Unit (Appendix 9). This will help you reflect on your experience and your students' experiences with the thematic book set.

UNIT OVERVIEW
Losing Hope: Talking About Depression

Day	Books	Discussion and Activities
1	**Introduction and Whole-Class Read-Aloud #1:** *Outside, Inside*	• Positives and Negatives • "Somewhere In-Between"
2	**Whole-Class Read-Aloud #2:** *After the Fall: How Humpty Dumpty Got Back Up Again*	• Word Gradient

3 and 4	**Small Groups Read-Aloud and Discuss #1:** *Big Bear Was Not the Same* *Maybe Tomorrow?*	• Goal Setting with Small Steps
5	**Whole-Class Read-Aloud #3:** *A Blue Kind of Day*	• Comfort Box List • Comfort Collage
6 and 7	**Small Groups Read-Aloud and Discuss #2:** *The Cat Who Couldn't Be Bothered* *When Sadness Is at Your Door*	• Stop and Notice • Comfort Box List Continued • Comfort Collage Continued
8	**Conclusion and Whole-Class Read-Aloud #4:** *Rain Before Rainbows*	• Three Good Things

Note: Each "day" of this unit is intended to take around 1 hour of class time. Time may vary slightly depending on student discussion, but please keep this time frame in mind as you move through the reading and activities.

BEFORE BEGINNING

1. Make sure you have completed the "Two Weeks Prior" and "One Week Prior" items on the planning checklist, including the Taking the Pulse of the Class: Before Unit and the Unit Pre-Check with Students forms.
2. Remember that the books within these units are specifically sequenced to build understanding. To have the greatest likelihood of success with these courageous conversations, we ask that you follow the order of the books, discussions, and activities and complete the entire unit.
3. Review Chapter 2 to help prepare for navigating the upcoming discussions you will be having with your students. As you complete the Daily Reflections at the end of each school day, consider revisiting Chapter 2 for helpful support in engaging in your own self-reflection and awareness, and ensuring your thoughtful and respectful approach to the topic.

DAY 1

Introduction and Whole-Class Read-Aloud #1: *Outside, Inside*

Discussion and Activities: Positives and Negatives; "Somewhere In-Between"

Time: 1 hour total

Introduction and Whole-Class Read-Aloud #1: *Outside, Inside*

Begin the unit by gathering students together for a whole-class read-aloud and discussion. Explain to your class that today you will be reading a story that was written in 2020, during the first part of the global pandemic. Ask students to raise their hands if they remember that time period. Then tell them to turn to their partner for a quick pair-share about their memories or what they have learned and heard about the pandemic from their families and friends. Allow for 2 minutes of sharing. (Depending on students' ages, they may have strong memories or more blurred ones.) Explain that this story by author and illustrator LeUyen Pham includes an "Author's Note" at its end recalling her experiences at that time.

- Show students the page spread that comprises the "Author's Note" and then read it aloud. (It is dense text, so you do not need to show the page to them while reading; however, make sure to show the "Author's Note" to them before you read it aloud.)
- Then show students the dust jacket. You will need to open the book and turn it around to show them the entire dust jacket cover as it is one full-spread picture. Ask students to point out a few things they notice that are specific to the pandemic (e.g., the face masks on hooks, a laptop with online schoolwork on its screen, the homemade bread, the teddy bear in a window, etc.). Then take the dust jacket off the book. Show students the single full-spread image that appears on the board pages (the hardcover) of the book. Ask them to comment on what they notice here (e.g., the little girl and her dad are wearing masks, there are no other people outside, a rainbow has been drawn in chalk on the sidewalk).
- Now turn to the endpapers (the inside of the front and back board covers) of the book. Show students the first inside page (before the title page), with the little girl inside hugging her cat, and then the last inside page, with the little girl outside running with her cat. Ask students how these two pictures match the title *Outside, Inside*. Do they think the little girl likes one better than the other?

Tell students that during the pandemic a general sadness existed among most people. Explain:

> *"Many people felt sad or stuck about having to be inside. But it was a complicated feeling because people were also worried; many people across the world were becoming very sick, and staying inside was something that might help keep the sickness from spreading. LeUyen Pham captures some of this feeling in her book."*

Then start to slowly read the book aloud. The text is sparse and lyrical, and the pages are full of images, so offer your students plenty of time to see each page. Welcome comments about what they are noticing.

- When you reach the last spread that opens up into a four-page image, give students time to look at the large scene, and then ask if they think this is an image of what actually happened or what Pham thinks would happen in the future. Help them understand that at the time she wrote this book, people were still mostly living under pandemic restrictions, so she was conveying what she hoped and believed *would* happen, rather than what was occurring in most places.

Discussion and Activities: Positives and Negatives; "Somewhere In-Between"

Have students return to their seats and pass out pieces of blank paper to them. Show students how to fold their papers into vertical thirds to make three columns. (They do not need to be exactly the same but try to have the students create three similar-sized columns.)

On the whiteboard or on large chart paper, draw three columns. At the top of the first one, write "Positives," and on the top of the last one, write "Negatives." Tell students to do the same on their papers and to leave the middle column blank. Then explain to students that they are going to write a list of **Positives and Negatives** from the pandemic that they might personally recall or that were described in the book. Explain that the negatives on the list are things that were challenging or made people (including themselves) feel sad or down or stuck, such as not being able to play with friends, or people getting sick. Positives would be some of the good things that happened, such as time for new hobbies or seeing more wildlife outside. Write these examples on the board as you share them. Then give students time to work on their lists, circling the room to support and encourage them.

> ***Note:*** The pandemic affected families in many different ways. Some students may have had relatives die or become very ill; some students' parents may have lost their jobs. Be aware that the emotional impact of this activity could greatly vary for your students.

After students have worked on their lists for about 5 minutes, call for their attention and ask them to put down their pencils. Explain:

> "*While there are some things on the list that are very negative, such as people being sick and dying, or some that are very positive, such as people running errands or getting food for neighbors more than they ever had before, some of the things on the list might be a bit 'in-between' and could even be related. For example, I might have on my list 'no soccer'* [write this on the board in the Negatives column] *because I missed not going to practices and games a lot. But on the positive side, I had 'learned to bake bread'* [write this on the board in the Positives column]. *These two are actually connected! I missed soccer, but I had more time, so I learned something I had never tried before. So, the negative and positive created a 'somewhere in-between.'* [Draw a

line connecting the two. Put a circle or star in the middle of the line where it crosses the middle column.] *A lot of you might have no school in one of the columns! If you have listed it as a positive, then there probably is also a related negative about not getting to see friends as much. If you have listed this as a negative, there is probably also a related positive about learning new ways of connecting online or seeing classmates' pets or family members online, and the like."*

- Ask students to now try and connect some of their positives and negatives: to identify those "**Somewhere In-Between.**" Explain that there might be some negatives or positives that do not seem to connect with items in the other column, but if students think about them more thoughtfully, they might be able to connect more of the items. Also add that there are a few things that might only feel negative and that is okay—not every item needs to be part of a pair. (***Note:*** This is an important point to include for those students who might have experienced events of extreme hardship during the pandemic.)
- Tell students to get started by drawing lines just like those you modeled between two items. They should also talk with their elbow or desk partners to give each other alternate ideas and find connections between the two columns.
- Circle the room, providing encouragement and support.

After about 7–10 minutes of work, stop students and have them put aside their pencils. Remind them that the pandemic was a worldwide event that was very difficult for many people. Explain that there was a general sadness at the time. Add:

> *"One thing that can help when you are experiencing sad and hard events is to try looking at what positives there might be as well. It does not mean you ignore all that is sad and say everything is okay, but rather you're just going to be aware that there are always 'somewhere in-betweens,' too! Finding a few positives about the situation, and thinking about the connections and 'somewhere in-betweens,' can help you look at a sad event with a slightly different mindset. Doing this helps you be a little more flexible in your thinking and encourages hope."*

- Again, show the students the large four-page spread at the end of *Outside, Inside.* Remind them that when Pham created this, it was her hope, rather than what was happening in the real world. Pham's book is a good example of "somewhere in-betweens," as it shows both the sad and negative things occurring but also offers a glimpse of the good things happening at the same time—things that encouraged her to have hope and imagine this future as shown on the spread.

Segue to Next Day and Daily Reflection

Advise your students that, over the next week, your class is going to talk about big emotions of feeling down, sad, and depressed. Let them know that you will now be moving on to the next part of the day, but tomorrow you will be returning to this topic of difficult emotions.

When the school day is over, take some time to fill out the Daily Reflection to reflect on this experience. Review it as you prepare for the next day's lesson.

DAY 2

Whole-Class Read-Aloud #2: *After the Fall: How Humpty Dumpty Got Back Up Again*

Discussion and Activity: Word Gradient

Time: 1 hour total

> ***Note:*** Today's reading, discussion, and activities will address directly the topic of depression as a mental health illness for the first time. When you worked through the Taking the Pulse of the Class: Before Unit (Appendix 2) document, you likely noted that your class included students with a family member suffering from severe mental health issues or whose family has been touched by tragedy, such as suicide. But these types of mental and behavioral health challenges in a family are sometimes kept quiet, and you might not know which of your students have been affected in this way. Be aware that the emotional impact of these discussions and activities in this unit could range across the full spectrum for your students. Chapter 2 is a good place to turn for reminders of how to support students; also reach out for advice from your school psychologists and counselors if needed.

Whole-Class Read-Aloud #2: *After the Fall: How Humpty Dumpty Got Back Up Again*

Gather students together for a whole-class read-aloud and discussion. Tell students that today you are going to read and discuss *After the Fall: How Humpty Dumpty Got Back Up Again* by Dan Santat. Explain that, like yesterday's *Outside, Inside*, this book uses its dust jacket cover, inside hardbound cover, and endpages to tell you quite a bit about the story before you even read it. These outside pieces of the book are called the *peritext*, and Santat is famous for using the peritext in his books.

- Start the class read-aloud by exploring this peritext. Show students the entire dust jacket cover like you did yesterday and ask what they notice about the text on one side of the wall ("Life begins when you get back up") and how that relates to the title on the other side. Ask what they think Humpty Dumpty is doing on the wall with his binoculars. Then take off the dust jacket and show your students the one full-spread picture that is on the board pages (the hardcover) of the book. Ask them to comment on what they notice here: What do they think happened? Now, turn to the endpapers (the inside of the front and back board covers) of the book. Only show the front endpaper at this point, and before you ask students what they notice, read aloud the inside flap text: "My name is Humpty Dumpty. I'm famous for falling off a wall. (You may have heard about it.)" Ask students if anyone knows and would like to recite the Humpty Dumpty rhyme by Mother Goose.
    - Here is the poem. After the student recites it, say the words again again while writing them on the whiteboard or on chart paper:

        Humpty Dumpty sat on a wall,
Humpty Dumpty had a great fall;
All the king's horses and all the king's men
Couldn't put Humpty together again.

- Now, read the entire inside front flap, repeating the first part you just read and continuing until you read "After the fall." Stop here and ask students to predict what might happen in the story. After a few predictions, explain that today's story is a "fractured" fairy tale. This means authors take a well-known fairy tale or folklore and fundamentally change it. They are counting on their readers to already know something about the original tale to catch the nuances and humor in their fractured tale. Tell students to keep the original poem in mind as they listen to *After the Fall.*
- Begin reading the book to the class, making sure that all can see its illustrations. You will be asking students frequently throughout the read-aloud to comment on what they notice. Use the prompts below to help draw attention to specific pages:
  - Title page: "What happened to Humpty here?"
  - On the second spread: "What was Humpty doing on the wall? (Notice the binoculars and what Humpty says about being close to the birds.)"
  - On the third spread: "What is the name of the hospital? What hints in Humpty's room show he is a birdwatcher? What do you notice in his room that might make him sadder?"
  - On the fourth spread: "What do you notice about the cereal? How might this make Humpty feel sadder?"
  - On the sixth spread: "What thought do you think Humpty is having?"
  - On the eighth spread: "What do you think about the plane that Humpty created? Is it what you expected? Why or why not?"
  - On the eleventh spread: "What is the accident that is happening?"
  - On the twelfth and thirteenth spreads: "How can you tell that Humpty is scared? How does looking at the illustration on the thirteenth spread make you feel? How has the author drawn the picture to make you feel that way?"
  - On the fifteenth spread: "What do you notice about the light on the wall?"
  - On the seventeenth spread (last pages of the book): "How do you feel looking at this page?"

Note: The end of the book is quite dramatic, so give your students plenty of time to examine the page. After you read and discuss the last page, show them the back endpaper and ask what they notice.

- Next, have a brief general share about the story. Ask students to turn to a partner sitting near them for a pair-share on their reaction to the book: sharing their favorite part of the story and explaining why they liked it.

Discussion and Activity: Word Gradient

Have students return to their seats. As they settle in, tell them that Humpty's sadness was specific to an event that had happened. Sometimes particular events, especially those that are big and traumatic, can make us feel very sad and scared, as if we are stuck. Reminders of the event can make us feel sad, even when things seem to be okay. For example, Humpty was reminded of his fear of heights every time he saw a ladder. He was reminded that he couldn't do the things he wanted to because he was afraid he might fall again.

- Explain that Humpty was feeling more than just a little sad. Ask students how they might describe Humpty's feelings. What words would they use to describe how he felt? As students offer ideas, write the words on a section of the whiteboard. (Students might suggest all sorts of feelings, such as being *afraid*, *anxious*, *scared*, as well as those that mean "sad," such as *depressed*, *blue*, or *down*. Write all words suggested on the board.)
- Then draw a line across the whiteboard and in the middle write the word *sad*. Tell students that they are going to create a **Word Gradient**. Ask them if they know what *gradient* means in terms of art. After students give suggestions, explain that in art, *gradient* usually refers to the amount of color. It is like a slope or ramp, where the colors are lighter on one side of the spectrum and darker on the other.
- Ask students to think about the emotion *sad*. What is a word they might use for a deeper type of sad? How about a lighter type of sad? Help students come up with different words that mean "sad" and place them together on the line, going from light to dark.
  - Assist students as needed by suggesting words like (feeling) *blue*, (feeling) *down*, *miserable*, *despairing*, *out of sorts*, *gloomy*, *bleak*, and the like. You might pull out a thesaurus to help, too! If a student has not suggested the word *depressed*, be sure to add that one to the line. For each word, have students tell you where it should go and explain why.
- After several words are listed on the line, ask students if everyone agrees with the placement of the words for the most part. If students would like, have them move words if they can convincingly explain their reasons why. When the gradient line seems set, find the word *depressed* and star it. Explain that *depressed* can mean a feeling—a type of sadness—but it is also used as a term for a mental health illness called *depression*. Ask students if they know what depression is and take a few answers. Then share the following definition of depression from the American Psychiatry Association, explaining that it is a definition used by doctors:
  - "Depression is a common and serious mental disorder that negatively affects how you feel, think, act, and perceive the world. Symptoms can vary from mild to severe and appear differently in each person. It is normal to experience moments of sadness or feeling down or blue as part of being a human. However, depression is when symptoms occur for most of the day, nearly every day, for more than two weeks, and change your day-to-day functioning. Depression is treatable."
  - Stop for a brief moment and explain a few words in the definition. Some of the words mean something a little bit different to doctors. For example, *common* in the definition means that depression happens a lot. Lots of people have it. It does not mean it is not severe or serious, but rather just that it is not a highly unusual or rare disease. *Treatable* means that there are medications and therapies available for relieving symptoms. It is important to understand that *treatable* does not mean that it is always cured; it simply means that there are many medications and types of therapies and treatments available that can help alleviate symptoms for many people.
- Explain that Humpty might have been diagnosed as having symptoms of depression by the

King's Men doctors at the beginning of the book because he was having a hard time every day. And in fact, that was something the author, Dan Santat, was mindful of when he wrote this book. Show students the dedication at the beginning of the book on the title page: "For Leah." Explain that Leah is Dan's wife. She suffered with postpartum depression after their children were born. Postpartum depression is a type of depression that can occur after a woman has a new baby. Dan dedicated this book to Leah after watching her journey with this illness and in admiration of her courage.

Tell your students that, over the next few days, the class will be reading more books that include characters who are very sad and might be exhibiting the symptoms of depression. As the class reads and discusses the books, they will also learn about ways to support people who might be experiencing depression, and some strategies that can help alleviate some of its symptoms.

Segue to Next Day and Daily Reflection

Explicitly help your students segue by letting them know that you will now be moving on to the next part of the day, but you will be returning to this topic of depression tomorrow.

When the school day is over, take some time to fill out the Daily Reflection to reflect on this experience. Review it as you prepare for the next day's lesson.

DAYS 3 AND 4

Small Groups Read-Aloud and Discuss #1: *Big Bear Was Not the Same* and *Maybe Tomorrow?*

Discussion and Activity: Goal Setting with Small Steps

Time: 2.5 hours total across 2 days

> ***Note:*** You can divide this time as works best for your class. Plan to spend 15–20 minutes for read-aloud and discussions with each of three smaller groups of students during center or station time for each of the books, for a total of about 1 hour and 45 minutes to 2 hours total. Then allow 30–40 minutes for whole-class discussion and the Goal Setting with Small Steps activity.

Small Groups Read-Aloud and Discuss #1: *Big Bear Was Not the Same* and *Maybe Tomorrow?*

> ***Note:*** Prior to class today, divide your students into three small groups. Across 2 days, work with each small group independently to read and discuss both of the two titles: *Big Bear Was Not the Same* and *Maybe Tomorrow?*. The goal is for each of the two books to be read and discussed by all the students but in smaller groups, rather than as a whole class.

Explain to students that they will move through small-group centers today (and tomorrow if applicable), and at one station they will do a read-aloud and discussion with you about either the book *Big Bear Was Not the Same* or *Maybe Tomorrow?*. They will then do a second round of stations and read the other book in a read-aloud and discussion with you. Tell students that both books will be available in the room throughout the rest of the unit if they would like to later look at them.

During the small-group read-aloud and discussion, prompt students to notice and make comments about what they are hearing and seeing. Use general prompts such as, "What do you notice about this page?" or "What do you think the author is trying to tell us about how [Big Bear or Elba] is feeling here?" throughout both books. When you finish the read-aloud, use the specific prompts below for each book as listed to engage in a brief final discussion.

Big Bear Was Not the Same

- "At the beginning of the story, Big Bear is shown as the one who makes Little Bear feel safe. That makes it hard for Little Bear to understand why Big Bear is now scared. What things does Little Bear do at first to try to help Big Bear? What does Little Bear finally say that helps Big Bear? After he says this, what happens?"
- "Like *After the Fall* and *Outside, Inside*, this book also has a different dust jacket image than the images on the board pages (the hardcover) of the book. What do you notice about the dust jacket image? What do you notice about the hardcover images? How do they relate? What do they tell us as readers about the story and what might happen in the future after the story takes place?"

Maybe Tomorrow?

- "Norris is an especially good friend to Elba. What are some of the little things he does throughout the book to help support her as she deals with her feelings of sadness and loss?"
- "When did you notice that Elba's block was getting smaller? Do you think it will ever disappear? Why or why not?"
- "Like *After the Fall* and *Outside, Inside*, this book also has a different dust jacket image than the images on the board pages (the hardcover) of the book. What do you notice about the dust jacket image? What do you notice about the hardcover images? How do they relate? What do they tell us as readers about the story and what might happen in the future after the story takes place?"

Segue to Next Day and Daily Reflection

When you break on Day 3, explicitly help your students segue by letting them know you are now moving to the next part of the day, but you will be returning to this topic of sadness tomorrow.

When the school day is over, take some time to fill out the Daily Reflection to reflect on today's experience. Review it as you prepare for the next day.

Discussion and Activity: Goal Setting with Small Steps

On Day 4, after all the reading has been completed, tell your students that the two books read over the last 2 days, *Big Bear Was Not the Same* and *Maybe Tomorrow?*, were similar. In both cases, one of the main characters was suffering a lot of sadness after a major event occurred in their life. Big Bear was saddened and scared by the forest fire; Elba was sorrowful because a friend had passed away. These events made both of them similar in certain ways to Humpty; something bad happened and they remained scared and sad afterward.

However, in the two books discussed here, the character in pain had a friend who helped them: by being present and listening. Norris seemed to know that was what Elba needed and was never frustrated. Little Bear didn't know at first what to do and became confused and frustrated, but then he began to understand Big Bear and helped support him.

These friends were able to inspire the hurting character who was depressed to take small steps to feel better. The board pages of both books hint that Big Bear and Elba are going to continue taking such small steps, partly because of their friend's support.

- Begin today's activity by telling students that when someone is depressed, goal setting can begin to make them feel more hopeful. For both Elba and Big Bear, the goal was to start to move forward and be able to do the things they used to in their day-to-day lives with less pain. (Note for students that this does not mean Elba and Big Bear will never be sad again. There will still be times when they feel sad or scared—and that is okay—but that sadness and fright will become more manageable.)
- Setting goals can give someone a path to get better at something that matters to them. It also gives them something to look forward to—reaching that goal! Even if they do not achieve their final goal for a very long time, any steps they achieve on the way to it are progress. And that makes them more confident, which in turn will make them more likely to keep reaching for their goal.
  - We can see this happening in *Maybe Tomorrow?*. Every day, Elba gets a little more comfortable going with Norris toward the beach. And over time, through small steps, she eventually gets there and starts feeling better along the way. In the book, we see that Norris gently encourages Elba and helps her take those small steps.
- Tell your students that today they are going to practice breaking down a goal into a series of small steps. This can help you reach a goal more easily! Pass out paper while asking students to think of one goal they would like to achieve in their lives within the next 4 weeks. This could be a goal for school, like completing a report on time, or learning a new song for the band concert, or it could be a goal for a sport or activity they participate in (e.g., running the 2-mile race without walking), or a personal goal (maybe making a new friend), or something at home (perhaps cleaning out and reorganizing their bedroom closet).
  - Ask students to write their goal at the top of their page. Encourage them to be specific about their goal in their writing so that it will be clear when they reach it. They might also draw a picture of themself achieving their goal.
  - Then remind students that it is important to break down **Goal Setting with Small Steps**. Otherwise, it can be hard to get going. Direct them to write down the numbers 1–10.

These will be the 10 steps they are going to take toward meeting their goal. Then have students assign those steps to the next 4 weeks as follows:

- Week 1 (for Steps 1, 2, and 3)
- Week 2 (for Steps 4, 5, and 6)
- Week 3 (for Steps 7 and 8)
- Week 4 (for Steps 9 and 10)

- Then ask students to start thinking about three very easy first steps that would help move them along toward their goal. These should be simple steps to help get them started and not feel overwhelmed. For example, they might start jogging 4 minutes without stopping, then 5 minutes without stopping, then 6 minutes without stopping the first week to prepare for running the 2-mile race. Or, they might write one paragraph of their report, go to the library and research at least one new source, and then write two new paragraphs. Have students brainstorm and then write down their first-week steps.
- Continue writing down steps by now going backward. The last step should be reaching the goal they want to achieve and celebrating! Have students imagine how they will feel when they reach their goal and draw a picture of themself celebrating as they achieve it with Step 10.
- Now, direct students to fill in the other steps for reaching their goal: Steps 4, 5, 6, 7, 8, and 9. Circle the room, encouraging students to make their steps specific and to keep them reasonable, especially Steps 1–6. You might have students plan to repeat a few steps (such as practicing a skill) when appropriate.

When students have all completed their goal setting, tell them they can share their goal and plan with their desk or elbow partner. Sharing goals is important as you can help support another person in reaching their goal. (If any of the students' goals are highly personal, it is okay to keep sharing optional.) After students share (if they choose to do so), direct them to keep their list in a folder or in their desks, so they can check in on their progress. Remind them that they will check in as a class next week to see how they are progressing toward their goals.

Segue to Next Day and Daily Reflection

After your students have stored their goal-setting sheets, explicitly help them segue by letting them know that you will now be moving on to the next part of the day, but you will be returning to this topic of sadness and depression tomorrow.

When the school day is over, take some time to fill out the Daily Reflection to reflect on this experience. Review it as you prepare for the next day's lesson.

DAY 5

Whole-Class Read-Aloud #3: *A Blue Kind of Day*

Discussion and Activities: Comfort Box List; Comfort Collage

Time: 1 hour total

Special Materials Needed:

- Posterboard or larger sheets of paper, construction paper, scissors and glue, magazines that can be cut up for collage

Whole-Class Read-Aloud #3: *A Blue Kind of Day*

Gather students together for a whole-class read-aloud and discussion of *A Blue Kind of Day*. Although in the last few books the main character was sad for a particular reason, the central character in this book shows symptoms of depression that are not related to any particular event or experience. We see him wake up with symptoms of depression, and no potential reason is given for why he is feeling this way.

- Begin by showing your students the dust jacket of the book. Ask them what they notice about the image of Coen on the front and on the back of the book. Also read aloud the text on the back cover: "When you get lost in feelings, your body is a map to help you find your way." Ask students to predict what might happen in the book based on these dust jacket cover images and words. (If students ask, explain that the pictures under the dust jacket in this book are the same as those on the dust jacket. But tell them it is always a good idea to check!)
- Start reading the text, encouraging students to share what they notice about the story and the images. At the beginning of the story, tell students to pay attention to how Coen describes the feelings of his body. Ask them how the images help convey these feelings as well.
- "What do Coen's family members try to do to help him? Does this work?"
- Eventually, the book says that his family members waited. "Why do you think the author takes special time to note that Coen's feelings were okay, and that they would not last forever? What is she saying about the depressive symptoms Coen exhibits in the book?"
- "How does the author show you that Coen is beginning to feel better? How does she describe his feelings? What does his family do that helps him?"
- "What feeling does Coen have at the end of the book? How do you know this?"
- When you have finished reading, ask the students what they think the overall message of the story is.

Discussion and Activities: Comfort Box List; Comfort Collage

Explain to students that Coen's family tried hard to help him feel better. In the end, they simply stayed by his side. They could not make him feel better. They simply were there for him. As he gradually began to feel less weighted down, he was able to ask for help to do something (read a book with his mom), which relaxed him. That comforting step helped him move on to the next day with a little hope.

- Tell students that today they are going to start creating two things that might be of comfort if they started to feel down. Make it very clear to them that these two things should be used before they feel as depressed as Coen was: The things ought to be used when they start to feel a little sad or are having a bad day. A friend could also bring them one of the things when they are feeling blue and maybe sit with them while they use it, just as Coen's mom read a book with him.
- Have students return to their seats; pass out pieces of lined paper to them. Tell students that they are going to create a list of items that will go into a Comfort Box. At home, they might take an old shoebox or small box and actually create the Comfort Box by placing the desired items in it. Then when they feel sad, they can retrieve the Comfort Box and hold these items, use them, or just look at them. But at school, they are simply going to create a list and place it in their desks (or a personal folder). Then they can take out the list and think about the pictures or items in the box during those times in school when they feel sad. They will have to use strong visualization skills to imagine each item.
- Now, ask your students to write their names at the top of the sheet of paper and the words **Comfort Box List**. Model this on the whiteboard while students are also writing. Begin your list on the whiteboard by modeling aloud, thinking of a few favorite items that make you feel better:
  - "I am going to write the word *Lucky* here because that's my dog's name and I love her very much. Or, I could draw a quick picture of her. In my actual box at home, I might put in a photo of her. She always makes me feel better when I pat her silky ears. If you have a pet, you might want to draw a picture of your pet or write their name on this list."
  - "My family. I am going to write down their names next, and at home I would put a photo of them in my box. I am going to add more info to this list item by including a description underneath. You can do this when you are writing a list; just indent the description a little bit under the main item. Or if you are numbering your list, you can put a lowercase "a" under the number or a bullet. Both of these lines would also be indented. [*Model this kind of layout on your whiteboard.*] I am adding this extra description because I know for sure that a big hug from my mother would make me feel a lot better, so I am writing down the phrase *Big Hug from Mom*. This will help me imagine getting a hug from her!
  - "The library. I love to go to the library, so this word will bring up happy feelings for me when I see it on my list. I am going to draw a picture of my library card here instead of drawing the library because I think it will remind me that reading a book often makes me feel better.
- Continue modeling for another item or two and then ask students what other items they think they might add to their lists. Remind them to draw pictures or to add an indented phrase or description below any list item. Now, circle the classroom, providing support as students work on their lists for the next 5 minutes.
- Tell students to put their lists aside for now. They will add to them during the next activity so they should still be easily accessible. Next, pass out larger pieces of paper.
- Inform your class that they are now going to create an item similar to their list: a **Comfort Collage.** On this large paper, they will glue pictures they cut out of magazines to make a

collage of images they like. They can also draw images on the paper directly, and/or draw pictures on other kinds of paper and cut them out and glue them on the large paper as well. The idea is to completely fill up the page with images that make them smile or remind them of things that make them smile. This is much like the Comfort Box List. You can pull out this collage to look at whenever you like or even hang it up in a special place. Say:

> *"For example, I might glue several images of dogs and pets on my Comfort Collage because they make me smile! I am also going to add this magazine image of a lake because it makes me feel peaceful when I look at it. Oh! And that reminds me that on my Comfort Box List, I am going to add pebbles that I found at the lake in the park because they feel so smooth in my hand and remind me of going to the park."*

- Invite students to take magazines for cutting piled in the front of the room, or paper to make their own drawings, and begin work on their collages.
- Again, circle the room, giving encouragement and support. As you do so, remind students to go back and forth between the list and the collage creation as each will remind them of items to possibly add.
- Let students work for about 10–15 minutes.

Segue to Next Day and Daily Reflection

After students have finished their work within the directed time frame, tell them to tidy up the classroom for now, but advise them that tomorrow they will have more time to work on both the Comfort Box List and the Comfort Collage.

Let them know that you will now be moving on to the next part of the day, but tomorrow you will be returning to this topic of comforting oneself.

When the school day is over, take some time to fill out the Daily Reflection to reflect on this experience. Review it as you prepare for the next day's lesson.

DAYS 6 AND 7

Small Groups Read-Aloud and Discuss #2: *The Cat Who Couldn't Be Bothered* and *When Sadness Is at Your Door*

Discussion and Activities: Stop and Notice; Comfort Box List Continued; Comfort Collage Continued

Time: 2 hours total across 2 days

> ***Note:*** You can divide this time as works best for your class. Plan for 15- to 20-minute read-aloud and discussions with each of four small groups of students during center or station time (about 1 hour to 1 hour and 15 minutes total). Finally, allow for about 45 minutes for the whole-class Stop and Notice activity and time to complete work on the Comfort Box List and Comfort Collage.

Special Materials Needed:

- Items from yesterday: Posterboard or larger sheets of paper, construction paper, scissors and glue, magazines that can be cut up for the collage

Small Groups Read-Aloud and Discuss #2: *The Cat Who Couldn't Be Bothered* and *When Sadness Is at Your Door*

> ***Note:*** Prior to class today, divide your students into about four small random groups. Across 2 days, work with each small group independently to read and discuss one of the two titles: *The Cat Who Couldn't Be Bothered* or *When Sadness Is at Your Door.* The goal is for each of the two books to be discussed by two smaller groups.

Explain to students that they will move through small-group centers today (and tomorrow if applicable), and at one station they will do a read-aloud and discussion with you about either the book *The Cat Who Couldn't Be Bothered* or *When Sadness Is at Your Door.* Tell students that both books will be available in the room throughout the rest of the unit if they would like to later look at the book that is not read to them today.

During the small-group read-aloud and discussion, prompt students to notice and make comments about what they are hearing and seeing. Use general prompts such as, "What do you notice about this page?" or "What do you think the author is trying to tell us about how [the cat or the child] is feeling here?" Throughout both books, use the specific prompts given next.

The Cat Who Couldn't Be Bothered

- Begin by showing the students the dust jacket of the book. Show them the front and back and read aloud the words on the back: "Hi Greg! Do you want to play? No, thanks." Read aloud the title "The Cat Who Couldn't Be Bothered." Ask students what "couldn't be bothered" means. What do they think of this dust jacket cover? How do they think the cat feels? Then explain that the board covers for this book are similar to but different from the dust jacket. Show them these images. Then ask students what they predict will happen in this book. Finally, begin reading the book.
- Ask the students: "What do you notice about how the cat is drawn? How do you think he is feeling? In the pictures where he is imagining himself accepting the invitation from his friend, how does he appear to be feeling?"
- Also ask: "What do you notice about the cat's [Greg/Gareth] friends? How are their actions similar to those of the other main characters' friends and family members we have met in earlier books?"
- When you reach the page where the cat yells "Stop," ask: "How do you think it feels for the cat to say this? Do you think it is hard or easy? Why? How do the friends react?"

When Sadness Is at Your Door

- Begin by showing the students the dust jacket of the book. Show them the front and back and read aloud the words on the back: "When sadness arrives, don't be afraid of it." Ask students what this means. What do they think of this dust jacket cover? How do they think the child feels? Then explain that the board covers for this book are the same, but the endpages have different images. Show the endpapers at the front of the book to the students and then show them those at the end. What do they notice? What do they predict will happen in this book? Finally, begin reading the book.
- Ask the students: "Do you notice how sadness is taking over the child's life in the first few pages of the book?"
- Read on and ask: "How does this change after the child names Sadness and says hello? How about after the child starts doing activities with Sadness? How would you describe these activities? How are they similar to those we observed in earlier books when the main character needed comfort?"

(***Tip:*** Students will notice that Sadness is growing smaller, but also the slight smiles on Sadness's face as well as the change in the child's face.)

- At the end: "Why do you think it is unknown if Sadness will come the next day?"
- Discussion and Activities: Stop and Notice; Comfort Box List Continued; Comfort Collage Continued

When all groups have had the chance to do their read-aloud and discussion, hold a whole-class discussion. Begin by telling students that, on the surface, the books they read in small groups appeared to be different from each other. One was about a cat realizing that he is experiencing symptoms of depression, and the other was about a young boy also navigating some of the symptoms of depression who sees his Sadness as an actual figure/person. But in both books, the main character (the cat or the child) comes to understand what is happening to them and speaks up about it. This recognition helps them name their unhappiness and makes it easier for them to ask others for help.

- Direct students to find a classmate who heard a different book than they did. Give them 3 minutes to pair-share about the books they read. "What was the story about? What did they like best about it? What do they think was the message of the book?" Then have all students return to their original seats after sharing.
- Explain to your students:

> *"In both books, these depression symptoms are not happening for a reason that the readers are told. The main character is simply feeling that way, much like Coen also woke up feeling depressed. This sometimes happens. One thing that can help is recognizing that it is happening so that you can take steps to ask for help or try to help yourself as well. If you notice these behaviors in a friend or family member one day, you can also take steps to try to help them."*

- Tell students:

  "When you are feeling these types of depressive symptoms, it can sometimes be hard to recognize the problem and especially hard to say something aloud about it. Experiencing these types of symptoms can make you feel very badly—you might feel tearful, feel like everything takes extra effort, not want to do the activities you normally enjoy, or even refuse to get out of bed. You might feel heavy and slow and tired, and at the same time you might feel restless or 'coiled up tight' like Coen mentioned. You might not have the energy to 'bother' to do anything. You might feel extra-irritable and snap at friends or family. You might even have physical pains like a headache or stomachache."

- Such symptoms can be difficult to recognize as being related to one's emotions, and this can make it tough for friends to recognize as well. But noticing one's emotions is very important.
- One step students can take themselves is to practice observing their thoughts. Pretend they are a scientific observer doing research. They are going to look at themself and say, "I am noticing that I am having the thought that . . . " and/or "I am noticing that my body feels like . . . " and/or "I am noticing that I am acting in this way. . . . "
- Tell students that when they are feeling symptoms of depression or having a big emotional reaction, it can be hard to express this. Thus, they need to practice this skill often. It will help them notice all their different emotions. Noticing as an observer can help them become able to recognize their state of mind and ask for help if needed. It can also prompt them to feel more settled as they recognize that it is an emotion and emotions are neither good nor bad. This practice can also sometimes help them feel a bit detached from the actual emotional experience and better able to calm down or take a break from their inner thoughts for a brief minute. They should try to do their noticing/observing in the present moment, but they can also do so after something has happened, reflecting on their actions or behaviors then.
  - Give the students an example. Say:

  "For example, yesterday after school, I had to take my dog to the vet. When I was driving there, I noticed that my heart was beating faster than normal and that I felt sweaty. I also was remembering a lot about when my older dog passed away several years ago and how sad that was. Then my daughter called just as I pulled into the parking lot. When I answered her call, I was very short with her. I noticed this after I hung up. Then I noticed that I was having the thought that something bad might happen at the vet's office. I realized that I was beginning to feel very sad about going to the vet."

- Explain to students that **Stop and Notice** is something they should try to do when they feel a big emotion. They should ask themselves what they are noticing about their thoughts, the ways their body is feeling, and the actions they are taking. While it can be difficult to make such an assessment at this moment, you are going to help them try to do this today when they get on the lunch line. Over the next few weeks, often direct your students to "stop and notice," observing and taking stock of themselves like a scientist.

- Now, ask your students to pull out their **Comfort Box Lists** and **Comfort Collage** for **Continuation.** Allow them about 30 minutes to work on these two items. Circle the room, giving encouragement and support and helping students to toggle back and forth between listing and creating the collage. You may want to stop the class after a few minutes of getting started and ask students to share their work with their desk or elbow partner. This can inspire some new ideas.
- Interrupt the students a few minutes before your class/activity time is over. Tell them that they should leave the lists in their desks or personal folders for now. They might want to create actual Comfort Boxes at home. But, the lists will stay there to help them imagine these items when at school. When they are having very sad thoughts or are feeling down or stuck, they can pull out the list and be reminded of the things that give them comfort. The collages will be hung for now on the walls of the classroom nearest their desks. That way during the day, the students will remain aware of what inspires them and makes them smile! Later, these collages can be taken home and hung there.

Segue to Next Day and Daily Reflection

After students have worked for an additional 10–15 minutes, ask them to clean up the work area for now, but remind them that tomorrow they will have more time to focus on both the Comfort Box List and Comfort Collage. Let them know that you will now be moving on to the next part of the day, but you will be returning to this topic of managing depression or sadness tomorrow.

When the school day is over, take some time to fill out the Daily Reflection to reflect on this experience. Review it as you prepare for the next day's lesson.

DAY 8

Conclusion and Whole-Class Read-Aloud #4: *Rain Before Rainbows*

Discussion and Activity: Three Good Things

Time: 1 hour total

Special Materials Needed:

- One small notebook for each student

Conclusion and Whole-Class Read-Aloud #4: *Rain Before Rainbows*

Gather students together for a whole-class read-aloud and discussion of *Rain Before Rainbows.* Ask them what they think this title means.

- Show the class the dust jacket of the book. Show them its front and back and read aloud the words on the back: "In the midst of the rain, rainbows can be hard to see. But with courage and the help of good friends, there is always a way out of the darkness." Ask students what this means. What do they notice about this dust jacket cover?

- Then explain that for this book, the hard cover of the book has the same images as the dust jacket, but the endpages have different pictures. Show the endpapers at the front of the book to your students and then show them the ones at the end. What do they notice? What do they predict will happen in this book? Finally, begin reading the book.
- Start with the title page. This is a strongly emotional page, as is the book's first spread. Ask students what they notice and think about the images chosen. What do they believe is happening to the little girl and the fox?
- Read slowly through the next few spreads, giving students time to look closely at the illustrations and share what they notice. When you reach the spread where the little girl and fox arrive on land, ask the students how these pages make them feel. What does the illustrator do with the images and colors that has such an impact on this page spread and the next one? (If the students do not make connections between the friendly animals supporting the little girl and the friends described earlier in the book, explain this connection.)
- The story is not over when the little girl and the fox reach the "treasure" (the big yellow field). Ask students if they thought the story would end here. Why or why not? Continue reading and then ask students why they think the author and illustrator kept the story going. What do they think about the story overall? Encourage students to share things they especially liked about the story and their overall ideas.

Discussion and Activity: Three Good Things

Have students return to their seats. Tell them that today you are going to create a new special routine that they will now do every day for the next month!

- Explain that they have learned a lot over the last several days about big emotions of sadness and the symptoms of depression. Remind them that depression is a mental health illness and it involves symptoms occurring over a longer period of time. Over the last 2 weeks, they have encountered various characters who exhibited some of the symptoms of depression. They also learned about ways to support people who might be experiencing such symptoms, such as listening or just being close by. They learned some strategies that can help reduce their own risk for developing depression or reducing the impact of some of the symptoms; for example, goal setting, creating items that can help give comfort and remind you of good things, and noticing emotions. Today, we are going to add another strategy to help reduce the risk of depression or that might help alleviate some symptoms: starting a daily practice of noticing three good things. This can help encourage a positive mindset overall and help us see the "somewhere in-betweens" that we know happen when we are having both positive and negative experiences.
- Pass out a small notebook to each student. Ask them to write down their name and **Three Good Things** on the cover.
- Then indicate that each day they will have a 5-minute period to write or draw a list of three

good things that happened at school that day. These do not have to be big events, and at first it might be hard to think of three. Tell students that we are going to brainstorm some possible ideas now to help us get ready for regularly doing this activity. (Also, tell them this task does get easier with practice!)

- On the whiteboard, write down ideas that students share. Start them off with a few examples, such as:
  - "We played soccer in PE!"
  - "[*Insert teacher name*] told me she liked the topic I chose for my report."
  - "The dry-erase marker I had for math was new."
  - "I ate pizza for lunch."
  - "The bus was on time this morning."
  - "We went to the school library."
  - "My friend told me a funny story."
- Tell students that some days when they might feel down, it could be extra-hard to come up with something to write. They are allowed to take an occasional "past" day. Tell students this is not a "pass" day (write this word on the board) but a "past" day (cross out the last "s" in *pass* and write "t" above it). This means that students can write down a good memory or favorite memory as one of their items, instead of something that happened that day.

- Make clear to students that the time for writing in their Three Good Things notebooks might vary a bit from day to day, but it will always be toward the end of the day. Today, they are going to do this writing task right now! Record the date on the whiteboard and have students copy that on the first page of their notebook. Then give students 5 minutes to write and draw their list. Tell them if they finish their list before the full 5 minutes are up, they can draw additional pictures around it or even write down more details if they would like to.
- Finally, inform students that some days they might want to go back and look at their prior lists when they have extra time, or they might flip through their notebooks on days they are feeling sad, just like they might look at their Comfort Box List or their Comfort Collage.

Conclusion of Unit and Segue to Rest of the Day

Explicitly help your students segue by letting them know you are now moving to the next part of the day, and this is the end of the unit on depression. Let them know that the books will remain in the classroom for some time and that they are welcome to revisit them. Also tell them that although the unit may have been completed, these conversations can always continue around its topic, and they should feel free to ask questions or discuss the topic in more detail.

When the school day is over, take some time to complete the Daily Reflection form. The next day or the day after that, ask your students to complete the Unit Post-Check with Students. Finally, about a week to 10 days after the unit was completed, fill out Taking the Pulse of the Class: After Unit to consider more broadly this experience for your current students, yourself, and your future students.

FINAL SUGGESTIONS

During the weeks following this unit, you might want to revisit some of these themes, books, or the conversations around them. This unit was intended as an introduction to, and the beginning of courageous conversations around, the difficult topic of the mental health issue of depression. It was meant to help students feel more comfortable talking about it and to increase understanding. It also introduced some preventive actions and general practices for increasing self-awareness related to emotional well-being.

Some students may want to continue to discuss this topic in class in a deeper way. Reach out to your school counselors, psychologists, and support faculty for individual help for students seeking more specific or individualized support in this area. The Unit Post-Check with Students will help you identify students needing or wanting this support.

You may decide to expand on this unit with further book sharing, discussions, and activities. The websites that follow may serve as good resources as you do this work.

ADDITIONAL RESOURCES

American Academy of Child and Adolescent Psychiatry: Depression in Children and Teens: *www.aacap.org/AACAP/Families_and_Youth/Facts_for_Families/FFF-Guide/The-Depressed-Child-004.aspx*

Centers for Disease Control and Prevention: Anxiety and Depression in Children: *www.cdc.gov/children-mental-health/about/about-anxiety-and-depression-in-children.html*

Child Mind Institute: Depression & Mood Disorders: *https://childmind.org/topics/depression-mood-disorders*

Johns Hopkins Medicine: Depression in Teens and Children: *www.hopkinsmedicine.org/health/conditions-and-diseases/depression-in-children*

Sesame Workshop: Emotional Well-Being: *https://sesameworkshop.org/topics/mentalhealth*

MEETING COMMON CORE AND CASEL STANDARDS

Common Core English Language Arts Standards for Grade 4

This unit meets specific Common Core State Standards for English Language Arts in grades 3, 4, 5, and 6. We have included the specific ELA standards for grade 4 below to illustrate the strands and items met (similar for all four grades third through sixth). The QR code here will link you to the specific lists for grades 3, 5, and 6.

CCSS.ELA-LITERACY.SL.4.1

Engage effectively in a range of collaborative discussions (one-on-one, in groups, and teacher-led) with diverse partners on grade 4 topics and texts, building on others' ideas and expressing their own clearly.

CCSS.ELA-LITERACY.L.4.4

Determine or clarify the meaning of unknown and multiple-meaning words and phrases based on grade 4 reading and content, choosing flexibly from a range of strategies.

CCSS.ELA-LITERACY.RL.4.1

Refer to details and examples in a text when explaining what the text says explicitly and when drawing inferences from the text.

CCSS.ELA-LITERACY.RL.4.6

Compare and contrast the point of view from which different stories are narrated, including the difference between first- and third-person narrations.

CCSS.ELA-LITERACY.RL.4.7

Make connections between the text of a story or drama and a visual or oral presentation of the text, identifying where each version reflects specific descriptions and directions in the text.

CCSS.ELA-LITERACY.W.4.2

Write informative/explanatory texts to examine a topic and convey ideas and information clearly.

CCSS.ELA-LITERACY.W.4.4

Produce clear and coherent writing in which the development and organization are appropriate to task, purpose, and audience.

CASEL Social and Emotional Learning Standards for Grades 3–5

This unit meets specific CASEL Core Competence Area goals for Social and Emotional Learning for grades 3–5. We have included the CASEL areas and specific example standards below to show the items met in this unit. (The items are similar for grade 6.)

Self-Awareness: The abilities to understand one's own emotions, thoughts, and values and how they influence behavior across contexts. This includes capacities to recognize one's strengths and limitations with a well-grounded sense of confidence and purpose.

- Identifying one's emotions
- Linking feelings, values, and thoughts
- Having a growth mindset
- Developing interests and a sense of purpose

Self-Management: The abilities to manage one's emotions, thoughts, and behaviors effectively in different situations and to achieve goals and aspirations. This includes the capacities to delay gratification, manage stress, and feel motivation and agency to accomplish personal/collective goals.

- Managing one's emotions
- Identifying and using stress-management strategies
- Setting personal and collective goals
- Using planning and organizational skills
- Showing the courage to take initiative

Social Awareness: The abilities to understand the perspectives of and empathize with others, including those from diverse backgrounds, cultures, and contexts. This includes the capacities to feel compassion for others, understand broader historical and social norms for behavior in different settings, and recognize family, school, and community resources and supports.

- Recognizing strengths in others
- Demonstrating empathy and compassion
- Showing concern for the feelings of others
- Understanding and expressing gratitude

Relationship Skills: The abilities to establish and maintain healthy and supportive relationships and to effectively navigate settings with diverse individuals and groups. This includes the capacities to communicate clearly, listen actively, cooperate, work collaboratively to problem-solve and negotiate conflict constructively, navigate settings with differing social and cultural demands and opportunities, provide leadership, and seek or offer help when needed.

- Communicating effectively
- Developing positive relationships
- Seeking or offering support and help when needed

Responsible Decision Making: The abilities to make caring and constructive choices about personal behavior and social interactions across diverse situations. This includes the capacities to consider ethical standards and safety concerns, and to evaluate the benefits and consequences of various actions for personal, social, and collective well-being.

- Identifying solutions for personal and social problems
- Anticipating and evaluating the consequences of one's actions
- Recognizing how critical thinking skills are useful both inside and outside of school
- Reflecting on one's role to promote personal, family, and community well-being
- Evaluating personal, interpersonal, community, and institutional impacts

Appendix of Reproducible Materials

ITEMS USED BEFORE THE UNIT

ITEMS USED DURING THE UNIT

UNIT WORKSHEETS

APPENDIX 1
Planning Checklist

We suggest the following timeline to prepare and then share and discuss the books and do the related activities with your students. Please note that timing for your individual class should be determined by your situation and your schedule and, most importantly, should be guided by your students' reactions to the books and activities. Plan generally, however, on about 1 hour of daily time with the unit for 7–10 days in a row.

Two Weeks Prior

- ☐ Complete Taking the Pulse of the Class: Before Unit (Appendix 2) for a general sense of your class at this time.
- ☐ Collect and read twice each of the books for the unit.
- ☐ Review the "Unit Plans: Reading, Discussions, and Activities" section of the unit.
- ☐ Send out the Administration Notification Slip (Appendix 3) and School Counselor/Psychologist and Support Staff Notification Slip (Appendix 4).

One Week Prior

- ☐ (Optional) Send out Family Notification Slips (Appendix 5) to the families of your students.
- ☐ Have students complete the Unit Pre-Check with Students (Appendix 6) and review the results carefully. Check in with any students with reactions that cause concern so that you can prepare for extra support.
- ☐ Review Chapter 2 of the book.
- ☐ Collect all materials needed for the unit:
  - ☐ **Daily Reflection forms (Appendix 7):** You will need one for each day.
  - ☐ **Books:** One copy is required, but you may prefer to secure two copies of each book. After each book has been shared during the unit, place it in an easily accessible display in the classroom. Please give students access to explore these books on their own during free-choice times. You will want to keep the display available for some time after the unit is completed.
  - ☐ **Materials already in your classroom:** Please have available and ready to use the following commonplace classroom materials:
    - Chart paper or a section of whiteboard that can remain posted for the duration of the unit
    - Unlined white paper
    - Pencils and pens; colored pencils, crayons, or markers
    - Construction paper or other colored paper
    - Scissors
    - Tape or glue
    - Any additional materials indicated within the unit chapter's detailed description

(continued)

During: Readings, Discussions, and Activities (approximately 7–10 school days)

- ☐ Follow the detailed plans for each day.
- ☐ One to 2 days after the unit is completed, have students complete the Unit Post-Check with Students (Appendix 8).

One Week Following

- ☐ After reviewing the Unit Post-Check with Students, check in with any students with reactions that cause concern.
- ☐ Refer any students expressing interest or for whom you have concerns at this point for additional, individual discussion with a school support professional. Also consider additional whole-class work if indicated.
- ☐ Complete and review Taking the Pulse of the Class: After Unit (Appendix 9). This will help you reflect on your experience and your students' experiences with the thematic book set.

APPENDIX 2

Taking the Pulse of the Class: Before Unit

Unit:		Date:
Directions: Two weeks before starting a new unit, think about who your students are and what they may need while discussing this topic in the coming weeks. Complete the following inventory to help you plan.		
Diversity in the Classroom		
Identities	**Representation in the Class**	**Names of Students**
Race		
Gender		
Ethnicity		
Disability		
Immigrant		
Refugee		
Religion		
Social class		
Languages spoken		

(continued)

Emotional Capacity
How are your students doing right now with handling emotionally charged conversations and situations?
Which students may need additional emotional support at this time?
Group Dynamics
How are your students getting along this year?
Which students may need additional support?
Based on cultural and group dynamics, how should students be divided during each activity? At this point in the school year, which works best?

Whole class	Works well	Works okay	Not going to work
Small groups	Works well	Works okay	Not going to work

(continued)

<table>
<tr><td colspan="4">Potential Small Groups (list names here):</td></tr>
<tr><td>Pairs</td><td>Works well</td><td>Works okay</td><td>Not going to work</td></tr>
<tr><td colspan="4">Potential Pairs (list names here):</td></tr>
<tr><td>Individual</td><td>Works well</td><td>Works okay</td><td>Not going to work</td></tr>
</table>

(continued)

APPENDIX 2 *(page 4 of 4)*

Political Climate
What current events may influence students' reactions to the unit?
What are your plans to help address students' concerns if they arise?
Additional Needs
What additional needs (e.g., support staff, parent volunteers) do you have for this unit?

APPENDIX 3
Administration Notification Slip

Date: ____________________________

Dear ____________________________________

Starting next week, our class will begin to read books and participate in activities related to the topic of ______________________________________. I will be reading aloud several picturebooks centered on this topic to the class, as well as holding group discussions and activities to help enrich students' understanding of this topic. The specific books being used in the unit are of high literary merit and provide opportunities for rich discussion on the topic, as well as general development of empathy and compassion. This unit works with national standards in the English language arts and standards for social and emotional learning.

Please let me know if you have any questions or would like additional information on the books and/or planned classroom activities.

Thank you in advance for your support.

Sincerely,

____

APPENDIX 4

School Counselor/Psychologist and Support Staff Notification Slip

Date: ______________________________

Dear ____

Starting next week, our class will begin to read books and participate in activities related to the topic of ____. I will be reading aloud several picturebooks centered on this topic to the class, as well as holding group discussions and activities to help enrich students' understanding of this topic. The specific books being used in the unit are of high literary merit and provide opportunities for rich discussion on the topic, as well as general development of empathy and compassion. This unit works with national standards in the English language arts and standards for social and emotional learning.

I have alerted our administration about this upcoming unit. I am also letting you know for two reasons. First, since I will be discussing this topic with my class, it is possible I will need to reach out to you for support for students who might demonstrate a need or desire for additional related support (e.g., space to talk more about the topic, referrals to external mental health providers or community resources). Second, I wanted to extend an invitation to you to stop by during some of the activities or reading and discussion.

Please let me know if you have any questions or would like additional information on the books and/or planned classroom activities.

Thank you in advance for your support.

Sincerely,

____

APPENDIX 5
Family Notification Slips

CLASS ANNOUNCEMENT

During the week(s) of ______________________, our class will be reading books and working on activities related to the topic of ____________________________. If you have any questions, please feel free to contact me at ______________________________.

CLASS ANNOUNCEMENT

During the week(s) of ______________________, our class will be reading books and working on activities related to the topic of ____________________________. If you have any questions, please feel free to contact me at ______________________________.

CLASS ANNOUNCEMENT

During the week(s) of ______________________, our class will be reading books and working on activities related to the topic of ____________________________. If you have any questions, please feel free to contact me at ______________________________.

CLASS ANNOUNCEMENT

During the week(s) of ______________________, our class will be reading books and working on activities related to the topic of ____________________________. If you have any questions, please feel free to contact me at ______________________________.

APPENDIX 6

Unit Pre-Check with Students

Name: ______________________________ Date: ______________

Unit Pre-Check with Students: ______________________________
Unit Name

1. I know a lot about ______________________________
Unit Name

No Kind of Yes

2. I want to learn about ______________________________
Unit Name

I don't want to I kind of don't want to I kind of want to I really want to

APPENDIX 7
Daily Reflection

Today's Date:
Unit Topic:
Day of Unit:
Students Absent:

Directions: At the end of each day, take 5–10 minutes to reflect on the following questions. This will help you prepare for the next day.

Learning Context	
What went well? Why?	
What did not go well? Why?	

(continued)

<table>
<tr><th colspan="2">Social, Emotional, and Group Context</th></tr>
<tr><td rowspan="2">What feelings came up during the activities?</td><td>For students?</td></tr>
<tr><td>For you?</td></tr>
<tr><td>What was tough for students to discuss?</td><td></td></tr>
<tr><td>What was easier for students to discuss?</td><td></td></tr>
<tr><td>Which students may need more of your attention tomorrow?</td><td></td></tr>
<tr><td>How did the cultural dynamics among students play out during the activities? [Refer to the Pulse of the Class: Before Unit form (Appendix 2) as needed.]</td><td></td></tr>
<tr><td>Do you plan to change any groupings for tomorrow based on today's experiences?</td><td></td></tr>
<tr><td>Additional notes</td><td></td></tr>
</table>

APPENDIX 8
Unit Post-Check with Students

Name: ______________________________ Date: ______________

Unit Post-Check with Students: ______________________________
Unit Name

1. I know a lot about ______________________________
Unit Name

No | Kind of | Yes

2. I learned about ______________________________
Unit Name

I didn't learn anything | I learned some things | I learned a lot

3. I still want to learn more about ______________________________
Unit Name

I don't want to | I kind of don't want to | I kind of want to | I really want to

APPENDIX 9
Taking the Pulse of the Class: After Unit

<table>
<tr><td colspan="2">Unit:</td><td>Date:</td></tr>
<tr><td colspan="3">Directions: One week after completing the unit, think about how your students responded to the topic and activities. Complete the following inventory for two purposes:
1. How did this unit work for this group of students? Reflect on the outcomes and how this will affect your work with these students throughout the rest of the school year.
2. How did this unit work overall? Reflect on the outcomes and plan ahead for the next time you cover this unit with a new group of students.</td></tr>
<tr><td colspan="3">Diversity in the Classroom</td></tr>
<tr><td colspan="3">Reflect on how various aspects of students' identities might have been discussed or addressed during this unit. Indicate what went well during these conversations. Then consider what did not go well. What would you do differently next time?</td></tr>
<tr><td rowspan="2">Race</td><td>Was this identity addressed or discussed in some way?
YES
NO</td><td>If no, what did not work well?</td></tr>
<tr><td>If yes, what worked well?</td><td>If no, what would you do differently?</td></tr>
<tr><td rowspan="2">Gender</td><td>Was this identity addressed or discussed in some way?
YES
NO</td><td>If no, what did not work well?</td></tr>
<tr><td>If yes, what worked well?</td><td>If no, what would you do differently?</td></tr>
</table>

(continued)

Ethnicity	Was this identity addressed or discussed in some way? YES NO	If no, what did not work well?
	If yes, what worked well?	If no, what would you do differently?
Disability	Was this identity addressed or discussed in some way? YES NO	If no, what did not work well?
	If yes, what worked well?	If no, what would you do differently?
Immigrant	Was this identity addressed or discussed in some way? YES NO	If no, what did not work well?
	If yes, what worked well?	If no, what would you do differently?

(continued)

<table>
<tr><td rowspan="2">Refugee</td><td>Was this identity addressed or discussed in some way?
YES
NO</td><td>If no, what did not work well?</td></tr>
<tr><td>If yes, what worked well?</td><td>If no, what would you do differently?</td></tr>
<tr><td rowspan="2">Religion</td><td>Was this identity addressed or discussed in some way?
YES
NO</td><td>If no, what did not work well?</td></tr>
<tr><td>If yes, what worked well?</td><td>If no, what would you do differently?</td></tr>
<tr><td rowspan="2">Social Class</td><td>Was this identity addressed or discussed in some way?
YES
NO</td><td>If no, what did not work well?</td></tr>
<tr><td>If yes, what worked well?</td><td>If no, what would you do differently?</td></tr>
</table>

(continued)

<table>
<tr><td rowspan="2">Languages Spoken</td><td>Was this identity addressed or discussed in some way?
YES
NO</td><td>If no, what did not work well?</td></tr>
<tr><td>If yes, what worked well?</td><td>If no, what would you do differently?</td></tr>
<tr><td colspan="3">Emotional Capacity</td></tr>
<tr><td colspan="3">How did your students handle emotionally charged conversations and situations during this unit?</td></tr>
<tr><td colspan="3">What activities, if any, were emotionally challenging for the students?</td></tr>
<tr><td colspan="3">Which students needed additional support during this unit?</td></tr>
<tr><td colspan="3">What kind of emotional support did you provide?</td></tr>
</table>

(continued)

How did they respond to this emotional support?
When using this unit in the future, what emotional support will you provide? When will these supports be needed?
Group Dynamics
How did students get along during this unit?
Which students needed additional support?
What kind of support did you provide?
How did they respond to this support?

(continued)

When doing this unit in the future, what group support will you provide? When will it be needed?
Political Climate
What current events influenced students' reactions to the unit?
If anything came up, what did you do to address students' concerns?
Additional Needs
What additional needs (e.g., support staff, parent volunteers) will you need next time?
Additional Reflections
What other reflections and thoughts do you have about using this unit as you think (1) about working with the current group of students in future units and (2) about using this unit in the future with a new group of students?

APPENDIX 10

Thinking About the Changemakers

Today, we read about ______________________________. They are a changemaker!

The social issue they are an activist for is ____.

Fill in the changemaker's name in the left column. In the right column, write down some of the responses from your group to the prompt.

Some words that could describe ________________ are . . .	
________________'s family, or close friends, or local community supports them by . . .	
________________ has demonstrated bravery by . . .	
________________ has sacrificed by . . .	
If I were __________, I would . . .	

APPENDIX 11

Directions to Make a Peanut Butter and Jelly Sandwich

1. Go to the pantry/closet/drawer.
2. Open the pantry/closet/drawer.
3. Take out the bread and peanut butter.
4. Close the pantry/closet/drawer.
5. Take the bread and peanut butter over to the counter/table.
6. Go to the closet/cupboard.
7. Open the closet/cupboard.
8. Take out a plate.
9. Close the closet/cupboard.
10. Take the plate to the counter/table.
11. Go to the fridge.
12. Open the fridge.
13. Take out the jelly/jam.
14. Close the fridge.
15. Take the jelly/jam to the counter/table.
16. Go to the silverware drawer.
17. Open the silverware drawer.
18. Take out a knife and spoon.
19. Close the silverware drawer.
20. Take the knife and spoon to the counter/table.
21. Open the bag of bread.
22. Take out two pieces of bread.
23. Set the two pieces of bread on the plate.
24. Open the jar of peanut butter.
25. Pick up the knife from the counter/table.
26. Insert the knife into the peanut butter jar.
27. Remove the knife from the peanut butter jar with peanut butter on it.
28. Spread the peanut butter on one of the slices of bread.
29. Put the knife with peanut butter on it in the sink.
30. Close the jar of peanut butter.
31. Open the jar of jam/jelly.

(continued)

32. Pick up the spoon from the counter.
33. Insert the spoon into the jar of jam/jelly.
34. Remove the spoon from the jar with jam/jelly on it.
35. Spread the jam/jelly on the piece of bread without peanut butter on it.
36. Put the jam/jelly spoon into the sink.
37. Close the jar of jam/jelly. Close the bag of bread.
38. Pick up both pieces of bread.
39. Put the two pieces of bread together, with the peanut butter and jam/jelly sides touching.
40. Set the sandwich down on the plate.
41. Pick up the jar of peanut butter and bag of bread.
42. Go to the pantry/closet/drawer.
43. Open the pantry/closet/drawer.
44. Put away the bread and jar of peanut butter.
45. Close the pantry/closet/drawer.
46. Pick up the jar of jam/jelly.
47. Go to the fridge.
48. Open the fridge.
49. Put away the jar of jam/jelly in the fridge.
50. Close the fridge.
51. Go to the plate with your sandwich on it.
52. Enjoy your sandwich!

APPENDIX 12

Five Senses Poem Work Sample: "In My Classroom, by a Teacher"

See	Colorful books piled in the corner Listening—mostly—faces of students
Hear	Rubber soles squeaking under the desk Pencils scritch-scratching across soft rustling paper
Smell	Spicy sweet corn chip smells from leftover lunches Sharp soap scent of hand sanitizer
Taste	Blue raspberry Jolly Rancher from my secret stash
Touch	The smooth marker spinning in my fingers Spongy construction paper Rough, thin paper towels

<u>Trial 1:</u>

Pencils scritch-scratching across soft rustling paper,
Colorful books piled in the corner of the room,
Smooth marker spinning in my fingers as I write on the board,
The listening faces of my students.

<u>Trial 2:</u>

The sharp soap scent of hand sanitizer,
Rubber soles squeaking under the desk,
Pencils scritch-scratching across soft rustling paper,
Spongy pile of construction paper tight in my hand,
And the sweet taste of a blue raspberry Jolly Rancher from my secret stash.

APPENDIX 13
A Story for the Next Generation

Name: ______________________________ Date: ______________________

The message I want my grandchildren to know about their family: Think about what you want your grandchildren to know about you and your (their!) family. Write it here:

____

____

____

____

The story that I will tell my grandchildren: Think about the story you will tell to share this message. Write a title or descriptive phrase about the story here:

____

____

____

____

Write a few details about the story that you will need to include.

Who are the people in this story? ______________________________

____

When did the story happen? ______________________________

____

Where did the story happen? ______________________________

____

How did you (or the family member) feel when the event started? ______________

____

What was the event? ______________________________

____

What was the most exciting part of the event? ______________________

____

(contined)

How did the event end or resolve? ____

____

How did you (or the family member) feel when the event ended? ______________________

____

How does this story illustrate the message you wish to tell your grandchildren? __________

____

____

Poetic Phrases to Tell My Story: Consider what poetic phrase you might use over and over when you are telling your story to your grandchildren. Make sure that the phrase helps you send the message you want your grandchildren to know about you and your (their!) family. Write down three possibilities here and circle the phrase you will use.

____

____

____

____

APPENDIX 14

Understanding Microaggressions: Words and Actions That Hurt

Name: ______________________________ Date: ____________________

In the table below, **match** the statement from Column 1 with an underlying and hurtful message in Column 2. Talk with your partner about where you have heard statements like those in Column 1 and discuss any thoughts or questions you have about each statement.

Column 1: Statements (Microaggressions)	Column 2: Underlying and Hurtful Message
1. You throw like a girl.	A. Only thin people are attractive.
2. Boys don't cry. Be a man!	B. Curly or kinky hair = bad hair. Straight hair = good hair.
3. I didn't think you could get an A. You're actually smart.	C. Your family's food or traditions are not normal.
4. I can't tell if you're a boy or girl. What are you?	D. Girls *should* have long hair and boys *should* have short hair.
5. Where are you *REALLY* from?	E. Crying is weak. Boys should hide their feelings because it means they are tough.
6. That's so gay.	F. Girls are typically bad at math and science.
7. Your lunch smells funny. (*Scrunches nose.*)	G. Only people from a particular group (e.g., race, gender, etc.) can be intelligent.
8. You look better with straight hair.	H. Being gender nonbinary or transgender is not okay.
9. You would be prettier if you lost weight.	I. Girls are not athletic or good at sports.
10. Why is your hair so short? You're a girl!	J. Being gay is weird or bad.
11. You're good at math and science, for a girl.	K. People who look like you couldn't be an American citizen. You must be from another country.

Note. Adapted from *Breaking the Prejudice Habit, http://breakingprejudice.org.*

APPENDIX 15

"This Is Us" Original Poem

Name: ______________________________________ Date: ______________________

Use the following instructions if you decide to write an original poem. Be yourself and have fun!

Choose a Topic: Think about what you want your poem to focus on. Consider all the messages and ideas you learned in this unit.

Brainstorm Ideas: Write down words and phrases connected to your topic. Think about how you feel and what you want to say to the audience.

Choose a Poem Type: Decide what type of poem you want to write. Here are a few options:

- *Free verse:* A poem with no strict rules about rhyme, meter, or structure.
- *Rhyming poem:* A poem where the lines rhyme with each other.
- *Haiku:* A three-line poem with a syllable pattern of 5-7-5.
- *Narrative poem:* A poem that tells a story.

Topic/Theme: ____

Words and Phrases You Want to Include: _____________________________________

____

____

____

Write Your Poem:

- Start writing your poem on the back of this sheet using the ideas and words you brainstormed.
- Use descriptive and feeling words to create images in your mind.
- If you're writing a rhyming poem, think of words that rhyme with each other to make your poem sound musical.

Edit and Revise:

- Read your poem aloud to see how it sounds. Make changes so it sounds better.
- Highlight words you want to emphasize or use different volumes: louder or softer.

Practice Reading Aloud:

- Practice reading your poem aloud several times. Pay attention to how it sounds and how you feel when you read it.
- Read out loud to a friend or classmate and ask them for feedback.

Finalize Your Poem:

- Make any final changes to your poem. It's okay to keep editing until you're happy with it.

APPENDIX 16

I Dissent: Ruth Bader Ginsburg Makes Her Mark Vocabulary and Comprehension Chart

Vocabulary Chart

Dissent:

Disapprove:

Not Concur:

Object:

Protest:

Resist:

Persist:

(continued)

APPENDIX 16 *(page 2 of 2)*

Comprehension Chart

Questions	**Answers**
What is this person's name?	
What career did she want? Why?	
How did people react to her wanting this career. Did they *disapprove*, *dissent*, or *not concur*? Why?	
What were her overall goals?	
Ruth faced some problems from others in trying to reach her goals. What were some of these obstacles? Would you say people were *objecting to*, *protesting about*, or *resisting* what she was doing?	
Despite obstacles, Ruth kept trying to reach her goals. Name two ways in which she *persisted* in trying to reach her goals.	

APPENDIX 17

The International Day of the Girl: Celebrating Girls around the World

ORGANIZATIONAL CHART

Liliya, pp. 14–15	
Questions	**Responses**
What career did your girl want? Why?	
How did people react to her wanting this career? Did they *disapprove, dissent*, or *not concur*? Why?	
What were her overall goals?	
She faced some problems from others in trying to reach her goals. What were some of these obstacles? Would you say people were *objecting to, protesting about*, or *resisting* what she was doing?	
Despite obstacles, she kept trying to reach her goals. Name two ways in which she *persisted* in trying to reach her goals.	

Sokanon, pp. 16–17	
Questions	**Responses**
What career did your girl want? Why?	
How did people react to her wanting this career? Did they *disapprove, dissent*, or *not concur*? Why?	
What were her overall goals?	
She faced some problems from others in trying to reach her goals. What were some of these obstacles? Would you say people were *objecting to, protesting about*, or *resisting* what she was doing?	
Despite obstacles, she kept trying to reach her goals. Name two ways in which she *persisted* in trying to reach her goals.	

(continued)

Abuya, pp. 12–13	
Questions	**Responses**
What career did your girl want? Why?	
How did people react to her wanting this career? Did they *disapprove*, *dissent*, or *not concur*? Why?	
What were her overall goals?	
She faced some problems from others in trying to reach her goals. What were some of these obstacles? Would you say people were *objecting to*, *protesting about*, or *resisting* what she was doing?	
Despite obstacles, she kept trying to reach her goals. Name two ways in which she *persisted* in trying to reach her goals.	

Flora, pp. 8–9	
Questions	**Responses**
What career did your girl want? Why?	
How did people react to her wanting this career? Did they *disapprove*, *dissent*, or *not concur*? Why?	
What were her overall goals?	
She faced some problems from others in trying to reach her goals. What were some of these obstacles? Would you say people were *objecting to*, *protesting about*, or *resisting* what she was doing?	
Despite obstacles, she kept trying to reach her goals. Name two ways in which she *persisted* in trying to reach her goals.	

(continued)

Hana, pp. 10–11	
Questions	**Responses**
What career did your girl want? Why?	
How did people react to her wanting this career? Did they *disapprove*, *dissent*, or *not concur*? Why?	
What were her overall goals?	
She faced some problems from others in trying to reach her goals. What were some of these obstacles? Would you say people were *objecting to*, *protesting about*, or *resisting* what she was doing?	
Despite obstacles, she kept trying to reach her goals. Name two ways in which she *persisted* in trying to reach her goals.	

APPENDIX 18

Picture Analysis Chart

Text +	Picture =	Story

APPENDIX 19

"How I Speak"

Name: ______________________________________

1. Listen to the way you talk! (Talk for 15 seconds and listen to yourself.) How do you sound?

____
____
____
____
____

2. What would happen if you concentrated on the feeling of speaking? Where do you feel words in your body? Do you speak without pauses or hesitations?

____
____
____
____
____

3. How often do you slip up, forget words, or have difficulty finding them in the first place?

____
____
____
____
____

4. Do you sometimes shy away from speaking?

____
____
____
____

5. Do you sometimes not want to say anything at all?

____
____
____
____

APPENDIX 20

Story Timelines

Name: ______________________________ Date: ____________________

Emmanuel's Timeline from *Emmanuel's Dream: The True Story of Emmanuel Ofosu Yeboah*

Year: Event 1:	Year: Event 2:	Year: Event 3:
Year: Event 4:	Year: Event 5:	Year: Event 6:

(continued)

APPENDIX 20 *(page 2 of 2)*

Name: ______________________ Date: ______________

Louis's Timeline from *Six Dots: A Story of Young Louis Braille*

Year: Event 1:	Year: Event 2:	Year: Event 3:
Year: Event 4:	Year: Event 5:	Year: Event 6:

APPENDIX 21
Question and Response

Name: ______________________________ Date: ____________________

1. Do you ever need to take medicine to be healthy? ____________________

2. My inhaler is like a tool to help my body. Do you use a tool to help your body? ____________________

3. How do you get from place to place? ____________________

4. How do you use your senses? ____________________

5. I also love reading and writing. What about you? ____________________

6. Are you really good at something? ____________________

7. What do you like to talk about? ____________________

8. Do you ever wonder if people understand you? ____________________

9. Do you ever feel frustrated? ____________________

10. What's helpful to you? ____________________

11. How do you use your voice? ____________________

12. What helps you learn? ____________________

13. What will you do with your powers? ____________________

APPENDIX 22
Story Map

Name: ______________________ Date: ______________

Book title: ______________________

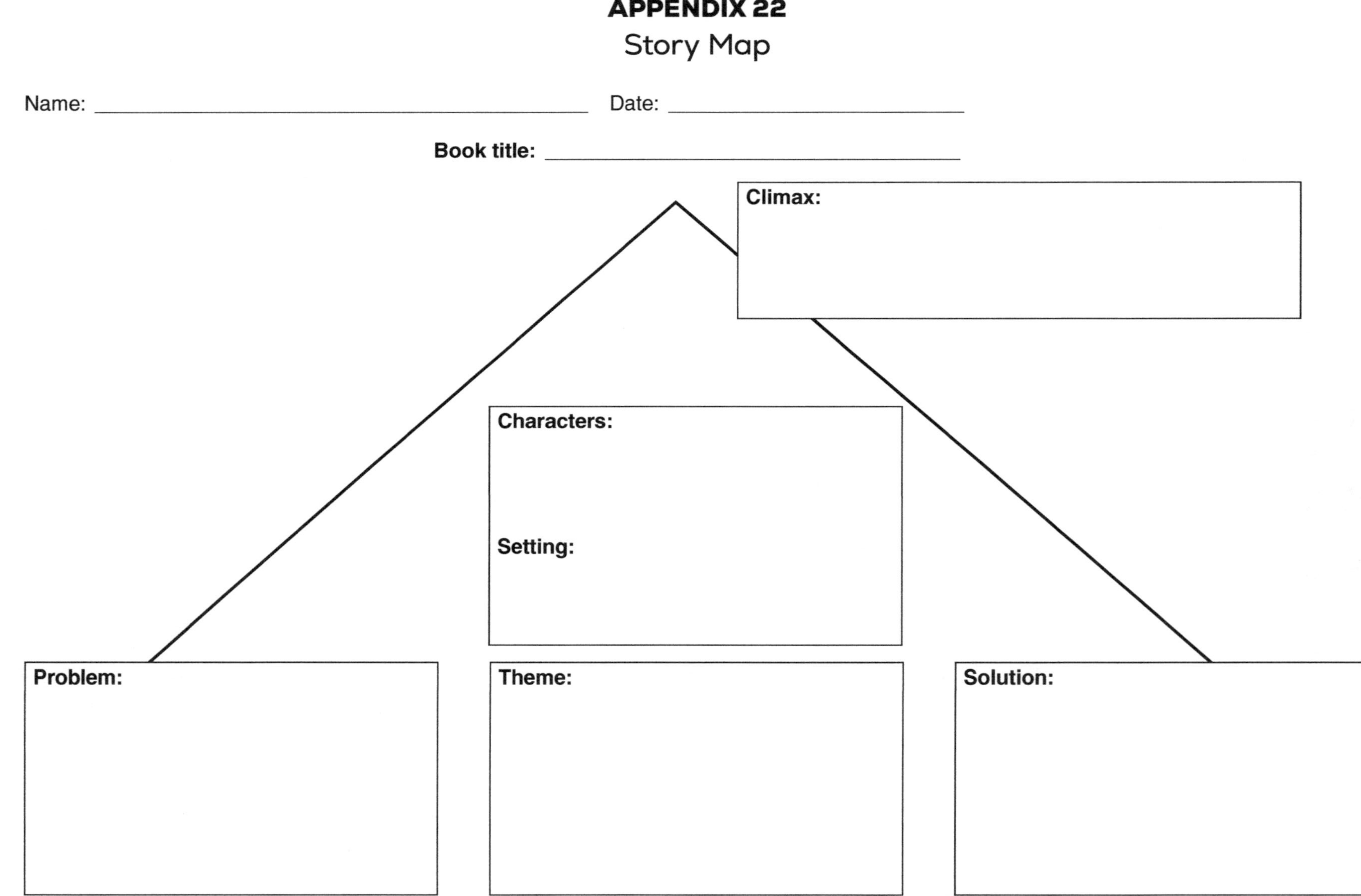

APPENDIX 23

School's First Day of School Quick-Write/Reflection

Name: ______________________________ Date: ____________________

What did you learn about anxiety today?

APPENDIX 24

Writing Prompt/Create a Comic Strip

Name: ______________________ Date: ______________

Writing Prompt: *Think of the first day of school. What feelings did you have? Was one of your feelings anxiety or worry? If you felt anxious, what did you do to conquer your anxiety? If you did not feel anxious, describe why.*

(continued)

APPENDIX 24 *(page 2 of 2)*

Create a comic strip to show your feelings on the first day of school this year.

APPENDIX 25

Character Webs

Name: ______________________ Date: ______________

Wemberly Worried

Wemberly's Worries

(continued)

APPENDIX 25 *(page 2 of 2)*

Name: ______________________ Date: ______________

The Day You Begin

Angelina's Worries

APPENDIX 26
Letter to a Character

Name: ______________________________ Date: ____________________

What advice would you give to Wemberly or Angelina about the first day of school? Use what you learned in our class discussions and your own experience to compose your letter.

Dear ____________________________,

____

____

____

____

____

____

____

____

____

____

____

____

____

____

Your friend,

____

APPENDIX 27

Mistakes! Research

Name: ______________________ Date: ____________

The "mistake": ____

Inventor and inventor background	The story	The result

APPENDIX 28
Compare and Contrast

Name: ______________________ Date: ______________

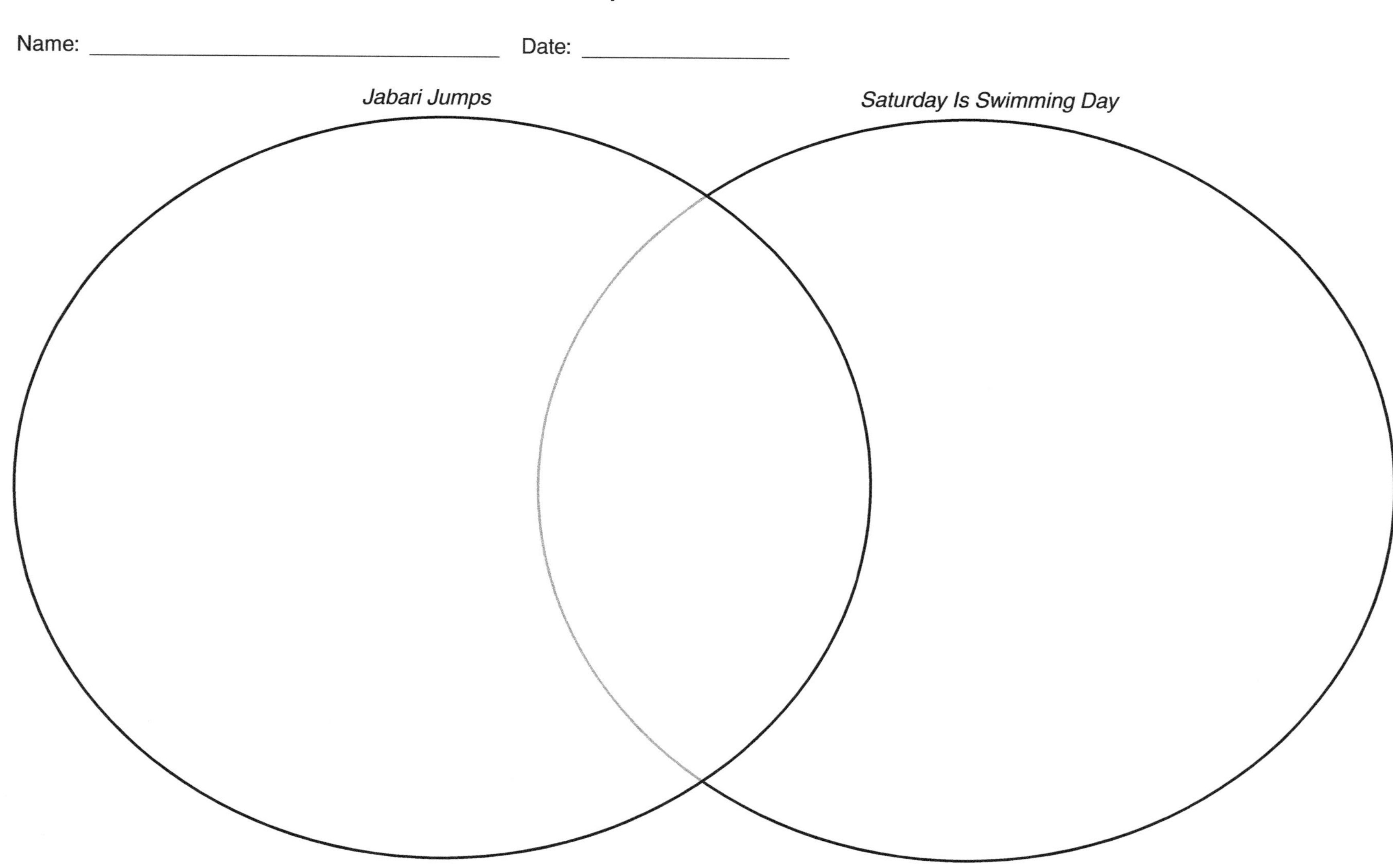

APPENDIX 29

Class Brainstorm: *Animals We Fear*

APPENDIX 30

Facing My Fears: *The Girl and the Wolf*

Name: ______________________ Date: ____________

If I were the author of this story, I would get lost in the woods with a ______________________.

First, ____

____

____

____

____

____

Next, ____

____

____

____

____

____

Finally, ____

____

____

____

____

____

(continued)

APPENDIX 30 *(page 2 of 2)*

Title: ______________________________

Cover Illustration:

References

Apol, L. (1998). "But what does this have to do with kids?": Literacy theory and children's literature in the teacher education classroom. *Journal of Children's Literature, 24*(2), 32–46.

Bassock, D., Latham, S., & Rorem, A. (2016). Is kindergarten the new first grade? *AERA Open, 2*(1), 1–31.

Bishop, R. S. (1990). Mirrors, windows, and sliding glass doors. *Perspectives: Choosing and Using Books for the Classroom, 6*(3), ix–xi.

Bitsko, R. H., Holbrook, J. R., Ghandour, R. M., Blumberg, S. J., Visser, S. N., Perou, R., et al. (2018). Epidemiology and impact of health care provider—diagnosed anxiety and depression among US children. *Journal of Developmental & Behavioral Pediatrics, 39*(5), 395–403.

Cooperative Children's Book Center (CCBC). (2014, April). *2023 CCBC diversity statistics news release: CCBC's diversity statistics show small changes in number of diverse books for children and teens published last year.* CCBC Diversity Statistics Media Kit. *https://uwmadison.app.box.com/s/rn4ccrdx8f8a2nbbqb6spx16kxcy52r1/file/1490478755959.*

DeVos, B., Nielsen, K. M., & Azar, A. M. (2018). *Final report of the Federal Commission on School Safety.* U.S. Department of Education.

Frye, N. (1970). *The stubborn structure: Essays on criticism and society.* Cornell University Press.

Galda, L., Liang, L. A., & Cullinan, B. E. (2017). *Literature and the child* (9th ed.). Cengage Learning.

Huyck, D., Dahlen, S. P., & Griffin, M. B. (2016, September 14). *Diversity in children's books 2015 infographic. https://readingspark.wordpress.com/2016/09/14/picture-this-reflecting-diversity-in-childrens-book-publishing*

Kauffman, G., & Short, K. G. (2001). Talking about books: Critical conversations about identity. *Language Arts, 78*(3), 279–286.

Lehman, B. A., Freeman, E. B., & Scharer, P. L., (2010). *Teaching globally, K–8: Connecting students to the world through literature.* Corwin Press.

Meredith, K., Robinson, L., & Togans, L. (2014). Microaggression activity. In M. Kite (Ed.), *Breaking the prejudice habit.* Ball State University. *breakingprejudice.org.*

Myers, C. (2013). Young dreamers. *The Horn Book Magazine, 89*(6), 10–14.

Nodelman, P. (1996). *The pleasures of children's literature* (2nd ed.). Longman.

Nodelman, P. (1997). Ordinary monstrosity: The world of Goosebumps. *Children's Literature Association Quarterly, 22*(3), 118–125.

Pope, D. C., Brown, M., & Miles, S. (2015). *Overloaded and underprepared: Strategies for stronger schools and healthy, successful kids.* Wiley.

Rajmil, L., Fernandez de Sanmamed, M.-J., Choonara, I., Faresjö, T., Hjern, A., Kozyrskyj, et al. (2014). Impact of the 2008 economic and financial crisis on child health: A systematic review. *International Journal of Environmental Research and Public Health, 11,* 6528–6546.

Reyes, M. R., Brackett, M. A., Rivers, S. E., White, M., & Salovey, P. (2012). Classroom emotional climate, student engagement, and academic achievement. *Journal of Educational Psychology, 104*(3), 700e712.

Romeo, R. R., Leonard, J. A., Robinson, S. T., West, M. R., Mackey, A. P., Rowe, M. L., et al. (2018). Beyond the 30-million-word gap: Children's conversational exposure is associated with language-related brain function. *Psychological Science, 29*(5), 700–710.

Souza, T. (2018, April 30). *Responding to microaggressions in the classroom: Taking ACTION.* Faculty Focus.

Teaching Tolerance. (2017). *Let's talk!: Discussing race, racism, and other difficult topics with students. www.learningforjustice.org/magazine/publications/lets-talk*

Twenge, J. M., Martin, G. N., & Campbell, W. K. (2018). Decreases in psychological well-being among American adolescents after 2012 and links to screen time during the rise of smartphone technology. *Emotion, 18*(6), 765–780.

van Geel, M., Vedder, P., & Tanilon, J. (2014). Relationship between peer victimization, cyberbullying, and suicide in children and adolescents: A meta-analysis. *JAMA Pediatrics, 168,* 435–442.

Willems, M. (2010). *Can I play, too?* Hyperion Books for Children.

Willems, M. (2014). *Waiting is not easy!* Hyperion Books for Children.

Yosso, T. J. (2005.) Whose culture has capital?: A critical race theory discussion of community cultural wealth, *Race Ethnicity and Education,* 8(1), 69–91.

Index

Note. f following a page number indicates a figure.

B

C

D

E

F

G

H

I

J

K

L

M

N

O

P

Q

R